EAST ASIA: HISTORY, POLITICS, SOCIOLOGY, CULTURE

edited by
EDWARD BEAUCHAMP
UNIVERSITY OF HAWAII

THE ROOTS OF JAPAN'S INTERNATIONAL ENVIRONMENTAL POLICIES

Anny Wong

Routledge
Taylor & Francis Group

LONDON AND NEW YORK

First published 2001 by Garland Publishing, Inc.

Published 2017 by Routledge
2 Park Square, Milton Park, Abingdon, Oxon OX14 4RN
711 Third Avenue, New York, NY 10017, USA

*Routledge is an imprint of the Taylor & Francis Group,
an informa business*

Copyright © 2001 by Anny Wong

All rights reserved. No part of this book may be reprinted or reproduced or utilised in any form or by any electronic, mechanical, or other means, now known or hereafter invented, including photocopying and recording, or in any information storage or retrieval system, without permission in writing from the publishers.

Notice:
Product or corporate names may be trademarks or registered trademarks, and are used only for identification and explanation without intent to infringe.

Library of Congress Cataloging-in-Publication Data is available from the Library of Congress.

ISBN 13: 978-0-8153-3950-2 (hbk)

Contents

Page

Acknowledgements vii
Abstract ix
List of Tables xi
List of Figures xiii
List of Abbreviations xv

Preface xix

Chapter 1: Introduction: The Global Environment and Japan 1
  Objectives of this study 1
  The global environment in international affairs: Japan's
  interests and goals 5
  The case studies: whaling, deforestation in the tropics
  and acid deposition in Asia 13
  Structure of the study 18

Chapter 2: Theory and Methodology 25
  Complex interdependence, regimes and two-level games 25
  Decision making: the bureaucratic politics model and
  Japan's foreign policy 33
  Methodology 36

Chapter 3: The Global Environment in Japanese Politics and
       the Major Domestic Policy Actors 45
  Evolution of environmental issues in Japanese
  domestic politics 46
  The Japanese government bureaucracy 50
  Japanese politicians 62
  Japanese business and industry 65
  Non-governmental organizations 69
  Japanese academia 74
  "Think tanks" or policy studies research institutes 75
  The Japanese mass media . . . . : 77
  Summary 79

Chapter 4: Whaling 89
  Modern whaling: a history and its present-day controversy 89
  The whaling controversy and Japan's whaling policies 91
  The international regime for whaling .92
  History of modern Japanese whaling 100

v

vi *Contents*

U.S. domestic legislation: its impact on the international
regime on whaling and Japan's whaling policy in the 1980s 107
Japan's policy on whaling 111
Policy actors in Japan's whaling policy .114
Chapter conclusion 126

Chapter 5: Deforestation in the Tropics 145

Tropical forests: timber source, biodiversity storehouse,
carbon sink and a home to many 145
Tropical deforestation and Japan's policy responses 147
The international regime for the conservation of forests
in the tropics 150
Japan and forest destruction in Southeast Asia 162
Japan's policy responses to deforestation in the tropics 173
Policy actors in Japan's policy on deforestation in the tropics . . .177
Chapter conclusion 187

Chapter 6: Acid Deposition in Asia 201

Acid rain: definition, dangers and characteristics 202
Acid rain in Asia and Japan's policy responses 203
Acid rain control in Europe and North America 207
China: number one pollution source in Northeast Asia 217
Japan's policy on acid rain control in Asia 228
Policy actors in Japan's acid rain policy 231
Chapter conclusion 239

Chapter 7: Conclusion 257

Policy making in Japan and the international environment 258

Appendix: List of Interviewees 267
Bibliography 275
Index 321

Acknowledgements

I was blessed with kind advice and generous support from many people throughout my doctoral program. First of all, I thank Dr. Carolyn Stephenson, the chair of my dissertation committee, for her rigorous guidance. I also thank other members of my committee, Drs. James Dator, Charles E. Morrison, James E. Nickum, and Patricia G. Steinhoff for sharing with me their scholarship and encouragement.

I extend my appreciation to Drs. Muthiah Alagappa, Haruhiro Fukui and Alvin So for their roles in various stages of my dissertation. I am, furthermore, indebted to all the people who have generously shared with me their time, knowledge, and insights in my research. The names are too numerous to mention, but I would not have been able to complete this dissertation without their valuable assistance.

For funding support, I thank the East-West Center for sponsoring my doctoral studies and the Center for Japanese Studies of the University of Hawai'i at Manoa for a generous grant to launch my field study in Japan. I am also grateful to many organizations for allowing my participation in academic conferences and other activities, which helped me to refine thoughts and expand my intellectual horizons.

Last, but not least, I am most grateful to my parents for their loving support and for preparing me for life's many challenges. I thank my friends everywhere for adding color to my life with their insights, humor, and culinary delights. Finally, a special *mahalo* to Sara Banaszak, my Wong family in Honolulu, and the Murooka family in Japan for opening their homes and hearts to me.

Abstract

This study draws on complex interdependence, regime theory, two-level games theory, and the bureaucratic politics model to examine foreign policy making in Japan. The focus is Japan's policies towards international environmental issues, with case studies on whaling, deforestation in the tropics and transboundary acid deposition in East Asia.

This study has two objectives. The first is to investigate how interactive dynamics between domestic and international politics affects foreign policy making in Japan, particularly the country's international environmental policies. The second is to identify motivations behind Japanese government policies towards the global environment. Whaling, deforestation in the tropics and transboundary acid deposition in East Asia are chosen as case studies because they illustrate how Japan views different kinds of international environmental problems. Each case also involves a different set of diplomatic relations for Japan, and together they present a broad outline of the ascent of environmental issues in international politics in the past three decades.

Environmental issues are useful to the study of foreign policy-making because they typically cut across conventional lines of jurisdiction in a government. Understanding motivations behind Japan's international environmental policies is particularly important because Japan is second largest economy in the world and is a top donor of development and environmental assistance. In other words, Japan has significant influence to do good as well as bad for the global environment.

This study supports the view that the bureaucratic politics model is useful in identifying major domestic forces behind Japanese foreign policy and the Japanese government's views of international environmental issues. However, application of concepts in complex interdependence, regime theory, and two-level games model helps to reveal a more penetrating and complex picture of foreign policy making. Dynamic interactions between systemic and subsystemic levels open opportunities for policy actors to build transnational alliances, redefine issues and exploit issue linkages—among other strategies—to increase their bargaining leverage at domestic and international levels. On motivations behind Japanese policies and actions towards the global environment, the end of Cold War confrontation presents new opportunities for an economic powerhouse like Japan to assert itself in international politics. Japan's success in domestic industrial development, pollution control, its advanced technologies and enormous official aid program are seen by Japanese policy makers as instruments to establishing Japanese leadership in global environmental affairs. However, Japan is nowhere closer to its objective despite high hopes and billions of dollars in environmental aid disbursements. A significant part of the problem lies in disparities between Japanese views and international opinions and regimes. Japan has a rather narrow interpretation of environmental issues. As a resource poor country, ensuring energy and resource security has always been the country's top national priorities. Thus, Japanese policies emphasize resource management for sustainable use over nature protection, and it has more proactive and progressive policies towards "brown issues" (e.g., energy, urban development) than "green issues" (e.g., biodiversity protection).

List of Tables

TABLE		Page
1.	Regional distribution of ODA	9
2.	Trends in environment-related coverage in 4 major newspapers in Japan	78
3.	Membership in IWC, 1972-92	96
4.	Whale oil production, 1935-39	102
5.	Production of pelagic whaling, LTCW and STCW	105
6.	Estimated net release of carbon to the atmosphere from tropical deforestation, by region, 1980	147
7.	Japanese log imports from Southeast Asia, 1970-87	164
8.	Trends in tropical hardwood imports, 1950-87	166
9.	Comparison of SO_x and NO_x emissions by country, 1990	205
10.	Original members of the 30% Club	213
11.	Coal consumption in Asia, 1990-2010	217
12.	Average annual electricity growth rates	218
13.	Electric power production	219
14.	Major recipients of Japan's bilateral assistance by aid type, 1996	224
15.	Coal-related projects supported by the Green Aid Plan	235

xi

List of Figures

FIGURE   Page

1. Areas of environmental ODA by area, FY 1995 4

2. Japan's bilateral ODA by area, FY 1996 10

3. Trends in procurement condition on Japan's ODA loans 11

4. Trends in Development Assistance Committee (DAC)
    countries' ODA, 1988-1998 12

5. Japan's environmental ODA, 1986-95 52

6. Shifts in Japan's consumption of domestic and imported
    timber and wood materials, 1986-92 148

7. Supply of domestic and imported timber and wood
    materials by area, 1992 170

8. Supply of domestic and imported timber and wood
    materials by type, 1992 170

9. International trade of wood, 1994 171

10. World CO_2 emissions, 1994 220

11. Projected new CCT capacity in Asia, 1990-2000 230

12. Trends of Green Aid Plan-related budget 235

xiii

List of Abbreviations

ADB	Asian Development Bank
APEC	Asia Pacific Economic Cooperation
ASEAN	Association of Southeast Asian Nations
ASW	Aboriginal Subsistence Whaling
BWU	Blue Whale Unit
CCTs	Clean Coal Technologies
CIFOR	Center for International Forestry Research
CITES	Convention on International Trade in Endangered Species of Wild Fauna and Flora
CLRTAP	Convention on Long-range Transboundary Air Pollution
CO_2	Carbon dioxide
COP 3	Third Meeting of the Conference of Parties to the Climate Change Convention
CSD	United Nations Commission on Sustainable Development
CTP	Cooperative Technical Program to Measure the Long-range Transport of Air Pollutants
DAC	Development Assistance Committee
EACN	European Air Chemistry Network
ECO ASIA	Environment Congress for Asia and the Pacific
EEZ	Exclusive Economic Zones
EMEP	Cooperative Program for Monitoring and Evaluation of Long-Range Transmission of Air Pollutants in Europe
ESCAP	United Nations Economic and Social Commission for Asia and the Pacific
ETP	Emissions Trading Program
FAO	United Nations Food and Agriculture Organization
FGD	Flue Gas Desulfurization
FoE	Friends of the Earth
FSC	Forest Stewardship Council
G-7	Group of Seven (grouping of developed economies)
G-77	Group of 77 (grouping of developing countries)
GATT	General Agreement on Tariffs and Trade

GEF	Global Environment Facility
GEIC	Global Environment Information Center
GIFA	General International Fisheries Agreement
GISPRI	Global Industrial and Social Progress Research Institute
GLOBE	Global Legislators Organization for a Better Environment
GNP	Gross National Product
GTCs	General Trading Companies
ha	hectares
ICETT	International Center for Environmental Technology Transfer
ICR	Institute for Cetacean Research
ICRW	International Convention for the Regulation of Whaling
IDE	Institute of Developing Economies
IFAW	International Fund for Animal Welfare
IFF	Intergovernmental Forum on Forests
IIASA	International Institute for Applied Systems Analysis
IPF	Inter-governmental Panel on Forests
IGES	Institute for Global Environmental Strategies
IMS	Initial Management Stocks
INC	Intergovernmental Negotiating Committee (for a global forest convention)
ISD	Initiatives for Sustainable Development toward the 21st Century
ISO	International Organization for Standardization
ITO	International Timber Organization
ITTA	International Tropical Timber Agreement
ITTO	International Tropical Timber Organization
IUCN	International Union for the Conservation of Nature and Natural Resources (also known as the World Conservation Union)
IWC	International Whaling Commission
JAS	Japan Agricultural Standard
JATAN	Japan Tropical Forest Action Network
JEA	Environment Agency of Japan

Abbreviations

JETRO	Japan External Trade Organization
JICA	Japan International Cooperation Agency
JIFPRO	Japan International Forestry Promotion and Cooperation Center
JIIA	Japan Institute for International Affairs
JIS	Japan Industrial Standards
JETRO	Japan External Trade Organization
JWA	Japan Whaling Association
KNCF	Keidanren Nature Conservation Fund
kwh	kilowatt-hours
LTCW	Large-Type Coastal Whaling
MAFF	Ministry of Agriculture, Fisheries and Forestry
MHW	Ministry of Health and Welfare
MITI	Ministry of International Trade and Industry
MMPA	Marine Mammals Protection Act
MoC	Ministry of Construction
MoE	Ministry of Education
MoF	Ministry of Finance
MoFA	Ministry of Foreign Affairs
MOI	U.S.-Canada Memorandum of Intent on Transboundary Air Pollution
MoT	Ministry of Transport
MSY	Maximum Sustainable Yield
Mt S	Megatons of Sulfur
NAAQS	National Ambient Air Quality Standards
NAMMCO	North Atlantic Marine Mammal Commission
NGOs	Non-governmental organizations
NIES	National Institute for Environmental Studies
NIRA	National Institute for Research Advancement
NMP	New Management Procedure
NO_x	Nitrogen oxides
NPOs	Non-profit organizations
ODA	Official Development Assistance

OECD	Organization for Economic Cooperation and Development
OECF	Overseas Economic Cooperation Fund
PS	Protection Stocks
RAINS-Asia	Regional Air Pollution Information and Simulation-Asia
RAN	Rainforest Action Network
RETROF	Research Association for Reforestation of Tropical Forest
RITE	Research Institute to Innovate Technologies for the Earth
RMP	Revised Management Procedure
RMS	Revised Management Scheme
rwe	roundwood equivalent
SMS	Sustained Management Stocks
SO_2	Sulfur dioxide
SOS	Southern Ocean Sanctuary
SO_x	Sulfur oxides
STCW	Small-Type Coastal Whaling
TFAP	Tropical Forest Action Plan
WHO	World Health Organization
WMO	World Meteorological Organization
UNCED	United Nations Conference on Environment and Development (also known as the "Rio Summit")
UNCHE	United Nations Conference on the Human Environment (or commonly known as the "Stockholm Conference")
UNCLOS	United Nations Convention for the Law of the Sea
UNCTAD	United Nations Conference on Trade and Development
UNECE	United Nations Economic Commission for Europe
UNEP	United Nations Environment Program
UNGASS	United Nations General Assembly on the Environment and Sustainable Development
U.S.	United States of America
WTO	World Trade Organization
WWF	World Wide Fund for Nature or World Wildlife Fund (as it is known in the United States)

Preface

What are global environmental problems and how does Japan propose to respond to them? A recent visit to the Ministry of Foreign Affairs' home page in March 2000 on the Internet showed 10 major areas under the heading of "Japanese approaches to the environment." Of these, five addressed energy issues, two emphasized technology transfer and recycling, one was a bilateral agenda for cooperation with the United States, and the remaining two were domestic public education programs. Not a single item was devoted to nature conservation or biological diversity preservation.

While this list was admittedly inadequate in representing the full range of interests and views in the entire Japanese government, it sufficed to demonstrate what the Japanese government, as a whole, considered as priorities in global environmental protection. "Brown" issues, or industrial pollution, energy use, and waste issues were the key concerns, and "green" issues, such as species and habitat conservation, were secondary.

Since this study was completed at the end of 1998, much has remained the same in the Japanese government's view of international environmental issues and responses to them. The government continues to make energy issues its top focus in international environmental discussions. This bias was reinforced by the conclusion of the Kyoto Protocol in December 1997. The protocol commits Japan and other industrialized economies to reduce greenhouse gas emissions to below their 1990 levels.

In Japan's case, it has to achieve a 6 percent reduction by the end of the first commitment period in 2012. Meeting this target through domestic efforts alone could be very costly because Japan has already gone through several rounds of emissions reductions. A less expensive way to meet this target would be to purchase carbon credits from other countries. Towards this end, Japan's official development assistance program provides loans and grants to help developing countries purchase clean coal technology from Japan. Japanese power companies, in particular, have become big

xix

buyers of carbon credits produced by greenhouse gas emissions reductions from more efficient fossil fuel combustion and carbon sequestration by trees and vegetation.

Energy and resource security, pursued by emphasizing sustainable use and management of resources, also remains a central policy objective for Japan. Japanese fisheries officials labor to assist Japanese deep-sea fisheries to cope with the full-scale implementation of the 200-nautical-mile exclusive economic zones under the United Nations Convention on Law of the Sea. Fisheries officials also work to negotiate bilateral fishing agreements with countries having rich fisheries grounds, such as Indonesia, and provide assistance and training to fisheries industries and communities overseas.

Finally, bureaucratic dominance in policy making remains true. Although the bureaucracy no longer commands the public's traditional sense of trust, the legal structure continues to bias in favor of the government. The bureaucracy governs Japanese society through its regulatory powers and uses them to resist outside intervention in policy processes. In addition, the bureaucracy remains a stronger policy actor than either politicians or civil society in national policy debates because of the existing infrastructure for policy research and the expertise of its individual officials. Until non-bureaucratic actors acquire independent ability to collect, analyze and disseminate information, they cannot significantly challenge the bureaucracy's dominance in policy discussions and decision-making.

Nonetheless, change is the only constant in life, and there have been some important changes in the past two years. The main driver of these changes is Japan's domestic economic recession, the longest and most stubborn in the country's post-World War II history.

Japan's official development assistance (ODA) program is the government's main instrument in international environmental cooperation. Despite severe budget deficits, the government had allowed decades of uninterrupted growth in its ODA allocations until the first cut was made in fiscal year 1998. The reduction, at more than 10 percent reduction, was not a big surprise since cuts have been made in all other areas of the national budget and public interest in international cooperation has been significantly dampened by the country's economic woes.

The more ominous setback in Japan's ODA program is its reversal to "tied" loans. Special ODA loans have been extended to neighboring Asian economies to help them to recover from the financial crisis. These special ODA loans charge an interest rate of 1 percent, which is lower than the 2.7 percent average of ordinary Japanese ODA loans, and they have extended grace periods for repayment. However, these cheap loans are tied, which means that recipients are required to purchase Japanese products and services. Japanese industry, suffering from the domestic economic downturn, has put intense pressure on politicians and the bureaucracy for assistance.

Preface

ODA loans thus become a form of subsidy in helping Japanese business to sell their products and services overseas.

The Japanese government's enormous deficit has also put pressure on the bureaucracy to introduce changes that will have serious ramifications on the quality and direction of its ODA program. In 1999, the Overseas Economic Cooperation Fund, which is responsible for making ODA loans, officially merged with the Japan Export Import Bank, which guarantees Japanese investments overseas. The new organization is known as the Japan International Cooperation Bank. Critics fear that the merger could become an institutional basis for the commercialization of Japanese aid.

On the bright side, government relations with non-governmental organizations (NGOs) have generally improved in the last several years. Budget cuts and hiring freezes have forced the government bureaucracy to enter into more cooperative relations with NGOs, making them "partners" in international cooperation activities. The Ministry of Foreign Affairs, which is most directly involved in international cooperation activities, now has regular policy dialogues with NGOs, particularly development—focused ones with experience in field projects. The Japan International Cooperation Agency, the office responsible for sending technical assistance personnel overseas and a body under the auspices of the Foreign Ministry, has also recently opened policy dialogues with NGOs. There have been other unprecedented actions. Joint missions of staff from NGOs and the Ministry of Foreign Affairs' Economic Cooperation Bureau visited Bangladesh and Cambodia to evaluate each other's projects. Another was a workshop in Okinawa in March 1999 that was co-sponsored by NGOs and JICA to increase mutual understanding and collaboration between Japanese and other Asian NGOs. The increased willingness of some NGOs to work with the government is also partly due to the economic recession. As public donations decreased, their dependence on government funds increases.

Another landmark in the development of civil society in Japan was the enactment of a non-profit organization law in December 1998. The new law removes the power of the central government bureaucracy to grant legal status—thus exercising control—over civil society organizations. Under the new law, a non-profit organization only has to apply to the prefectural government for where it operates, or to the Economic Planning Agency if it works in more than one prefecture. The new law also removes the bureaucracy's administrative authority to "approve" (*ninka*) legal status. Instead, legal status need only be "authenticated" (*ninsho*) by the prefectural government or the Economic Planning Agency. Authentication must also be given within two months after an application is filed, if the organization meets the provisions set forth in the legislation. Finally, the requirement for 300 million yen in endowment for incorporation, was eliminated. As of August 1999, a total of 1,130 organizations had applied *xxii*   *Preface*

for incorporation and 469 have been authenticated, receiving the status of "specified non-profit corporation" (*tokutei hiero hojin*).

Having obtained a revision in the law governing their legal status, NGOs target tax reform in the second stage of their legislative lobby. This will begin at the end of its third year of implementation when the new law is up for a scheduled review. Obtaining tax-exempted status and other reforms in the tax system is critical to the long-term survival and development of NGOs in Japan. At present, individual contributions to NGOs are not tax deductible. Corporate donations can only get tax deduction for amounts up to 0.125 percent of their capital and 1.25 percent of their annual profit. In comparison, corporate donations to government-operated organizations or those specially registered by the government are not bound by this ceiling. This not only favors organizations with government ties; it is also part and parcel of the patron-client relationship that exists between the government bureaucracy and industry.

Looking into the future, amendment of the civil law would likely be the top goal of NGOs in their third phase of legislative lobbying. The civil law provides the basis for legal entities, such as foundations (*zaidan hojin*) and civil association (*shadan hojin*). The current law was written over a hundred years ago in the Meiji era. The only significant amendment ever made came after World War II, which put each type of organization (medical, social, religious, educational, etc.) under its respective government regulatory bodies. This change gave the government bureaucracy gained enormous power to control society. Therefore, amendments to the civil law are necessary to provide a new general legal and philosophical basis for non-profit organizations in Japan.

One final important effect of the prolonged economic recession is a much tighter job market for young professionals. College graduates may find work in the non-profit sector more attractive when jobs in private firms have become extremely hard to find. However, the ability of NGOs to hire more staff is questionable. A weak economy reduces public interest and donations to the non-profit sector. The Internet explosion in Japan since 1998 could also draw young professionals and enterprising individuals to new Internet-based business ventures rather than working as low paid staff with few benefits or volunteers in NGOs.

On the subject of the Internet, NGOs in Japan found in it a cheap instrument for research, information exchange and communication. The Internet has helped civil society groups to form alliances and undertake joint actions in influencing policy debates both inside and outside of Japan. Even the Japanese government, particularly the smaller bureaucratic bodies, has shown greater appreciation of the Internet as an instrument of influence. For example, the Environment Agency disseminates information about its work and policy proposals through the web site of the Global Environment Information Center, the agency's public relations arm. Raising public

Preface *xxiii*

awareness and support for the agency's work and policy proposals help to increase influence in intra-governmental negotiations. The Ministry of Health and Welfare has also been active in using the Internet to educate the public about dioxin pollution in Japan, and even soliciting public input via the Internet for its policy proposals.

Economic pressure has also compelled a restructure of the government under the Basic Administrative Reform Law of 1998. The current 21 ministries will be reduced to only 12. A Ministry of Environment will be created to replace the Environment Agency on 1 January 2001. The new ministry will retain jurisdiction over areas currently covered by the Environment Agency, such as pollution prevention regulations for air, water, and soil, and conservation of natural environment, including management of national parks and wildlife protection. The new ministry will also have expanded jurisdiction, sharing oversight in some areas with other ministries. Its new responsibilities include promotion of recycling, regulation of carbon dioxide emissions, ozone layer protection, prevention of marine pollution, examination and manufacturing regulations for chemicals, monitoring radioactivity in the environment, wastewater treatment by sewerage system, conservation of rivers and lakes, and conservation of forests and green areas.

Elevation to the ministerial level will put the new Ministry of Environment on equal footing with the big and powerful ministries for international trade, construction and agriculture. However, it does not mean equal leverage. The new Ministry of Environment will still be much smaller in size and budget, and the jurisdictional boundaries drawn and maintained over the past five decades will not be erased overnight.

Although the new ministry will have a new legal basis for broader participation in policy debates, its limited resources and expertise will restrict involvement to those areas which it has already established policy leadership, namely, global warming, acid deposition, and ozone layer protection. Also, as a coordinating body under the Prime Minister's Office, the Environment Agency has more direct access to the chief executive. Hence, it is not entirely clear whether becoming a ministry will improve the Environment Agency's leverage in intra-government negotiations.

Relations between politicians and civil society also have had important changes in the past several years. Politics has become more competitive in Japan even as the Liberal Democratic Party continues to dominate in national politics. Debates in the Parliament are now televised and cabinet members, political appointees, can no longer rely on their career bureaucrat deputies to answer questions for them in the Diet. Political debates leading up to the passing of the new non-profit sector law have attracted many politicians who wanted to demonstrate their democratic beliefs in a new era of more adversarial politics in Japan. Many politicians, both old and young, realize that they must be more responsive to civil society, as a

xxiv   *Preface*

whole, and not just their home constituents. For example, in August 1999, a Parliamentary League to Support Non-Profit Organizations was formed to push for amendments to the non-profit organization law, including the NGO lobby for tax reforms.

As for the international environmental issues examined in this study, the Japanese government has not fundamentally altered its policies towards them. In whaling, the Fisheries Agency maintains its insistence on the principle of sustainable use, as well as respect for cultural diversity and science–based policies to guide the management and use of whales and other resources. Japan's desire to end the temprorary ban on commercial whaling continues to be resisted by anti-whaling nations, and Japan continues—and fails—to downlist certain whale stocks and species that are governed by the Convention for the International Trade of Endangered Species of Wild Fauna and Flora (CITES).

Anti-whaling groups and the media continue to criticize Japan's research whaling program. The harassment of Japanese research whaling vessels by Greenpeace, the most vocal of anti-whaling groups, in the southern oceans made international news headlines in February 2000 when the new prime minister in New Zealand openly declared her unqualified political support for Greenpeace. This announcement has strained diplomatic relations between New Zealand and Japan.

On deforestation in the tropics, the Asian financial crisis since 1997 has slowed consumption of forest products of all types in Japan. Debates on a global forest convention will continue under the new United Nations Forum on Forests. This forum will succeed the Intergovernmental Forum on Forests, which concluded its work at its final meeting in February 2000. The new forum will address the work left unfinished by its predecessor, which include efforts to explore conditions will lead to international consensus on a global forest convention.

Forest has proven to be an extremely intractable environmental issue. Nearly 10 years after the Rio Earth Summit, the international community has made scarce progress in reaching agreement on how to address forest destruction and conservation. During this period, international agreements have been concluded on deserts, climate change, biological diversity conservation, biosafety and transport of hazardous materials. A treaty on persistent organic pollutants will conclude by the year 20001.

While negotiations continue at the international level, forests of all types are disappearing. Where tropical forests are concerned, illegal logging has been especially rampant in Indonesia and Cambodia. New governments in both countries have introduced new laws on forest concessions and other forest management measures, but they need resources to implement laws and regulations. Indeed weaknesses in institutions and governance are the most significant obstacles to forest conservation.

Preface

While forest imports of all types have declined in Japan, the country is still a major producer of wood panels, paper and paperboard, and Japan, Korea and China together account for over 90 percent of Asia's industrial wood imports. In fact, Chinese consumption of all types of forest products, including pulp and paper, is growing very rapidly and a domestic ban on logging will increase pressure on all types of forests around the world.

While it is interesting to observe the Forestry Agency, which is opposed to further liberalization of forest product trade, reaching out to conservation NGOs in Japan, North America and Europe, these actions are still reflective of the turf battles within the Japanese government. In international trade talks on forest products under the Asia Pacific Economic Cooperation (APEC) and the World Trade Organization, the Forestry Agency did not oppose further liberalization in paper and pulp trade because these goods are under the jurisdiction of the Ministry of International Trade and Ministry. The Forestry Agency instead proposed to take trade discussions on forest products outside of the industrial goods category and to establish new discussion forums that emphasize the multiple functions (economic, environmental, cultural) of forestry. If this happens, Forestry Agency would exercise greater influence *vis-a-vis* the Ministry of International Trade and Industry in inter-ministerial negotiations on national policies.

Overall, the Japanese government continues to emphasize international **forestry** cooperation as its core activity towards the conservation and sustainable management and use of forest resources. The government and industry are keen to support reforestation and afforestation activities as means to acquiring "carbon credits" to help Japan meet its greenhouse gas reduction commitments under the Kyoto Protocol. For example, Japanese power companies have invested in commercial tree plantations in Australia in exchange for carbon credits and a new program was launched in 1998 to send forestry experts overseas to offer training in reforestation.

Furthermore, Japanese policy also shows little improvement in appreciating linkages among different types of forests, focusing its actions on tropical forests, and the International Tropical Timber Organization (ITTO) and the United Nations Food and Agriculture Organization (FAO) are the main international forums for Japanese involvement and financial contributions. Finally, the Japanese government (as well as NGOs) has done little to change domestic consumption patterns through regulatory or market mechanisms. However, such criticism also applies to most governments and NGOs in industrialized economies. Most have been quicker to condemn unsustainable forest policy and forestry practices in timber exporting countries than to push for positive reductions in domestic timber and paper use.

On transboundary acid pollution in Asia, China has become more responsive to this problem as information increases about the extent of damage and the economic costs to the country. Chinese citizens, especially those in urban areas where industrial pollution has become a major political issue, are demanding better environmental quality. Many experts have called for the replacement of coal burning boilers by oil or low sulfur burning boilers in Beijing, and the city has switched to unleaded gas. On 7 December 1999, the Chinese government hosted a conference for international and Chinese experts to talk about sulfur dioxide emissions prevention methods. The Chinese government hoped that this would spark interest in foreign investment and cooperation with Chinese companies to develop and install better sulfur dioxide control technologies.

Despite these positive actions, acid pollution in China and its transport to other parts of Asia are still increasing. Nationwide acid rain surveys in Japan found that in parts of the country, acid pollution has worsened to the level experienced in Europe and North America. Most of these most vulnerable areas are on the Japan Sea side of the country that faces mainland Asia.

Following agreement to form an Acid Deposition Monitoring Network in East Asia, the network has been implementing its preparatory phase activities since 1998. From October 1999 on, countries will report their monitoring data during the preparatory phrase to the Interim Network Center in Niigata, Japan. This will hopefully establish a basic and common understanding of the state of the problem in each participating country. In mid-2000, a second Intergovernment Meeting will take the monitoring network towards the next stage of work, which includes an assessment of transboundary transport and effects.

There is no doubt that Japan will continue to be a major player in international environmental affairs because of the size of its economy and its ODA program. However, it is still to be seen whether Japan's view of international environmental issues will mature beyond the narrow definitions and interests determined by its domestic bureaucratic policy framework. A restructuring of the government and more competitive politics hold potential for changes that would make the policy process more open and transparent.

CHAPTER 1

Introduction:
The Global Environment and Japan

The state of the global environment once again came to the fore of international politics in the mid-1980. Japan, as the world's second largest economy, came under intense international scrutiny for the environmental effects of its policies and actions. Western industrialized economies pressed Japan to share the responsibilities of developed countries. Developing countries called for more Japanese aid. Conservation groups demanded Japan to change its ways and stop environmental destruction.

Japan responded. Not only because it had to, it wanted to. New policy announcements and increased official assistance for environment-related activities soon followed. However, most Japanese actions fell short of its own goals and international expectations. What could explain this outcome? Answering this question, this study posits, requires an investigation of the roots of Japanese policies.

To do so, this study draws on concepts from several theoretic models to create a framework for analysis. Three case studies of different types of environmental issues are used as vehicles to find out about Japanese government perspectives towards the international environment as well as the motivations and dynamics in decision making.

The four parts in this chapter lays out the objectives and structure of this study, introduces the three case studies, and examines how concern for the global environment has developed as a political and policy issue in the last three decades, both within Japan and at the international level.

OBJECTIVES OF THIS STUDY

This study has two main objectives. The first is to examine how interactive dynamics between domestic and international politics affects foreign policy making in Japan, and focusing in particular on Japan's international envi-

I

ronmental policies. The second is to investigate motivations behind Japanese government policies and actions towards the global environment.

On the first objective, why focus on Japan's international environmental policies? There are three major reasons. The first is that although the global environment is conventionally seen as a foreign policy matter, in essence it is still a domestic policy issue. The assertion here is that all policies are basically domestic policies because the key policy makers and the most important policy constituents are, with rare exception, found in the domestic setting. Thus, international concerns, including the global environment, have little relevance in national policy until they become politicized in the domestic setting.

Second, studying Japan's policies towards the international environment helps to understand interactive dynamics in domestic politics and foreign policy making because, as Caldwell puts it, "..environmental issues cut across conventional categorical jurisdictions, the implementation of environmental policies is difficult without the cooperation of various administrative agencies, each with its own mission and priorities."[1]

Third, environmental issues are useful for studying domestic politics and policy making in Japan because they have had some impact in penetrating a policy making process that is tightly controlled by the government bureaucracy. For instance, domestic citizen movements in the 1960s and 1970s, launched in reaction to severe industrial pollution, were critical to pressuring the Japanese government to adopt new environmental legislation and implement pollution control measures.[2] In the 1980s, increasing popular Japanese interest in the global environment was also a catalyst to the growth of non-governmental organizations (NGOs) in Japan. Although NGOs have yet to be truly influential in Japanese government processes which are lacking in openness and transparency,their endorsement as legitimate actors in development and environmental conservation by international organizations and Western governments put pressure on the Japanese government to relinquish absolute monopoly on policy decision making.[3] In November 1993, the Japanese government allowed, for the first time, public consultation of a policy draft—Japan's national Agenda 21 plan. Another unprecedented decision was an invitation to Japanese NGOs to join a Japanese government delegation to an international meeting (the United Nations Conference on Population and Development in Cairo in September 1994).

The majority of research on policy making in post-war Japan has favored either systemic or domestic level approaches in analysis.[4] This study follows a more recent trend to focus on dynamic interactions between internal and external forces in policy making.[5] This study supports the view that the Japanese bureaucracy dominates in policy making, but it is not immuned to outside pressure nor is it dominated by it. Instead, participation and influence in policy making depend greatly on the place and

Introduction

definition of a policy issue within the policy framework. Also, the interests and leverage of the Japanese bureaucracy, as well as other interested actors, are influenced by multi-level and interactive dynamics within and across issues and jurisdictions. Thus, policy decisions are rarely the dictate of any one actor, even a dominant one, but rather products of bargaining and negotiations among interested actors.

On the second objective of this study, it is important to examine Japanese policies and actions because they have serious impact on the global environment. Apart from being the world's second largest industrial economy, Japan is also a leading donor of environmental assistance. In fact, the Japanese government considers its Official Development Assistance (ODA) program a major instrument in responding to environmental problems worldwide. As one Ministry of Foreign Affairs publication declares, "ODA is likely for some time to remain as an effective means for Japan to realize its aspirations to play a role, which is commensurate with its position and economic strength for international peace, security and prosperity."[6] Japan is the top donor to over 55 countries in Asia, Africa, and the Middle East. Japan also makes large contributions to multilateral organizations. These include programs of the United Nations Environment Program, the International Tropical Timber Organization, the International Maritime Organization and the World Bank's Global Environment Facility, the International Development Association, and the Multilateral Ozone Fund.

What should the world expect of Japan? The country's new Basic Environmental Law, which was passed in 1993 and sets the country's guiding principle and framework for cooperation in environmental affairs, states that Japan should "provide environmental preservation assistance to developing countries when such aid contributes to ensuring the health and civilized life of the Japanese people."[7]

Moreover, Japanese ODA continues to favor development-related activities over those emphasizing environmental conservation as the primary objective. Figure 1 below shows that over half (54.9%) of all Japanese environment-related ODA spending in 1995 focused on "the living environment," which includes road building and energy generation (and another 7.7 percent was allocated for pollution control). In contrast, only 10.7 percent of all funds were given to forest conservation and 7.5 percent to nature conservation. Nature protection and biological diversity clearly have not been priorities for the Japanese government.[8]

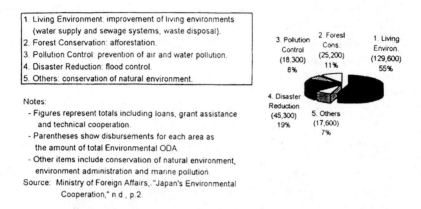

Figure 1. Areas of environmental ODA by area, FY1995 (million yen)

There is also ample evidence of adverse social and ecological distress resulting from Japanese ODA-funded projects. One common criticism is that Japanese aid often supports infrastructure and resource development projects that are essentially more pertinent to Japanese economic interests than the needs and welfare of aid recipient countries or the future of the environment.[9]

A bias for economic growth, as well as a belief in technology as a panacea for environmental problems, is also evident. The Japanese government's environmental ODA policy, which was announced in 1991, emphasizes that the purpose of Japanese aid is to help developing countries to achieve environmental conservation—without sacrificing economic growth—through transfers of Japanese technology and experience. The ODA Charter echoes a similar view that "in implementing environmental ODA, Japan will make the best use of the technology and know-how that it has acquired in the process of successfully making environmental conservation compatible with economic development." Such views have prompted critics to question if this broad application of the term "sustainable" in Japanese official announcements is not a disguise for conventional development, which stresses economic growth above all else.[10]

Japan's belief in the power of technology is deeply rooted in its domestic economic development and pollution control experience. A Ministry of Foreign Affairs publication states that "Having confronted and overcome serious pollution problems in the past, Japan is in a position to assist developing countries by making its technical know-how, personnel, and other resources available."[11] Thus, Japan sees relevance in transferring technol-

Introduction

ogy and its own experience to help developing countries to overcome contradictions in development and environmental conservation.[12]

THE GLOBAL ENVIRONMENT IN INTERNATIONAL AFFAIRS: JAPAN'S INTERESTS AND GOALS

North America, Western Europe, and Japan all had rapid industrial growth after World War II. Incomes grew and the quality of life improved, but the environmental and health effects of industrial pollution had to be acknowledged by the 1960s. A new wave of literature linking development and the environment appeared. Writings by Reid and Carson, for example, drew broad public attention to the social and environmental effects of industrial development.[13] Public demands for pollution control produced stricter environmental standards and gave momentum to citizen movements to protect nature.

A major event took place in 1972. The United Nations Conference on the Human Environment (UNCHE) held in Stockholm put environmental problems, for the first time, on the international political agenda.[14] Questioning how unrestrained consumption of resources can threaten human survival encouraged a new perspective on the relationship between development and the environment. For example, the works of Hardin, the Ehrlichs, and Meadows embraced and advanced this new perspective.[15] People in developed and developing countries began to share a new sense of common vulnerability. Seeing that there is "only one world," as Caldwell puts it, environmental protection would be an international endeavor transcending race, religion, national boundaries, political ideologies, and economic conditions.[16]

Philosophical debates and scientific research over the next decade deepened understanding of the problems and what is required for their solution. New environmental laws were passed and regulations put into effect in many countries. However, the world also learned that domestic actions were not enough. Addressing the causes of these problems as well as their effective solution would require international cooperation. Among the most influential publications of the 1970s and 1980s were *The Global 2000 Report to the President*, the *World Conservation Strategy*, *Our Common Future* (report of The World Commission of Environment and Development) and *Staying Alive*.[17]

The easing of East-West tensions by the mid-1980s had sufficiently reduced public fears of a nuclear holocaust so that North-South conflicts, particularly disparities in development, regained prominence in international politics. Since development is tied to resource use and management, the state of the global environment soon took center stage in international discussions. More information about environmental damage worldwide underscored the urgent need for international cooperation to prevent irreversible ecological destruction and outbreaks of violence over resources.[18]

Such international concern culminated with the United Nations Conference on Environment and Development (UNCED) in 1992.[19] Over 180 countries and 102 heads of states attended the meeting. There were high hopes for significant progress in building consensus on responses to international environmental problems, but major breakthroughs were obstructed by the persistence of long-held differences over fundamental issues, including responsibility and equity, among others. Governments could not, however, allow the meeting to end as a complete failure because of domestic political pressures. Industry and conservation forces wanted to show some modicum of success. As a result, several new environmental agreements were agreed upon and mechanisms for international cooperation adopted, such as national Agenda 21 plans for action and new funds to support technology transfer.[20] Another important outcome was the recognition of a legitimate role for non-governmental organizations in international environmental policy discussions by governments and multilateral organizations.

The world and Japan itself, too, thought the country could contribute towards reconciling conflicts between development and the environment. As the world's second largest economy, Japan consumes a disproportionate share of the world's energy and resources and contributes heavily to environmental degradation. Japan also has the economic means and technological capabilities to help address environmental problems. In response to this international pressure, Japan introduced new policy guidelines in overseas assistance and substantially increased aid to environment-related activities.

At UNCED, for example, the Japanese prime minister headed the largest national delegation to the meeting. He asserted that "The prosperity Japan has achieved through the utilization of the resources of the earth makes it incumbent upon Japan to play a leading role in the international efforts for both environment and development."[21] To back his words, he pledged that Japan would spend between 900 billion and 1 trillion yen (the largest sum committed by a single country) on official development assistance in environmental fields over five years from 1992.[22]

Although international pressure was crucial to pushing Japan to take actions on global environment issues, Japan was also keenly aware of the intimate connections between the global environment and its national interests. Japan's dependence on external sources of energy and raw materials has been a main force in shaping the Japanese view of national security.[23] The 1981 Japan Defense White Paper summarizes this thinking,

> Japan is dependent for its survival and prosperity on imports of the bulk of its resources and energy. Among the possible threats to its

Introduction

> safety and existence are the restrictions or suspensions of supplies of resources, energies, and foodstuffs, etc., as well as armed aggression.[24]

Such a perspective easily casts Japan as a "passive" or "reactive" state in international politics. However, this could only be true if interpreted in a simplistic fashion. Careful analysis shows that strategic logic and rationality are clearly evident in the minds of Japanese policy makers when they craft and choose policy options. In fact, Japanese policies are unusually direct in their ties to the two overarching national objectives of promoting economic growth and ensuring national security, and their conceptions of security can heavily influence the definition of national interests and policy preferences.[25] In the case of modern Japan, the Japanese government has long held economic welfare as central to national security and Japanese people are broadly concerned about access to natural resources and energy.[26] Consequently, environmental issues are largely seen as resource issues by Japanese policy makers.

This linking of the international environment to national security is not new or unique to Japan. Brown, Matthews, Myers, and Westing, among others, have added an environmental components to their definitions of national security.[27] What makes Japan exceptional is the extent to which the advancement of its narrowly defined national interests is openly acknowledged by Japanese policy elites inside and outside of the government. This sentiment is especially strong within the Japanese bureaucracy, which is one of the oldest institutions of modern Japan and created with the mission to guide the country's transformation into a modern, industrialized nation-state.

Hence, Japanese policies towards international environmental issues are most strongly driven by its core interest in access to resources and energy. Conserving nature and biodiversity is not an end but means to sustainable resource development and use. This explains Japanese government wariness for sentiments that emphasize protection of nature and resources without equal acceptance for access and use. Therefore, "sustainable growth" and "sustainable development," in particular, quickly became popular catch phrases in Japanese diplomacy. Environmental conservation, from the Japanese government perspective, must recognize and support human consumptive needs of natural resources.[28]

Apart from its basic reliance on the global environment for national survival and prosperity, Japan has other reasons to take interest in international environmental issues. First, as Ikle and Nakanishi said in their 1990 article, "The time has come for Japan to develop a sense of purpose for contributing to a peaceful world on a scope commensurate with its enormous economic and technological strength."[29] Expansion of the Japanese economy throughout much of the 1980s had increased international pressure on Japan to assume greater responsibilities in world affairs, and protecting the environment was considered a positive cause by the Japanese government. Unlike defense and peacekeeping activities, the global environment is a broadly popular and less politically controversial issue for Japan domestically and internationally.[30] Japan might even erase its image as an "economic animal" and "environmental outlaw." Japan also has great economic wealth and technological capabilities to tackle international environmental problems. Hence, Japanese policy makers felt confident that Japan could meet this challenge, as well as international expectations.

Second, for a country that has become the second largest economy in the world, Japan hosts a very small number of international organizations. This is a reminder that despite the country's wealth, Japan still lacks status in international affairs. This was a driving factor behind the Japanese government's rigorous campaign to bring the International Tropical Timber Organization's secretariat to Japan.

Japan also welcomed the opening of international environmental technology centers in Osaka and Shiga by the United Nations Environment Program in November 1992. These were the first United Nations environment-related offices in Japan.[31] Their mission was to facilitate the transfer of technology from industrialized to developing economies. United Nations offices are particularly valued by the Japanese government because the Japanese public has a fairly high opinion of the United Nations and consider Japanese participation in United Nations activities a symbol of positive membership in the international community.

Third, considerations of economic costs and benefits are also major forces behind Japan's interest in the global environment.[32] For example, helping developing countries to improve energy efficiency is much cheaper than reducing greenhouse gas emissions domestically. Since Japan has already gone through several rounds of energy efficiency improvement. Further domestic improvement would be extremely costly.

As for benefits, Japan could profit from sales of environmental goods and services. The demand for environmental business has been growing worldwide. The reasons behind this phenomenon include social pressure for environmental cleanup, availability of technological solutions, changes in lifestyle, "subsidized" demand created by the presence of environmental aid, introductions of regulations and deregulation to encourage environmental improvement, and preferential treatment and financing from international agencies for environment-related projects.[33] The 1992 report of the Organization for Economic Cooperation and Development (OECD) entitled *Environment Industry: Situation, Prospects and Government Policies* estimated that the global market for environmental technologies will grow from US$200 billion in 1990 to US$300 billion by the year 2000.[34]

At present, 85 percent of this market is found in OECD member countries, and the United States alone represents 40 percent of the market. Developed countries will remain the top markets, but demand for environ-

Introduction 9

mental technologies is expected to increase substantially in other parts of the world. Asia, in particular, could be a highly profitable market. The region has been growing rapidly, and its markets for environmental goods and services are less competitive than in Western Europe, North America, and Japan. Hong Kong, South Korea, Singapore, and Taiwan would be the first tier of Asian economies to invest in environmental technologies, and Thailand, Indonesia, and China would follow. Most of this environmental clean up in Asia and elsewhere around the world will be funded by development assistance, and the transfer of clean coal technologies to tackle global warming and acid rain is a priority.[35] "Toward an Environmental Strategy for Asia," a 1993 World Bank report, estimated that the region may spend up to US$40 billion annually by the year 2000. Improving water supply and sanitation would be the biggest areas for "environmental investment" (reaching US$12.2 billion), followed by soil conservation and afforestation (reaching US$8.6 billion).[36]

Japanese businesses could profit substantially from this demand for environmental goods and services. Domestic enforcement of stringent pollution control regulations and extensive implementation of clean technologies since the early 1970s have helped to produce an advanced and competitive Japanese environmental industry. In fact, Japanese firms are world leaders in advanced air and water pollution control technologies.[37] Japanese businesses would also be in a good position to penetrate Asian markets with the help of Japanese ODA. Table 1 and Figure 2 below show that Asia continues to receive the largest amount of Japanese ODA despite a decline in its total percentage share as a result of Japan's more diversified international interests.[38]

Table 1. Regional distribution of ODA, (net disburstments, %)

Region	1970	1980	1985	1990	1992	1996
Asia	98.3	70.6	67.7	59.3	65.1	49.6
Middle East	3.3	2,5	1.7	1.5	2.0	6.7
Africa	2.3	18.9	15.0	15.4	12.2	12.8
Latin America	-4.0	6.0	8.8	8.1	9.1	11.8
Europe	-0.2	0.2	1.1	6.9	1.5	2.4
Oceania	0.0	0.5	0.9	1.6	2.0	2.4
Unclassifiable	0.3	1.2	4.8	7.1	8.2	14.3

Note: "-" indicates recovery surplus.

Source: *Japan Almanac 1995*, Tokyo: Asahi Shimbun, 1995, p.115; and JICA, *An Introduction to JICA*, September 1997, p.3.

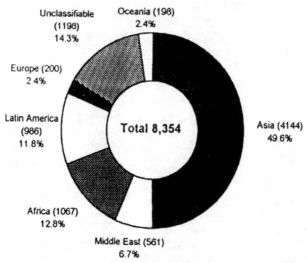

Source: JICA, *An Introduction to JICA*, September 1997, p.3.

Figure 2. Japan's bilateral ODA by area, FY 1996 (US$ million)

Japanese government allocations for environment-related activities, in particular, have increased considerably in the past decade. Numerous governmental and quasi-governmental bodies and programs have been established to help Japanese businesses. For example, the Ministry of International Trade and Industry created the Global Industrial and Social Progress Institute in 1988 to help industry in overseas transfers of environmental technologies in ODA-funded projects. The ministry's programs to combat global warming, such as the Action Plan to Arrest Global Warming, the Green Aid Plan, and the Green Aid Initiative announced in 1997, also explicitly involve the private sector.

Adjustments in Japan's ODA policy on environmental assistance loans provide further evidence of support for private industry. To increase purchases by aid recipient countries, in May 1995 the Japanese government lowered the interest rate on its bilateral assistance loans for environment-related projects to 0.2 percentage points below the usual.[39] In January 1998, intense pressure from Japanese industry forced the Japanese government to reverse its policy on untying ODA loans for environment-related projects in developing countries. Figure 3 below shows a rapid improvement in procurement conditions for Japanese ODA loans from 1985 to 1996. This policy change could restore obstacles for non-Japanese firms obtaining contracts for Japanese ODA-funded projects.[40]

Introduction

Figure 3. Trends in procurement conditions on Japan's ODA loans

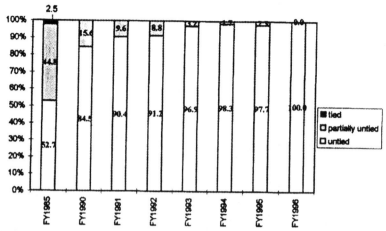

Source: <<www.mofa.go.jp/policy/oda/summary/1997/chart9.html>> viewed on 11 May 1998.

Fourth, some parts of the Japanese government have interest in the global environment because bureaucratic interests are involved. Japan's ODA program and its environment-related allocations, in particular, have grown steadily despite freezes and cuts in other areas of the government budget. As Figure 4 shows below, by 1995, Japan led the world in total ODA disbursement. The sum was approximately US$14.5 billion, making Japan by far the world's largest ODA donor.[41] It was not until 1998 that Japan's ODA budget was reduced for the first time in its history as a result of severe government budgetary constraints. In other words, the country's ODA budget has been a source of new funds for the bureaucracy.

Figure 4. Net disbursement of ODA among major industrialized nations, 1986-1995

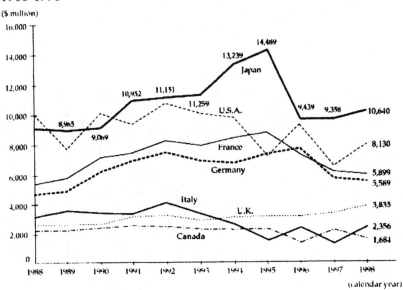

Source: 1999 DAC Press Release.

Fifth, responsibility for the environment is diffused throughout the government bureaucracy, so ministries and agencies consider involvement in environment-related decision making a way to expand their powers and influence. This includes clever definitions of issues and problems to fit existing divisions of power and the building of complex relationships with other interested policy actors inside and outside of the government to advance their own bureaucratic goals.

Finally, for Japanese society, supporting global environmental protection gives them a sense of common identity with the world community. Having attained material wealth, Japanese people became more interested in a place and mission for their country in world affairs. Public support is widespread for Japanese participation in international environmental issues as an expression of the country's efforts in internationalization and international cooperation. Moreover, the issue proffers an opportunity for Japan to overcome its limitations in defense and peacekeeping activities. Surveys have shown that a majority of Japanese considers the global environment an area in which Japan could make positive contributions. This public interest was also reflected in the number of global environment-related articles in the four major newspapers in Japan between 1987 and 1992, the

Introduction 13

year of the Rio Earth Summit. In one case, it grew from zero to 1,321 articles within this five-year period.[42]

In summary, domestic and international level forces have shaped Japan's interests and goals in the global environment. Although Japan's ambitions in and commitment to international environmental issues have declined in recent years, the international environment is still prominent in the country's foreign policy agenda because international expectations and the domestic roots of its interests and goals in the issue continue to persist.

THE CASE STUDIES: WHALING, DEFORESTATION IN THE TROPICS AND ACID DEPOSITION IN ASIA

Case studies on whaling, deforestation in the tropics, and acid deposition in Asia were selected for their individual distinction and collective complementarity in explaining Japanese perspectives and policies toward the global environment. Each case covers two key Japanese policy responses. While they are reflective of Japan's perspectives, interests, and goals in these particular issues, they also render insights into Japan's perspectives, interests, and goals towards the larger issue of global environmental protection. The following are brief descriptions of these three cases and the policy responses studied.

Whaling

The policy responses studied are (1) Japan's 1982 objection to the International Whaling Commission's temporary ban on commercial whaling and its later acquiescence, and (2) its decision to launch a scientific research whaling program in 1987.

Japan's whaling policy makes an interesting case study because the country has consistently and unequivocally refused to give up commercial whaling. When an international whaling moratorium was passed in 1982, Japan immediately filed an official objection to it. International pressure forced Japan to withdraw this objection, but Japan opposes it and has worked laboriously to lift this moratorium. Such explicit display of determination is not only rare for Japan, it also appears odd considering that commercial whaling has no national economic importance and outside criticisms have been damaging to Japan's international prestige and credibility in environmental conservation.

Nonetheless, Japanese policy makers consider their position critical to defending access to natural resources and their consumptive and commercial use. To them, this is a fight for legal principles and scientific integrity in international conservation and management regimes, as well as respect for cultural diversity.

Whaling, as a case study in intra-government rivalry in decision making, shows how a single policy actor could exercise dominant influence. The Fisheries Agency has been the most powerful actor because all fisheries matters, including whaling, fall under its official jurisdiction. Only vital linkages of whaling to other policy issues compelled Fisheries Agency officials to accept policy compromises. The United States had to tie Japanese whaling to Japanese fishing rights in U.S. waters in order to force Japan to relinquish its objection to the commercial whaling ban.

In this connection, whaling highlights how bilateral issues in Japan-U.S. relations can affect Japanese policy making. The two countries were the biggest players on opposite sides of this issue. The Japanese prime minister and most other politicians and bureaucratic actors would rather give up whaling than incur any damage to bilateral relations. Japan-U.S. relations, in particular, were beset by bilateral trade tensions in the years when these two policy decisions were made.

Therefore, there were serious concerns of how whaling, or specifically insisting Japan's right to whale, could make Japan more vulnerable in bilateral trade negotiations. Prime Minister Yasuhiro Nakasone took the unusual step to independently amend the Fisheries Agency's research whaling proposal. Such acts are extremely rare for Japanese prime ministers who do not generally take active participation in the policy process and not especially in issues outside of economic and security areas.

As an environmental issue, whaling provides many useful insights. First, as one environment scholar puts it,

> [whales are]...the most poignant symbol of the world environmental movement...the survival of whales continues to be an object of international anxiety...and perhaps better than any other issue illustrates the difficulty in reconciling multiple conflicting interests and values of nations in management and protection of the biosphere.[43]

In fact, whaling is widely regarded as the first true international environmental issue. Rapidly declining whale populations worldwide by the 1960s gave impetus to the growth of conservation movements, especially in North America. Anti-whaling campaigns grew rapidly into a worldwide phenomenon by the 1970s and gave thrust to the ascendancy of conservation groups and issues in national and international politics. The passing of the moratorium in 1982 was a critical turning point in the international regime for whaling for it signaled the triumph of the anti-whaling movement.

In addition, the issue of whaling (and whales) sheds light on evolution of the common property resource concept, which is central to the development of international regimes for the conservation, management, and use of resources.[44] Other questions on conservation seen through this case study are debates on the place of science, culture, and morality in conservation,

Introduction

indigenous rights, commercial use of renewable natural resources, and the use of totems in conservation movements.

Deforestation in the tropics

The Japanese policy responses studied in this case are (1) the allocation of Japan's ODA for forestry conservation in the tropics and (2) Japan's decision to host the International Tropical Timber Organization (ITTO). Together they represent Japan's basic perspectives and approach to deforestation in the tropics (and other types of forests around the world).

Shifting agriculture, poverty, and the conversion of forests into plantation estates and other uses have been held largely responsible for the destruction of tropical forests. However, the international tropical timber trade initiates the process of destruction because these cuts are the most commercially valuable. So although the international tropical timber trade accounts for less than five percent of the total volume of tropical timber consumed worldwide, it fuels logging expansion, opens lands to migrant settlers, and makes land available for conversion to commercial plantations.

Japan has been the world's top importer of tropical hardwood for many decades and Southeast Asia has been its main supply source. Hence, Japanese domestic demand has been a main impetus behind the expansion of commercial logging and timber industries in the region. In addition, Japanese government assistance and business loans and investments have helped to build infrastructure, purchase heavy machinery, and procure other essentials for logging and timber exports in these tropical hardwood-producing countries.

Changes in the domestic demand and overseas supply structure since the late 1970s had greatly reduced Japan's import of tropical timber. As a result, these policy responses had more to do with defense of Japanese interest in resource use and the realization of diplomatic ambitions in international affairs than tropical forest conservation.

In studying policy making in Japan, this issue provides further evidence of the Japanese government's views and policies towards the environment, particularly natural resource issues. In contrast to whaling where the Fisheries Agency dominated, three large ministries shaped Japanese policies in this issue. They all used their official powers and influence over related issues, as well as forces outside of the government, to advance their respective goals and interests in intra-governmental negotiations. Remarkable, too, was the success of domestic conservation groups in raising public awareness of tropical forest destruction as well as Japan's role in it through their anti-tropical timber campaign. Although NGOs still have a long way to go in truly penetrating the policy process, the government bureaucracy, politicians and big business in Japan could no longer refute that NGOs are legitimate voices in civil society.

In diplomacy, this study of Japan's policy responses to deforestation in the tropics highlights Japan's economic ties with its Southeast Asian neighbors and the role ODA plays in tropical timber (and other resource) exploitation. Japan's 1985 decision to host the ITTO secretariat also reflects its aspiration for greater international stature. In an issue that is easily cut by the North-South divide, it would be a serious test of Japan's ability to bring together often opposing perspectives and interests to realize sustainability in natural resource conservation and use.

As an environmental issue, protecting forests in the tropics replaced whaling as a priority issue for many international conservation groups following the passing of the commercial whaling ban in 1982. Concern for the rapid and extensive destruction of tropical forest first emerged in the 1970s as a result of increased scientific understanding of their importance to ecology and global climate change. By the 1980s, concern grew into alarm as the world learned more about the impact of deforestation on the environment and human communities in these forests.

Like whaling, tropical deforestation also raises questions on the conservation, management, and use of renewable natural resources. However, forests are not common property resources, and banning the use of forests or timber is not a viable solution because human consumptive needs of these resources cannot yet be terminated or fully replaced by other commodities. Moreover, forests are a source of food and medicines and they are home to millions of hunting and gathering tribal peoples and other forest inhabitants.

Consequently, achieving sustainability in timber production and consumption has been the general consensus among international organizations, governments, industry and conservation groups. Yet, the current international trade regime poses many obstacles to achieving sustainable forestry. The building of an international regime for forests has also been hampered by ideological, political, and economic differences between the developed and developing countries and between producers and consumers of timber.

Acid deposition in Asia.

The two key policy responses examined in this case are (1) Japan's decision in 1988 to create an Acid Deposition Monitoring Network in East Asia and (2) Japan's assistance to China's energy sector and efforts to engage China in multilateral cooperation.

In Asia, rapid economic growth in the last decade has greatly increased energy consumption in the region. Dependence on coal in energy production and the lack of pollution control devices have increased emissions of sulfur and nitrogen oxides, which are causes of acid pollution. In fact, acid

Introduction

deposition has become a major domestic and transboundary environmental problem in Asia. Japan's worries about its vulnerability as a net importer of acid pollution from China, which is now the world's largest producer of sulfur dioxide.

In contrast to whaling and deforestation in the tropics, acid rain is not a problem that Japan can distance itself from physically. The transboundary movement of air pollutants made Japan realize the importance of international cooperation to effectively address this problem. Hence, Japan aims to build a multilateral acid rain control regime in Northeast Asia and actively assists China to improve its energy sector.

The Environment Agency of Japan is the leading bureaucratic actor in this issue. It has managed to establish and maintain bureaucratic leadership in policy making by defining acid rain as a pollution matter, one that falls distinctly within its jurisdiction. (Instead of allowing the Ministry of International Trade and Industry, which has formal authority over energy issues, to take control.) As a small body with limited financial and human resources, the Environment Agency has to exercise creative assertiveness and cautious cooperation with the bigger bureaucratic actors to pursue its goals. One way is to use its official role as a policy coordinating body within the Japanese government; another is to emphasize the use of scientific expertise—which it commands—to minimize intervention by other policy actors inside and outside of the government who do not have this capability.

In diplomacy, this has been a rare instance of Japan taking initiatives to respond to an external problem. The potential threat of large-scale environmental and health damage from transboundary air pollution from the Asian continent has been an important cause of this pro-active behavior. Although Japan has a clear objective, the material wealth, and technology to help reduce sulfur emissions in China and other parts of Asia, Japanese policy makers have acted with caution and sensitivity because of the country's history of relations with its Asian neighbors. This is also another situation where Japanese leadership is being tested. Many difficulties are present. For instance, unlike Western Europe, the region lacks a tradition in multilateral cooperation and regional frameworks for multilateral cooperation were sorely inadequate. Moreover, sovereignty disputes between mainland China and Taiwan as well as on the Korean peninsula greatly complicate regional cooperation.

As an environmental problem, transboundary acid pollution was first confirmed in Europe in the 1960s. Since acid pollution is tied to industrial development, its emergence as a major environmental problem in Asia in the 1990s is clearly a by-product of the region's rapid economic growth throughout much of the 1980s and 1990s. Growth of the Chinese economy has been particularly striking. According to a United Nations Conference on Trade and Development report, foreign direct investment in China more

The Roots of Japan's Environmental Policy

than doubled from US$11.1 billion in 1992 to US$25.8 billion in 1993, making China the second largest recipient of foreign direct investment after the United States.[45] Hence, measures to curb air pollution in Asia are drastically needed to avoid more severe costs on human health and the environment.

Acid rain differs from whaling and deforestation. Its a pollution problem and a transboundary one. Since the transport of acid pollutants is dictated by regional wind and climate conditions, regional—not global—approaches to the problem may be most effective. The invisibility of acid pollution and the lack of apparent physical damage in Asia at this time, compared to forest loss and decline in whale populations, also increase the importance of science to establish the problem and to move parties to action.

In summary, these three cases together document the rise of environmental issues in national and international political agendas since the end of World War II and international and Japanese responses. The three cases are complementary in their emphasis on aspects of environmental issues that may be present or prominent in one case and absent or non-relevant in another to allow analytical comparisons and contrasts. For instance, an international conservation regime exists in whaling, while one is still in the making for forest conservation, and none exists or is called for in acid rain control. Differences, too, are evident in the role or function of science as a policy driver and tool of policy actors in the three cases. Finally, the cases highlight a multitude of issues associated with environmental conservation, including equity in access and use of natural resources, achieving sustainability, the efficacy of development assistance and technology and the rights of indigenous peoples.

For the study of Japanese politics and policy making, the distinctive nature, history and importance of each issue reveal how the Japanese government responds to different kinds of environmental problems. They show that the potentials and limitations for the exercise of power depend not only on the size and capabilities of an actor, but also on the peculiarities of an issue and the policy framework in which it is found or set. Hence, the policy actors, their influence and the preferred policy choices could change as an issue evolves in the domestic and international policy framework.

STRUCTURE OF THE STUDY

There are seven chapters in all. Chapter 2 covers the theoretical concepts and models used in this study. Chapter 3 focuses on how environment (domestic and international) evolved as a policy issue in domestic Japanese politics and identifies the major actors in Japan. Chapters 4, 5 and 6 are

Introduction 19

the case studies on whaling, deforestation in the tropics and transboundary acid pollution in Asia. The final chapter presents conclusions to this study.

Notes

[1] Lynton K. Caldwell, *Between Two Worlds: Science, the Environmental Movement and Policy Choice*, Cambridge: Cambridge University Press, 1991, p.79.

[2] For more on citizens movements and the democratic process in Japan, see Kurt Steiner *et al.*, eds., *Political Opposition and Local Politics in Japan*, Princeton: Princeton University Press, 1980.

[3] David Potter, ed., *NGOs and Environmental Policies: Asia and Africa*, London and Portland: Frank Cass, 1996; and John Farrington *et al.*, eds., *Non-governmental Organizations and the State in Asia*, London and New York: Routledge, 1993.

[4] A sample includes Kent E. Calder, "Japan's Foreign Economic Policy Formation: Explaining the Reactive State," *World Politics*, Vol.40, July 1988, pp. 517-41; Daniel I. Okimoto, "Political Inclusivity: The Domestic Structure of Trade," *The Political Economy of Japan: The Changing International Context*, ed. by Takashi Inoguchi and Daniel I. Okimoto, Vol.2, Stanford: Stanford University Press, 1988, pp.305-344; T.J. Pempel, *Policymaking in Contemporary Japan*, Ithaca: Cornell University Press, 1977; Chalmers Johnson, *MITI and the Japanese Miracle: The Growth of Industrial Policy*, Tokyo: Charles E. Tuttle Press, 1982; and Michele Schmiegelow, ed., *Japan's Response to Crisis and Change in the World Economy*, Armonk: M.E. Sharpe, 1986.

[5] For example, Michael W. Donnelly, "Conflict over Government Authority and Markets: Japan's Rice economy," in *Conflict in Japan*, ed. by Ellis S. Krauss, Thomas P. Rohlen and Patricia G. Steinhoff, Honolulu: University of Hawaii Press, 1984, pp.355-374; Stephen M. Weatherford and Haruhiro Fukui, "Domestic Adjustments and International Shocks in Japan and the United States," *International Organization*, Vol.43, No.4, Autumn 1989, pp.586-623; Robert M. Orr, Jr., *The Emergency of Japan's Foreign Aid Power*, New York: Columbia University Press, 1990; and Leonard Schoppa, "Two-level Games and Bargaining Outcomes: Why *Gaiatsu* Succeeds in Some Cases and Not Others," *International Organization*, Vol.47, No.3, Summer 1993, pp.353-386.

[6] *Ibid.*

[7] Yoshihiro Nomura, "History, Structure and Characteristics of Japan's Environmental Law" in Reeitsu Kojima *et al.*, eds., *ibid.*, p.141.

[8] MoFA, "Japan's Environmental Cooperation," n.d., p.3.

[9] For example, see Richard Forrest, "Japanese Aid and the Environment," *The Ecologist*, Vol.21, No.1, January/February 1991, pp.24-32; Yo Kimura, "The Environmental Impact of Foreign Aid," Program on U.S.-Japan Relations, Harvard University, Occasional Paper, 1990; and Rene E. Ofreneo, "Japan and the Environmental Degradation of the Philippines," *Asia's Environmental Crisis*, ed. by Michael C. Howard, Boulder: Westview, 1993, pp.201-233.

[10] For instance, William E. Rees criticizes the concept's distortion by the political mainstream and calls for a new definition in his article, "The Ecology of Sustainable Development," *The Ecologist*, Vol.20, No.1, January/February 1990, pp.18-23.

[11] MoFA, "Looking Ahead...," *op cit.* This also explains Japan's willingness to host the United Nations Environment Program's International Environmental Technology Center in Osaka City and Shiga Prefecture. See <<www.mofa.go.jp/policy/global/environment/pamph/1994/coop.html>>. Viewed on 9 May 1998.

[12] Examples of this kind of thinking can be found in the following: Hiroshi Inose, "Technological Innovation and Japan's International Contribution," *Japan Review of International Affairs*, Vol.6, No.3, Fall 1992, pp.255-274; Shigeaki Fujisaki, "Environmental Issues in Developing Countries and the Role of ODA," *Japan Review of International Affairs*, Vol.7, No.1, Winter 1993, pp. 68-83; and Michio Hashimoto, "Some Thoughts on Japan's Role in Tackling Environmental Problems in Developing Countries," *Technology and Development*, No.3, 1990, pp. 5-15.

[13] L. Reid, *The Sociology of Nature*, London: Penguin Books, 1962; and Rachel Carson, *Silent Spring*, Boston: Houghton Mifflin, 1962.

[14] Also commonly known as the Stockholm Conference.

[15] Garret Hardin, "The Tragedy of the Commons," *Science*, No.162, 1968, pp.1243-1248; P. Ehrlich and A. Ehrlich, *The Population Bomb*, New York: Ballantine, 1968; and D. Meadows *et al.*, *The Limits to Growth: A Global Challenge, A Report for the Club of Rome Project on the Predicament of Mankind*, New York: Universe Books, 1972.

[16] See Caldwell, *Between Two Worlds...*, *op cit.*, p.1; and David A. Kay and Harold K. Jacobson, eds., *Environmental Protection: The International Dimension*, New Jersey: Allanheld Osmun, 1983.

[17] *The Global 2000 Report to the President*, Washington, D.C.: U.S. Government Printing Office, 1980; International Union for Conservation of Nature and Natural Resources (IUCN and also known as the World Conservation Union), *World Conservation Strategy: Living Resource*

Introduction

Conservation for Sustainable Development, Gland: IUCN, 1980; World Commission on Environment and Development, *Our Common Future*, Oxford: Oxford University Press, 1987; and V. Shiva, *Staying Alive: Women, Ecology and Development*, New Delhi: Zed Books, 1988.

[18] For more on environmental conflicts, see Stephan Libiszewski, "What is Environmental Conflict?" Occasional paper of the Environment and Conflicts Project, No.1, July 1992; and Volker Boge's "Proposal for an Analytical Framework to grasp `Environmental Conflict,'" in the same publication.

[19] Held in Rio de Janeiro, Brazil; also commonly known as the Rio Earth Summit.

[20] They include Agenda 21 and its action programs for the sustainable use of natural resources in development; the Forest Principles, a non-binding agreement on forest conservation and use; and conventions on global climate change and biodiversity.

[21] Ministry of Foreign Affairs, "Looking Ahead: A Foreign Policy for a Changing World," *Japan's Policy Series*, No.9302E, July 1993, pp.2-5.

[22] The actual sum exceeded this pledge by more than 40%, reaching 1.44 trillion yen (or US$13.3 billion). See <<www.mofa.go.jp/policy/oda/summary/1998/8.html>>. Viewed on 10 March 2000. Also see Sigeki Nishihira *et al.*, eds., *Environmental Awareness in Developing Countries: The Cases of China and Thailand*, Tokyo: Institute of Developing Economies, 1997, p.24.

[23] See for example, Robert S. Ozaki and Walter Arnold, eds., *Japan's Foreign Relations: A Global Search for Economic Security*, Boulder: Westview Press, 1985.

[24] *White Paper of Japan, 1981-82*, Tokyo: The Japan Institute of International Affairs, 1981, pp.37-38.

[25] Arnold Wolfers, *Discord and Collaboration*, Baltimore: Johns Hopkins University Press, 1962, p.150.

[26] Until the end of World War II, *fukoku kyohei* or "rich nation, strong army" was a central tenet behind Japanese policies for the main lesson leaders of modern Japan drew from observations of Western colonialism and imperialism was that economic might is the basis of national power.

[27] See Lester Brown, *Redefining National Security*, Washington, D.C.: Worldwatch Paper No. 4, October 1977; Jessica T. Matthews, "Redefining Security," *Foreign Affairs*, Vol.68, No.2, 1989, pp.162-177; Norman Myers, "Environmental Security," *Foreign Policy*, No.74, 1989, pp.23-41; and Arthur H. Westing, "The Environmental Component of Comprehensive Security," *Bulletin of Peace Proposals*, Vol.20, No.2, 1989, pp.129-134. There are also voices opposing this view. Daniel Deudney, for example, defined threats to national security strictly as inter-state violence and warns that harnessing "the emotive power of nationalism to help mobilize environmental awareness and action may prove counter-produc-

tive by undermining globalist political sensibility." See Deudney's "The Case Against Linking Environmental Degradation and National Security," *Millenium: Journal of International Studies*, Vol.19, No.3, 1990, pp.461-476.

[28] The concept was coined by IUCN in its World Conservation Strategy and later popularized by the *Our Common Future* report. The report defines it as "Development that meets the needs of the present without compromising the ability of future generations to meet their own needs."

[29] Fred Charles Ikle and Terumasa Nakanishi, "Japan's Global Strategy," *Foreign Affairs*, Vol.69, No.3, Summer 1990, p.81.

[30] On the other hand, Japanese participation in United Nations peace-keeping missions began with hopes but ended with disappointments. There was not enough domestic support to sustain this commitment. In addition, the Japanese government had to balance between foreign expectations and foreign anxieties. The former criticized Japan for only providing non-military support services in low-risk areas. The latter, mostly from countries that had suffered from past Japanese aggression, voiced concerns for Japanese remilitarization.

[31] See D.C. Liu *et al.*, *Huanjin Wenti, Cong Zhong Ri Bijiao Yu Hezuo De Guandien Kan* (Environmental Problems: A Comparative View of Sino-Japanese Conditions and Cooperation), Beijing: People's University Press of China, 1995, p.195.

[32] See Neil Gross, "Charging Japan with Crimes against the Earth," *Business Week*, 9 October 1989, pp.108 and 112.

[33] Masanobu Kaizu and Shigeo Hiratsuka, "Environmental Business Opportunities in Japan," *NRI Quarterly*, Vol.1, Summer 1992, p.2.

[34] These figures include expenditures on equipment, systems, physical plants, and services. OECD, *The OECD Environment Industry, Situation, Prospects and Government Policies*, Paris: OECD, 1992, p.16.

[35] *Ibid.*

[36] This compares with the OECD estimate of US$31 billion for Asia (excluding China) by the year 2000. *Ibid.*; and The "Asian economies exact environment toll," *The Japan Times*, 7 December 1993, p.20.

[37] For more details, please see Makoto Natori, "Japan's Pollution Control Technologies and Their Role in the World," *Japan Review of International Affairs*, Vol.7, No.1, Winter 1993, pp.51-67.

[38] Having a regional preference is not unique to Japan. 70% of British aid goes to Commonwealth countries, 90% of French aid goes to its foreign provinces, territories and former colonies, and 40% of U.S. aid went to Israel and Egypt in the 1980s. See Katsuya Mochizuki, "Economic Development and Environmental Issues in Asia: Focusing on Official Development Aid," *Development and the Environment: The Experiences of Japan and Industrializing Asia*, ed. by Reeitsu Kojima *et al.*, Tokyo: Institute of Developing Economies, 1995, pp.411 and 413.

[39] Hisane Misaki, "China sinks deeper into ecological cesspool," *The Japan Times*, 23 June 1995.

Introduction

[40] Japan's Foreign Ministry announced that 100% of ODA loans were untied by the 1996 fiscal year. This complies with the OECD ban on tying aid loans when the interest rate is around the group's average of 2.5% Consequently, Japanese businesses only obtained 30% of those international tenders and the rest were won by European and North American firms. By lowering the interest rate to just 0.75% in November 1997, Tokyo can legally reinstate tied aid to give Japanese firms a monopoly in ODA-funded environment-related projects in developing countries. See Ministry of Foreign Affairs, "Japan's Official Development Assistance Summary 1997," n.d., p.43.

[41] *Ibid.*

[42] Shigeaki Fujisaki, "The Global Environment and North-South Relations: Considering the Future of the Earth," *Environmental Awareness in Developing Countries: The Cases of China and Thailand*, ed. by Sigeki Nishihira *et al.*, Tokyo: Institute of Developing Economies, 1997, p.2.

[43] Lynton K. Caldwell, *International Environmental Policy: Emergency and Dimensions*, 2nd ed. Durham and London: Duke University Press, 1990.

[44] On common property theory and case studies, see Fikret Berkes, ed., *Common Property Resources: Ecology and Community-based Sustainable Development*, London: Belhaven Press, 1989; Elinor Ostrom, *Governing the Commons: The Evolution of Institutions for Collective Action*, Cambridge: Cambridge University Press, 1990; Daniel W. Bromley *et al.*, eds., *Making the Commons Work: Theory, Practice and Policy*, San Francisco: Institute for Contemporary Studies, 1992; and Bonnie J. McCay and James M. Acheson, eds., *The Question of Commons: The Culture and Ecology of Communal Resources*, Tucson: University of Arizona Press, 1987.

[45] Nishihira *et al.*, eds., *op cit.*, p.17.

Chapter 2

Theory and Methodology

How are international environmental issues characterized in the international system? How do international institutions for the environment evolve? How and to what extent do they affect the policies of individual governments and *vice versa*? What are the causes of foreign policy? Is it dictated by systemic forces, driven by foreign pressure or domestic politics, or a product of the idiosyncratic preferences of individual decision makers? Or perhaps a combination of all of these? More specifically, what explains foreign policy making processes in Japan?

To answer these questions, this study draws on several sources to construct a conceptual framework for analysis:

- the theory of complex interdependence to demonstrate linkages between bureaucratic politics and transgovernmental relations;
- regime theory to understand how and why international institutions of governance and cooperation are formed and how they affect sub-systemic policy making, particularly as it pertains to the environment;
- Putnam's two-level games theory to study the inter-level dynamics that affect the making of foreign policy; and
- the bureaucratic politics model, to examine domestic policy process in Japan.

COMPLEX INTERDEPENDENCE, REGIMES AND TWO-LEVEL GAMES

The question of the level of analysis has long preoccupied scholars of international relations and foreign policy. Time and again, approaches that focus on a single level of analysis were found inadequate in explaining the roots of foreign policy.

Systemic level approaches enable observations of patterns of interaction and generalizations about relationships in the international system, but they can exaggerate systemic influences on national actors and underestimate the impact of actors on the system. They also have the tendency to produce a sort of "black box" or "billiard ball" concept of the national actors, that is, a high degree of uniformity in the foreign policy operational codes of the national actors is automatically presumed.

State level approaches, on the other hand, take an in-depth look at national actors and allow comparative generalizations. They highlight the goals, motivations, and purpose of actors who act on behalf of the state in formulating and executing foreign policy. The main drawback is their potential to overstate differences among sub-systemic actors.[1]

Another limitation of single level approaches is that they ignore the notion that linkages among issues are endemic and can render the domestic-international distinction meaningless. Revolutions in communication, transportation, and technology, for instance, have greatly weakened the realist paradigm's assumption of the division between these two spheres. Single level approaches also do not recognize the importance of issues, and bureaucratic actors are simply aggregated into their respective national governments when governments are not single, unitary entities.

Hence, theorists of international relations and foreign relations have moved towards multi-level approaches in explaining a world of increasing interdependence and where they see foreign policy as integrally related to domestic structures and processes.[2] Among them, Rosenau pioneered the concepts of domestic-international "linkages," "penetrated" societies, "issue areas," and states as "adaptive entities," that is, adapting simultaneously to internal and external influences.[3]

Under situations of interdependence, governments are still the main actors, but their primacy diminishes because of increasing participation in international politics by a multiplicity of subnational, transnational, and supranational actors.[4] Furthermore, the power or influence that an actor yields in one issue may not apply in another issue because degrees of interdependence can vary from one issue to another. Issues of interdependence, due to their technical nature and decentralized structure, can also cause greater fragmentation and intra-governmental conflicts in decision making. Thus, intensive bargaining often occurs among actors seeking solutions to conflicts and control over issues. Scientific knowledge also gains importance as a tool of persuasion. Under interdependence, redefinition of issues and the building of new international institution can alter even long-established patterns of interaction.[5]

Gourevitch's notion of a "Second Image Reversed" deepened conceptual understanding of the interactive ties between the systemic and state levels. By suggesting that the international system is both a consequence of domestic politics and structures, and a cause of them, Gourevitch's work

Theory and Methodology

helps to explain how the international system affects regime types and coalition partners within individual nations.[6]

"Complex interdependence"

Further refinement by Keohane and Nye produced the concept of "complex interdependence." With roots in the liberal-institutionalist tradition, complex interdependence opposes several basic realist assumptions: that states are coherent units and dominant actors in the international system, that force is a usable and effective instrument of policy, and that a hierarchy of issues exists in world politics.

Complex interdependence posits a world in which actors other than states participate directly in world politics. Multiple channels of contact open up to expand non-governmental and transnational contacts.[7] Samhat found that non-governmental groups, such as Greenpeace International, Friends of the Earth, and Amnesty International, are significant forces in international politics because they raise public consciousness towards issues, provide representation for minorities, and bring together local communities worldwide for a common cause.[8] Governmental bureaucracies, too, may alter their perspectives and form transgovernmental coalitions on particular policy questions as a result of contacts. Under complex interdependence, the potential role of international organizations is also greatly enhanced in international politics. This allows small and weak states, as well as non-state actors, to use these multilateral fora to present and assert their views.[9]

Complex interdependence also posits that military force losses its effectiveness as an instrument of policy. This is because the defense of national interest becomes more complicated with the breakdown of sharp boundaries between domestic and systemic levels. However, Keohane and Nye did not dismiss the idea that military force remains as a policy instrument. The main difference compared to realism is that "military force is not used by governments toward other governments within the region, or on the issues, when complex interdependence prevails," and it may be "important in these governments' relations with governments outside that region, or on other issues."[10] Therefore, complex interdependence is more characteristic of economic and environmental issues than military ones, and that it is more common among advanced, industrialized countries than developing ones.

Finally, a clear hierarchy in actors and issues does not exist. The agenda is affected principally by changes in the distribution of resources within the issue areas and a variety of processes. These include the evolution of international regimes and their ability to cope with changing economic and technological circumstances, changes in the importance of transnational actors, linkages from other issues, and issue politicization as a result of domestic politics.[11] Since gains and losses are not a zero-sum game, actors

The Roots of Japan's Environmental Policy

can exploit asymmetrical interdependence as a source of power. Goals, too, would vary by issue area and the distribution of power within it.

Regimes, issue areas, and national interests

Since a clear hierarchy of actors and issues does not exist and goals could vary by issue area and the distribution of power within it, the relevance of regimes increases in issues of complex interdependence. Krasner defined regimes as:

> sets of implicit or explicit principles, norms, rules, and decision making procedures around which actors' expectations converge in a given area of international relations. Principles are beliefs of fact, causation, and rectitude. Norms are standards of behavior defined in terms of rights and obligations. Rules are specific prescriptions or proscriptions for action. Decision making procedures are prevailing practices for making and implementing collective choice.[12]

By providing a context for interaction (or cooperation), regimes serve to organize issue areas, reduce uncertainty, reduce transaction and information costs, and facilitate negotiations among groups with substantially different interests. The collective enforcement mechanisms of a regime also lessen the likelihood of autonomous defection and permit selective punishment of violations of norms.[13]

Since regimes are basically social institutions, they can occur naturally as a set of norms and rules that have evolved over time and are implicitly or explicitly accepted or they can be created deliberately to give order to an issue area.[14] One hypothesis on regime formation suggests that knowledge and values can play a direct role in regime formation. The importance of shared values and knowledge of causal connections is stressed. A network, or an epistemic community, would emerge to link those who share a common understanding of the problem and its solutions and allow them to communicate their ideas persuasively to policy makers.[15] Transnational coalitions, domestic politics, and ideas can also be important.[16] Finally, contextual factors, such as events and conditions in the international setting and science and technology, can significantly improve chances of success in regime formation.[17] Since regimes can change over time in response to economic and political pressures, changes may be basic shifts in a system's power structure, internal contradictions that are inherent in a system or which develop over time, as well as major revisions in domestic priorities.[18]

In Keohane and Nye's view, the structure of the international system profoundly affects the nature of an international regime. The international regime, in turn, affects and, to some extent, governs the political bargaining and daily decision making that occur within the international system.[19] Regimes, or the fabric of one, may provide the foundation for other

Theory and Methodology 29

regimes. The linking of regimes can also "have significant consequences for the outcomes flowing from the operation of each of the affected regimes."[20] Thus, the effectiveness of a regime—international or domestic—varies depending on the issue area and its linkages, as well as changes in a regime's issue structure and the distribution of power within it. Finally, regimes will continue to exist and remain effective only as long as the groups or actors utilizing them find it in their interest to maintain them.[21]

On the matter of issues and issue areas, the core idea is that issues and issue areas are created when a phenomenon or problem persists or continues. The specific policy/issue at stake will determine who will become involved in policy making.[22] Lowi observed that the kinds of behavior actors engage in depends on the issue and that each issue area will develop its own "political structure, political process, elites and group relations.".An understanding of the policy content thus becomes essential.[23] Gowa's work supports this by her assertion that state strength can be distinguished along issue-area lines.[24]

Different forces can affect a government's definition of state interests and national roles and its decisions for actions. These forces include international institutions and regimes, individual and group learning, as well as domestic political change.[25] While survival of the state is the most basic goal, a state also has other important national interests. Hence, a state's role can differ from one issue to another and be active in some and passive in others.[26]

In issues of complex interdependence, Keohane and Nye proposed that how policy actors respond depends on their "sensitivity" and "vulnerability" interdependence in that situation. "Sensitivity" interdependence can be social, political or economic. It is created by interactions within a framework of policies and "contagion" effects can occur to increase that sensitivity. A state's sensitivity interdependence involves "degrees of responsiveness within a policy framework," which can be measured by the volume of flows across borders, as well as "the costly effects of changes in transactions on the societies or government." Moreover, "sensitivity interdependence is created by interactions within a framework of policies" (and this framework is assumed to remain unchanged). As a result, sensitivity interdependence reflects the immediate effects of external changes.

Vulnerability interdependence, on the other hand, depends on the relative availability and costs of the alternatives faced by actors. An actor's vulnerability can be measured by its ability to bear costs imposed by external events after changes in policies. While sensitivity reflects the immediate effects of external changes, vulnerability interdependence reflects the costs of "making effective adjustments to a changed environment over a period of time."

Players can attempt to manipulate sensitivities and vulnerabilities in a situation to improve their bargaining positions at either level. Success in

30 The Roots of Japan's Environmental Policy

exploiting vulnerabilities is more important because they are critical to providing power resources for a player in situations of interdependence. However, manipulating sensitivities and vulnerabilities is not risk-free because it could prompt counter-strategies by other players. As a result, there are limits to the ability of players to manipulate asymmetrical interdependence.[27]

International regimes can have different kinds of impact at the domestic level. For example, they can influence a government's definition of its national role, change standard operating procedures for national bureaucracies, and present new coalition opportunities for subnational actors to improve access for third parties. They can also encourage incremental learning, change the attitude of participants through contact with institutions, and provide information about compliance with rules to increase knowledge about the behavior of other actors.[28]

While internal and external pressures may compel a government to act or respond to a situation or issue, leadership does not automatically occur. Internal and external pressures also would not be effective at all times and under all conditions. In issues of interdependence, issue linkages exist and non-state actors are present in the political system. Hence, "...leadership is not so much a matter of some powerful actor structuring the incentives of others through the use of negative and positive sanctions, though such efforts undoubtedly do occur on a regular basis, as the deployment of entrepreneurial skills or creativity in identifying and putting together mutually beneficial deals."[29]

Two-level games theory model

In issues of complex interdependence and regimes, the game theoretic approach provides a descriptive and analytical framework to analyze the motivations and preferences of states in an issue area. Under game theory, a mixture of conflicting and complementary interests prompts negotiations among policy actors. Cooperation results when actors adjust their behavior to the actual or anticipated preferences of others.[30] In this negotiation process, actors can employ a variety of strategies to increase their bargaining leverage and to push opponents to reach an agreement.

Interest in the connections between the systemic and domestic levels of analysis gave rise to the two-level games approach proposed by Putnam in his article "Diplomacy and Domestic Politics: The Logic of Two-level Games" in 1988.[31] Several principal concepts in this approach can find roots in international relations and decision making literature of the past three decades. Among them are games, organizational and bureaucratic politics, interdependence, and linkage politics.[32]

Interest in the two-level games model generated a larger project that resulted in an edited volume by Evans, Jacobson and Putnam in 1993 with 11 case studies on security, economic, and North-South conflict issues.[33]

Theory and Methodology

Other works have also tried to refine and expand this theoretical model's conceptual ideas, investigate its potentials and limitations, and add new elements to strengthen and enrich it.[34]

Unlike traditional game theory, which concentrates on bargaining among players (policy actors) within a single level of analysis, the two-level games model assumes that players are simultaneously engaged in negotiations on two levels (domestic and international). Games in the two levels occur in parallel and connections between them can impact on bargaining within each level.

In fact, this "double-edged" quality of the two-level games model is its most distinctive feature. This model emphasizes that policy makers simultaneously calculate the implications of international and domestic implications of decisions in working to achieve their policy (and personal) goals.[35] What may be rational for a player at one level of bargaining may not be so for the same player at another level. At the same time, the connections between levels can also open opportunities for players in either level. This stress on the interaction between the two levels (the domestic "table" and the international "table") makes it an "interactive" approach, which recognizes that domestic policies can be used to affect the outcomes of international bargaining and that international moves may be aimed at achieving domestic goals.

The two-level games approach also differs from traditional views in its treatment of internal divisions, which are not seen to necessarily weaken a state's bargaining position at the international level. In some situations, internal divisions may even strengthen a state's bargaining position. For instance, when both sides have an interest in reaching an agreement, "a differential in the relative size of the win-sets shifts the distribution of costs and benefits in favor of the player with the more constrained win-set."[36]

The interactive nature of the two-level games approach means that many strategies and conditions that may be exploited at the domestic table may also be used at the international table. To begin with, negotiators can take advantage of their freedom to act autonomously within the domestic win-set. Moravcsik posits that "the statesman has exclusive power to negotiate internationally, and to submit items for domestic ratification. This affords the statesman a tacit veto over any agreement, which can be exercised simply by refusing either to negotiate in earnest or to submit any accord for ratification."[37]

Another way is to expand or constrict the win-set at his and his opponent's table.[38] Schoppa finds that "participation expansion" and "alternative specification" could, respectively, increase pressure on a decision and encourage consideration of policy proposals not previously studied.[39] Participation expansion, in particular, can force bureaucrats, who previously reigned supreme in their issue areas, to coordinate their bargaining with officials from other ministries. Participation is also broadened when interest in the issue expands to include higher levels of government as well as new interest groups or important constituencies outside of the government.

A common way to expand participation is through issue redefinition, which changes the character of an issue, and it can be done by any of the following means:

- "internationalize" a domestic issue at either table to broaden public concern and increase the level of participation in the domestic arena;[40]
- make an issue bigger, more inclusive, and significant to security and national core values to help negotiators to garner political support from domestic constituencies to accept (or reject) an agreement;[41] and
- redefine an issue into one with implications for an important bilateral relationship.[42]

A third strategy is to use issue linkage and "synergistic issue linkage." The latter specifically links previously unrelated issues in the domestic arena to the issue at stake in international negotiations. This also has the effect of expanding participation and may open up the process of international negotiations for a broad cross-sectoral compromise.[43]

Fourthly, foreign pressure can increase public awareness of a problem or a previously neglected domestic issue. With the aid of the media, foreign pressure can become a rallying point for the unorganized and ignored general public.[44] Schoppa concluded that foreign pressure tend to produce the most positive results when the strategies resonate with domestic politics.[45]

This is how "reverberations" can alter constraints for the other side and affect expectations about an agreement held by domestic groups there. In Putnam's view, these are a negotiator's silent allies in an opponent's domestic table. International pressure may even transform these groups from a minority into a majority. Such reverberations may result from either deliberate attempts at persuasion or they may be the unintended result of public reaction to the course of negotiations. Transnational allies are seen as crucial in this interactive approach because domestic groups, such as nongovernmental organizations and business interests, can substantively undermine or strengthen domestic support for the opponent and affect his or her "acceptability set" and bargaining strategy.[46]

Another strategy is to affect the costs and benefits of agreement to key constituents. Raising the costs of non-agreement would make unfavorable agreements relatively more attractive, while offering specific benefits to powerful domestic constituencies or swing groups through linkages and side-payments may also induce agreement.[47] Two-level games theory assumes that domestic coalitions form on the basis of an assessment of the relative costs and benefits of negotiated alternatives to the status quo.

Hence, the more diffused the costs and benefits of the proposed agreement, the more possibilities there are for them to target swing groups and gain their support at relatively low costs.

Finally, the exploitation of information asymmetries can strengthen the bargaining position of the negotiator and the state. The negotiator may wish to preserve a distribution of information and knowledge that favors his/her interests or change it if the current balance is perceived to favor the adversary. He/she also needs knowledge about knowledge, which includes how much the others know.[48] A negotiator may also manipulate public perceptions at the domestic and international levels by selectively releasing information. This strategy may be more effective when there is substantial uncertainty about the content of an agreement.[49]

DECISION MAKING: THE BUREAUCRATIC POLITICS MODEL AND JAPAN'S FOREIGN POLICY

Having examined the evolution of thinking on interdependence, regimes, and two-level games theory, this section takes a step down to the domestic level to look at decision making under the bureaucratic politics model and in Japan's foreign policy in particular. Milner concluded in her review of Grieco's *Cooperation Among Nations* and Haas' *Saving the Mediterranean* that the "biggest gains in understanding international cooperation in the future are likely to come from domestic-level theories."[50] When domestic structures, such as political institutions, state-society relations and political culture, can determine success in access to the policy process and in building domestic and transnational coalitions.

The bureaucratic politics model

The bureaucratic politics model began with Hilsman's 1959 article "The Foreign Policy Consensus: An Interim Research Report."[51] Foreign policy "products" (decisions and behavior) are seen as outcomes of a bureaucratic-political process in which bargaining takes place among players (actors) positioned hierarchically in the government. The games theoretic approach is central to analysis and "decision games" are played in converting activities into decisions.[52]

Allison's work explicitly challenged the realist assumptions of the unitary nature of governments. Bureaucracies and individual officials are seen as acting independently or even competing with the central decision maker, even if they do not form transnational coalitions.[53] Allison's bureaucratic politics model hypothesizes intensive bargaining among decision making entities. There is no consistent master plan but "conflicting perceptions of national bureaucratic and personal goals." Policy is seen not to emanate from a centralized, objective decision maker, but from a conglomeration of powerful organizations with different missions, perceptions and priorities.

34   *The Roots of Japan's Environmental Policy*

In other words, where you sit influences what you see and where you stand.[54]

Moreover, although perception is central to the definition of a situation, a decision maker's preferences are rarely based entirely on objective understandings of an issue area. With rationality bounded by cognitive and information limits and egotism, actors can only achieve near rationality or make choices that are "satisficing."[55] Perceptions about issues, linkages and pay-off structures are influenced by a host of subjective factors, including partisan definitions, political obligations, memories of individuals and organizations and personality attributes.[56] Decision makers also do not only focus on a single strategic issue or have any consistent set of strategic objectives to guide their actions. Instead, they look simultaneously at many diverse intra-national issues and act according to various conceptions of national, organizational and personal goals.

Nonetheless, bureaucratic organizations (and its sub-units) have an inherent desire to build governing coalitions with other actors in the policy making process because they can be levers to strengthen their own bargaining power and position for immediate benefit or future gains. Consequently, a policy outcome is not a single, rational choice but the result of competition and compromise (the pulling and hauling) forged through bargaining at the micro-level and the position reached may not be what the individual players exactly wanted or anticipated. Hilsman also noted that "very often policy is the sum of a congeries of separate or only vaguely related actions. Sometimes it is an uneasy, even internally inconsistent, compromise among competing goals or an incompatible mixture of alternative means for achieving a single goal."[57]

Although the bureaucratic politics model is not without problems,[58] it provides a useful conceptual framework to understand why bargaining takes place and explain how or why different goals and interests can find compromise to produce policy positions or decisions on a given issue.

Decision making and Japan's foreign policy

The bureaucratic politics model has been extensively used in studying Japan's post-World War II foreign policy because the Japanese government bureaucracy holds a central position in policy making. However, it is not a unitary monolith and it is not perfectly insulated from outside forces.[59] Muramatsu and Krauss described the contemporary policy making system in Japan as "patterned pluralism" by stating that,

> Pluralism exists because influence is dispersed among a wide variety of competing actors. There are many points of access to the policy making process and interest groups can penetrate the government and yet remain free of governmental control. At the same time, policy making is 'patterned' in that political alliances with interest groups are relatively fixed due to the one-party dominance, the framework provided by the bureaucracy and the ideological cleavages.[60]

Theory and Methodology

Therefore, the bureaucracy may have control over vital flows of information, cumulative experience, and expertise, as well as regulatory powers over the financial system, but negotiations take place with powerful constituencies outside of the government to win compliance in areas beyond regulatory control.[61] Some scholars have even gone further to suggest the idea of "reciprocal consent" of mutual influences by state and private sector on state and market choices.[62]

The bureaucratic politics model also suggests that the extent to which bureaucracies can shape public policies vary over time, by issue area, and according to bureaucratic jurisdiction. Research has confirmed this characteristic in Japanese policy making.[63] In addition, ministries within the Japanese government are co-equals (in status, if not in actual power and influence) and loyalties divide along ministerial (and even smaller unit) lines. Since each has its own jurisdictions, goals, interests, and constituencies, conflicts and differences are always present. Intensive bargaining and negotiations often occur within the government and with outside actors whose support is important to reaching consensus on policy decisions and implementation.

In the case of Japan, studies have shown that policy actors highly value consensus in decision making because they usually have to interact with each other over long periods of time and across a broad range of issues. Hence, their negotiations and bargaining are usually set within the context of their long-term relationships and these long-term relationships can affect the outcome of the bargaining process.

Increasing evidence also suggests that the powerful bureaucracy can serve as a communication link between domestic and foreign groups, as mediator of domestic disagreements and as coordinator of the overall negotiating process.[64] Growing interdependence by the 1980s also meant more signs of pluralism and transnational linkage between Japanese domestic interest groups and their counterparts overseas as Japanese foreign policy and domestic politics, too, is increasingly exposed to the effects of interdependence.[65] Domestic issues turn into foreign issues and *vice versa*. An increasing number of ministries and agencies, including non-governmental actors, outside of the Ministry of Foreign Affairs have become involved in foreign policy matters. As a result, what is a foreign policy issue from one point of view may be a domestic issue from another.[66]

In its foreign policy, Japan has long been characterized as a "reactive state" that responds only when there is outside pressure and then it still only copes with the international environment.[67] Japanese leadership also tends to be technical and sector-specific rather than broadly political. This inability to respond to outside demands is largely attributed to narrowly defined perceptions of self-interests in the international arena, the fragmented character of state authority in Japan, and the lack of strong top leadership to make policy initiatives.

Nonetheless, outside pressure or *gaiatsu*, though seemingly critical to induce Japanese responses, does not appear to be effective at all times and in all issues. Studies with approaches that examine inter-level dynamics in policy making have found that foreign pressure tends to produce the most positive result when these strategies resonate with domestic politics. In other words, outside pressure works only when the domestic balance of power already factors or shifts on its own to favor the outside position.[68] Domestic politics determines how costs are calculated and national interests would prevail over international pressure.[69]

In this connection, there are questions as to whether bilateral or multilateral pressure may be more effective in obtaining Japanese cooperation, under what circumstances, in what particular issues, and to what extent. Although Japan highly values good relations with the United States because of their defense and economic ties, multilateral pressure could be more effective in situations of growing interdependence in world politics. Japanese public would more likely view a multilateral decision as a "world opinion" and more willing to defer to "world opinions" than to bilateral pressure from the United States.[70]

METHODOLOGY

All policies are basically domestic policies because the most important constituents are within the domestic setting. The challenge then is to identify the domestic roots of foreign policy decisions. The discussion above presented arguments on the merits of the two-level games theory over those based on a single level of analysis in explaining the causes of foreign policy and how the bureaucratic politics model has elucidated understanding on policy making in Japan.

Hence, this study draws on concepts from both approaches to identify and explain the domestic roots of Japan's international environmental policies. Emphasis is also placed on the issue itself. The international environment, as an issue of complex interdependence, has its own characteristics. Each international environmental problem or issue can have its own characteristics, history, regime, and set of interested policy actors.

A search for the domestic roots of Japan's international environmental policies can expand understanding in many ways. First, it helps to illuminate how policy issues, particularly those of complex interdependence, are set in the domestic political context and ascertain the influence of outside forces (international regimes and agreements, bilateral and multilateral pressures, transnational and non-governmental actors, and public opinion).

Second, it helps to identify participants in the policy process, their interests, and influence. Since shared and divergent interests among policy actors can affect their interactions with each other, negotiations could significantly affect resulting policy choice and actions.

Theory and Methodology

Third, it could help to explain disparities, if any, between international expectations and Japan's responses. For instance, international conservation groups and the Japanese government have, on the whole, differed on their views and responses to most nature conservation issues. For these groups, biodiversity conservation is their major concern. For the Japanese government, nature is seen primarily as a source of raw materials for consumption. Hence, its policies have focused more on supporting human/commercial access and use over conservation. The Japanese government also generally opposed to proposals that could curtail or terminate human/commercial use of nature/natural resources.

Fourth, the roles and influence of transnational epistemic communities in policy making would be subjected to evaluation. It has been suggested that epistemic communities, generally consisting of scientists, government officials, and secretariat members from specialized international agencies, can become influential enough in the domestic arena to affect a government's acceptance and compliance with international treaties and regimes. Nonetheless, domestic political considerations also matter and political leaders would not hesitate to put them above scientific findings or coalitions.[71] The U.S. government's response to transboundary acid pollution problems with Canada throughout much of the 1980s is evidence of this tendency.

Therefore, using the two-level games theory and the bureaucratic politics model with an issue-centered focus may better explain the motivations and objectives behind Japanese government responses to international environmental issues. In this manner, Japan's policies towards international environmental issues would help to explain domestic political dynamics and *vice versa*.

The theories discussed are examined in the three case studies of Japanese foreign environmental policies. Each case focuses on two major policy responses which are representative of Japanese government motivation and objectives in the issue studied. Each case also examines the nature of the problem and international responses to them (in the form of regimes that are existing or evolving) to enable comparisons of international and Japanese government responses.

Field study was conducted in Japan from August 1994 to December 1995. Over a hundred interviews were conducted. They included meetings with Japanese government officials chiefly responsible for the policy issues studied in this dissertation (e.g., the Ministry of Foreign Affairs, the Environment Agency of Japan, and the Ministry of Agriculture, Forestry and Fisheries) and staff in Japanese and international conservation NGOs in Japan (e.g., Japan Tropical Forest Action Network, Elsa, Friends of the Earth and the World Wide Fund for Nature). Interviews were also conducted with academics, researchers, and scientists in Japanese government-affiliated institutions and private organizations (e.g., Tsukuba University,

Mitsui Marine Research Institute, Institute of Developing Economies, the Japan Institute for International Affairs), journalists (e.g., *The Japan Times, Bungei Shunju*), and staff in business enterprises and associations (e.g., Sumitomo, Keidanren, and Keizai Doyukai).

Between the end of the field study in Japan and the end of December 1997, additional meetings took place in person with experts and officials from various organizations in Tokyo, Jakarta, Beijing, Edmonton and Hawaii. The Internet also facilitated communications with researchers around the world.

Most meetings were conducted in English, or a mix of Japanese and English, and a few were in Mandarin Chinese in Beijing. Nearly all interviews were conducted in person and usually at the interviewee's work place. Questions focused mainly on the perceptions and objectives of the organizations, groups, and individuals responsible for or interested in the issues examined in this study. Questions also addressed relations among these organizations, groups or individuals to investigate the dynamics of their interaction within the parameters of the issues studied, as well as in areas that are linked to them. The interviewees were informed that the purpose of the interviews was for academic research. Only in a few instances did interviewees request anonymity for their comments.

Secondary research materials were mainly gathered from libraries at the University of Hawaii at Manoa and the East-West Center in Honolulu, the International House of Japan, Keio University, Tsukuba University, the United Nations University, and the Institute for Developing Economies in Japan. Towards the end of this study, the Internet and the World Wide Web were also useful tools in data collection.

The primary and secondary sources used were mainly books, articles in academic journals and newspapers, and published and unpublished reports of government offices, international organizations, and non-governmental organizations in the United States, Europe, Japan, and Indonesia. English-language materials make up the bulk of the resources used, and Japanese and Chinese language materials were also used.

Theory and Methodology

Notes

[1] J. David Singer, "International Conflict: Three Levels of Analysis," *World Politics*, Vol.12, April 1960, pp.453-461; and J. David Singer, "The Level-of-Analysis Problem in International Relations," *World Politics*, Vol.14, October 1961, pp.77-92.

[2] Stephan Haggard and Beth A. Simmons, "Theories of International Regimes," *International Organization*, Vol.41, No.3, Summer 1987, pp.491-517.

[3] See James N. Rosenau, "Pre-theories and Theories of Foreign Policy" in *Approaches to Comparative and International Policies*, ed. by R. Barry Farrell, Evanston: Northwestern University, 1966, pp.27-92; James N. Rosenau, *Linkage Politics: Essays on the Convergence of National and International Systems*, New York: The Free Press, 1969; James N. Rosenau, ed., *Domestic Sources of Foreign Policy*, New York: The Free Press, 1967; and James N. Rosenau, "Adaptive Polities in an Interdependent World," *Orbis*, Vol.16, Spring 1972, pp.153-173.

[4] James N. Rosenau, *International Studies in a Transnational World*," *Millennium: Journal of International Studies*, Vol.5, No.1, Spring 1976, pp.1-20.

[5] James N. Rosenau, "Capabilities and Control in an Interdependent World," *International Security*, Vol.1, October 1976, pp.32-49.

[6] Peter Gourevitch, "The Second Image Reversed: the International Sources of Domestic Politics," *International Organization*, Vol.32, No.4, Autumn 1978, pp.881-911.

[7] See James N. Rosenau, "International Studies in a Transnational World," *Millenium: Journal of International Studies*, Vol.5, No.1, 1997, pp.1-20.

[8] Nayef H. Samhat, "International Regimes as Political Community," *Millenium: Journal of International Studies*, Vol.26, No.2, 1997, pp.349-378.

[9] Keohane and Nye, *op cit.*, pp.25 and 26.

[10] *Ibid.*, p.25.

[11] Robert O. Keohane and Joseph S. Nye, *Power and Interdependence: World Politics in Transition*, New York: Little, Brown and Co., 1977, p.24.

[12] Stephen Krasner, ed., *International Regimes*, Ithaca and London: Cornell University Press, 1980, p.2.

[13] See James N. Rosenau, "Before Cooperation: Hegemons, Regimes, and Habit-driven Actors in World Politics," *International Organization*, Vol.40, No.4, Autumn 1986, pp.849-894; and Kenneth A. Oye, ed., *Cooperation under Anarchy*, Princeton: Princeton University Press, 1985.

[14] Regimes may be imposed or negotiated, but Young asserts that the incidence of imposed orders is inversely related to the level of interdependence in societies. Oran R. Young and Gail Osherenko, eds., *Polar Politics: Creating International Environmental Regimes*, Ithaca and London:

Cornell University Press, 1993, pp.19-20. Also, Richard Cooper, "International Cooperation in Public Health as a Prologue to Macroeconomic Cooperation" in *Can Nations Agree? Issues in International Economic Cooperation*, ed. by Richard Cooper *et al.*, Washington, D.C.: Brookings Institution, 1989, pp.178-254.

[15] Sikkink also calls them "principled issue networks." See Kathryn Sikkink, "Human Rights, Principled Issue-Networks, and Sovereignty in Latin America," *International Organization*, Vol.47, No.3, Summer 1993, pp.411-442; Peter Haas, "Do Regimes Matter? Epistemic Communities and Mediterranean Pollution Control," *International Organization* Vol.43, No.3, Summer 1989, pp.378-403; Peter Haas, *Saving the Mediterranean*, New York: Columbia University Press, 1990, pp.55-56; and Emanuel Adler and Peter M. Haas, "Conclusion: Epistemic Communities, World Order and the Creation of a Reflective Research Program," *International Organization*, Vol.46, No.1, Winter 1992, pp.367-390.

[16] Thomas Risse-Kappen, "Ideas Do Not Float Freely: Transnational Coalitions, Domestic Structure and the End of the Cold War," *International Organization*, Vol.48, No.2, Summer 1994, pp.185-214.

[17] There are arguments that regime formation is more likely when parties have a greater propensity to focus on scientific or technical considerations, when negotiators with a scientific technical background have a greater role in negotiations and when the issues to be dealt with in creating the regime are highly technical (in contrast to issues that are openly political). See Young and Osherenko, *op cit.*, pp.16 and 20.

[18] See Oran R. Young, *International Cooperation: Building Regimes for Natural Resources and the Environment*, Ithaca and London: Cornell University Press, 1989, p.100; and Oran R. Young, *Resource Regimes: Natural Resources and Social Institutions*, Berkeley: University of California Press, 1982, pp.107-110.

[19] Keohane and Nye, *op cit.*

[20] Oye, ed., *op cit.*; and Oran R. Young, "Institutional Linkages in International Society: Polar Perspectives," *Global Governance*, Vol.2, No.1, 1996, pp.1-24.

[21] For more on interdependence and regimes, see Robert Gilpin, *War and Change in World Politics*, Cambridge: Cambridge University Press, 1981; Robert Axelrod, *The Evolution of Cooperation*, New York: Basic Books, and 1984; Robert O. Keohane, *After Hegemony: Cooperation and Discord in the World Political Economy*, Princeton: Princeton University Press, 1984. On the effectiveness of international regimes, environmental ones in particular, see Oran R. Young and Konrad von Moltke, "The Consequences of International Environmental Regimes: Report from the Barcelona Workshop," *International Environmental Affairs*, Vol.6, No.4, Fall 1994, pp.348-370.

[22] Charles W. Kegley, Jr. and Eugene R. Wittkopf, *American Foreign Policy: Pattern and Process*, New York: St. Martin's Press, 1987.

[23] Theodore Lowi, "American Business, Public Policy, Case Studies and Political Theory," *World Politics*, Vol.16, No.4, July 1964, pp.677-715.

[24] Joanne Gowa, "Public Goods and Political Institutions: Trade and Monetary Policy Processes in the United States," *International Organization*, Vol.42, No.1, Winter 1988, pp.14-32.

[25] David A. Baldwin and Helen V. Milner, "Economics and National Security," in *Power, Economics and Security: The United States and Japan in Focus*, Boulder: Westview Press, 1992, pp.29-50.

[26] K.J. Holsti, "National Role Conceptions in the Study of Foreign Policy," *International Studies*, Vol.14, No.3, September 1970, pp.233-309.

[27] Keohane and Nye, *op cit.*, pp.12-14.

[28] *Ibid.*

[29] Young, *International Cooperation...*, *op cit.*, pp.234-235; Keohane and Nye, *op cit.*, pp.229-232. For more on leadership in international regimes, see also Young and Osherenko, *op cit.*, p.18.

[30] See James G. March and Herbert A. Simon, *Organizations*, New York and London: John Willy and Sons, 1958.

[31] Robert D. Putnam, "Diplomacy and Domestic Politics: The Logic of Two-level Games," *International Organization*, Vol.42, No.3, Summer 1988, pp.427-460.

[32] These include those mentioned above and others, such as: Wolfers, *op cit.*,; James N. Rosenau, *Domestic Sources of Foreign Policy*, New York: The Free Press, 1967; Graham T. Allison, *Essence of Decision: Explaining the Cuban Missile Crisis*, Boston: Little, Brown and Co., 1971; Jonathan Wilkenfeld, ed., *Conflict Behavior and Linkage Politics*, New York: David McKay Co., 1973; John Steinbruner, *A Cybernetic Theory of Decision: New Dimensions in Political Analysis*, Princeton: Princeton University Press, 1974; Peter J. Katzenstein, ed., *Between Power and Plenty: Foreign Economic Politics of Advanced Industrial States*, Madison: University of Wisconsin Press, 1978; Robert D. Putnam and Nicholas Bayne, *Hanging Together: Cooperation and Conflict in the Seven-Power Summits*, London: Sage, 1987; and Michael Mastanduno, David A. Lake and John G. Ikenberry, "Toward a Realist Theory of State Action," *International Studies Quarterly*, Vol.33, December 1989, pp.457-474.

[33] Peter B. Evans, Harold K. Jacobson and Robert D. Putnam, eds., *Double-Edged Diplomacy: International Bargaining and Domestic Politics*, Berkeley: University of California Press, 1993.

[34] Examples are Peter F. Cowhey, "Domestic Institutions and the Credibility of International Commitments: Japan and the United States," *International Organization*, Vol.47, No.2, Spring 1993, pp.299-326; H. Richard Friman, "Side-Payments versus Security Cards: Domestic Bargaining Tactics in International Economic Negotiations," *International*

Organization, Vol.47, No.3, Summer 1993, pp.387-410; Harold P. Lehman and Jennifer L. McCoy, "The Dynamics of the Two-level Bargaining Game: The 1988 Brazilian Debt Negotiations," *World Politics*, Vol.44, No.4, July 1992, pp.600-644; Frederick W. Mayer, "Managing Domestic Differences in International Negotiations: The Strategic Use of Side-Payments," *International Organization*, Vol.46, No.4, Autumn 1992, pp.793-818; and Schoppa, *op cit*.

[35] Although the two-level games approach focuses on the international and domestic levels, the individual level is also understood to play a significant role. This is because the "negotiator" is the central actor in negotiation and has the power to choose his strategies to manipulate interaction between international and domestic levels to achieve his policy objectives. See Putnam, *op cit.*, p.436; and Andrew Moravcsik, "Introduction: Integrating International and Domestic Theories of International Bargaining," in Evans *et al.*, eds., *op cit.*, pp.15-17.

[36] A "win set" is defined as "the set of potential agreements that would be ratified by domestic constituents in a straight up-or-down vote against the status quo of no agreement." See Moravcsik, *ibid.*, pp.23 and 28.

[37] Putnam uses the term "negotiator" in his 1988 article, while "statesman" is used in the 1993 edited volume by Evans, Jacobson and Putnam. The two, however, are basically the same. See *Ibid.*, pp.24-25.

[38] *Ibid.*, pp.25 and 28.

[39] See Leonard Schoppa, "Two-level Games and Bargaining Outcomes: Why *Gaiatsu* Succeeds in Some Cases but Not Others," *International Organization*, Vol.47, No.3, Summer 1993, p.373.

[40] *Ibid.*, p.372; and Lowi, *op cit.*, pp.677-715.

[41] Friman, *op cit.*, pp.391 and 402-403.

[42] Schoppa, *op cit.*, p.384.

[43] Putnam, *op cit.*, pp.455-458.

[44] Schoppa, *op cit.*, p.372.

[45] *Ibid.*, p.384.

[46] An "acceptability set" is the set of agreements preferred by the negotiator to the status quo. It may reflect the negotiator's interest in enhancing his/her domestic position, decision to respond to international imperatives regardless of domestic factors and individual policy preferences about the issues in question. See Moravcsik, *op cit.*, p.30.

[47] Side-payments are compensatory measures aimed at facilitating agreements between actors. It could be in the form of direct monetary compensation or indirect compensation in material concessions on other issues. Friman finds that the weaker the domestic resistance is to the proposed compensation, the more likely policy makers are willing to offer side-payments. See Friman, *op cit.*, pp.391 and 402-403.

Theory and Methodology

[48] Yaacov Vertzberger, *The World in their Minds: Information Processing, Cognition and Perception in Foreign Policy Decisionmaking*, Stanford: Stanford University Press, 1990.

[49] Moravcsik, *op cit.*, p.34.

[50] Helen Milner, "International Theories of Cooperation Among Nations: Strengths and Weaknesses," *World Politics*, Vol.44, No.3, April 1992, pp.466-496. See also Joseph Grieco, *Cooperation Among Nations*, Ithaca: Cornell University Press, 1990; and Haas, *Saving the Mediterranean, op cit.*

[51] Roger Hilsman, "The Foreign Policy Consensus: An Interim Research Report," *Journal of Conflict Resolution*, No.3, 1959, pp.361-82.

[52] Lincoln P. Bloomfield, *The Foreign Policy Process: Making Theory Relevant* London and Beverly Hills: Sage Professional Papers, International Studies Series, Vol.3, No.02-028, 1974.

[53] Allison, *op cit.*

[54] *Ibid.*

[55] Herbert A. Simon, *Administrative Behavior: A Study of Decision-Making Processes in Administrative Organization*, 3rd ed., New York: The Free Press, 1976.

[56] For instance, the Sprouts talked of a psychomilieu and the "operational environment" in James E. Dougherty and Robert L. Pfaltzgraff, Jr., *Contending Theories of International Relations: A Comprehensive Survey*, 3rd ed., New York: Harper and Row, 1990. See also Harold and Margaret Sprout, *Foundations of International Politics*, Princeton: Nostrand, 1962.

[57] Roger Hilsman, *The Politics of Policy Making in Defense and Foreign Affairs*, New York: Columbia University Press, 1971.

[58] Commonly criticized are its assumption that bureaucratic actors behave in a rational manner and the vagueness of any boundary between the institutional role performance and idiosyncratic behavior. For more, see Yale H. Ferguson and Richard W. Mansbach, *The Elusive Quest: Theory and International Politics*, Columbia: University of South Carolina Press, 1988, pp.174-178.

[59] For example, T.J. Pempel, *Policy and Politics in Japan: Creative Conservatism*, Philadelphia: Temple University Press, 1982; T.J. Pempel, "The Unbundling of `Japan, Inc.': The Changing Dynamics of Japanese Policy Formation," *The Journal of Japanese Studies*, Vol.13, Summer 1987, pp.271-306; J.A.A. Stockwin *et al.*, *Dynamic and Immobilist Politics in Japan*, Honolulu: University of Hawaii Press, 1988; Haruhiro Fukui, "Studies in Policymaking: A Review of the Literature," *Policymaking in Contemporary Japan*, ed. by T.J. Pempel, Ithaca and London: Cornell University Press, 1977, pp.22-59; Chalmers Johnson, *op cit.*; and Michio Muramatsu and Ellis S. Krauss, "Bureaucrats and Politicians in Policymaking: The Case of Japan," *The American Political Science Review*, Vol.78, No.1, March 1984, pp.126-146.

[60] The Japanese political landscape has seen some great changes in the 1990s, including a disruption of nearly half a century of the Liberal Democratic Party rule. However, the Liberal Democrats continue to have the strongest ties with the bureaucracy as a result of their long and intimate working relationship in the past decades. See Muramatsu and Krauss, *ibid.*

[61] John O. Haley, "Governance by Negotiation: A Reappraisal of Bureaucratic Power in Japan," *Journal of Japanese Studies*, Vol.13, Summer 1987, pp.343-357

[62] Richard Samuels, *The Business of the Japanese State: Energy and Markets in Comparative and Historical Perspective*, Ithaca and London: Cornell University Press, 1987.

[63] Okimoto, *op cit.*, p.318.

[64] *Ibid.*

[65] For instance, I.M. Destler *et al.*, *The Textile Wrangle: Conflict in Japanese-American Relations, 1969-1971*, Ithaca: Cornell University Press, 1979; Orr, *op cit.*; Schoppa, *op cit.*, and Leonard Schoppa, *Bargaining with Japan: What American Pressure Can and Cannot Do*, New York: Columbia University Press, 1997.

[66] Haruhiro Fukui, "Too Many Captains in Japan's Internationalization: Travails at the Foreign Ministry," *The Journal of Japanese Studies*, Vol.13, Summer 1987, pp.359-381.

[67] For example, Calder, *op cit.*; and Gerald Curtis, ed., *Japan's Foreign Policy After the Cold War: Coping with Change*, New York: M.E. Sharpe, 1993, pp.1-42.

[68] Examples are Frances McCall Rosenbluth, *Financial Politics in Contemporary Japan*, Ithaca: Cornell University Press, 1989; Dennis Encarnation and Mark Mason, "Neither MITI nor America: the Political Economy of Capital Liberalization in Japan," *International Organization*, Vol.44, No.1, Winter 1990, pp.25-54; Mayer, *op cit.*; and Schoppa, "Two-level Games and Bargaining Outcomes...," *op cit.*

[69] As observed by T.J. Pempel in "Japanese Foreign Economic Policy: The Domestic Bases for International Behavior" in Katzenstein, ed., *op cit.*, pp.139-190. A study by Sprinz and Vaahtoranta on stratospheric ozone layer protection and transboundary acid rain control in Europe also found that domestic factors are most important in shaping a country's position in international environmental negotiations. See Detlef Sprinz and Tapani Vaahtoranta, "The Interest-based Explanation of International Environmental Policy," *International Organization*, Vol.48, No.1, Winter 1994, pp.77-105.

[70] Haruhiro Fukui, "The GATT Tokyo Round: The Bureaucratic Politics of Multilateral Diplomacy" in *The Politics of Trade: U.S. and Japanese Policymaking for the GATT Negotiations*, ed. by Michael Blaker, New York: Columbia University Press, 1978, pp.75-169.

[71] Lawrence E. Susskind, *Environmental Diplomacy: Negotiating More Effective Global Agreements*, New York and Oxford: Oxford University Press, 1994, pp.73-76.

CHAPTER 3

The Global Environment in Japanese Politics and the Major Domestic Policy Actors

Since all foreign policies are basically domestic policies and the most important constituents are in the domestic setting, examining how environmental issues evolve in the Japanese domestic policy setting helps to illuminate the key forces that shape Japan's international environmental policies. As this study will show, politicization of international environmental issues in the Japanese domestic policy setting has open up new competition among policy actors.

This chapter has two parts. The first part outlines the evolution of environmental concerns as a policy issue in Japan's domestic setting, in particular, the laws, institutions, and official policies that have developed over the past three decades. The second part examines several domestic policy actors inside and outside of the Japanese government to identify the major actors by evaluating their interest (or non-interest) in this issue, their perspectives, their place in the foreign policy process, and how they can assert themselves in policy discussions.

For many ministries and agencies the global environment is important because as a new issue to Japanese politics it can promise new resources and expanded powers and influence. On the other hand, most politicians have cared little about the global environment because it is non-essential to their political careers. Japanese media, too, have yet to seriously address global environmental issues. As for big business, they see potential profits and ramifications for their corporate image. Finally, the issue has excited Japanese citizens who would like to see more open public debates and participation in policy making.

Outside pressure, or *gaiatsu*, can be relevant, but it does not usually affect the entire country or government. It is the individual actor that is susceptible to outside pressure and would likely yield to outside pressure only when his/her interests are threatened. At the same, outside pressure can also be used to advance one's own motives if properly exploited. This is

45

especially true for policy actors who do not have enough leverage on their own. Hence, the effectiveness of *gaiatsu* must be considered in terms of the specific policy actor that it targets, to what extent it affects the preferences and actions of that policy actor, and the policy issue that is involved.

EVOLUTION OF ENVIRONMENTAL ISSUES IN JAPANESE DOMESTIC POLITICS

Following the end of World War II, industrialization and economic growth were the Japanese government's priorities. Environmental consequences were ignored or accepted as inevitable side effects. Such abuse gave rise to many environmental and human tragedies throughout the country from the 1940s to the 1960s. The most notorious of these were the "big four" of methyl-mercury poisoning (Minamata disease) in Kumamoto and Niigata, cadmium poisoning (*itai-itai* disease) along the Jintsu River in Toyama Prefecture, and asthma in Yokkaichi.[1] The government's initial refusal to recognize these problems or to respond to them provoked widespread local protests and citizens movements to demand compensation for victims and fundamental changes in government policies. The mass media's broad and sympathetic reporting also gave strength to these citizen movements. As a result, new environmental legislation began to appear after the mid-1960s.

Among the first sets of comprehensive ministerial, legal, and planning measures for environmental protection in Japan, the Basic Law for Environmental Pollution Control (hereafter "Basic Environmental Law") was the most important. Promulgated in August 1967, the Basic Environmental Law provided the fundamental principles and framework for environmental pollution control measures. The law stipulated seven environmental pollution symptoms and explicitly stated the responsibilities of the national government, local authorities, and enterprises, including the division of medical costs for certified pollution victims.[2]

However, these laws only emphasized industrial pollution control. Government and public awareness or concern for environmental protection in the broader sense of the term remained weak. The Japanese government also did not abandon its bias for industrial growth. Evidence of this is the "harmonization principle" found in the Basic Environmental Law, which implied that the need for pollution control was not absolute, and counseled that the promotion of economic activities should take precedence in some cases.

Growing public dissatisfaction pressured the bureaucracy and politicians to accept a fundamental change in 1970 when a special session of the Japanese Diet was convened to debate environmental pollution control measures. A total of 14 laws were enacted or revised. Many anti-pollution regulatory measures were strengthened and many institutional arrangements were expanded.[3] The most significant amendment was the removal of the "harmonization principle" from the 1967 Basic Environmental Law.

Global Environment in Japanese Politics 47

This change indicated that the Japanese people would no longer tolerate government policies that put industrial growth above all else. The law was also brought closer to the principles adopted by the Tokyo metropolitan government's Pollution Prevention Act in 1969, which recognized environmental rights as a basic right of citizens in Tokyo. Finally, the new amended law allowed local governments to independently introduce more stringent regulations.[4]

Another outcome of the "Pollution Diet" of 1970 was the decision to establish a special agency for the environment. The Environment Agency was established in 1971 to formulate and promote basic principles for environmental conservation and to coordinate the activities of other administrative agencies in this field. Its formation was also in anticipation of the Stockholm Conference in 1972.

The Stockholm Conference was a turning point for Japan and many other countries. For the first time, pollution and the environment assumed prominence in international affairs. This highlighting of global environmental problems also encouraged a shared global consciousness among peoples in developed and developing countries and across ideological boundaries. The year 1972 also marked another important milestone in Japanese environmental legislation: the passing of the country's first Nature Conservation Law indicated a new recognition that nature protection is important and distinct from pollution control.[5]

However, the Oil Crisis quickly overshadowed this new international interest in the environment. For most countries, national attention refocused on domestic affairs, especially energy security and economic growth. Japan was not an exception. The only bright light in this was that Japan's domestic cleanup did not stop. Enough public pressure persisted and the energy crisis became a catalyst for improving energy efficiency. The results were impressive successes in pollution control. The Environment Committee of the Organization for Economic Cooperation and Development (OECD) conducted a review of Japan's environment policy between 1976 and 1977 and reported that pollution in many parts of the country had declined significantly. Japan's Gross National Product (GNP) and employment was practically unaffected, and Japan even did best among OECD countries in reducing sulfur dioxide and nitrogen oxides emissions because of its massive application of acid scrubbers throughout the country.[6]

Nevertheless, it was not until the second half of the 1980s that a renewed Japanese interest in the global environment appeared. By this time, global warming, ozone depletion, and other environmental problems were making headlines around the world. As the second largest capitalist economy, Japanese responsibility could not be denied, nor could Japan be content as only an economic giant. The Plaza Accord of 1985 doubled the value of the yen, and the Japanese government faced increased domestic and outside pressure to assume a larger role in world affairs. Global environment protection greatly appealed to the Japanese government and the Japanese people because it appeared as a positive and non-controversial issue—compared to peacekeeping. In addition, it also enabled them to feel a shared consciousness with the rest of the world.

The country was also riding on the crest of a domestic economic boom and wanted to define a new world role for itself as the Cold War drew to a close. In 1987, the Upper House passed a resolution declaring that Japan should take initiatives in environmental issues. Following this, the Environment Agency's White Paper in 1988 made one of the earliest official articulations of Japan's role. It declared that as an economic power, Japan must fulfill its responsibility and assume a "leadership role" in global environmental protection.[7] To bridge contradictions between development and environmental conservation, the White Paper drew heavily on the 1987 Brundtland Commission Report and embraced its idea of "sustainable development."[8] Two other Environment Agency expert reports also came out in the same year and both urged the Japanese government to exercise leadership in solving global ecological problems.[9]

Japan's conceptualization of its new role was eventually unveiled at a major international conference on global environmental protection in Tokyo in September 1989. Prime Minister Noboru Takeshita offered Japan as a voice for developing nations and a bridge between them and the industrialized ones.[10] Some Japanese policy makers even proposed the formation of a "United Nations Environment Security Council." This, they thought, could guarantee Japan a place in an exclusive body and put Japan on equal footing with other major world powers.

Global environmental protection as a new foreign policy focus changed the basic trend of Japan's environmental policies at home and overseas. One is a fundamental shift from the conventional policy framework of domestic pollution control measures to a new framework whose core theme is global environmental protection. Japan's first major Official Development Assistance (ODA) pledge to the global environment was made at the Arche Summit of the Group of Seven (G-7) in 1989 where the Japanese prime minister promised 300 billion yen in environment-related aid for the 1989-91 period.[11] At the G-7 Summit in London in 1991, Japan announced its new environmental ODA guidelines. The new policy recognized poverty and pollution as closely related to environmental problems. Forestry conservation and afforestation, energy conservation and energy technology, pollution control, wildlife conservation, and soil conservation were listed as targeted fields for Japanese assistance.

Nonetheless, the official Japanese view of the environment changed little in essence. Not only were there no concrete plans or vision to tackle international environmental problems, the new environmental ODA policy continued to treat economic growth as a priority; and technology, the cure

Global Environment in Japanese Politics

for environmental ills. Developing countries, the Japanese government reasoned, can achieve environmental conservation without sacrificing economic growth with the aid of Japanese technology transfer and experience.[12]

In June 1992, the Cabinet approved a new ODA Charter, which explicitly advocated increased national commitment to research on global environmental problems and finding technological solutions to these problems. The ODA Charter also called for expanding the involvement of the Japanese public and non-governmental organizations (NGOs) in international development and environmental issues.[13] By this time, both public interests in the global environment and the number of NGOs involved in environment activities were increasing. There was also increasing worldwide endorsement of NGO participation in the policy process in international forums. The Japanese government recognized that it could not ignore this new trend. Thus, the Japanese government, as well as industry, established special funds to support NGO activities.

At the United Nations Conference on Environment and Development (UNCED) in 1992, Japan made its pledge of nearly 1 trillion yen for environmental assistance. Domestic excitement about UNCED greatly influenced the drafting of new environmental legislation. First, the Japanese government put up Japan's national action plan (a follow-up to UNCED's Agenda 21) for public consultation in mid-November 1993. Although the public had only three weeks to review the proposed national action plan before its submission to the United Nations, this was the first time the Japanese government had ever allowed public comment on a policy draft. Over 100 groups and individuals from across the country submitted comments and more than 100 points were revised, including commitments to strengthen the roles of non-governmental organizations, women, and youths in policy making.[14]

Second, deliberation over a new Basic Environmental Law began just a month after UNCED, and a new Basic Environmental Law was passed in the Diet on 12 November 1993. As the coordinating agency for government environment policies, the Environment Agency drafted this new law. However, obtaining consensus from other government ministries and agencies was difficult because they were wary that the new law might expand the power base of the Environment Agency. Business leaders, too, were anxious that environmental constraints might have economic repercussions. By this time, the Japanese economy was beginning to show signs of strain after the so-called "economic bubble" had exploded two years earlier. Hence, the 1993 Basic Environmental Law was made more moderate in its final form. A major weakness, critics have charged, is the lack of public participation under this new Basic Environmental Law.

Nonetheless, the 1993 Basic Environmental Law was the first Japanese legislation that formally commanded the country to utilize its economic power to cooperate with other nations to protect the global environment. This new law established the basic framework and principles for Japanese environmental policy. It also designated the national government to lay out a "basic environmental program" to articulate its long-term policy and direction.[15] The law treated global environmental problems as the common concern of all people and the goal is to realize a sustainable global society. The law also provided the first integrated legal coverage for pollution control and natural environment conservation.[16] Two years later, on 16 December 1995, the Cabinet approved the Basic Environment Plan, which outlined the government's overall direction and policies towards environmental conservation through the first half of the twenty-first century.[17]

In June 1997, Japan's "Initiatives for Sustainable Development toward the 21st Century" (ISD) was unveiled by Prime Minister Ryutaro Hashimoto at the United Nations General Assembly Special Session on the Environment and Sustainable Development (UNGASS) to be the basis for a new package of comprehensive environmental cooperation activities. The objective of assistance, under this initiative, is to realize sustainable development, and its action program targets air and water pollution, global warming, "fresh water" problems, conservation of nature, and promotion of public awareness.[18]

Finally, Japan's hosting of the Third Conference of the Parties (COP 3) to the Framework Convention on Climate Change in Kyoto in December 1997 can be considered successful for producing agreements on quantitative reductions of greenhouse gases. However, domestic interest in the global environment had significantly declined as domestic attention largely shifted to the nation's economic problems. Despite rhetorical commitments, the domestic economic situation was so dire that the ODA budget was cut—for the first time ever—by 10 percent in the 1998 fiscal year. Japanese industry also pressed the government to reverse its policy on untying loans for environment-related ODA projects beginning 1998.

THE JAPANESE GOVERNMENT BUREAUCRACY

Among the domestic policy actors, the strongest is the government bureaucracy. With over 850,000 people working in 12 ministries and 10 administrative-level agencies, the national bureaucracy is, with infrequent exceptions, the true force that rules the country. Bureaucratic dominance in the policy process is rooted in the centralized and vertical structure of the Japanese government. Numerous studies confirmed this observation with their propositions of a ruling triumvirate (the government bureaucracy, politicians, and big business), sophisticated interpretations of "creative conservatism," inter- and intra-bureaucratic rivalries, and bureaucratic and political coalitions with interest groups.[19] The *1994 OECD Japan Environment Performance Review* observed that transparency is lacking in the Japanese policy process. Policy making mainly involves intense inter-

Global Environment in Japanese Politics

ministerial negotiations, and there are few channels for public intervention. In addition, the report found that indirect influence on the policy process comes from nearly 25,000 ministry-affiliated private entities that are staffed by former bureaucrats.

Structural paternalism has prevailed largely because the drafting of laws is in the hands of the Japanese bureaucracy and not its legislators. The bureaucracy has superior command of vital information flows and technical expertise on policy matters. In comparison, Japanese politicians do not receive budget to hire research aides or experts to gather data, study issues, and draft policies. Neither would most devote resources to these activities.

Politicians of the Liberal Democratic Party (LDP), in particular, did not need to distinguish themselves or the party in domestic or policy debates. The LDP had solid control as the ruling party for nearly half a century. As a result, the key battles for LDP politicians were internal party rivalries. Foreign policy issues, in general, would not command their attention until they have become highly politicized domestically.

With politicians uninterested in policy debates and party policy organs recommending policy positions, the participation of Japanese politicians in the foreign policy process was limited mainly to consultations with ministries and agencies, leaving the drafting of policies and laws to the bureaucracy. For the Liberal Democratic Party, its Policy Research Committee, *shingikai* (consultative council), and numerous *"zoku"* (or "policy tribes" in which politicians organize themselves into issue/area study groups) have been the key points of contact between elected representatives and the bureaucracy.[20] Approval for policy drafts is usually obtained with few amendments from politicians. Senior or high level politicians, in particular, rarely interfere in routine policy matters. To do so would appear ill form as both sides consider relationships of trust and respect to have formed over the years. It was also difficult to challenge this bureaucratic dominance in policy making in the last several decades when policies appeared to have created and sustained Japan's post-war economic prosperity. Thus, consultations are usually formal, not substantial, and policy drafts would then move on to cabinet conference.[21]

Another source of power for the bureaucracy is its regulatory powers over the financial system. One last important reason for the dominance of the bureaucracy is that Japanese voters have few effective means to challenge their regulatory powers and policy preferences. Record of legislators' voting pattern is not available to the public and there are no laws to give the public the right to request information from the government.[22]

Thus, this look at the domestic policy actors in Japan's international environmental policies will focus heavily on the Japanese bureaucracy, particularly those ministries and agencies within it that are relevant to the policy issues examined in this study.

Japanese government bureaucracy.

For the Japanese bureaucracy, the global environment is a new policy initiative, and a new policy initiative often means an increase in public expenditure. Since ODA, particularly environment-related ODA, has grown steadily in the government budget even in times of severe budgetary constraints, the environment has enough policy drive to cause many ministries and agencies to want a role in this policy area.

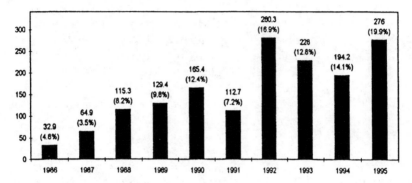

Note: parentheses show Environmental ODA as a percentage of total ODA.
Source: MoFA, "Japan's Environmental Cooperation," n.d., p.2.

Figure 5. Japan's environmental ODA, 1986-1995

The ministries and agencies involved could gain new funds, new powers as well as positive publicity. Of course, defining what is "environmental" is largely contextual, depending heavily on where one sits. For instance, the Ministry of Construction considers its road widening projects "environmental" under the new environmental construction law (*Kankyo Kensetsu Taiho*) passed in January 1994. Another example is the attachment of the terms "welfare" and "environment" by the ministries of Construction and Agriculture, Forestry and Fisheries to secure appropriations for their projects proposed under the country's 17 trillion yen economic stimulus package announced in April 1998.[23]

As in most modern governments, various ministries and agencies responsible for agriculture, land use, natural resource development, human health, and the environment shared jurisdiction over environmental concerns. In Japan's case, responsibility for the environment is also diffused within the government. The Environment Agency was created as the coordinating agency for the entire Japanese bureaucracy over all environment-related matters. Its powers are principally in pollution control and nature conservation. The Ministry of Health and Welfare (MHW) covers a large portion of waste issues and matters where human health is concerned. The Ministry of International Trade and Industry (MITI) covers environment-related technologies and management of industrial environmental issues.

Global Environment in Japanese Politics   53

The Ministry of Agriculture, Forestry and Fisheries (MAFF) has jurisdiction over the management of forests, the conservation of fisheries resources, and the approval of agricultural chemicals. The Ministry of Transportation (MoT) addresses pollution control due to all forms of transport in the air, land, and sea. The Ministry of Construction (MoC) is responsible for urban planning and public works, such as sewage, urban parks and roads, and the preservation of rivers.

As in most governments, ministries and agencies often jealously guard their jurisdictions and continuously strive to expand their powers. For example, the Ministry of Foreign Affairs (MoFA) and MITI each set up independent research facilities on the environment within two weeks of the 1989 Arche Summit; each with a mission to reflect the perspectives and strengths of its sponsor. However, the formulation of an integrated set of global environmental policies in Japan has also been hampered by the absence of political leadership.

As a result, the policy preferences and actions of each ministry and agency are guided primarily by their own narrowly defined bureaucratic agenda. For instance, MoFA, MITI, and the Environment Agency each reacted differently to a Chinese verbal agreement on a draft treaty for bilateral cooperation to combat pollution and nature conservation in 1993. Both MoFA and MITI had reservations about how it might impact their jurisdictions and interests. MoFA feared that China might take advantage of it to secure greater ODA allocations, while MITI was wary of how it might complicate conduct of its Green Aid Plan with China that began in 1991 to support the installation of desulfurization devices in power plants. On the other hand, the Environment Agency, the smallest player and one with no resources at its disposal to lose, welcomed the treaty because it would facilitate environmental studies and research in China.

In this complex structure, sectionalism reigns and politics and history usually dominate in deciding who has a role, especially leadership, in a foreign policy issue. Interested policy actors must find at least elements in it that fall under its jurisdiction to justify their claim for bureaucratic leadership or involvement in the policy process. Such behavior can be seen in the actions of the Environment Agency, the first bureaucratic policy actor examined here.

Environment Agency of Japan (JEA).

JEA is an agency in the Prime Minister's Office and headed by a director general who is a minister of state. JEA is possibly the most sincere supporter of the environment in the Japanese government. However, JEA—contrary to what its name suggests and the best intentions of its officials—has not been a strong player in environmental protection at home or overseas.

The reasons for its creation and division of bureaucratic jurisdictions within the Japanese bureaucracy limit JEA's powers primarily to matters related to pollution control. The agency was established in 1971 largely due to the need for a new body to coordinate government response to pollution problems and to have such a body in place to represent Japan at the Stockholm Conference in 1972.

Being a small body, JEA has little leverage to negotiate with other ministries and agencies. JEA policy drafts are usually watered down by intragovernmental consultations. Nonetheless, several JEA officials and experts interviewed for this study concurred that JEA can be more effective as an agency under the Prime Minister's Office than as a ministry. First, JEA has better access to the Prime Minister's Office. Second, as a coordinating agency, JEA can speak officially on all environment-related policies within all parts of the Japanese government. For example, JEA's director general can exercise the "right of recommendation." The Ministry of Finance, which monopolizes the budget process, is the only other government body that has this right.[24] In this regard, the passing of the Basic Environmental Law of 1993 has increased JEA's limited powers by expanding the scope of policy issues that are deemed to have an environmental component. For example, the new law designates whaling as a matter in biodiversity conservation.[25] This gives JEA, for the first time, official authority to speak on the country's whaling policy. However, JEA has chosen not to assert itself in this policy issue. Instead, JEA has focused its limited human and material resources on a few "new" international environmental issues, including acid rain and global warming, in which it has greater potential for real influence in the policy process.

Limits to JEA's powers and influence have been present from the start. Other ministries and agencies that risked losing some of their prerogatives and regulatory powers opposed creation of the agency. In order to maintain some control they installed their own staff in key positions of influence, including bureau and section chiefs and secretary general of the secretariat, within JEA. At its inception, MHW sent 283 officials, MAFF sent 62, MITI sent 26, and the Economic Planning Agency sent 21.[26]

One consequence is that loyalties are split within the Environment Agency.[27] Officials who do not have their beginnings at JEA sometimes prioritize the interests of their "home" ministries and agencies. Those officials whose entire careers have been at the Environment Agency struggle to break free from this "colonial system." Yet, in Japan's lifetime employment system where promotion is based on seniority, ridding this outside influence means basically waiting for such officials to be "grandfathered" out. Although original JEA recruits now reach between 70 to 80 percent of the staff, and many are rising to higher positions of authority (such as directors of bureaus), the highest key positions are still occupied mainly by officials from outside ministries.[28]

A small staff and limited budget also seriously curtail JEA's influence. Since JEA began in 1971 with a small staff and a small budget, even uninterrupted incremental increases in staff and budget have not significantly improved its relative size and position within the government bureaucracy. The entire budget of the agency is only a tiny fraction of those of the large ministries. For a country that has pledged to take an active role in global environmental protection, the entire JEA has less than 1100 staff. This number includes park rangers and personnel in training and research centers across the country. Only around 500 JEA officials are administrators at JEA headquarters in Tokyo. This compares, for example, to a staff of 17,000 at the U.S. Environment Protection Agency. This manpower shortage fundamentally constraints JEA's ability to be in active in more than a few policy issues.[29]

Another handicap for not being a full-fledged ministry is that JEA cannot present bills without consent from other ministries. Seeking their agreement often requires compromises that weaken JEA's already limited influence in policy making.[30] For example, inter-ministerial differences and opposition from business circles prevented the passing of Japanese environmental impact assessment legislation until June 1997.[31]

Traditional ministries also protect their jurisdiction by restricting JEA's enforcement powers. JEA's principal function is to coordinate rather than to implement environmental protection policies. Even in pollution control, its strongest mandate, JEA has only statutory powers to establish ambient emission and related standards in air, water, noise, and other fields. Ambient or environmental quality standards are not legally binding in Japan. They serve only as policy objectives by indicating levels of pollution that an area may not exceed. Emission standards, on the other hand, fix the quantity of pollutants that a source may discharge per unit of time. These standards are legally binding and are enforced by administrative and criminal sanction.

With these inherent weaknesses, JEA has to rely on its official role as the coordination agency for all environment-related matters in order to access policy processes that are frequently dominated by the big ministries. In assessing environmental ODA, for instance, JEA has acquired some influence.[32] In global warming, JEA disputed MITI's attempt to establish comprehensive control. By treating global warming an energy issue, MITI puts its strictly within its jurisdiction. JEA sided with the Forestry Agency's argument that reforestation and afforestation are needed to help reduce greenhouse gases. This gave both agencies a foothold in the issue.[33] On MITI's Action Program to Arrest Global Warming, which aims to stabilize carbon dioxide emissions at 1990 levels, JEA intervention altered the program's priorities to urban system, transportation, energy demand, and energy supply. The Ministry of Construction and the Ministry of Transportation, favored the first two, respectively. Drawing in these two big domestic ministries prevented the Action Program from having an undiluted energy-centered focus that would allow the virtual dictate of MITI.[34]

In addition, JEA created a Global Environment Department specifically to plan, formulate and promote the government's basic policies towards international environmental issues. This gives JEA a more visible presence in government policy discussions on international environmental issues. Nonetheless, with limited resources and a restricted mandate, JEA can practically focus on only a few issues. Global warming, ozone layer depletion and acid deposition are its top three priorities. JEA also sponsors its own research centers to generate expert studies that it can present to the public and use to assert itself in intra-governmental discussions. They include the National Institute for Environmental Studies and the Institute for Global Environmental Strategies.

A majority of JEA staff also have environment-related academic backgrounds and training. This scientific and technical expertise in environment-related matters has given JEA some leverage in policy discussions, as well as protection against bullying and encroachment by the big ministries.

Forces outside the Japanese government have also been used to help it to gain access to and bolster its leverage in the foreign policy process. JEA actively builds coalitions with international environmental groups and environmental departments in other countries to raise the prominence of environmental issues in domestic politics and to ensure for itself a place at the domestic and international bargaining tables. JEA officials have also used the 1994 OECD review of Japan's environmental policy and UNCED outcomes to argue for more transparency and openness in Japan's policy process. As a small and weak body, greater transparency and openness are the only sure ways to improve JEA's access to policy processes without a fundamental change in its official mandate.

Another way in which JEA improves its bargaining position *vis-a-vis* the big ministries is to rally public support for its policy preferences.[35] Public opinion is not usually a formidable force in Japanese politics, but past pollution tragedies gives it potency where environmental matters are concerned as well as a sense of moral support and urgency.[36] For example, media reports of potential dangers from transboundary acid pollution helped JEA to push for a more pro-active approach to the problem and to secure support for its initiatives from other ministries and the administration.

In this connection, JEA has also worked to foster a positive relationship with NGOs. As Caldwell puts it, "...NGOs could provide a constituency for the official agencies for environmental protection now established in most countries."[37] Although NGOs are another credible but not generally influential force in Japanese politics, JEA sees them as allies in dealing with the large and traditional ministries. NGOs can also be a helpful source of information.

The Institute for Global Environmental Strategies (IGES) hired the former head of the leading Japanese anti-tropical timber NGO that is sharply

Global Environment in Japanese Politics

critical of Japan's policy (or more specifically those of MITI, MOFA and MAFF) on timber issues. The Japan Fund for Global Environment was created to support NGO activities. The fund grew to 5.5 billion yen in fiscal 1995-96 and disbursed 650 million yen to support 160 projects (out of a total request of 2.2 billion yen by 360 applications from Japanese and foreign groups). Low interest rates in Japan has restrained the fund's growth. To maintain a stable level of disbursements, direct government subsidies from the general account have supplemented interests earned in the last several years. It is notable that JEA had informal consultation with NGOs on the establishment of this fund.[38]

The Global Environment Information Center (GEIC) is another bridge between JEA and civil society. GEIC was created as a joint program with the United Nations University as a result of the Tokyo Conference on Global Environmental Action in October 1994. Its objective is to promote sustainable development and it does so by providing support to social groups identified in Agenda 21, which includes NGOs. Through its physical facility at the United Nations University in Tokyo and the Internet, GEIC provides information to the public and facilitates network building among international, national, and subnational bodies.

One last important way for JEA to stretch its limited financial and human resources is to hire private enterprises and to use advisory groups for expert advice. The 1993 Basic Environmental Law replaced the former advisory councils with the Central Environmental Council. Consisting of professors, scientists, and other knowledgeable persons, these councils have played a more active role in environmental policy making than is typical of advisory bodies in the Japanese bureaucracy.[39]

All of the above demonstrates that JEA, as a small upstart with severely constrained resources and powers in the Japanese bureaucracy, must be creative and diligent in order to penetrate the policy process that is dominated by the big and powerful ministries.

Ministry of Finance (MoF).

MoF basically "has no thinking of its own on the environment."[40] Generally regarded as the most powerful of Japanese ministries, MoF finds the environment too trivial to deserve its attention. Holding the purse strings of the entire Japanese government, MoF can quite easily have great influence over the country's international environmental policies, but it has chosen not to.

First, unlike the other ministries and agencies which see potential for increased budgets and expanded powers in addressing environmental issues, MoF has "no incentive to be involved at all"[41] because MoF has no jurisdiction or regulatory powers where international environmental conservation is concerned. Only in ODA policy making is MoF exposed to environmental issues because of its influential role in deciding the country's aid policy. Yet, even in this, ramifications of Japanese ODA on the global

58   *The Roots of Japan's Environmental Policy*

environment, international development, or the country's political image has not been major concerns for MoF.

The only area of ODA, environment or otherwise, that really interests MoF is multilateral contributions to inter-governmental organizations because MoF is most directly responsible for this and Japan—or MoF—stands to gain expanded power or influence in these multilateral institutions. Only in this instance, too, does MoF find itself directly vulnerable to pressure from international organizations or from the United States and other industrialized economies.[42]

Secondly, MoF has not taken any interest in environment issues in general. Doing so helps it to remain free from political bargaining with other policy actors inside and outside of the Japanese government. Since MoF officials see their ministry's independence as its strength, the ministry would not interfere with pledges made by the Prime Minister and other ministries as long as they are true to the ODA principles and within the negotiated ODA budget. For example, the ministry did not support proposals for a carbon tax to curb greenhouse gas emissions by JEA and other ministries. Taxes are politically sensitive and controversial issues, and especially hard to justify in times of domestic economic slowdown.[43] In fact, the ministry's tax bureau was one of the staunchest opponents to a carbon tax because it would be responsible for tough negotiations with politicians, business, and other interested parties, as well as selling it to the public. The Finance Ministry would likely consider a carbon tax only after its adoption by other OECD countries and after its political and economic ramifications become clearer.[44]

Thirdly, the global environment is something that is beyond MoF's expertise. The ministry speaks the language of economics. When an issue is heavily laden with science and technical matters, the ministry prefers to avoid involvement rather than to admit ignorance. The ministry has not appeared keen to remedy this handicap. There is yet no environment department and there has been no call to set one up from within the ministry. Only a counselor position has been created to manage general coordination in this area. Although this position ranks quite high within the ministry, it's incumbent is charged with many other responsibilities and there is very limited staff support.

All of the above shows that the global environment has not been a priority to MoF.[45] Nonetheless, as the ministry that holds the nation's purse strings, MoF can be influential, particularly in deciding ODA allocations.

Ministry of International Trade and Industry.
For MITI, "environmental issues are energy issues."[46] Global warming is the top international environmental issue for the ministry because within the government, MITI is chiefly responsible for energy matters. As a result, protecting the environment is thus basically a matter of increasing domestic energy efficiency and transferring technology overseas to help others to

Global Environment in Japanese Politics

do the same. Although addressing the impact of international trade, consumption, and production processes on the environment are not among MITI's priorities, there are reasons for MITI to take want to participate in policy processes on other international environmental issues.

First, it could bolster its declining influence in aid policy. MITI especially emphasizes its role in facilitating technology transfer from Japan's private industries to development countries. Second, technology transfer or the sale of environmental goods and services could mean big profits for Japanese industry, which is MITI's chief constituent. ODA grants and loans could give Japanese business a competitive edge their North American and European rivals. MITI's Grant Assistance for Grassroots Projects scheme is another example of this objective in promoting sales of Japanese goods and services overseas. The scheme supports projects carried out overseas by NGOs, by providing financial assistance mainly for hardware purchases. Third, helping developing countries to improve their energy efficiency would be much cheaper than further efforts in Japan, which could require big investments by Japanese businesses.

Many programs have been established to promote the export of environmental goods and services. One example is the Green Aid Plan, which was launched in 1991 to improve energy efficiency and environmental conditions in developing countries through the transfers of Japanese technology. In this connection, MITI also set up its own quasi-government research centers, such as GISPRI (Global Industrial and Social Progress Research Institute), to help the government and private industry in promoting and undertaking technology transfers to developing countries. There were also investments in environment-related research and development. MITI established the Research Institute to Innovate Technologies for the Earth (RITE) in 1990 to launch a hundred-year plan for sustainable development.[47] The International Center for Environmental Technology Transfer (ICETT) aims to train 10,000 developing country officials from 1994-2004 in energy issues and pollution control technology.[48] MITI money has also been behind a United Nations University program to study urban energy issues in Asia.[49]

These efforts all aimed to build markets for pollution control technology for Japan in the long-term. Asia is a top priority because of its geographic proximity. The region is Japan's economic backyard, providing resources, markets, labor, and land. It is also home to over half of the world's population and is the fastest growing region in the world. Within Asia, China is its biggest concern because of its rapidly growing energy demand. MITI's chief response is to transfer technologies that will help to simultaneously meet this demand and reduce pollution.

Although energy is MITI's chief concern when it comes to the environment, the ministry is really responsible for more than this. As the trade ministry, MITI oversees the implementation of the Convention on the

International Trade of Endangered Fauna and Flora (CITES). There are clear conflicts of interests for MITI in being CITES chief administrator in Japan, instead of other ministries or agencies with direct responsibility for conservation matters. For MITI, trade is the priority, not the protection of endangered species. However, other ministries and agencies have not been keen to challenge MITI leadership in this matter because there is little money and power in biological diversitry conservation as a policy matter. This helps to explain the lack of Japanese actions in nature conservation.

Ministry of Agriculture, Fisheries and Forestry.

Japan considers the environment foremost as a source of raw materials to feed the material needs of Japan—and the rest of the world. MAFF's chief concern in global environmental protection is to ensure access to and use of the environment, which are to be achieved through sustainable management and use. The case of whaling aptly reflects MAFF's anxiety about how the commercial whaling ban could have a domino effect on other forms of commercial fisheries and other uses of global commons.

Another important reason for MAFF's interest in global environment protection is, of course, the potential for increased budget and influence. MAFF is not a policy actor in Japan's ODA, but it wants to have a slice of this growing pie. The ministry has a massive budget deficit because of its subsidies to various domestic constituents in farming, forestry, and fisheries. Almost every one of these sectors in Japan is not competitive.

MAFF's participation in international environmental policy discussions is based on its jurisdiction over all matters governed by the Fishery Law and the Forest Law. In global warming, MAFF's Forestry Agency stresses reforestation as a way to reduce greenhouse gases in order to assert itself in policy discussions. The ministry also supports reductions in tropical timber imports, because it could help to increase sales of domestic timber. Finally, on transboundary acid pollution from the Asian continent, MAFF secured a position in the foreign policy process on the basis of its powers over Japanese forests and inland waters, which could suffer from acid damage.

Like other ministries and agencies, MAFF defines environmental issues in a manner that suits its objectives and expertise. The ministry thus underlines the importance of technical assistance in the country's ODA program, using its expertise on agriculture, forestry and fisheries to assert its voice in policy discussions.

Ministry of Foreign Affairs.

For MoFA, committing Japan to international environmental protection is a "diplomatic instrument for expansion of Japanese power."[50] Environmental protection is considered a positive and relatively non-controversial issue. External demand for Japanese actions is complemented by domestic support to respond to this challenge. Japan's wealth, technology,

Global Environment in Japanese Politics

and experience in domestic economic development and pollution control together provide MoFA the basis to push for Japanese leadership in international environmental affairs.

MoFA's position in deciding the country's ODA policy and activities is most directly critical to the ministry's objectives. Apart from supporting activities it favors, MoFA can use its position in intra-governmental ODA negotiations to leverage its bargaining position in other policy matters.

However, this is not enough. MoFA must also explore other avenues for influence. MoFA's chief responsibility is in coordinating foreign policy. Having no regulatory control over policy implementation domestically means that it lacks a domestic base of supporters. Another implication of being the country's chief liaison with the world is that MoFA is most exposed to foreign demands, and addressing these external demands cannot be done without cooperation from the domestic ministries.

One tactic is to use foreign pressure to press for responses and cooperation from other domestic policy actors. Another is to use contacts with NGOs and public opinion to help deflect foreign pressure, give legitimacy to its policy initiatives, and press other policy actors in the domestic arena.

In summary, although the Japanese bureaucracy is the most powerful policy actor, it is not a monolithic entity. Factions exist within and between ministries and agencies. Since each jealousy guards its bureaucratic jurisdictions, there is intense rivalry among them. In addition, alliances may occur across bureaucratic boundaries between those sharing similar responsibilities and perspectives on an issue. Consequently, seeing how an issue is set and defined within the Japanese bureaucratic policy structure is imperative to understand the key policy actors that are involved, the interplay of their objectives and interests, negotiations at subnational and international levels, and the logic behind policy choices.

The policy actor with chief bureaucratic leadership usually has the greatest influence over the policy. However, the opinions of others would not generally be ignored unless the chief bureaucratic actor needs no support or fears no opposition from other policy actors. Linkages among issues can cross bureaucratic lines and repeated interactions occur among policy actors over a broad range of issues. Thus, policy actors consider it wise to consult with relevant actors to build consensus or at least to minimize intra-governmental conflicts.

In addition, consultation has another useful purpose. It improves the potential for cooperation (or at least non-interference) in implementation, thus giving added strength to a policy choice. Each negotiation between policy actors thus becomes an investment in the issue at hand as well as in linked issues. The give-and-take that occurs becomes bargaining chips for use in present and/or future negotiations. Consequently, policy decisions result from the interplay of overlapping and divergent interests among rel-

JAPANESE POLITICIANS

Japanese politicians, on the whole, have not been interested in international environmental issues because as a foreign policy issue they have not been important to their political careers. In contrast to politics in North America and Western Europe, the lack of strong environmental consciousness among Japanese voters means that there are few green points (or votes) to gain from supporting environmental causes.

Japanese politicians can also afford to ignore international environmental concerns for other reasons. First, Japan's location protects it from most environmental effects of its economic actions overseas. Public demand for government or industry responsibility is thus minimal. Second, voices advocating conservation causes are usually too small and too weak to press for political responses. Third, politicians see no reason to support initiatives that may be detrimental to the interests of their major contributors, that is, Japanese big business. For these reasons, most Japanese legislators have scarce interest in the international environmental issues.

Two prominent exceptions are Wakako Hironaka (a former Director General of the Environment Agency) and Takashi Kosugi. Yet, not being senior politicians, they can have only minor influence in deciding policy priorities within the party and in consultations with the powerful government bureaucracy. For example, Kosugi, succeeded U.S. Vice President Al Gore as chairman of GLOBE (Global Legislators Organization for a Better Environment) in 1992. Although this gave Kosugi a prominent platform to propose his policy agenda and assert personal leadership, he was unable to mobilize greater support or propose policy alternatives from within his own LDP, big business, or the bureaucracy.

Japanese politicians are also handicapped by a lack of knowledge and an ability to gather information even when they have interest in an issue. Japanese legislators do not have funds or staff to conduct their own research or make policy proposals. Within the political parties, there are so-called "policy tribes" (zoku) in which legislators could specialize and have particular influence on specific areas of policy,[51] However, environmental issues are largely unknown to them and rank low in their priority of interests.[52]

Having scarce expertise and resources to draft policies and legislation, politicians must also rely on the bureaucracy to undertake these tasks. Japanese legislators can only push for policy changes by articulating their personal philosophies, indicating a preferred direction, or giving a rough overview of a policy, and then letting the responsible bureaucratic office to put their thoughts into policy drafts.[53] Yet even this has been difficult for most Japanese legislators to do because so much of their time and energy

Global Environment in Japanese Politics 63

is devoted to social/political obligations and never-ending preparations for the next election.

In fact, only a small group of Japanese senior politicians has some impact on the government's international environmental policies. These senior politicians are interested because they recognize the prominence of the environment as a policy issue in international politics and its implications for Japan's international status. Their position also makes them more vulnerable to outside criticism if they choose to ignore environmental issues. Supporting environmental protection thus makes a good political investment for Japanese diplomacy and for their own political careers.

Among these senior politicians, former Prime Minister Noboru Takeshita was crucial in getting the Liberal Democratic Party to put global environmental issues on its agenda.[54] Takeshita was also a major force in other ways. As chair of an international environment conference in September 1989, he openly offered Japan as a voice for developing countries and as a bridge between them and the industrialized economies. Takeshita supported building of the Sino-Japanese Friendship and Environmental Cooperation Center in Beijing and he personally opened the center in 1996.

Two other prime ministers who gave some prominence to the global environment in their political agendas are Toshiki Kaifu and Ryutaro Hashimoto. Kaifu headed a Japanese delegation of government officials, politicians, and businessmen to Beijing in 1993 for a major bilateral environmental cooperation symposium, and both Hashimoto and Takeshita backed creation of the Japan Fund for Global Environment to support NGO activities.[55]

Nonetheless, it was Prime Minister Yasuhiro Nakasone who showed a clear example of direct executive intervention in the policy process. In the controversy on Japanese whaling, Nakasone used his position to override the powerful bureaucracy and other domestic forces to protect his own political agenda.[56]

Nakasone was afraid that MAFF's opposition to the 1982 international moratorium on commercial whaling would negatively affect U.S.-Japan relations. The United States was the strongest proponent of the moratorium. Nakasone felt that confronting with the United States in the whaling debate could increase tension in their bilateral relations.[57] Neither would Nakasone allow this controversy to jeopardize his ambitions to raise Japan's international stature or that of his own.

Under Nakasone's leadership, the Liberal Democratic Party did not speak out to support whaling. In fact, a Diet bill introduced in 1984 to support Japanese whaling was aborted. In 1986, another bill proposed as a response to U.S. threats of sanctions (the removal of Japanese fishing rights in U.S. waters) against Japanese whaling was blocked. From Nakasone's view, the United States appeared determined to expel all foreign fisheries interests from its exclusive economic zone and the United States could use the whaling issue to increase leverage in bilateral trade talks. Thus, he found it hard to defend Japanese whaling when the industry has no economic significance to Japan or his own constituency.[58]

Nakasone's personal intervention was even more evident in Japan's scientific whaling program. After Japan agreed to terminate all commercial whaling in 1987, the Fisheries Agency, the chief policy actor, moved to initiate research on the minke whale stocks in the Antarctic because they hold the greatest potential for renewed commercial exploitation. Nakasone personally tried to dissuade the Fisheries Agency from carrying out this plan. Before his official visit to the United States in April 1987, Nakasone met with the Director General of the Fisheries Agency. Nakasone expressed his concern that scientific whaling could give Japan an "unfair image" and that the United States could accuse Japan of "continuing commercial whaling" under the guise of research whaling.[59]

Determined to pursue its own objectives, however, the Fisheries Agency submitted a draft of its "Research whaling preparation plan" in October 1987 to take 825 minke whales and up to 50 sperm whales per season in the Antarctic. Talks between the Prime Minister's Office and the designers of the program soon reached an impasse. The former determined that the numbers were too high for acceptance by the United States, and the latter refused amendment to safeguard the integrity of their research plans.

To assert his own preference, Nakasone publicly stated—without prior consultation with the Fisheries Agency—that he considered the numbers too high. This was an extremely uncommon act by a Japanese chief executive. Furthermore, subsequent to this public announcement, the Prime Minister's Office "requested" that the Fisheries Agency cut the number of minke whales to 300 and to drop sperm whales entirely from the program in order to improve its chances of acceptance in the West.

Many scientists and bureaucrats—even those outside of the Fisheries Agency—were appalled by this disrespect for their expert authority and jurisdiction over policy matters. Yet, there was nothing they could do except to adjust to this unexpected turn of events.[60] Therefore, Nakasone's decision to intervene directly was not driven so much by a goal to protect whales as it was a choice to sacrifice Japanese whaling in order to control tensions in U.S.-Japan trade relations and to protect himself and the country from attacks by anti-whaling advocates.

For those government offices supportive of the environment, such interest by senior politicians can be very helpful in resolving intra-governmental battles. This is particularly true for the smaller policy actors, who on their own would not have the leverage to bargain with the bigger and more powerful ministries and offices. For instance, Hashimoto and Takeshita's support for the Japan Fund for Global Environment was critical to its establishment.[61] In another instance, Takeshita personally stepped in to ask

Global Environment in Japanese Politics

JEA and MITI to settle their differences in order to push through the Action Program to Arrest Global Warming in 1990. Takeshita underlined the importance of the environment and by doing so gave support to JEA. The outcome also settled intra-ministerial disputes between MITI's Bureau of Environment and Bureau of Energy and Resources. The former pushed for the Action Program, and the latter resisted because of potential ramifications on Japan-U.S. trade relations.[62]

Such interventions by Japanese politicians are rare. It takes a politician of substantial stature and influence, such as Takeshita, to exert sufficient leverage against the powerful bureaucracy for changes in national policies and to broker different interests inside and outside of the government.[63]

JAPANESE BUSINESS AND INDUSTRY

The medium- and small-sized Japanese firms that make up the majority of Japanese companies have little interest in international environmental issues except where stability in the supply and prices of energy and natural resources are concerned. These medium- and small-sized Japanese firms find little reason to be interested in the international environment because they produce mainly for the domestic market where green consumption is still insignificant. Also, as suppliers to the large conglomerates, they are not directly exposed to green consumption demands by individual consumers at home or overseas.

Large conglomerates like the *sogo sosha*, or general trading companies, on the other hand, have to be sensitive to international environmental issues because they have become important to their business. As transnational companies, they must be attentive to changing trends and issues in international politics and the global economy. The *sogo sosha* are particularly vulnerable because they are the main importers of natural resources and energy to Japan as well as the top exporters of Japanese goods. With business interests around the world, most especially in North America and Europe where their investments increased sharply in the 1980s, they are highly visible internationally and exposed to outside criticisms. Therefore, endorsing global environment protection became politically and economically sensible for their corporate image and company bottom lines.

Riding high on the domestic bubble economy and in the run up towards UNCED in 1992, many Japanese companies set up offices for international environmental affairs and introduced company environment guidelines. The attitude of Japanese big business towards the global environment is best reflected by the actions of Keidanren, or the Federation of Economic Organizations, which represents about one thousand of the largest Japanese companies. Keidanren adopted its Global Environment Charter in 1991. The Charter offers guidelines not only for business activities within Japan, but also for Japanese enterprises operating overseas. This initiative

66   *The Roots of Japan's Environmental Policy*

and its timely announcement were even praised by Maurice Strong, who was chair of UNCED.

In addition, just one month before UNCED in June 1992, the Keidanren Nature Conservation Fund (KNCF) was established as a major symbol of Japanese big business commitment to international environmental conservation. KNCF would support nature conservation activities carried out by NGOs in developing countries and provide information and training on environmental matters to Keidanren member companies and their staff.

At UNCED, Japan had the largest delegation—seven persons—attending meetings of the Business Council for Sustainable Development, the business equivalent of the inter-governmental UNCED. In anticipation of Third Meeting of the Conference of the Parties to the Climate Change Convention in Kyoto in December 1997, Keidanren announced its Voluntary Action Plan on the Environment with a goal of reducing industrial sector carbon dioxide emissions to below 1990 levels by the year 2010.[64]

Yet what does the international environment mean to Japanese big business and how meaningful are their activities? A report on strategies to arrest global warming produced in October 1991 by the Keizai Doyukai (Japan Association of Corporate Executives)[65], whose members are generally executives in Keidanren member companies, sums it up nicely,

> ...corporations must now understand the element of the "environment" as a top priority in corporate philosophy. Corporations must change their stance on the environmental problem from the traditional one of merely treating environmental pollutants, which is part of their business activities, to one that is linked to the overall business activity that broadly encompasses development, production, sales, services and treatment of wastes. This change is not based on the concept of protecting the environment by sacrificing growth, but is a shift to "sustainable development" which promotes business activity by placing top priority on environmental preservation.[66]

In other words, the environment continues to be valued only in terms of its importance to corporate business activities. The only difference is an explicit expansion of environmental preservation from waste and pollution control to include energy and resource input efficiency. Growth is not to be dispensed with and the application of sustainable development, a term itself wrought with contradictions, is shallow and self-serving.

Furthermore, technology is emphasized as the key to achieving sustainable development. The Keidanren Global Environment Charter explicitly called for "the development and supply of innovative technologies, products and services to promote the conservation of energy and resources and the preservation of the environment." There has been no talk or emphasis on fundamental changes in political institutions at local, national, and

Global Environment in Japanese Politics

international levels or the economic mechanisms that govern the management and use of environmental resources. After all, protecting biodiversity and nature conservation require more than tree planting projects to increase green coverage, save a coastal area, or to avert desertification.[67]

The creation of KNCF substantiates charges by critics that these Japanese corporate giants were more for its demonstrative effects than any genuine long-term commitment to the environment. KNCF was set up with 300 million yen, the minimum necessary to obtain legal status as a non-profit entity under the country's stringent association laws. Without any significant endowment, KNCF must seek voluntary donations from Keidanren member companies to support its activities.[68] Donations have fallen drastically following the bursting of the Japanese economic bubble and a steep decline of corporate interest in the global environment after UNCED in 1992. As a result, KNCF has given out a total of only US$2 million as of 1996, even though Keidanren companies are among the biggest and richest in the world.[69]

Lack of staff and expertise is another problem. The KNCF administrative staff is small and borrowed from a Keidanren member company whose president chairs KNCF. One remedy has been to work with outside groups, including The Nature Conservancy, Conservation International, World Resources Institute, The Smithsonian Institution, and the John D. and Catherine T. MacArthur Foundation, to carry out projects in developing countries. NGOs have criticized this KNCF preference to work with large and conservative groups in the United States and United Kingdom over smaller and/or domestic groups. NGOs have also cited this as evidence of Keidanren's interest in earning wider publicity. KNCF contributions to these international groups follow the example of Western companies, allowing them to project themselves as good corporate citizens.

It is not surprising that KNCF finds it easier to collaborate with these larger, more established groups. These groups have long experience in working with business corporations. Their collaboration gives Japanese business staff opportunities to expand skills and knowledge on environmental affairs. Many of these activities, including project missions to Indonesia and Papua New Guinea, have had Japanese NGOs participation. KNCF considers its sponsorship of these activities an effort to facilitate exchange between Japanese and international NGOs. Nonetheless, on the whole, Japanese business interest in the global environment still has to mature and words need to be translated into actions.

Japanese big business is influential in government policy making because it is simultaneously the top constituent and patron of the powerful ministries, namely the MoF, MITI, MoC, and MAFF. The practice of "*amakudari*" or "the descent from heaven," in particular, sustains an informal structure, which ties Japanese business to their regulatory bodies. *Amakudari* allows bureaucrats to obtain executive posts in private firms after retirement from the civil service. Each year hundreds of ex-bureaucrats move from being regulators of an industry/business into becoming advisors and liaisons with their former employer.[70] At the same time, these human links also extend bureaucratic influence beyond the formal structure. A National Personnel Authority report released in March 1995 reported that a total of 203 senior government officials found jobs in companies formerly under their jurisdiction in 1994. The Ministry of Finance topped the list for the 30th consecutive year with 58 retired officials joining the private sector, followed by MITI with 23. Within the business community, manufacturing took in the largest number of retired bureaucrats (57), followed by finance and the insurance sector (45).[71]

The country's domestic economic slowdown since the early 1990s and the concurrent resurgence of the U.S. economy have severely dampened Japanese business interest in the global environment. At the international level, talk of global economic competitiveness has also eclipsed international environmental cooperation. Only two environment-related issues still hold some corporate interest. First, in the long term, it is the sale of environmental goods and services. Japan has an advance environment technology industry, especially in clean air and water, as a result of domestic pollution clean up. Japanese companies have a long-term view that Asia-Pacific economies will become new markets for their environmental goods and services. In addition, Japanese companies may have advantages over North American and European firms because of their significant investments throughout the region and Japan's ODA program to facilitate sales. Programs such as MITI's Green Aid Program have aided the transfer (or sale) of desulfurization technology to China.

The second, more immediate environmental issue attracting corporate interest is compliance with ISO 14000 for environmental management and environmental auditing which took effect in October 1996.[72] Under ISO 14000, certified organizations have to set up a framework for continuous improvement to maintain their certification status.[73] Although certification is voluntary and requires several hundreds of thousands of dollars, stricter domestic environmental laws have made big business (and increasingly medium- and small-sized firms) keen to obtain ISO certification. For example, ISO 14000 has been adapted into the Japan Industrial Standards (JIS) and it has been in effect since September 1996. Some corporations also expect cuts in operating costs as a result of improved environmental practices. Finally, many companies industry thinks that having ISO 14000 certification could benefit as their corporate image. Green consumption has been slowly gaining popularity in Japan and it is already important in key markets in North America and Europe where consumers have stronger environmental awareness.[74]

NON-GOVERNMENTAL ORGANIZATIONS

Unlike in America and Western Europe where political traditions look favorably upon voluntary action and citizen access to government, NGOs in Japan "could not take for granted notions of citizen participation, local autonomy, or access to the government.... These are their practical goals, not means to more distant ends."[75] Their development and access to the policy process is restricted because, "there is an underlying assumption among government officials that NGOs are basically unauthorized actors in a society where the government is the only authorized organization to promote public interest."[76] As a consequence, the powerful bureaucracy has for the longest time viewed NGOs as a potential threat or at least a nuisance.

The rising influence of NGOs and their recognition as legitimate actors in environmental conservation by national governments and multilateral organizations has put pressure on the Japanese government and other influential domestic policy actors to gradually concede to this new phenomenon. For instance, the Agenda 21 national action plan was the first government policy draft to be put up for public debate.[77] The Japanese official delegation to the United Nations Conference on Population and Development in Cairo in September 1994 was the first occasion in which NGOs were invited by the Japanese government to join a government delegation.

Domestic pressure for bureaucratic acceptance of NGOs has been increasing. The introduction of environment-related information to the Japanese public by NGOs, most especially immediately before and after UNCED, greatly expanded their visibility in Japanese society. The public image of NGOs was further enhanced after the Great Hanshin Earthquake in Kobe in 1995 when many citizens groups actively carried out rescue and care efforts while the government was slow to act under the burden of its massive bureaucratic structure.[78]

Japanese politicians, the bureaucracy, and big business, too, see that NGOs can be useful to their own agendas. Supporting NGOs can help to improve their public image and compensate their handicap in grassroots networks and activities. Giving money to finance NGOs activities is also cheaper than undertaking these activities on their own.

Finally, for bureaucratic actors who do not have strong home constituencies or powers, such as the Ministry for Foreign Affairs and JEA, support from NGOs can sometimes improve their leverage in intra- and inter-ministerial negotiations. Enlisting NGO cooperation may also be useful in situations when speaking directly on an issue is difficult or countereffective for a bureaucratic agency. For instance, Makiko Tanaka, former Director-General of the Science and Technology Agency, urged Greenpeace to stop France's plans to conduct nuclear tests in the Pacific. In another example, JEA welcomed NGOs efforts to raise public awareness of the dangers of transboundary air pollution from mainland Asia. Increased public concern helped JEA to argue for more pro-active responses and to obtain government funds for its activities.

Thus, the Japanese government and big business have created new funds to support NGO activities.[79] MoF created small funds in 1989 to support Japanese NGO project activities in developing countries. The Subsidy System for NGO Projects reached a total disbursement of 540 million yen in 1994, and the Grant Assistance for Grassroots Projects grew to 1.5 billion yen in 1994. JEA's Japan Fund for Global Environment supports NGO activities in Japan and overseas.[80] The priority has been on Asia and in areas of reforestation and conservation of tropical forests, desertification, wildlife protection, and air and water pollution.[81]

The Ministry of Posts and Telecommunications launched its Voluntary Postal Savings for International Aid scheme in 1991. Holders of postal savings accounts can give 20 percent of interest payments to NGO activities. Donations jumped from 910 million yen in 1991 to 2.3 billion yen in 1992, and 2.4 billion yen in 1993. By the end of July 1994, there were over 15 million account holders participating in this program. As of March 1994, the scheme had given to 197 NGOs for 261 projects in 56 countries.[82] However, low interest rates in recent years have caused disbursements to fall. Decline of popular interest in international environmental activities has also affected donations to the scheme. In 1996, disbursements fell to 1.5 billion yen and then just one billion yen in 1997.

However, for ministries that are big and heavily domestic-oriented in their jurisdictions, such as the Ministry of Education, MoF, MAFF, and MoC, their adversity towards NGOs has not lessened. For instance, while MoF provides funds for NGO activities overseas—largely to appease outside demands—it "pays no attention to them and does not even want to pay attention to them."[83]

The number of NGOs active in international environmental issues in Japan increased in the late 1980s. It was a time of domestic prosperity and growing public interest in global affairs that was matched by increasing government ambitions in the international arena. Most Japanese NGOs are small groups with origins in Japan. A few are branches of international conservation groups, such as Greenpeace, which came to Japan to recruit membership and donations. Nonetheless, the total number of NGOs in Japan is small considering the size of Japan's population, economy, and ODA disbursements. This is particularly true for those involved in international issues. An NGO directory produced by the Japan Fund for the Global Environment reported that of the 4,000 groups in the country, only 427 are active in international environment and development work, and only 283 of them engage in activities overseas.

This small number reflects primarily the severe legal and institutional barriers imposed by the government bureaucracy. Until recently, the legal

Global Environment in Japanese Politics

framework basically does not allow the majority of NGOs to be legally incorporated or to have tax-exempt privilege. This has been a formidable obstacle to developing a strong organizational base. NGOs in Japan, as incorporated foundations or incorporated associations, fall under the category of "non-profit public interest corporations" and are governed by Article 34 of the Civil Code. For an organization to be eligible for incorporation, it is required to have an endowment of 300 million yen (approximately US$3 million), an annual budget of approximately 30 million yen, an activity plan, and a board consisting of publicly esteemed individuals.

Furthermore, the applicant must have the "approval of the competent governmental office," that is, the government authority with jurisdiction over the area of work which the NGO seeks involvement. With no objective criteria to guide "approval," the granting of legal status is left to arbitrary discretion even after an applicant has fulfilled all the legal requirements.[84] If a group works in more than one area, it would have to receive approval from all relevant government offices.[85] After all of this, it still takes several months to explain the detailed documents accompanying the application to the appropriate ministry before public interest corporation status is granted. Thus, it is not surprising to find that, according to the *1994 NGOs Directory*, only 28 NGOs in the entire country have received legal status from a list of 186 independent citizens organizations.[86]

With the promulgation of a new non-profit organization law in 1998, many more are seeking legal status. Prior to the passing of this law, the majority of NGOs are registered as personal limited companies and must pay taxes for money raised (or income earned) from the sale of subscriptions and other merchandise.[87] Even formally registered NGOs in Japan are subject to a high tax rate of 27 percent (versus 37.5 for profit-making corporations). Consequently, significant portions of NGO funds go to taxes and operating costs.

Non-profit organizations in Japan also do not enjoy many of the benefits available to their counterparts in other countries, such as discounted postage rates.[88] Hence, even the largest NGOs in Japan operate on annual budgets that are only a fraction of their Western counterparts. For example, the Nature Conservancy Society of Japan employs about 20 people and operates on an annual budget of about US$3 million. This is just about one-tenth of The Nature Conservancy in the U.S. which has a staff of 1,300 and an annual budget of around US$300 million.

Fund raising has also been extremely difficult for these groups because charitable giving is not a tradition in Japan. Japanese citizens are also less inclined to give to non-profit organizations because the tax system does not encourage donations by corporations or individuals. In general, companies in Japan can only claim tax deductible donations up to 0.125 percent of their capital, plus 1.25 percent of their annual profit.[89] Individual donations to NGOs are not even tax-exempted. Only contributions to government-owned or government-authorized organizations qualify for tax deduction, and the ceiling is 25 percent of an individual's income.

As a result, most Japanese NGOs exist virtually on the verge of bankruptcy. A JEA survey in 1992 found that up to 30.6 percent of the 368 NGOs that responded had only an average annual budget of 100,000 to 1 million yen. Another 11.6 percent and 20.7 percent had average annual budgets of less than 100,000 yen and only 1 million to 10 million yen, respectively. Hence, nearly half (49.2%) of them have no full-time staff and another 16.6 percent have only one to three persons.[90] Among Japanese NGOs, the larger ones include the Japan Union for Nature Conservation, the Nature Conservation Society of Japan, the Wild Bird Society of Japan, the World Wide Fund for Nature (Japan), and Defense of the Green Earth Fund. Yet membership in the vast majority of these groups is no more than a few hundred compared to the millions of members in the major groups in North America and Europe.

Shortage of funds severely hampers organizational capacity building and the ability of NGOs to engage the institutional forces in policy debates. Without adequate resources, they cannot conduct independent research and analysis to challenge industry and government positions. They are also unable to offer policy alternatives and demonstrate themselves as credible policy actors that can go beyond merely opposing or criticizing government policy proposals.

Such weaknesses make it easy for the government bureaucracy to restrict NGO participation in policy processes. Even when the role of NGOs is acknowledged, the government does not generally treat NGOs as equals. Government funds for NGO activities are biased towards serving the interests of the bureaucratic sponsor. NGO staff is not regarded as professionals or experts, but as volunteers to serve community and international welfare. Hence, Japanese government grants generally pay for project costs only; administrative expenses, including salaries for NGO staff, are not covered. For example, the 1995 Basic Environment Plan urges all sectors and groups of the society to "voluntarily and actively participate in environmental conservation."[91] Furthermore, government grants are usually disbursed after a project is finished to ensure that approved projects are executed. This means that NGOs without adequate pre-existing funds would have difficulty trying to take advantage of government funds.

Such realities explain why NGOs in Japan have remained skeptical of the government even if many more now accept the necessity of dialogue with the bureaucracy. NGOs worry about their dependence on government funds and independence of their organizational goals, philosophy, and actions. Some NGO leaders have also been wary that close contacts with the bureaucracy would weaken the credibility of their organizations and support from their members.

Global Environment in Japanese Politics

NGOs in Japan face other difficulties. Political lobbying is not considered useful because Japanese legislators do not regard the global environment an important political issue. In addition, NGOs and voters cannot rate and pressure politicians through campaigns and ballots because voting records are not available to the public.

The community-based and issue-oriented approach of most Japanese NGOs makes them more successful in the local arena than in national politics. This helps to explain why Japanese NGOs do not generally have strong national coalitions and networks that can increase their leverage *vis-a-vis* the central government. Few are capable of carrying out large scale and multi-year projects because they lack resources and manpower.

Ideological differences among Japanese NGOs constitute another major obstacle to making these groups a more formidable force in the Japanese political arena. Ideological differences can paralyze these organizations internally and frustrate cooperation with other groups. For instance, within the NGO community, there were vastly divergent opinions on the necessity and appropriate contents of a new law for non-profit organizations.

Advocates for a new law felt it was necessary to the growth of the non-profit sector and to encourage the professional development of NGOs. On the other hand, many were reluctant to support a new law because they feared it could result in stricter government regulation. Some even considered the professionalization of NGOs a threat to the ideological character and spirit of NGOs. Quite a few NGOs were anxious about legal requirements under a new law. The issue of financial reporting was particularly controversial. Some NGO leaders believed that financial reporting was essential to establishing accountability for the long-term growth of the non-profit sector. Others feared it could undermine their personal authority and expose their organization to outside scrutiny.[92] In fact, the concept of accountability was largely unknown and unheard of in Japan until several years ago and a full equivalent of this word/concept is absent in the Japanese language.[93]

For many foreign NGOs, their experience of working with Japanese groups has not been highly rewarding. Much of this outcome can be attributed to their ignorance of Japanese politics, culture and language, Japan's harsh domestic policy setting, and the high costs of living and operating in Japan. Tensions and disappointments also arise between foreign and Japanese groups because of differences in their goals, expectations, and working styles.

Japanese NGOs have complained about competition from foreign groups for government and private sector support. Many Japanese groups have alleged discrimination by these institutional donors, which are keen to demonstrate their largess to the outside world. Financial contributions from KNCF to The Nature Conservancy has often been cited as an example of such donor bias.

Another common complaint is the unequal working relationship with international conservation groups, particularly those from the United States.[94] Having a global reach, substantial financial resources, expertise, and political leverage, these groups are sometimes perceived as overbearing in their tendency to teach or guide their Japanese partners. Japanese groups have also charged that foreign groups ignore the objectives and working styles of their Japanese partners, because their work in Japan is seen only as one part of their global strategy.

However, from the perspective of foreign NGOs, many have been disappointed by the lack of funding and support in Japan. Quite a few have been frustrated by their perception of ambiguity and passivity among Japanese NGOs. As a result, some have decided that it would be more effective to directly pressure the Japanese government and big business from outside rather than in Japan or in cooperation with Japanese NGOs.

Therefore, cooperation between Japanese and foreign NGOs has been hampered by differences in their size and capacity. The weaker side fears losing control to the stronger one. Conflicts arise from different strategies and concerns about visibility for their organizations in joint campaigns. Visibility is important because it can affect subsequent membership recruitment and fund-raising activities.[95]

JAPANESE ACADEMIA

Academics have no real or independent role in national policy making on international environmental issues because there is basically no demand for their input by the government bureaucracy.[96] There are also other reasons why Japanese academics are insignificant in the national policy process. First, there are the peculiarities of Japanese academia. By choice or outside pressure, Japanese professors often live in the proverbial "ivory tower." Academia in Japan is often a refuge for those who do not want to join the money-oriented corporate world or the power-obsessed civil service. Many Japanese professors value their independence and are not interested in the everyday problems of modern society. Those who choose to address current topics could risk dismissal by their peers as lackeys of journalism and second-rate thinkers. The outcome is that those in the natural sciences generate a massive volume of data but make no effort to find application in real-life issues. Those in the humanities shut themselves off from the world, and immerse in studies that only serve their own satisfaction.[97]

Structural barriers in Japan's tertiary education sector are a second restriction on their participation in the policy making process. The rigid division of faculties and departments by subject areas is as strictly guarded as the official demarcations within the bureaucracy. This bars exchange of ideas and free flow of information.

Thirdly, the Ministry of Education (MoE) oversees all universities in Japan. MoE has an especially tight rein over the national universities

Global Environment in Japanese Politics 75

because it controls their budgets. Even outside financial sources must be channeled through the ministry. Thus, MoE exercises tight control over the institutional ties of all Japanese universities and their staff, keeping them within the ministry's bureaucratic boundaries. In addition to the ministry's control over funding, Japan's lifetime employment system also discourage Japanese professors from voicing dissent against MoE for fear of jeopardizing their careers and promotion prospects.[98]

Finally, where individuals do participate in policy making, such as in special study groups and projects sponsored by the ministries, their presence or views are valued primarily for the validation and credibility they give to the policy preferences of their government sponsors. This effectively makes them part of intra- and inter-bureaucratic rivalries. Working with one ministry or agency automatically makes them as supporters of that bureaucratic office. As a consequence, Japanese academia has very limited objective and independent participation in policy processes.

"THINK TANKS" OR POLICY RESEARCH INSTITUTES

One Ministry of Finance official put it bluntly "there are no policy research institutes in Japan."[99] The same view was echoed by many others who were interviewed for this research. All concurred that think tanks in Japan play no real role in national policy formulation on international environmental issues or practically all other issue matters.

Although there has been a proliferation of private and quasi-governmental think tanks throughout Japan, practically none conduct independent and objective public policy and problem-oriented research. Think tanks in Japan are not part of a revolving door system for researchers and scholars or ex-government officials and political appointees to participate in the policy process outside of the government. The reasons for this will be examined further below. In environment-related research, in particular, the focus has generally been on specialized technical subjects, such as pollution control, with scarcely any work on policy or the human dimensions of global change. Expertise on a broad range of international environmental is lacking even at national institutes for research, such as JEA's National Institute for Environmental Studies.[100]

The fist wave to create privately-owned policy research organizations occurred in the late 1960s and early 1970s, when Japanese companies established their own research institutes to emulate their western counterparts. The second wave came in the 1980s during the economic boom when many Japanese companies created think tanks as status symbols. The biggest and most prominent among these private think tanks are the Nomura Institute and the Mitsubishi Research Institute. However, they are large-scale consultants in reality. Since their budgets are controlled by their parent company (or their parent company is their biggest client if they "sell" their services), they cannot conduct independent and non-biased policy research. Instead they are expected to meet the research and development needs of the corporate activities of their sponsors. Economic policy and trend forecasting and analysis make up the bulk of their work and the quality of research among the smaller ones is debatable. As a consequence, their work has little influence on public policy debates and policy making.[101]

Commissions for research by ministry offices are quite common, but the work also generally validates or supports a ministerial view, instead of proposing policy options and identifying risks and advantages. The strict demarcation of bureaucratic jurisdictions also carries over so that these think tanks would generally work only for the ministerial office that oversees them and their parent company. A researcher in a private think tank sums it up in this manner, "They [the private research institutes] are part of the *keiretsu* [vertically integrated business such as the *sogo sosha*] system and are also subcontractors for the bureaucracy."[102]

There is also a multitude of quasi-governmental research institutes. These "public-interest corporations," as they are officially classified, are in reality affiliates of their parent ministries. Examples are the Japan External Trade Organization (JETRO), the Institute of Developing Economies (IDE), and GISPRI under MITI; the National Institute for Research Advancement (NIRA) under the Ministry of Education; the National Institute for Environmental Studies (NIES) and the Institute for Global Environmental Strategies under JEA; and the Institute for Cetacean Research (ICR) and Research Association for Reforestation of Tropical Forest (RETROF) under MAFF.

The ministries usually provide these groups with the bulk of their budgets, as well as a number of the research staff. A survey in 1993 found that of the 292 executives surveyed at 49 of these public interest corporations, 217 were former ranking government officials. Among these 217 executives, 34 came from MITI, 32 from MAFF, and 25 from MoF.[103] Thus, these think tanks are another *amakudari* haven for retired officials. This practice reinforces the tendency for research topics to be specific to the jurisdiction and interests of the sponsoring institutions and supportive of their perspectives. Researchers cannot propose policies nor can they be critical of their sponsoring institutions.[104] MoFA's Japan Institute for International Affairs (JIIA), for instance, did practically no research on Taiwan for nearly two decades following the normalization of diplomatic ties between Japan and China. There was also no serious research on Hong Kong because the territory was not an independent sovereignty with which MoFA must interact. Bureaucratic demarcations of jurisdictions also spill over to these government-sponsored think tanks. As a result, they do not work with each other, including those that may be under the same ministry or agency, because their primary allegiance (or budget and staff) is owed to a specific department or bureau.

Global Environment in Japanese Politics

In addition, the lifetime employment system also makes researchers subservient to the demands of their employers. Researchers are careful not to espouse views that could displease their masters and jeopardize personal career prospects.

THE JAPANESE MASS MEDIA

Although the Japanese mass media have been quite influential in mobilizing public opinion on domestic environmental problems, particularly in pollution-related ones, it has not been highly significant in shaping Japan's foreign environmental policies.[105]

One would expect the Japanese mass media to be more influential considering that illiteracy is practically non-existent in Japan, and the Japanese people are among the world's biggest consumers of newspapers. For a population of 126 million, Japanese newspaper daily circulation in 1995 (morning edition alone) was 10.1 million copies for *The Yomiuri*, 8.3 million for *Asahi*, 4 million for *Mainichi*, 2.9 million for *Nihon Keizai Shimbun*, and 1.9 million for *Sankei*. In comparison, the biggest newspaper in the United States, the *Wall Street Journal*, has a daily circulation of only 1.8 million and is followed by *The New York Times* with a daily circulation of 1.1 million copies.[106]

Another source of the media's influence is the widespread belief by policy elites in the media's potency in shaping public opinion. In a policy process that is severely lacking in access and transparency and where government officials, not elected representatives, are the main policy makers, public opinion is highly valued for its power to legitimize policy choices. Sometimes it goes so far as to "take press attention as a surrogate for public opinion."[107]

However, newspaper editors do not consider global environmental protection important in comparison to domestic political and economic news, sports, and reports on U.S.-Japan trade conflicts. There was little reporting on global environmental issues until the late 1980s and early 1990s when the number of environmental protection-related articles quickly rocketed as a result of growing public interest. The table below shows this rapid increase.

Table 2. Trends in Environment-Related Coverage in Four Major Newspapers in Japan

	1987	1988	1989	1990	1991	1992	1993	1994	1995
(1) Environmental Problem									
Nikkei	51	112	714	1,133	1,321	1,539	932	608	662
Asahi	37	87	456	787	1,186	1,538	936	828	760
Mainchi	4	17	95	124	229	298	280	519	637
Yomiuri	66	71	415	375	453	632	338	241	191
(2) Global Environment									
Nikkei	0	24	985	1,195	1,040	1,321	673	509	615
Asahi	14	24	364	606	829	1,217	589	429	455
Mainchi	0	3	114	140	259	466	167	277	280
Yomiuri	35	40	524	376	427	697	244	211	158

Nonetheless, these reports had only moderate impact on educating the Japanese public or encouraging public debate on the country's foreign environmental policies. Since most Japanese reporters had limited expertise on global environmental issues, their reporting has been highly dependent on their news sources. In addition, the history and public perception of a foreign policy issue in the domestic setting often affect the focus of news stories.

For instance, Japanese media reports on whaling in the critical years between 1982 and 1987 usually showed Japan as the victim of western bullying tactics because of the verbal and physical assaults on Japanese delegates by anti-whaling protesters. These reports helped to give credence to the Fisheries Agency's claims of Japan-bashing. Instead of more balanced reports to inform the Japanese people of the many sides of the whaling debate or the rationale of anti-whaling advocates, most news stories and editorials argued for the defense of Japanese pride and cultural traditions.[108]

In contrast, news reports on deforestation in the tropics and the devastating effects of the tropical timber trade rapidly shifted from a pro-establishment tone to a more balanced position as environmental groups became a new source of information for journalists. Also, the anti-tropical timber campaign's targeting of the role of Japanese big business in tropical forest destruction provided a perspective that is familiar to Japanese reporters and public.

Beyond the lack of interest and abilities to report on the global environment, there are fundamental weaknesses in the institutions of Japanese journalism. A harsh criticism comes from one of its own, who says that "there are few real journalists in Japan, most are only workers for the mass media company."[109] Since Japanese reporters are not given by-lines, they have no independent identity or incentive to conduct investigative reporting or state their own opinions. Original news stories are practically absent

Global Environment in Japanese Politics

in the dailies because the reporter club (*kisha kurabu*) system controls virtually all news sources.

Journalists in Japan must belong to reporter clubs to access news sources. Reporter clubs are attached to each of the Japanese government ministries, labor unions, major corporations, business federations, prominent politicians, political parties, and party factions, as well as leading social and cultural institutions. The number of these reporter clubs ranges from 440 identified in 1993 to as many as 1,000 throughout the country.[110] Most news is filtered through formal (on-the-record press conferences) and informal (off-the-record background briefings) with individual or institutional sources. Briefings are organized by, and restricted to, members of the respective reporter club.[111] Since Japanese reporters spend most of their working time in spaces provided by their news sources, including the ministries and agencies, they form interdependent relationships with their news sources and sometimes are no more than mouthpieces for the decision makers.[112]

Two other reasons deter investigative and original reporting. First, news stories must conform to house style and tone to obtain approval by editors. Second, the lifetime employment system discourages reporters from developing independent interests and views to avoid repercussions on their careers.[113]

Although independent and investigative reporting can be found in the tabloids (e.g., *Gendai*, *Flash*, *Arena*, *Focus*) and intellectual monthlies (e.g., *Bungei Shunju*), tabloid stories are usually not taken seriously and the environment is still not considered a worthy topic in either medium.[114]

Finally, a note on English language newspapers in Japan. English language Japanese newspapers like *The Japan Times* and the *Asahi Evening News* are more sympathetic to conservation arguments. This difference can be attributed to the fact that their reporters and editors as well as readers are more likely to be foreigners or Japanese who have greater familiarity with international opinion. However, the English media has a very limited reach in Japan so that it has a negligible impact on Japanese public opinion and public policy making.

SUMMARY

In the final analysis, the government bureaucracy is the country's most powerful foreign policy actor in international environmental issues. Its domination of the foreign policy process has allowed little room for outside participation. Nevertheless, citizen demand for accountability and representation has increased in Japan. Government officials know that not being elected representatives seek outside support to legitimize their policy choices and actions. Thus, consultations are held with key policy bodies of the ruling political party, its top leaders, and its policy tribes. With private business, "administrative guidance" is used to induce voluntary compliance and cooperation instead of direct regulatory control.[115] Increasing public demand for access and transparency in the policy process has compelled the government and industry to open contacts with NGOs and provide resources to support NGO activities.

Notes

[1] Scientific uncertainty, cover-ups by private industry and bureaucratic foot-dragging sometimes kept these diseases from formal recognition by the government for years after the first cases were detected. Reports of mercury poisoning in Minamata appeared by 1956 and suits in Niigata were filed in 1967. Cadmium poisoning was observed as early as the 1920s and cases erupted again around 1946, while in Yokkaichi complaints were lodged beginning 1959 but the problem was not formally recognized until 1967. For more on these and other cases, see Norie Huddle *et al.*, *Island of Dreams: Environmental Crisis in Japan*, New York: Autumn Press, 1975; and McKean, *op cit.*

[2] The seven symptoms were air pollution, water pollution, noise, vibration, ground subsidence, offensive odor, and soil contamination. Medical treatment expenses for certified victims of designated pollution diseases were split among the central government (25%), local governments (25%), and the firm(s) responsible for the pollution (50%). See <<www.mofa.go.jp/policy/environment/pamph/1992/2_front.html>>. Viewed on 9 May 1998.

[3] Broadbent's detailed case study of Oita prefecture's experience in handling the growth/environment dilemma in the 1970s illustrates how progrowth and pro-environment coalitions mobilized and struggled to affect government policies at all levels in Japan. See Jeffrey Broadbent, *Environmental Politics in Japan: Networks of Power and Protest*, Cambridge: Cambridge University Press, 1998. For victims of pollution, however, court judgments made between 1971 and 1973 on the "big four" cases were most decisive in assisting them to establish their claims. All judgments in these cases ruled in favor of the victims. The rulings also accelerated the establishment of basic legal principles governing damage claims and a national compensation system for personal injury caused by environmental pollution. See Shiro Kawashima, "A Survey of Environmental Law and Policy in Japan," *North Carolina Journal of International Law and Commercial Regulations*, Vol.20, No.2, 1995, p.242; and Julian Gresser *et al.*, *Environmental Law in Japan*, Cambridge: Massachusetts Institute of Technology Press, 1981, p.413.

Global Environment in Japanese Politics

81

[4] Ridgley observed that Japan's national laws function as a "floor," while local governments usually adopt much stricter, site-specific standards. This is partly the result of earlier unresponsiveness on the part of national government to industrial pollution problems and the more direct exposure of local governments to public pressure. Ridgley offers another explanation: that, in Japan, "a 'fair' standard is not necessarily one which treats everyone the same, but rather one which takes into account all the unique local preferences and peculiarities." See Susan Ridgley, "Environmental Protection Agreements in Japan and the United States," *Pacific Rim Law and Policy Journal*, Vol.5, No.3, July 1996, p.640.

[5] The law requires a basic survey of the natural environment in Japan once every five years and imposes new regulations to conserve the natural environment.

[6] OECD, *op cit.*, p.16.

[7] Morrisette and Plantinga, *op cit.*, pp.18-19.

[8] Formally entitled "Our Common Future," This World Commission on Environment and Development report was prepared under the guidance of its chair Mrs. Gro Harlem Brundtland, former Prime Minister of Norway.

[9] "Japan's activities to cope with global environmental problems: Japan's contribution toward a better global environment" by the Ad Hoc Group on Environmental Problems and "The Interim report on global warming" by the Expert Panel on Global Warming.

[10] Nomura, *ibid.*, pp.129-130.

[11] The Group of Seven refers to the top seven economies of the world: the United States, Japan, Germany, the United Kingdom, France, Italy and Canada. Takeshi Shirasu, "In Search of Closer Collaboration between Japan and US in the Aid Sphere: A Japanese View," Washington, D.C.: Overseas Development Council, 1990, p.12.

[12] Mochizuki, *op cit.*, p.415.

[13] MoFA, "Japan's Official Development Assistance Summary 1997," *op cit.*, pp.20-21 and 44-47.

[14] "Nation's Agenda 21 plan finalized," *The Japan Times*, 25 December 1993.

[15] This includes prescriptions of specific measures to internalize the external costs of pollution and to provide technological assistance to industry. See Kawashima, *op cit.*, p.250; and Hidefumi Imura, "Japan's Environmental Balancing Act: Accommodating Sustained Development," *Asian Survey*, Vol.34, No.4, April 1994, pp.356 and 357.

[16] Nomura, *ibid.*, pp.130-131.

[17] Environment Agency, "Basic Environment Plan Established," *Japan Environment Summary*, Vol.22, No.5, 10 January 1995, pp.1-3.

[18] A full statement by the Japanese Prime Minister at UNGASS can be found at <<www.eic.or.jp/eanet/e/jeq/v0002-03.html>>. Viewed on 9 May 1998.

[19] A sample of these thoughts includes Ezra F. Vogel, ed., *Modern Japanese Organization and Decision-Making*, Berkeley: University of California Press, 1975; T.J. Pempel, *Policy and Politics in Japan: Creative Conservatism*, Philadelphia: Temple University Press, 1982; John C. Campbell, "Policy Conflict and its Resolution within the Governmental System," in *Conflict in Japan*, ed. by Krauss *et al.*, *op cit.*, pp.294-334; Peter P. Cheng, "Japanese Interest Group: An Institutional Framework," *Asian Survey*, Vol.30, No.3, March 1990, pp.251-265; and Muramatsu and Krauss, *op cit.*

[20] Frank Schwartz, "Advice and Consent: The Politics of Consultation in Japan," USJP Occasional paper No.91-11, Program on U.S.-Japan Relations, Harvard University, 1991, p.8.

[21] Fukui, "The GATT Tokyo Round...," *op cit.*

[22] Japan does not have a freedom of information act similar to that in the United States. The new Information Disclosure Law only applies in Tokyo.

[23] "Japan's Next Stimulus Package to focus on Public Works," *The Nihon Keizai Shimbun*, 9 April 1998.

[24] Interviews with H. Kobayashi, Uitto and Nishioka.

[25] Interview with Matsushita.

[26] MWH was able to install the greatest number of officials because prior to the formation of the Environment Agency, pollution was a policy issue only in its effects on human health, a policy area that was—and still is—governed by MWH. Interviews with Matsushita and Kobayashi.

[27] This was also observed by Kawashima, *op cit.*, p.255.

[28] Interview with Matsushita.

[29] Interviews with Matsushita, Kobayashi and Kuroda.

[30] See Brendan F.D. Barrett and Riki Therival, *Environmental Policy and Impact Assessment in Japan*, London and New York: Routledge, 1991, p.14 and p.75.

[31] An Environmental Impact Assessment Law (EIA) received approval the Japanese Diet in June 1997, and will take effect in two years. Differences between JEA and MITI have held back the passing of Japanese EIA legislation since 1981. MITI's main contention is that power plants should not be included for assessment because they are part of the national energy policy for power security, while JEA insists that all businesses should be covered by the law. The new EIA law authorizes JEA to order EIA reviews on infrastructure projects and check on the contracting companies. However, the EIA law is not effective for those projects that have already started.

[32] Interview with Matsushita.

[33] Interview with Nishioka.

[34] Gresser *et al.*, *op cit.*, pp.229-242.

[35] Interview with Matsushita.

Global Environment in Japanese Politics

[36] Fukui suggested the importance of public support to the Ministry of Foreign Affairs, another bureaucratic actor that has no powerful domestic constituencies under its jurisdiction. See Fukui, "Too Many Captains in Japan's Internationalization...," *op cit.*

[37] Caldwell, *International Environmental Policy, op cit.*, p.314.

[38] The fund was created with an initial endowment of one billion yen from the government and contributions from private industry and the general public. The Japan Environment Corporation, a quasi-governmental non-profit organization under JEA guidance, manages the fund and its disbursements.

[39] Kawashima, *op cit.*, pp.254-255.

[40] Interview with Kato.

[41] *Ibid.*

[42] The International Finance Bureau, responsible for cooperation with multilateral organizations has no official role in representing the ministry in intra-governmental dialogues on ODA policy. This is the responsibility of the Budget Bureau. Interview with Kato.

[43] As proposed by expert reports commissioned by the Environment Agency.

[44] Interview with Kato.

[45] *Ibid.*

[46] Ai Nakajima, "Aid offered to clean environment abroad," *The Nikkei Weekly*, 27 July 1991, p.3.

[47] Emily T. Smith *et al.*, "Growth vs. Environment," *Business Week*, 11 May 1992, p.73.

[48] U.S. House of Representatives, Committee on Merchant Marine and Fisheries, Subcommittee on Environment and Natural Resources, Hearing on Business Opportunities in Environmental Technology and Trade, 25 February 1993, p.8.

[49] Interview with Uitto.

[50] Interview with Nishioka.

[51] Kenji Hayao, *The Japanese Prime Minister and Public Policy*, Pittsburgh and London: University of Pittsburgh Press, 1993, p.11.

[52] There are studies that suggest a rising influence of Japanese politicians in policy making as a result of the inability of the bureaucracy to articulate broad national goals for policy and the gradual institutionalization of party government. In addition, many more bureaucrats are entering politics and bringing with them some expertise into the *zoku*. However, consultation and consensus may continue to be the norm until drastic political changes occur and the *zoku* may only be important in giving support to the bureaucracy. See Okimoto, *op cit.*, pp.320-322; and B. C. Koh, *Japan's Administrative Elite*, Berkeley: University of California Press, 1989.

[53] Interview with Wada; and Hayao, *op cit.*, pp.143-144.

[54] Miranda Schreurs, "Japan's Changing Approach to Environmental Issues," *Environmental Politics*, Vol.6, No.2, Summer 1997, p.152.

[55] Interview with Matsushita.

[56] Nakasone's attempt to initiate a more active and executive-led leadership style has been extensively studied. First, he tried to overcome the powerful bureaucracy through the use of consultative committees composed of academics and industry leaders. In foreign policy, Nakasone showed a Japanese lead on international economic and security issues through his active participation at the summits of the industrialized economies. See for example, Hayao, *op cit.*; Robert D. Putnam and Nicholas Bayne, *Hanging Together: The Seven-Power Summits*, Cambridge: Harvard University Press, 1984; and J.A.A. Stockwin *et al.*, *Dynamic and Immobilist Politics in Japan*, Honolulu: University of Hawaii Press, 1988.

[57] Interview with Wada.

[58] Tatsuhiko Shiba, *Kujira to Nihonjin* (Whales and the Japanese), Tokyo: Yousensha, 1988, pp.24-25.

[59] *Ibid.*, p.23.

[60] Interviews with numerous officials in the Fisheries Agency and MoFA who were responsible for whaling. The same was also reported in many Japanese and English language publications. See for instance Shiba, *ibid.*; and Kazuo Sumi, "The `Whale War' between Japan and the United States: Problems and Prospects," *Denver Journal of International Law and Policy*, Vol.17, No.2, 1989, pp. 317-372. Nakasone attempted a top-down leadership style and took active role in other policy areas as well. For more, see Hayao, *op cit.*

[61] Interview with Matsushita.

[62] Interview with Nishioka.

[63] Interview with Kato.

[64] <<www.keidanren.or.jp/>>. Viewed on 10 May 1998.

[65] Membership in Keidanren is company-based, while in Keizai Doyukai it is individual-based.

[66] Keizai Doyukai, "Strategies to Arrest Global Warming," Tokyo: Keizai Doyukai, October 1991, p.7.

[67] KNCF to date has supported several tree-planting projects in Inner Mongolia, Vietnam, the West Bank of the Jordan River and Thailand.

[68] Interviews with KNCF and Keidanren staff.

[69] KNCF, "The Keidanren Nature Conservation Fund," Tokyo: KNCF, n.d.

[70] Although government officials are banned from getting jobs in companies that are closely related to their public jobs for two years after leaving the office, senior officials can seek exemption from the National Personnel Authority.

[71] "Bureaucrats find more executive jobs," *The Japan Times*, 30 March 1995, p.3.

Global Environment in Japanese Politics

[72] ISO 14000 succeeds ISO 9000. It is issued and regulated by the International Standardization Organization, a non-governmental organization of some 120 countries, that set various standards governing goods and services, which are traded internationally. ISO standards govern goods and services that are traded internationally. The difference between ISO 14000 and its predecessors is that ISO 14000 targets not just corporations and industry, but also government and financial institutions. The standards are generic and applicable to both service and manufacturing industries so that it provides an international benchmark for evaluating environmental performance in international markets.

[73] For details on ISO 14000, read James L. Lamprecht, *ISO 14000: Issues and Implementation Guidelines for Responsible Environmental Management*, New York: Amacom, 1997.

[74] Interview with Saito of Keidanren.

[75] McKean, *op cit.*, p.73.

[76] Toshihiro Menju and Takako Aoki, "The Evolution of Japanese NGOs in the Asia Pacific Context," *Emerging Civil Society in the Asia Pacific Community: Nongovernmental Underpinnings of the Emerging Asia Pacific Regional Community*, ed. by Tadashi Yamamoto, Tokyo: Japan Center for International Exchange, 1995, p.149.

[77] Interview with Matsushita.

[78] Interview with Yonemoto.

[79] Philanthropic contributions from Japanese big business grew most dramatically during the 1980s. By 1991, for the first time, the number of grant-making "incorporated foundations" (at 13,229) exceeded the number of non-grant-making "incorporated associations" (at 12,194). Although funds for NGO activities have increased during this and following periods, the vast majority of the money from these incorporated foundations goes to support their own programs. Also, only a small handful has annual incomes to provide grants to outside groups. See Takako Amemiya, "The Nonprofit Public Corporation in Japan, Part III," *SPF Newsletter*, No.4, October 1994, pp.3-4.

[80] The money comes from charitable contributions from citizens through their postal accounts, also a percentage of their charge cards. See Japan Fund for Global Environment, *Newsletter* (in Japanese), No.3, 6 December 1994, p.3.

[81] For a detail breakdown, see Japan Fund for Global Environment, *Newsletter* (in Japanese), No.2, 20 May 1994, pp.2-4.

[82] Menju and Aoki, *op cit.*, p.151.

[83] Interview with Kato.

[84] This approval system gives the government greater power, as compared to the "recognition system" which is applied to private school corporations and religious corporations. Once legal documents and applications are fulfilled, the government office must give its recognition.

[85] Takako Amemiya, "The Nonprofit Public Corporation in Japan," *SPF Newsletter*, No.2, May 1994, pp.1-3.

[86] Most NGOs in Japan then are really private corporations registered under an individual's name, usually that of its founder or leader, and enjoy no tax breaks. As a result, the individual must bear personal legal liability for the group and his membership is critical to the group's survival. Interviews with NGO leaders and staff; and Menju and Aoki, *op cit.* p.150.

[87] Interviews with staff of various NGOs in Japan.

[88] Amemiya, "The Nonprofit Public Corporation in Japan, Part III," *op cit.*

[89] Corporate giving to government-operated organizations is not restricted by this ceiling, and the ceiling is twice as high for donations to government authorized "special public interest promotion organizations."

[90] Environment Agency of Japan, *Quality of the Environment in Japan 1993*, p.28.

[91] Details on the Basic Environment Plan may be found at <<www.eic.or.jp/eanet/e/ bplan/leaflet3.htm>>.

[92] Under the new law, registered non-profit organizations must have one or more auditors as its officer(s) and an annual report of activities, inventory of assets balance sheet, statement of revenues and expenditures must be submitted to the government office from which it obtained approval.

[93] Interviews with K. Kuroda.

[94] Interviews with staff of different NGOs in Japan. Many Indonesian NGOs share a similar sentiment. Interview with Tjahjono.

[95] Bernard Eccleston, "Does North-South Collaboration Enhance NGO Influence in Deforestation Policies in Malaysia and Indonesia?" in Potter, ed., *op cit.*, p.87; and Margot Cohen, "Cautious Cooperation," *Far Eastern Economic Review*, 16 November 1995, p.67; and interviews with Tjahjono and Hasanuddin.

[96] Interview with Nakai.

[97] Shohei Yonemoto, "Japan and the global environmental crisis," *Japan Echo*, Vol.18, No.3, 1991, p.2104.

[98] The lifetime employment system in Japan provides a worker a guarantee of income and retirement pensions, but it also imposes severe restrictions on his/her freedoms. Only the obedient ones are rewarded with promotions and the associated hikes in wage and benefits. As long as lifetime employment prevails and the monetary sums involved remain substantial, few workers—whether in the public or private sector—few would chose to jeopardize their careers. See the views of Kazuo Yawata, a former career bureaucrat in MITI, in *"Saraba Tsusansho"* (Farewell to MITI) in *Bungei Shunju*, December 1997, pp.146-156.

[99] Interview with Kato.

[100] Interview with Nishioka.

[101] Interviews with Yonemoto, Neuffer and Tofflemire.

Global Environment in Japanese Politics

[102] Interview with Yonemoto.

[103] "'*Amakudari*' positions widespread," *Yomiuri Daily*, 4 November 1994, p.2.

[104] Interview with Kato.

[105] There are varied opinions on the relationship between mass media and politics in Japan. An extensive comparative study covering the 1980s and early 1990s portrays the Japanese mass media as a "trickster." They are seen to have substantial influence toward changing the state over time but serve no particular interests, including inde.pendence from the state. See Susan J. Pharr, "Media as Trickster in Japan A Comparative Perspective" in *Media and Politics in Japan*, ed. by Susan J. Pharr and Ellis S. Krauss, Honolulu: University of Hawaii Press, 1996, p.34.

[106] Ivan Hall, *Cartels of the Mind: Japan's Intellectual Closed Shop*, New York and London: W.W. Norton, 1998, p.49. See chapter on journalism in Japan.

[107] John C. Campbell, "Media and Policy Change in Japan" in Pharr and Krauss, eds., *op cit.*, p.190; and Krauss concurs in his essay in the same volume, Ellis Krauss, "Media Coverage of U.S.-Japanese Relations," in Pharr and Krauss, eds., *op cit.*, p.362.

[108] Interview with Obara.

[109] Interview with Shimoyama.

[110] Hall, *op cit.*, pp.45-46.

[111] *Ibid.*, p.52.

[112] Kristin Kyoko Altman, "Television and Political Turmoil: Japan's Summer of 1993" in Pharr and Krauss, eds., *op cit.*, p.167.

[113] Interview with Shimoyama.

[114] Interview with Shimoyama. Farley also observed that the tabloids sometimes function as tip sheets to expose problems. Once official investigation begins, the issue is legitimized for the mainstream press. See Maggie Farley, "Japan's Press and the Politics of Scandal," in Pharr and Krauss, eds., *op cit.*, p. 141.

[115] Gresser *et al.*, *op cit.*, pp.229-242.

CHAPTER 4

Whaling

"Whales are endangered animals," many of us have been told. The popular image of the whale is that of a unique creature, a marine mammal of great beauty and intelligence that was nearly hunted to extinction. Whaling symbolizes the blind greed and destructive power of modern industry. Ending commercial whaling in the name of protection and animal rights thus became the rallying call of conservationists. In fact, terminating commercial whaling was the first true international environmental campaign of the conservationist movement. Although a worldwide ban on commercial whaling since 1986 has helped many whale species and stocks to recover, whales remain a powerful symbol of the conservation movement.[1]

MODERN WHALING: A HISTORY AND ITS PRESENT-DAY CONTROVERSY

The use of whales as a resource for food, fertilizers, fuel, and other commodities has a long history. Many coastal communities are known to have consumed beached whales from their shores, but the lack of vessels and equipment deterred active catches of these large animals. The first records of whaling in the West belong to the Basques in the 11th century.[2] Coastal whaling also occurred in many other places. Organized commercial whaling began with the Dutch and the English around the 1600s, while American whaling commenced in the 1700s. As towns and industries grew, so did the demand for whale oil and spermaceti as lighting fuel and lubricant.

Norway's invention of the harpoon whaling technique in 1864 marked the beginning of modern whaling. Harpoons, together with faster boats and the use of factory ships, enabled whalers, for the first time, to pursue the faster-swimming species and to hunt in the Antarctic where whale

89

90 *The Roots of Japan's Environmental Policy*

resources were abundant.[3] The first shore hunts in the Antarctic took place in 1904.

The Southern Hemisphere became the main whaling grounds as stocks in the old hunting grounds were depleted.[4] By the end of the 1930s, the Antarctic seas produced 85 percent of the world's catch, and whale oil production was at a record high. The pre-World War II peak was reached in 1938, when nearly 55,000 animals of different whale species were caught. Of the 10 major pelagic whaling nations, Great Britain and Norway were the true leaders. The two together accounted for more than 95 percent of the world's annual catch.[5]

The introduction of substitutes for whale oil and other products gradually diminished the importance of whaling to industry and defense. In response to declining demand, most whaling companies cut back their fleets. Most eventually ceased operation when whaling was no longer profitable.[6] By the 1970s, only the former Soviet Union and Japan still had large whaling fleets because their whaling industry derived profits primarily from the sale of whale meat.[7] Nevertheless, several countries, including Norway, Iceland, and Greenland, continued to have small-scale coastal whaling after their large-scale commercial whaling ended. These small-scale operations are usually found in remote coastal villages. They have also survived because profits also depended on the sale of whale meat, which is traditionally consumed and traded in these places.[8]

Indiscriminate exploitation by the whaling industry throughout the 1950s and 1960s severely decimated many species and stocks of whales.[9] Scientists had cautioned against unsustainable harvests. However, the dominant voice of the whaling nations, driven by industrial and defense needs, overwhelmed most calls for conservation. Another weakness of the international whaling regime was the absence of management schemes or institutions with sufficient power to enforce catch quotas and to control illegal, or pirate, whaling.

Thus, whales became a key symbol of the conservation movement in the mid-1960s, when entire stocks of whales faced threats of extinction and uncertain futures after barely a century of modern whaling. For more than two decades, conservation groups aggressively campaigned to publicize the plight of the whales. In 1982, a temporary moratorium against commercial whaling was passed, and it took effect in 1986. Many whale stocks have recovered and a more sophisticated management scheme is also available. Considering these positive developments, should the temporary ban on commercial whaling continue?

Whaling opponents argue on the basis of animal rights that whales should be barred from any form of human exploitation. The protection of whales has become a moral and ethical issue. Whales must not be killed for commercial and consumptive use, even if catch quotas are given for aboriginal and subsistence purposes. Some proponents of this view even con-

Whaling

sider whales are special creatures deserving exceptional treatment. New Zealand's Commissioner to the International Whaling Commission is one such proponent. "Whales," he declared, "are the most highly developed form of life in the sea, just as man is on land. They are too valuable to end up as a steak..."[10] Such sentiment is widely found in places where there are virtually no interests in whaling or where past exploitation leaves behind feelings of guilt.[11]

This contrasts with the position of those who do not see whales as special or unique creatures deserving exceptional treatment or absolute protection. Whales are seen as a renewable natural resource. Their use by humans, including commercial and consumptive use, should be permitted under the principle of sustainable use. Proponents of this view include many scientists, some conservation advocates, whalers, and many countries with traditional whaling communities, including Japan, Iceland, Norway, Greenland, and Canada.

It is critical to underline that the current international regime on whaling does not prohibit the use of whales for commercial or consumptive purposes. Many international agreements offer protection to whales and other marine mammals, but none explicitly forbid their use. Widely accepted international agreements and principles on conservation also support the sustainable use of renewable natural resources. However, opponents of whaling are now the dominant voice, and those who dare to challenge the orthodoxy of the majority find themselves a maligned minority in an emotionally charged controversy.

THE WHALING CONTROVERSY AND JAPAN'S WHALING POLICIES

Japan belongs to the minority in this debate. Whales, to the Japanese, are a renewable resource that is basically no different from trees, cattle, or fish. Thus, whaling is seen as a fisheries and resource use issue. Most other whaling nations did, too, until they gave up whaling and embraced whales almost solely as a conservation matter.

Two policy decisions represent Japan's basic position on whaling. The first is Japan's objection to the temporary moratorium on commercial whaling, which was adopted by the International Whaling Commission in 1982. Japan did not agree the ban was needed and entered a formal objection. Although Japan was forced to withdraw its objection, it has remained determined to end this ban. This led to the second key policy to launch a research whaling program in 1987. The objective of the program is to identify whale stocks for sustainable use under a new scientific management regime.

Japan's refusal to give up commercial whaling has been taken as proof by whaling opponents that the country is an economic animal and environmental outlaw. Whaling opponents have also questioned why Japanese would not give up eating such beautiful, intelligent, and endangered animals.[12] If whales were merely a source of animal protein, why not switch to the cheaper and more plentiful alternatives like beef or chicken? If eating whales was a tradition, then the Japanese people should abandon this unnecessary and outdated practice to conform to international norms. Finally, if Japanese savor whale meat as an expensive delicacy, then it is surely a grotesque display of wealth.

Whaling opponents have also attacked Japan's research whaling program. First, they allege it is a cover for commercial whaling, because it allows the Japanese government to keep its whaling industry alive until commercial whaling resumes. Second, they consider the sale of whale meat a violation of the ban. Third, they find the catch excessive in number and they oppose lethal research because they believe that sightings, flesh samples, and other non-lethal methods can supply scientists with adequate information.

Despite incessant attacks by whaling opponents, the Japanese government has remained steadfast in its challenge of the moratorium. What explains this uncharacteristic adherence to a policy that invites so much international criticism? What do these responses say about the Japanese government's view of the environment? What do they say about the Japanese foreign policy process where environmental issues are concerned? Answers to these questions could be found in both the international and domestic settings in which this issue has evolved, specifically, the international whaling regime, U.S. anti-whaling legislation, the history of modern Japanese whaling, and the Japanese policy making framework.

THE INTERNATIONAL REGIME FOR WHALING

The earliest modern attempt at managing marine resources was the creation of the International Council for the Exploration of the Sea in 1925. A League of Nations meeting in 1927 raised the need for international rules to govern exploitation of marine resources. However, nothing happened until 1931, when the Convention for the Regulation of Whaling was adopted to stabilize world prices for whale oil and spermaceti following a crash of the whale oil market crash in 1930.[13] Having no real enforcement powers, the Convention was unable to deter excessive exploitation of whale stocks worldwide.

World War II temporarily halted large-scale industrial whaling in the high seas and the Antarctic. This interruption allowed some stocks to recover. In 1946, the United States proposed, and adopted, a new regime for whaling under the International Convention on the Regulation of Whaling (ICRW).[14] Two years later, the International Whaling Commission (IWC) was created to serve as the convention's implementation organ.

Several other international agreements and organizations also have some interest in conserving and managing whale resources, including the United

Whaling 93

Nations Food and Agriculture Organization (FAO), the United Nations Convention on the Law of the Sea (UNCLOS), and UNCED's Agenda 21. Nonetheless, they all recognize IWC as the chief international organ to regulate whale conservation and utilization worldwide.[15] Hence, ICRW and IWC have been at the core of the post-war international regime on whaling. To provide the international backdrop for this study of Japan's whaling policy, the following is a brief history of IWC and the whaling regime it has maintained from its inception in 1948 to the present. This synopsis demonstrates how IWC was transformed from a "whalers' club" into a protectionist stronghold.

ICRW and IWC: purpose and organization.

In 1946, 15 nations signed the International Convention on the Regulation of Whaling, and in 1948 the International Whaling Commission was formed to implement the ICRW. To the drafters and signatories of the Convention, whaling was but one form of fisheries. The Convention states in its preamble that its purpose is "to provide for the proper conservation of whale stocks and thus make possible the orderly development of whaling industry."[16]

Nature, whales, and all other natural resources were traditionally valued almost strictly in terms of their functional value to humans. Since conservation was to enable the vitality of resources for economic and nutritional needs, "...whale fisheries should be confined to those species best able to sustain exploitation in order to give an interval for recovery of certain species of whales now depleted in numbers."[17]

Since whales are recognized as a common resource, membership to IWC has always been open to all nations regardless of their whaling interests. Each country has one vote. There is no waiting period for membership or any substantial restriction on withdrawal from the Convention. This makes IWC one of the most liberal inter-governmental organizations. On the organizational structure of IWC, a commissioner represents each country and experts and advisers may assist him. Amending the Schedule requires a three-fourths majority, and decisions are binding on all contracting governments of the Convention. However, a contracting government can file an objection within 90 days of a decision to free itself from obligation.[18] Since IWC has no enforcement or sanctioning powers, the national government of each contracting country is responsible for implementing IWC rules and regulations where they apply to their territories and nationals.

The IWC Chairman and Vice Chairman are elected from among the commissioners (heads of national delegations) and usually serve for three years. A full-time secretariat was set up in Cambridge, England in 1976. Annual meetings of the commissioners are held in member countries, and three permanent committees perform the actual work of the organization.

94   *The Roots of Japan's Environmental Policy*

First, the Scientific Committee reviews catch data and research programs, and subsequently make recommendations to the Commission. Membership in this committee is voluntary for all member countries.[19] Second, the Technical Committee develops recommendations from the Scientific Committee into regulations, and proposals (requiring only a simple majority) are made to the Commission. The Technical Committee has two sub-committees. One is on aboriginal subsistence whaling and the other is on infractions.[20] Finally, the Finance and Administration Committee, made up of five representatives nominated by the IWC chairman, oversees operations of the Commission.[21]

From "whalers' club" to anti-whaling lobby.

An early attempt at managing whale fisheries was the Blue Whale Unit (BWU).[22] The main purpose of a management regime at this time was to protect whale oil prices. Annual catch quotas were based on the number of blue whales taken or their equivalents. No distinction was made among different species and there were no national quotas.[23] Whaling companies only had to report their catches to IWC, and all whaling activity would cease for the year once the total annual quota was reached.

What ensued came to be known as "Olympic whaling" as whaling companies raced to take the greatest number of whales or the greatest volume in BWU before the annual quota was filled. This fierce competition made it rational for whaling companies to acquire as many vessels as economically feasible to maximize their catch. For whale populations worldwide, this attempt at management resulted in a rapid and devastating decline that threatened the future of many whale stocks.

In the whaling season of 1961-62, a peak kill of 66,900 large whales was registered with the IWC.[24] The larger species, such as the blue and sperm whales, were severely depleted because they were preferred for economic efficiency.[25] By the mid-1960s, there was less than 1,000 blue whales left in the Southern Hemisphere. In response to this emergency, IWC banned blue whale hunts in the 1963-64 season and in 1966 established catch limits on all species in the Antarctic.[26] Whaling, in this form, represented the worst of the tragedy of the commons.[27]

Illegal whaling, too, depleted several whale stocks before an international observer system was instituted.[28] Whaling fleets harvested protected species and stocks and under-reported their catches of approved whales. The former Soviet whaling fleet was allegedly one of the worst offenders. During the 1960s, it took more than 700 protected right whales, and its actual blue whale catches were 10 times more than reported.[29]

Since there was little environmental awareness at this time and pro-whaling interests dominated IWC, the organization did not carry out its mandate to protect whale resources and properly manage the whaling industry. Scientific Committee recommendations were usually ignored by

Whaling 95

the Commission. In some cases, scientists sympathetic to the whaling industry even used scientific uncertainty to argue that there was no good evidence that large catches could not continue.[30]

However, things changed by the mid-1960s. As whaling became less profitable, most whaling nations downsized their whaling industry and softened their objections to quota reductions.[31] At the same time, the conservation movement was rising in the West. The plight of whales and their symbolism as victims of modern industry became a top campaign issue for many conservation groups; Greenpeace was the most high profile critic among them. Its skillful use of the media to show its activists in action, such as public protests and motor boat chases and obstruction of whaling ships, helped to win supporters worldwide.[32]

The first major international attempt to stop large-scale commercial whaling was the U.S. proposal to impose a complete and immediate 10-year moratorium on commercial whaling at the United Nations Conference on the Human Environment in Stockholm in 1972. The resolution was adopted with a 52 to 0 vote.[33] Since most IWC members at this time were supportive of commercial whaling, the IWC rejected this proposal. However, it gave up the BWU in the 1972-73 season in favor of species management when threat of extinction for several whale stocks became clearer. Species quotas were an improvement over the BWU, but poor quota enforcement did not effectively deter excessive exploitation of these marine mammals.[34]

Another outcome of the Stockholm Conference was the adoption of the Convention on International Trade in Endangered Species of Wild Fauna and Flora (CITES) in 1973. Many whale species came to be classified as endangered under CITES, which prohibited the international trade of their meat and other products. Subsequently, all catches of classified species— where hunting was still permitted—could only be used domestically.[35]

Whalers and conservation advocates, for different reasons, both supported a better management scheme to protect the long-term sustainability of whale stocks. The New Management Procedure (NMP) was proposed in 1974 and was fully implemented by the 1977 season to monitor the populations of 82 stocks from 11 species worldwide. The principle behind NMP is that all whale stocks should be stabilized at the level of maximum sustainable yield (MSY).[36] By managing each species on a stock-by-stock basis, NMP was a great improvement over the BWU and species quotas. Using NMP to study the 82 stocks also led to a further tightening of quotas and expanded the number of protected stocks to 52 in 1977.[37] In the same year, an International Observer Program was implemented to end illegal whaling. Another sign of greater concern for conservation was the commencement of the International Decade for Cetacean Research in 1978 to deepen research on the population status of these marine mammals and their habitats.[38]

96 *The Roots of Japan's Environmental Policy*

This new environmental awareness within IWC was also the result of a critical change in the organization's membership in the mid-1970s. New Zealand, a conservation advocate, joined IWC in 1976.[39] This marked the beginning of IWC's change from a "whalers' club" of the 1950s and 1960s into a stronghold of the anti-whaling lobby. Table 3 shows this change in IWC membership between 1972 and 1992.

Table 3. Membership in IWC, 1972 to 1992

Year	IWC quota	No.	Members
1972-73	42,500	14	USA, Britain, Mexico, France, Argentina, Australia, Canada, Panama, Denmark, Japan, USSR, Norway, Iceland, South Africa
1973-74	40,979		
1974-75	39,864	15	Brazil joins
1975-76	32,578		
1976-77	28,050	16	New Zealand joins
1977-78	23,520	17	Netherlands joins
1978-79	20,428		
1979-80	15,653	23	Seychelles, Sweden, Chile, Peru, Spain, Korea join
1980-81	14,523	24	Switzerland and Oman join; Panama withdraws
1981-82	14,233	32	Jamaica, St. Lucia, Dominica, Costa Rica, Uruguay, China, St. Vincent, India, Philippines join; Canada withdraws
1982-83	12,263	37	Egypt, Kenya, Senegal, Belize, Antigua, Monaco, Germany join; Jamaica, Dominica withdraw
1983-84	9,393	39	Finland, Mauritius join
1984-85	6,623		
1985-86	0*	41	Ireland, Solomon Islands join
1986-92	0	36	Ecuador, Venezuela join; Solomon Islands, Mauritius, Belize, Egypt, Philippines, Uruguay, Dominica, Jamaic Iceland withdraw
1994	0	35	Seychelles withdraws

* discounting aboriginal and scientific whaling quotas.
Source: D. Day, *The Whale War*, Vancouver: Douglas and McIntyre, 1987, p.97.

Most importantly, between 1976 to 1982 (the year New Zealand joined IWC and the passing of the moratorium, respectively), membership in IWC grew from 15 to 39 as a result of the admission of several non-whaling and anti-whaling nations. Among these new members were many small island nations, including Antigua, Belize, Dominica, St. Lucia, St. Vincent and the Grenadines, the Seychelles, and Mauritius, and several of them were recruited by anti-whaling groups to join IWC.[40] By 1982, 28 of 39 IWC members did not whale, and all of these island nations voted in favor the ban.[41]

Whaling

Passing the IWC commercial whaling moratorium and its aftermath.

Two important events in 1982 marked the beginning of a new era in the IWC regime. The first was the signing of the United Nations Convention on Law of the Sea, which covered practically all areas of marine affairs. Specifically, its recognition of the sovereign rights of coastal states within their 200-nautical mile exclusive economic zones (EEZ) brought to question the competence of IWC with respect to activities within this area.[42]

The second major event was the passing of the U.S.-proposed moratorium on commercial whaling when whaling opponents in IWC attained the crucial three-fourths majority. It is important to underline that this moratorium was not to be permanent or indefinite. Commercial whaling was to be suspended for a five-year period starting in 1986 and a Comprehensive Assessment was to be completed by 1990 as a basis to reconsider the moratorium. It was expected that by this time a new management regime would be developed and installed. An exemption was made for aboriginal subsistence whaling (ASW) upon U.S. insistence in order to secure bowhead whale quotas for the Alaskan Inuit population.[43] ASW was permissible, the United States argued, because "subsistence" activities contain no commercial element. This definition was useful in overcoming objections from many opponents of commercial whaling, but it was inaccurate. Human societies, including aboriginal subsistence communities, have long records of cash and barter trade over great distances.[44] Nonetheless, from this point on, the question of commerce became a central component in discussions on the use of whales and other resources.

The moratorium was controversial from the start. The IWC Scientific Committee never recommended the blanket moratorium.[45] Critics also cautioned that the ban could work against the principle of sustainable use, which has become widely accepted by international organizations and national governments. Canada, for example, left IWC in the same year as the moratorium was passed to protest against protectionist attacks on sustainable use.[46] Other IWC members with interests in whaling, namely, Japan, South Korea, Norway, and the former Soviet Union, also lodged reservations against it. This freed them from obligation and allowed them to continue whaling legally under quotas set by their own governments. Whaling opponents were determined to stop all commercial whaling. International censure and threats of economic sanctions by the United States and many European countries soon forced this minority to withdraw their objection or accept voluntary compliance.

Since an anti-whaling majority was firmly in place in the IWC, the pro-whaling countries felt that conducting the scheduled review of the moratorium in 1990 would be the only way to lift the ban. Towards this end, Japan launched its research whaling program in 1987 to assess the sustainability of specific whale stocks. Norway, too, while accepting a volun-

98   *The Roots of Japan's Environmental Policy*

tary compliance of the ban, initiated its own research whaling in the north Atlantic.

Comprehensive assessment of whale stocks was completed in 1990. It found that many whale species and stocks were not endangered. Opponents of the moratorium were hopeful that this finding, along with the application of the Revised Management Procedure (RMP) would compel IWC to carry out the schedule review of the moratorium, and maybe lift the moratorium. This new management scheme was considered by many scientists to be the most cautious and conservative management scheme ever introduced in natural resource management.

Strong anti-whaling majority within IWC rejected adoption of RMP in 1992. One reason cited for their objection was that the scheduled review of the moratorium, which they did not support, had not yet been carried out. This decision produced strong reactions from several IWC members. Iceland immediately left the organization in protest, and Norway announced it would end its voluntary compliance of the moratorium and resume commercial whaling in 1993.[47] The Faroe Islands, Norway, Greenland, and Iceland established the North Atlantic Marine Mammal Commission (NAMMCO) in Nuuk, Greenland that same year. Canada, Japan, and Russia did not pull out of IWC or obtained membership in this new organization, but they have attended NAMMCO's Council Meetings as observers since its inception.

NAMMCO's formation prompted some regime scholars to question if this signals a breakdown of the IWC regime.[48] Since only about 3 percent of the whales taken annually are caught under IWC quotas or with IWC approval, IWC may become irrelevant to IWC member nations that oppose whaling or do not whale. Nations that are supportive of whaling and sustainable use principles have also either left IWC or have threatened to leave it because they feel that IWC is not living up to the spirit and objectives of ICRW.

The Commission's rejection of RMP also infuriated many of its scientists. The chairman of the Scientific Committee resigned after the 1993 IWC meeting to protest against "the Commission's contempt for the recommendations of its Scientific Committee." He added that IWC's actions had "nothing to do with science."[49] Scholars also observed this move away from science in conservation by both supporters and opponents of whaling within IWC and in other conservation forums.[50]

These strong reactions from IWC members and scientists prompted the Commission to adopt RMP as the Revised Management Scheme (RMS) at the IWC meeting in 1994. However, opponents of the ban have generally dismissed this action as meaningless. This is because implementation of RMS requires an amendment in the ICRW Schedule and it is highly unlikely given the anti-whaling majority in IWC.[51] In fact, the Commission

Whaling 99

can defer a review of the moratorium and indefinitely prolong this temporary moratorium.

Whaling opponents have also put forth other measures to guarantee that commercial whaling would not resume even if the moratorium is lifted and a new management regime is implemented. First, they passed a resolution to create the Southern Ocean Sanctuary (SOS) at the IWC meeting in 1994 by a vote of 23 to 1 and 6 abstentions. (Japan made the sole opposing vote).[52] SOS bans all commercial whaling activities in the Southern Ocean for at least 10 years, and a review will be carried out at the end of the first 10-year period.[53] This ban also bars other forms of whaling in these waters, including the Antarctic minke whale stocks which have been well studied and considered sustainable for use under RMS.

Second, whaling opponents have been seeking to end small-scale whaling operations by asking IWC to expand its governance to include small cetaceans. The Scientific Committee and many scientists have not endorsed this proposal because IWC does not have expertise in this area, nor does it have the resources to develop it. There have also been questions on whether small cetaceans would not be better managed by regional fishery regulations because their presence and use are largely confined to regional locations.

Third, the Commission has continued to reject Japan's request for a relief quota of minke whales. The Commission decided that Japanese small-type coastal whaling comes under the moratorium because it contains a commercial element. It has also passed non-binding resolutions asking Japan to end its lethal research whaling program and Norway to halt its whaling activities. Both countries have chosen to ignore these requests because their activities are legal under ICRW. Finally, the Commission asked Canada to cease granting licenses for aboriginal subsistence whaling and to rejoin IWC in order to put all whale-related activities in Canada under ICRW.[54]

The tide is clearly against those who wish to whale. Nonetheless, there appears to be some recognition of a commercial element in aboriginal subsistence and hunting in recent years. Japan and Norway have been important in bringing about this development.[55] Whaling opponents have found it increasingly difficult to deny that commercial exchanges have a long history in all human communities. They also risk clashes with principles of equity and human rights. Hence, many whaling opponents now accept commercial use of whales in non-consumptive ways. (Commercial use of whales in consumptive manners, however, is still seen as morally wrong.) The economic value of whales is redefined in their attraction as live entertainment in whale-watching tours.[56] In fact, whale watching has been put on the official IWC agenda as a result of the worldwide proliferation of whale watching operations in the past decade.[57]

100   *The Roots of Japan's Environmental Policy*

Most recently, Ireland attempted to bridge differences between those who wish to whale and those who do not at the annual meeting of IWC in 1997 in Monaco. The five key negotiating points of the "Irish Proposal" are adopting RMS, restricting whaling quotas to coastal areas only (which in effect creates a global whale sanctuary), limiting whaling to catches for local consumption, phasing out lethal scientific research over time, and developing IWC regulations for whale watching. (The final point was dropped at the annual IWC meeting in 1998). Since the proposal failed to satisfy either side in this debate.[58] No breakthrough came about at the IWC annual meeting in Oman in 1998 and the impasse continues.

In summary, the rise and decline of commercial whaling worldwide and the increasing influence of conservation groups since the 1960s have significantly affected transformations in the international whaling regime. Today, a key question for the international whaling regime, in the form of IWC, is whether or not it should be abandoned and replaced by a new regime. The objectives of ICRW have been to conserve and enable the use of whale resources. It failed at conservation when membership was largely confined to nations with active whaling industries. Now it fails to guarantee use when most members do not whale or want to whale and anti-whaling interests dominate in the Commission.

HISTORY OF MODERN JAPANESE WHALING

The sea has always been a rich source for food for the Japanese people. "Passive whaling," or the taking of beached whales and incidental catches, was long practiced by coastal fishing communities in Japan (as in many other places) before the advent of active whaling by nets and harpoons. Although some evidence suggests that hand-harpoons were used in parts of Japan as early as the 12th century, most studies agree that active Japanese whaling began in the 16th century.[59] On the other hand, modern Japanese industrial whaling did not began until the early 20th century, but Japan became a major whaling nation within a few decades. As a result, Japan's whaling policy has had significant impact on whale populations worldwide. Moreover, Japan's whaling policy not only affects the international regime on whaling but also important debates over sustainable management and use of natural resource and commons.

The section focuses on growth of modern Japanese whaling, its importance to Japan, and its distinctive characteristics to demonstrate how international forces and domestic needs have affected the rise and decline of modern Japanese whaling.

Early Japanese whaling.

Records of whale hunting in Japan reveal hand-harpoon coastal whaling in the village of Taiji in the 16th century.[60] By the late 1600s, whalers in Taiji began net whaling, a technique that soon spread to several other coastal

Whaling

whaling communities. The lack of more advanced hunting technology and faster ships kept whaling within Japan's coastal seas until the end of the 1800s and restricted catches to species found in these waters.[61] Traditional coastal whaling in Japan was not a small enterprise. Often hundreds of people (practically entire villages) were involved in hunting and in land stations to clean, cut, and process the catch.

The arrival of American whalers in Japanese waters sparked a pivotal change in Japanese whaling.[62] Depletion of whale stocks in the New England waters, which was the traditional hunting grounds of the U.S. whaling fleets, drove American whalers to sail to the Pacific Ocean. They found catches in the Hawaiian waters and from there pushed further west, reaching Japan in 1820. British whalers soon followed. Within a few years, hundreds of whaling ships from the U.S. and other western powers were hunting in Japanese waters. In 1846, there were almost 300 ships from the U.S. alone.[63] In fact, Commodore Perry and his "black ships" came to Japan in 1853 with the primary objective of securing ports, supply and assistance for U.S. whalers, who by that time were expanding rapidly into the western Pacific.[64]

The rise and growth of modern Japanese whaling until World War II.

The new Meiji government was quick to realize the strategic and economic value of modern industrial whaling. Following the Sino-Japanese War of 1894-95, pelagic fisheries were seen as a way to assert Japanese influence in the Sea of Japan and the Korean peninsula. Japanese anxieties over the Russian threat were also rising.[65] The death at sea of 111 Taiji whalers around this time helped to convince Japanese whalers of the greater safety to be gained from a shift to modern whaling.

The Japanese adopted the Norwegian harpoon technique, which was then the most advance and efficient method. Faster ships also expanded hunting grounds and catch species. In 1896 the first Japanese whaling company using the Norwegian method was established,[66] and in 1904 the first Japanese pelagic whaling ship sailed to the North Pacific.[67] Other companies followed, but they were generally small and not very successful.

Japan's victory in the Russo-Japanese War of 1904-1905 opened a new chapter in modern Japanese whaling. Expulsion of the Russian fleet from Korean waters gave Japan virtual dominance in these whaling grounds. Japan also captured almost the entire Russian whaling fleet. The vessels were sold to private entrepreneurs who formed Toyo Gyogyo, the first large and modern Japanese whaling company. The company began operation in 1906.[68] In the same year, Japan's first modern whaling land station was completed in Ayukawa. As more whaling companies were established, the Japanese government began to regulate whaling in order to rationalize resource use and to avoid over-capitalization.[69]

A number of measures were introduced. First, the Japanese government ordered the four largest whaling companies to merge in 1909 to form Toyo Hogei. Second, a year later, the Japanese Whaling Association (JWA) was established to develop the industry, conserve stocks, and improve earnings for the industry. All whaling companies were required to join the association. Third, all catcher boats had to be licensed by the Ministry of Agriculture, Commerce and Administration (predecessor to the post-war Ministry of Agriculture, Forestry and Fisheries) and only thirty licenses were granted. Fourth, the Japanese government issued species specific whaling licenses in 1911, and regulations were introduced to set whaling seasons and demarcated hunting areas.[70]

Modern Japanese whaling has three basic forms: pelagic whaling, large-type coastal whaling (LTCW), and small-type coastal whaling (STCW). Pelagic and LTCW whaling—or industrial whaling—made Japan a major whaling nation by reaching new whaling grounds and expanding the volume and variety of catch species. Their catches supplied the nation with whale meat for consumption and whale oil and other by-products for export. STCW, in contrast, was economically important only to local and regional communities where traditional coastal whaling had long existed.[71]

Japanese industrial whaling expanded in these years while whaling waned in the West.[72] Growth of Japan's pelagic whaling fleet in the 1930s was especially dramatic. Before the collapse of the whale oil market in 1930-31, Norway had one of the largest pelagic whaling fleets. Japanese pelagic whaling began with the purchase of a surplus Norwegian ship and the hiring of several Norwegians as experts to train Japanese whalers. With this ship and crew, Japan made its maiden voyage to the Antarctic in 1934.

Following this trip, several more vessels were added to expand its pelagic whaling capacity. By 1941 Japan had become a major whaling nation. Whale meat and other by-products were consumed domestically as food and raw materials, while exports of whale oil and spermaceti earned valuable foreign exchange. As shown in Table 4 below, Japan's earnings from these exports grew over 40 fold between 1935 and 1939.[73]

Table 4. Whale oil production; 1935-39

Year	Value of Production Volume (in yen)
1935	473,639
1936	2,180,149
1937	8,662,277
1938	14,272,698
1939	19,710,000

Source: Nihon Suisan Nenpo, 1941.

With diminishing competition from the West, Japanese industrial whaling grew and prospered. World War II, however, disrupted the industry

Whaling

when whaling ships were commissioned for the war and the high seas became too dangerous.

Post-World War II Japanese whaling.

After World War II, the Allied Occupation authority approved the revitalization of all types of Japanese whaling to ease serious domestic food shortages. The Japanese government again kept close watch on this industry. New licenses were issued, along with new regulations on catch species, hunting seasons, vessel size, and hunting grounds and the country joined the International Whaling Commission in 1951.

While STCW was largely untouched by the war, LTCW and pelagic whaling were severely decimated and Japan had lost many of its old whaling grounds. However, Japanese government support gave them a quick recovery: LTCW catches returned to their pre-war level by 1947 and the first post-war pelagic fleet sailed to the north Pacific in 1952.

Since global demand for whale oil had greatly diminished and Japan was a hungry nation after the war, the post-war importance of both LTCW and pelagic whaling for Japan shifted to whale meat for the domestic market. In 1947, whale meat constituted as much as 47 percent of animal protein in the Japanese diet.[74] Even by 1964, when the country entered its decade of rapid economic expansion, whale meat constituted 23 percent of all animal protein consumed.[75]

There are several important considerations regarding whale meat consumption in Japan. Whale meat was never a national dish, but whale meat and other by-products have a long history in traditional whaling communities and their surrounding regions.[76] The spread of whale meat consumption nationwide before and after World War II was primarily the result of economic difficulties and government promotion. Whale meat was a cheap source of animal protein, which Japan could obtain without reliance on foreign sources.[77] In fact, whale meat was served in public school lunches until the 1970s.[78]

Throughout most of the post-war years, the size and catches of STCW remained fairly small and stable because they mainly supplied the traditional coastal whaling communities. The LTCW fleet grew slightly in size and catch volume in its post-war recovery, but also remained fairly stable until its decline in the 1970s. The greatest expansion was in Japan's pelagic whaling, which reached its peak in the 1961-62 season. Three companies with a total of seven fleets, each with its own factory ship, hunted in the Antarctic.[79]

Critical changes occurred for Japanese whaling and in the international whaling regime in the 1960s. As world demand for whale oil continued to decline, most whaling nations had to reduce their fleets. The depletion of several whale stocks also prompted IWC to reduce catch quotas. Since Japanese whaling was not dependent on the sale of whale oil, the Japanese whaling industry was not pressed to cut back. On the contrary, it expanded because IWC allocations at the time were determined by total annual tonnage under the BWU scheme.[80] Hence, Japanese whaling companies purchased surplus vessels from Norway and other whaling countries to enlarge its share of the annual catch.

However, these investments became a costly burden in the 1970s when IWC annual catch quotas were too small be profitable for any large whaling fleet. In response, the Japanese government called for a consolidation of the industry. The three leading whaling companies were merged in 1976 to form Nihon Kyodo Hogei. Only three factory ships, 20 catcher boats, and a work force of about 1500 were retained from the original companies.

Further cuts in quotas forced Nihon Kyodo Hogei to operate only one factory ship from 1977 until the last whaling season for Japan in 1987. By 1987, the industry had only 308 workers.[81] This was a dramatic drop from the peak of Japanese whaling when some 50,000 were employed in pelagic whaling and another 50,000 in LTCW.[82] Japanese industrial whaling was ending. Table 5 below shows the rise and fall of Japanese whaling in the last several decades.

Table 5. Production of pelagic whaling, LTCW and STCW
(1,000 tonnes)

Year	Pelagic	Coastal LTCW	STCW	Total	Year	Pelagic	Coastal LTCW	STCW	Total
1932	0.0	22.5	n.a.	n.a.	1963	340.9	24.1	2.0	367.0
1933	0.0	23.1	n.a.	n.a.	1964	336.4	23.6	2.5	362.5
1934	0.0	25.4	n.a.	n.a.	1965	341.3	21.0	2.7	365.0
1935	2.0	27.7	n.a.	n.a.	1966	254.3	23.3	2.3	279.9
1936	7.6	28.5	n.a.	n.a.	1967	233.5	28.5	1.8	263.8
1937	26.4	29.3	n.a.	n.a.	1968	213.8	39.5	1.6	254.9
1938	66.2	26.6	n.a.	n.a.	1969	184.0	38.4	1.6	224.0
1939	85.1	26.1	n.a.	n.a.	1970	191.5	34.6	1.4	227.5
1940	107.3	24.4	n.a.	n.a.	1971	188.9	33.1	1.3	223.3
1941	127.7	30.7	n.a.	n.a.	1972	166.6	26.8	1.1	194.5
1942	0.0	19.1	n.a.	n.a.	1973	140.2	22.5	1.2	163.9
1943	0.0	25.7	n.a.	n.a.	1974	122.7	21.9	0.9	145.5
1944	0.0	34.8	n.a.	n.a.	1975	105.3	20.6	1.0	126.9
1945	0.0	9.3	n.a.	n.a.	1976	54.2	22.4	0.6	77.2
1946	0.0	23.8	n.a.	n.a.	1977	51.3	19.7	0.7	71.7
1947	34.5	28.6	n.a.	n.a.	1978	23.7	17.5	0.9	42.1
1948	45.4	26.8	n.a.	n.a.	1979	16.8	13.2	0.8	30.8
1949	55.0	25.0	n.a.	n.a.	1980	16.4	15.1	0.6	32.1
1950	68.1	22.6	n.a.	n.a.	1981	15.0	12.9	0.7	28.6
1951	58.6	26.4	2.8	87.8	1982	17.9	9.0	0.7	27.6
1952	77.5	28.8	3.4	109.7	1983	16.7	8.9	0.7	26.3
1953	72.1	25.4	3.0	100.5	1984	15.6	8.5	1.1	25.2
1954	107.9	25.9	2.6	136.4	1985	10.2	7.5	0.9	18.6
1955	134.6	26.9	2.9	164.4	1986	10.6	5.5	0.9	17.0
1956	157.3	33.4	3.5	194.2	1987	10.6	5.7	0.9	17.2
1957	199.4	28.3	2.4	230.1	1988	0.0	0.0	0.5	0.5
1958	241.7	33.3	2.9	277.9	1989	0.0	0.0	0.4	0.4
1959	257.0	33.8	2.1	292.9	1990	0.0	0.0	0.4	0.4
1960	266.7	27.9	1.9	296.5	1991	0.0	0.0	0.4	0.4
1961	304.3	26.1	2.1	332.5	1992	0.0	0.0	0.4	0.4
1962	370.9	25.3	1.9	398.1					

Note: Totals may differ from the reported source by 0.1-0.2 due to decimal rounding.

Source: "Small-type Coastal Whaling in Japan," prepared by The Beneficiaries of the Riches of the S and Japan Small-Type Whaling Association, n.d.

Forced by the United States to withdraw its objection to the 1982 IWC moratorium decision, Japan's pelagic fleet sailed its last voyage to the Antarctic in 1986. The last LTCW shore stations were closed in 1987, and all STCW minke whale hunts stopped at the end of the 1988 season.[83]

Japanese research whaling, post-moratorium STCW and the whale meat trade.

With the end of pelagic whaling and LTCW, Nihon Kyodo Hogei was dissolved and replaced by Kyodo Senpaku in November 1987. Since whaling is now prohibited, the new company conducts no commercial hunts. Instead it charters vessels and crews to the Fisheries Agency for surveillance and the Institute of Cetacean Research (ICR) for research whaling.[84]

Minke whales in the Antarctic have been the main focus of Japan's research whaling program. The object is to study their population dynamics and relationship with other cetacean species and the Antarctic marine ecosystem. Under a 16-year plan, Japan takes approximately 300 minke whales each year from this stock. Results, thus far, have shown that this stock of about one million animals could be sustainably harvested under the Revised Management Scheme. This was one reason for Japan's objection to the Southern Ocean Sanctuary. It even sought an exemption for this stock, but its request was rejected.[85] Japan has continued its research whaling program in these waters and has expanded it in 1994 to cover minke whale stocks in the north Pacific.[86]

Other than research whaling, STCW is the only other type of whaling in Japan today. The Japanese government stopped issuing licenses for all IWC-protected species when the moratorium came into effect for Japan in 1987. This includes the minke whale stocks in Japanese coastal waters. A zero quota for this species has had a great impact on Japanese STCW. For instance, total catches of STCW fell by 46 percent in 1988 without the minke whale quota. Since then Japanese whalers could only take species that are not governed by IWC, STCW catches now concentrate on Baird's beaked whales and pilot whales. The Japanese government issues an annual quota for each species.

The Japanese government issued its first official appeal to IWC for special relief quotas of 50 minke whales annually for its STCW communities in 1987 following the end of large-scale Japanese commercial whaling that year. The delay and timing of this request have helped critics of Japanese whaling to question the authenticity of Japanese claims and motivations behind this request. Thus, the IWC Commission has consistently rejected this Japanese request on the grounds that Japanese STCW should be subjected to the moratorium because it contains a commercial element.

Japan introduced an "Action Plan for Community-based Whaling" at the 1993 IWC annual meeting in Kyoto hoping that this could circumvent the issue of commerce. It proposed a new category of whaling under abo-

Whaling 107

riginal subsistence whaling. The Japanese government also, on its own and through other agencies such as the Institute for Cetacean Research, has sponsored numerous studies, workshops, and seminars. Numerous papers on Japanese STCW have also been submitted to IWC.[87] The Commission accepted this Action Plan as a "constructive element" in a 1995 resolution, another resolution was made in 1996 to call for a workshop to "review and identify commercial aspects of socio-economic and cultural needs."[88] However, the anti-whaling majority within IWC would not allow any form of whaling other than the narrowly defined aboriginal subsistence category. The low-level representation by anti-whaling countries at the IWC workshop on community-based whaling in Sendai, Japan in March 1997 reflected their resistance against a new category of whaling based on social and cultural definitions.[89]

The moratorium, along with the CITES ban, has also terminated the import of whale meat and other by-products from countries still whaling, such as Norway, Iceland, and Greenland.[90] As the ban came into effect for Japan, all whale meat from IWC-protected species in Japan would either be from inventory accumulated during the whaling days or are by-products of Japanese research whaling.[91] Since the Japanese government sees potential for minke whaling in the Antarctic, it proposed a down listing of the minke whale from Appendix I to Appendix II at the CITES meeting in Zimbabwe in June 1997.[92] Japan's request was rejected after it failed to obtain a two-thirds majority within the Commission. At the same meeting, Japan's proposal to reconsider the relationship between IWC and CITES (adopted by CITES in 1979 to regulate the international trade of whale meat and other products) was also rejected.

This review of the history of modern Japanese whaling shows that its development has been closely tied to both domestic needs and international changes. Until the 1960s, the Japanese government considered the whaling industry important to national security. Whale oil and spermaceti exports earned valuable foreign exchange and supported self-sufficiency in animal protein. The Japanese whaling industry did not suffer severe cut backs until the mid-1970s because there was a stable domestic demand for whale meat. Since whale meat is consumed in Japan (as well as in Norway, Iceland, and some aboriginal subsistence communities in North America), whales continued to be valued as an economic and nutritional resource. Hence, scientific conservation and sustainable use of whale resources are seen as the means and goal of protecting whale stocks.

U.S. DOMESTIC LEGISLATION: ITS IMPACT ON THE INTERNATIONAL WHALING REGIME AND JAPAN'S WHALING POLICY

It is important to examine U.S. domestic legislation against whaling because they have significantly affected the development of the IWC

The Roots of Japan's Environmental Policy

regime, as well as Japan's whaling policy. This section reviews U.S. anti-whaling legislation and examines how these laws have been used to target Japanese whaling in particular.

Anti-whaling legislation in the United States.

U.S. domestic legislation on whaling has been influential in shaping the international whaling regime for two main reasons. The first is U.S. leverage in global affairs. In whaling, in particular, the United States had one of the largest whaling fleets and was the leading force behind creation of ICRW and IWC. The second is that IWC itself has no enforcement and sanctioning powers.

The U.S. Congress passed no laws hostile to whaling when the United States was a whaling nation. The simultaneous decline of U.S. commercial whaling and rise of the U.S. conservation lobby in the 1960s fundamentally changed U.S. policy and perspectives on whaling, and the year 1972 was the most critical turning point.[93] The U.S. Congress expressed "unanimous opposition to the resumption of commercial whaling" and passed the Marine Mammals Protection Act (MMPA), which bans the taking and import of marine mammal products. Exceptions are granted only to native Americans for subsistence purposes and where special waivers are given.[94] In the same year, the U.S. voted for a resolution to end commercial whaling at the Stockholm Conference.[95]

More restrictive measures to end commercial whaling and the international trade of whale meat were introduced in 1973. First, the U.S. Congress passed the Endangered Species Act to prohibit the taking, importing, exporting, and interstate commerce of all endangered species, their parts, and products.[96] Waivers were given only for scientific research, breeding to sustain survival of species, economic hardships, and subsistence use purposes by Alaskan natives.[97] In the same year, the Pelly Amendment to the Fishermen's Protection Act was used to impose trade embargoes on Russia and Japan to keep them from violating IWC quota allocations. The Pelly Amendment also supports the authority of the MMPA and allows the Secretary of Commerce to certify to the president any activity of the nationals of a foreign country that diminishes the effectiveness of international wildlife conservation programs.[98] The president may prohibit imports from the offending nation to the extent that such prohibition is sanctioned by the General Agreement on Tariffs and Trade (GATT).[99] Finally, by becoming a member of CITES, the United States accepted the CITES ban on the international trade of virtually all whale meat and by-products.

Domestic legislation and its use to end commercial whaling worldwide continued. The U.S. Congress expanded the Pelly Amendment in 1978 to allow certification of foreign nationals for "engaging in trade or taking which diminishes the effectiveness of any international program for endangered or threatened species whether or not such conduct is legal under the

Whaling

laws of the offending country." This, in effect, challenged the sovereignty of other nations. In the case of IWC and whaling, it meant that any country that has made reservations for any IWC decision could face certification and sanctions from the U.S. even if they are legally free from obligation under ICRW.

The United States used this expanded certification power to pressure other nations (both non-IWC member whaling countries and non-whaling ones) to submit to ICRW and to comply with IWC decisions. Certifications were issued in 1978 against Peru, South Korea, and Chile for whaling outside ICRW. The U.S. president only withdrew the threat of sanctions after these nations agreed to become parties to ICRW.[100]

In 1979 the Packwood-Magnuson Amendment to the Magnuson Fishery Conservation and Management Act (or the Magnuson Act) was passed.[101] The Amendment automatically removes a foreign nation's fishing allocations in U.S. waters granted under the Magnuson Act if the Secretary of Commerce determines that nationals of that country are engaged in whaling operations which diminish the effectiveness of ICRW. Rights to receive fishing allocations can be restored only after the certification is lifted.[102]

Since 1982 virtually every certification made under the Pelly Amendment and the Packwood-Magnuson Amendment has been related to the IWC moratorium—and with varying outcomes.[103] Norway, Japan, and Iceland were all certified for violating the IWC moratorium. Less than a month after certification, Norway announced a voluntarily suspension of commercial whaling after the 1987 season and a reduction of its catch for that year.[104] Japan was threatened with sanctions and a removal of its fisheries allocations in U.S. waters. A bilateral agreement in 1984 allowed Japan to recover its fishing rights on the condition that it withdraws its objection to the moratorium. Iceland was threatened with sanctions in 1986 to stop its export of whale meat. After two years of heated exchanges and high-level negotiations, Iceland agreed to export not more than 49 percent of whale meat and by-products from its research whaling program.[105] Even Canada, which left IWC in 1982, was threatened with sanctions in 1996 under the Pelly Amendment for issuing a license to hunt a single bowhead whale in the eastern Arctic for subsistence purposes.[106]

Since the IWC moratorium came into effect in 1986, U.S. legislation shifted to target the international trade of whale meat and other by-products. The fishery penalty under the Pelly and Packwood-Magnuson Amendments were modified in 1988 to include "any aquatic species" exported from a country determined to have compromised the effectiveness of ICRW, regardless of whether or not its nationals made the catch. The Pelly Amendment was further revised in 1992 to ban non-fisheries products from nations, which are deemed to have compromised international conservation principles.[107] In this broadened form, Norway was certified in 1990 and 1993, respectively, for resuming research whaling and small-scale commercial whaling; Japan was certified in 1995 for expanding its research whaling into the north Pacific.[108] Although these laws declare that sanctions would be applied only to the full extent permitted by international laws, specifically the General Agreement on Tariffs and Trade (GATT) and its successor, the World Trade Organization (WTO), the legality of these sanctions remains open to debate. Hence, their application has yet to go beyond certification.

In summary, the United States has used its enormous leverage in international trade to influence development of the international regime for whaling and the actions of other nations. Moreover, domestic economic needs and political considerations have been the key forces shaping U.S. whaling policy, whether it is in encouraging or curtailing whaling.

U.S. laws and Japan's whaling policy.

The passing of the IWC moratorium against whaling in 1982 alone would not have stopped Japanese whaling. Filing a reservation would allow Japanese whaling to legally continue and the Japanese government setting its own annual catch quotas. Given that Japan was one of two remaining large industrial whaling nations (the other being the former Soviet Union), whaling opponents could see Japan almost single-handedly defeating the moratorium.

Since the IWC was unable to force Japan to give up whaling, the U.S. government and U.S. conservation groups, two of the most ardent opponents of whaling, turned to using domestic U.S. laws to pressure Japan. As Japan's closest security ally and largest trading partner, the United States could exercise great leverage over Japan by putting whaling within the context of their bilateral relationship. Tying Japanese fishing rights in U.S. waters to whaling would be an especially effective way to pressure Japan. At this time, Japanese catches in U.S. waters of pollack alone were worth 10 billion yen annually. In comparison, Japanese whaling was valued only at 1 billion yen. Since Japanese fishing companies control the country's whaling companies, the U.S. government and conservation groups were confident that Japan would abandon whaling to protect their fishing interests.[109]

The General International Fisheries Agreement (GIFA) determined Japan's annual fisheries allocation in the U.S. In 1982, the timing of the moratorium coincided with the annual renewal of this agreement. Keenly aware of Japan's predicament in having to choose between fishing and whaling, the U.S. Senate threatened to terminate GIFA if Japan objected to the moratorium. Backing this threat was the 1979 Packwood-Magnuson Amendment, which would automatically remove Japan's fishing rights.[110]

The U.S. government saw a valuable opportunity to achieve multiple goals. Pressing Japan to discontinue whaling would score "green" points for itself internationally and domestically. It would also ease pressure from

Whaling

conservation groups in the country and silence some of their outcries against U.S. commercial fishing. Furthermore, removing Japan's fishing rights would give the U.S. fishing industry a virtual monopoly over fishing grounds within the U.S. EEZ and bolster U.S. fisheries exports.[111]

To the surprise of the United States and other whaling opponents, Japan decided to object to the moratorium on whaling. Knowing that the United States had plans to end all foreign fisheries allocations by 1988, the Japanese government considered that it would be more rational to protect whaling. Japan, in turn, was shocked by the instant U.S. reaction. As the objection was made, the Packwood-Magnuson Amendment was activated to immediately bar all Japanese fishing vessels from the U.S. EEZ.

To resolve this conflict, the two countries entered into negotiations and produced the Murazumi-Baldrige Agreement in November 1984.[112] The Agreement obliged Japan to withdraw its objection to the IWC sperm whale quotas and the moratorium. In return, after the moratorium was to come into effect in 1986, Japan would have two extra seasons of pelagic whaling in the Antarctic, two extra seasons of coastal whaling of minke and Bryde's whales, and three extra seasons of sperm whaling in the North Pacific. Japan ended all commercial whaling by the end of the 1988-89 season.[113] Effective exploitation of linkages between Japanese whaling and fisheries interests by the U.S. government thus brought an abrupt end to Japanese whaling.

JAPAN'S POLICY ON WHALING

It is remarkable that despite severe U.S. pressure and the presence of an anti-whaling majority in the IWC, the Japanese government has maintained steadfast commitment to its basic objectives of lifting the moratorium and resuming commercial whaling. Two particular decisions have been central to this Japanese policy towards whaling, and they are Japan's decision to file a reservation to the moratorium in 1982 and to commence research whaling in 1987.

Objectives and rationale.

Since resource security has always been a vital element in the Japanese government's view of national security, it is easy to understand why the Japanese government considers the moratorium on commercial whaling a threat to its interest in protecting access to natural resources. This also explains why the Japanese government does not agree with the anti-whaling majority that whales should be preserved, that is, untouched and separated from human needs. Rather, the Japanese government considers sustainable use of natural resource, including whales, as imperative to conservation.

Furthermore, contrary to allegations by anti-whaling advocates, economic profits from whaling have not been a key reason for the Japanese government's opposition to end the moratorium. The Japanese whaling industry had already lost its economic importance by the early 1980s.[114] Japanese policy makers have been more apprehensive about the effects of the moratorium and other developments within the IWC and the international whaling regime on other resource use regimes. The future of Japanese fisheries and the international fisheries regime, in particular, has been their greatest concern.

The importance of fisheries to Japan, and *vice versa*, cannot be underestimated. As a fish-eating culture, 40 percent of animal protein in the Japanese diet is derived from fish and other marine products.[115] Japanese fisheries, some of the largest in the world, meet two-thirds of this demand.[116] Having only 2 percent of the world population, Japan consumes 8 percent of global fisheries resources. Japan is also the top importer of marine products. It imports, in value, twice as much as the second largest importer, the United States. Marine products account for 6 percent of total imports each year.[117] The Japanese government was afraid that the IWC moratorium would undermine the spirit of other internationally agreed principles and agreements supportive of sustainable use of resources. For example, protection of bluefin tuna in the north Atlantic had developed into a major issue by the early 1980s.[118]

Apart from interests in fisheries and access to natural resources, the Japanese government wants to lift the moratorium because it considers this ban the result of political maneuvers and unsubstantiated by scientific justification. Since a powerful majority imposed the moratorium on Japan and other pro-whaling countries, the Japanese government worries that accepting such political arm-twisting in whaling could set a bad precedent for similar prejudice in other international arenas. A member of the Japanese IWC delegation once remarked, "[supporting sustainable whaling] is not an issue concerning whaling. Giving in to anti-whaling demands means other international issues can also be controlled by politics and emotions, without respecting other cultures."[119]

Furthermore, the absence of scientific justification for the moratorium would threaten the integrity of other international conservation and management regimes. Since the IWC Scientific Committee had stated that certain stock could be sustainably used, the Japanese government sees no reason to forego whales for consumptive purposes.

There are several reasons why the Japanese government places great value on science in this debate. The first is that science is the only reliable means to make its views heard in a controversy that is dominated by the political propaganda of the anti-whaling majority. Second, the Japanese government considers science a useful tool to counter the abuse of legal principles. Third, science—a rational and non-culture biased approach—could be more effective in settling differences and encouraging cooperation

Whaling

in an issue that has become heavily politicized, emotional, and laden with distrust.[120]

Indeed the Japanese government considers international attacks on Japanese whaling and the push to end all forms of whaling as a hazard to mutual respect for divergent cultural and ethical values in conservation and lifestyles.[121] Seeing that values and habits of a people are products of environmental and historical forces, the Japanese government considers accusations of "immorality" (in commercial whaling), "brutality" and "cannibalism" (in the human consumption of whale meat) as direct assaults on Japanese culture. While whaling opponents have often argued that whales deserve protection on the grounds that they are mammals (like humans), most Japanese do not share such a bias. To them, whales are no different from other resources in nature. In fact, whales are conventionally viewed as fish and the Japanese have no religious or traditional taboos against eating whales.[122]

In this connection, the Japanese government has also argued that consuming whale meat is more ecologically sound than eating commercially raised farm animals and produce since whales are not farmed. No forest has to be cut down or people displaced for its cultivation. These animals live freely until they are taken and death occurs within minutes. Hence, the Japanese government has asserted that it is chauvinistic for those who traditionally did not or had not chosen to whale or eat whale meat to dictate their preferences to the rest of the world. It would be equally hypocritical for those who consume commercially produced meat, dairy, and vegetables to criticize Japan (and other countries) for wanting to whale and consume whale meat.

The Japanese government's decision to sell the whale meat from its research whaling program has invited substantial criticism. The Japanese government defends this decision with several reasons. First, whale meat should not be wasted given that it is a resource and that there is a domestic demand for it. Second, the Japanese government does not profit from research whaling. ICR manages sales of this whale meat and its national distribution, and prices are determined by past consumption levels. Third, since IWC has no money to support research, receipt from sales help to supplement Japanese governmental funding for the research whaling program. Fourth, the research data and findings generated by the research whaling program are submitted to the IWC.

The rise of non-governmental organizations in international affairs has been difficult for the Japanese government to accept. Within the IWC, in particular, the Japanese government believes that the political tactics of anti-whaling groups were crucial to producing the two-thirds majority required to pass the moratorium in 1982.[123] On the whole, the Japanese government has been wary of the influence of conservation groups in international discussions on the conservation and sustainable use of whale resource. These groups are seen to have their own political agendas, whether as observers within IWC or lobbyists on national delegations. Therefore, the Japanese government considers these groups an unwelcome challenge to the national sovereignty of IWC member and the integrity of ICRW.[124] For these reasons, the Japanese government has regarded its opposition to the moratorium and the launching of its research whaling program as necessary actions to protect the country's interests in diplomacy and natural resource use.

POLICY ACTORS IN JAPAN'S WHALING POLICY

In the making of Japan's policy on whaling, the bureaucracy has been the strongest actor, particularly the Fisheries Agency of the Ministry of Agriculture, Fisheries and Forestry. Politicians, in general, have had scant interest in whaling and Prime Minister Yasuhiro Nakasone actively intervened only when whaling was seen to jeopardize his interests in other matters.

As for anti-whaling groups in Japan, they have had minimal success in affecting Japanese government decision making and public opinions on whaling. Groups outside of Japan, too, have been successful in pressuring the Japanese government only through their lobbying efforts in the IWC and with governments sympathetic to their cause. The Japanese fishing industry had been able to press key policy actors to give in to their demands only because of the urgency of the situation, and the whaling industry has been barely audible.

The governmental actors.

The bureaucracy was the most influential of three governmental actors that have been influential in deciding Japan's objection to the moratorium and the launching of a research whaling program.

The Japanese bureaucracy.

The making and implementation of these two policy decisions basically involved only two ministries, namely, the Ministry of Ministry of Agriculture, Fisheries and Forestry (MAFF) and the Ministry of Foreign Affairs (MoFA).

In the Japanese government, whaling is designated a fishery activity and has been under the control of the Fisheries Law since 1949. This puts the regulation of all whaling activities under the jurisdiction of MAFF, or more specifically its Fisheries Agency.[125] MoFA's involvement, on the other hand, is due to its official position as the Japanese government's chief liaison with the outside world. MoFA has to represent Japan at IWC, respond to outside criticisms, and soothe conflicts with foreign countries that arise from Japan's whaling policy.

The Environment Agency of Japan (JEA) has no say in this issue for several reasons even though whaling has a conservation element. Foremost is

Whaling

that JEA simply has no official authority over whaling. As explained in chapter three, MAFF basically exercises bureaucratic leadership over all natural resource matters related to Japan domestically and overseas within the Japanese bureaucracy. Secondly, JEA was created in 1971 to respond to the domestic pollution crisis. So JEA can assert itself in bureaucratic policy discussions only where pollution or "brown issues" are concerned. Thirdly, as a policy matter, whaling long predated JEA so that an established set of policy actors, policies, and dynamics already exist. This seriously obstructs involvement by JEA. Fourthly, as a small agency, JEA has little leverage in policy discussions with the older and larger ministries, including MAFF.

The Ministry of International Trade and Industry (MITI) has not been an important voice in setting Japan's whaling policy. Several of the same reasons cited for JEA above also apply. In addition, MITI recognizes that the Fisheries Agency is the lead bureaucratic player in this issue. MITI intervenes only where the economic ramifications of whaling would spill over into areas under its jurisdiction.

Thus, the Fisheries Agency has been the dominant policy actor and it has worked to protect its virtual monopoly on the whaling issue. Guarding its jurisdiction over whaling is not only important to protecting its bureaucratic turf and priorities in whaling, but also its dominance over most other natural resource use matters. Since Fisheries Agency officials regard themselves as the most qualified experts on the matter, outside opinions are not generally welcomed. Therefore, JEA, MITI, and all other bureaucratic actors—except for MoFA—have had no relevant role in making Japan's whaling policy. Their views and actions are not truly reflective of the Japanese government. Only the Fisheries Agency can make this claim.

Fisheries Agency.
Fisheries Agency controls the licensing, monitoring, and taking of cetaceans in Japanese waters or by Japanese vessels for commercial or research purposes. Regulation of LTCW and pelagic whaling are specifically the responsibility of the Oceanic Fisheries Department. The Fisheries Agency has also been the strongest supporter of Japan's research whaling program.

Since the Fisheries Agency has the authority to draft all policy proposals on all forms of fisheries, including whaling, it has a practical monopoly in deciding the national policy on whaling. The Fisheries Agency's priority is to protect access to fisheries resources worldwide and their conservation is driven by this goal. Whaling had lost practically all economic importance by the early 1980s. Nonetheless, Fisheries Agency officials were anxious that accepting the IWC moratorium could seriously affect other Japanese fisheries policies as well as the development of fisheries regimes worldwide. Of particular concern was the way that the moratorium came about and forced upon Japan. As a result, Fisheries Agency officials rejected the moratorium and have continued to work for its removal. Towards this end, they have devoted much energy and resources. Official delegations are present in all IWC meetings, research whaling was launched and continues, and the country has submitted many scientific and anthropological research papers to IWC.

Although the Fisheries Agency has the strongest voice in setting the country's policy on whaling, it could not act without support from other important governmental and non-government actors. Its decision to lodge an objection to the IWC moratorium in 1982 demanded extensive intra- and inter-ministerial talks to prevent domestic disputes. For this, Fisheries Agency officials responsible for whaling had two main tasks. One was to persuade other colleagues in charge of fisheries within the Fisheries Agency to accept their decision to file the objection. They had to explain how anomalies in the whaling regime could affect other fisheries regime so that defending whaling would benefit Japanese fisheries interests in the long term. At the same time, they had to allay anxieties of Japanese fisheries over possible repercussions. The greatest fear was the removal of Japanese fishing rights in the U.S. exclusive economic zone. This threat was real because U.S. legislation tying whaling to fisheries was already in place and had been unleashed against Japan.

Their second task was to convince MoFA to support the decision to file an objection to the moratorium. MoFA, as the Japanese government's chief bureaucratic liaison with the international community, would be in the front line of outside criticisms. An endorsement from MoFA's North American Bureau was especially important because the U.S. could carry out the most significant sanctions against Japan. For officials in the North American Bureau, smooth Japan-U.S. relations was the priority. In their view, filing an objection to the moratorium would provoke strong reactions from the U.S. and complicate their work in handling Japan-U.S. relations, especially at a time of worsening bilateral trade relations.

Outside of the bureaucracy, whaling officials in the Fisheries Agency had to persuade the Japanese fishing industry to accept their decision. At this time, Japanese fisheries in the U.S. alone were worth hundreds of millions of dollars annually and employed thousands of people. Since the fishing industry owns the whaling industry, it was clear that the former would readily abandon the whaling. The fisheries industry had to believe that benefits from defending whaling would justify the risks involved.

Whaling officials from the Fisheries Agency nearly ran out of time for their lobbying. Persuading each of these groups took several months of arduous discussions. The objection was officially filed on 2 November 1982, only two days before the 90-day IWC deadline for reservations. However, Japanese officials had to withdraw their hard-won objection almost immediately after it was filed because the United States had activated the Packwood-Magnuson Amendment to bar all Japanese fishing vessels from entering or operating in the U.S. EEZ. This quick and severe

Whaling

U.S. response shook the Japanese fishing industry. To protect their fishing rights, the Japanese fishing industry pressured Fisheries Agency officials to withdraw the objection.

Recovering Japan's fishing rights was not automatic. Japan had to withdraw its objection to the IWC moratorium and stop all commercial whaling by 1988 under the terms of the Murazumi-Baldrige Agreement, which was signed in 1984. This meant that Japanese whaling was sacrificed for Japanese fishing interests in the United States. Nevertheless, U.S. negotiators were quite sympathetic to the Japanese situation. Allowing Japan to end commercial whaling by 1988 gave Japan two extra seasons for small-type coastal whaling beyond 1986, when the IWC ban was to come into effect. Japanese negotiators requested this as a grace period to help settle the future of whaling crews.

Some Japanese officials involved in negotiations with the United States believed that the terms of the agreement could have been more favorable to Japan if there were higher level dialogues. Although a few Diet members urged ministerial-level meetings at the later stage of negotiations, no one of such stature came forth, nor was there any support from the Prime Minister's Office or the Cabinet. In fact, the prime minister distanced himself from the issue entirely because of negative publicity generated by this affair.[126]

Despite this setback, Fisheries Agency officials supporting whaling were still determined to challenge the moratorium. Their strategy was to launch a research whaling program in 1987 to gather scientific evidence to assess whether certain stocks are capable of sustainable harvests. First, they mobilized support from politicians to obtain Diet approval for research whaling on 28 March 1985. By this time, the end of Japanese fishing interest in the United States was near and the Murazumi-Baldrige Agreement was already in place. This made politicians protective of fisheries interests less anxious of potential repercussions from whaling, whether it is research or commercial. The U.S. strategy linking whaling and fishing had also made Japanese politicians more aware of connections between the two issues. Defense of whaling thus came to be viewed as a defense of fishing.[127]

Prime Minister Nakasone was worried about negative U.S. reaction and damage to Japan's international image. He tried to persuade the Fisheries Agency to give up the idea of research whaling. He even told the Director General of the Fisheries Agency on 25 April 1987, before his trip to the United States, that research whaling would give Japan an "unfair image" and that the U.S. would accuse Japan of "continuing commercial whaling" under the guise of research whaling.[128]

The Fisheries Agency ignored the prime minister's appeal and submitted in 1987 a draft of its "Research Whaling Preparation Plan" to take 825 minke whales and up to 50 sperm whales per season in the Antarctic. Although Japan was close to losing all of its U.S. fishing quotas, the fisheries industry remained anxious and pressed designers of the program to cut the number to 525 minke whales each season.[129]

For the prime minister, this number was still too high for acceptance by the United States, but the Fisheries Agency refused further cuts to protect the integrity of its research plan. The two sides eventually reached an impasse that was broken only with an unexpected move by the prime minister. Nakasone publicly stated, without consultation with the program's designers, that he considered the numbers too high. Subsequent to this announcement the Prime Minister's Office "requested" the Fisheries Agency to slash the number of minke whales to 300 and drop sperm whales from the program. Nakasone's actions infuriated the Fisheries Agency, but its officials and scientists could do little more than to adjust to this sudden turn of events.[130]

In summary, the Fisheries Agency's dominance in this issue was most significant in deciding Japan's objection to the moratorium in 1982 and launching of research whaling in 1987. Fisheries Agency had almost exclusive jurisdiction over the country's fisheries policy, of which whaling is a part. Large, powerful, and domestically oriented, the Fisheries Agency, or MAFF for that matter, was quite resistant to intervention from other domestic policy actors or censure from foreign critics.

How whaling, as a policy issue, was framed and treated by the responsible Fisheries Agency officials also deterred input from other governmental and non-governmental policy actors. It is not uncommon for Fisheries Agency officials to have a technical education background. In fact, many officials for whaling graduated from the fisheries department of Tokyo University. Their education background strongly influenced their perspectives and their preference to set the whaling issue in a heavily science-based context for policy discussions. The opinions of those without such scientific training were less respected and effectively excluded from any meaningful participation in policy discussions.

For the Fisheries Agency, its virtual monopoly on whaling policy has its benefits and costs. On the one hand, it has been able to better shield whaling from outside intervention and political bargaining that may dilute its influence. On the other, this monopoly has weakened the credibility of its policy within the international arena and leaves it vulnerable to criticisms that it only represents the will of a small band of Fisheries Agency officials and industry interests.

Ministry of Foreign Affairs.

MoFA, on the whole, would not oppose an end to Japanese whaling. Being in the front line of foreign attacks, MoFA officials have had to defend a policy that they have little input in making and implementing. Most troubling to them has been the adverse impacts of a pro-whaling position on U.S.-Japan relations.

Whaling 119

Their worries were especially aggravated during the worst years for Japanese whaling from 1982 to 1987, which coincided with serious conflicts in U.S.-Japan trade relations as well as rising foreign anxieties about Japanese economic power. MoFA feared that a decision to lodge the objection could tarnish Japan's international image—which it did.

Just as whaling has its supporters and detractors within the Fisheries Agency, MoFA, too, has not been united in its resistance to whaling. Within MoFA, its North American bureau has been least supportive of Japanese whaling. This is because it is most directly responsible for responding to reactions from the U.S. and whaling could complicate its work on the broad range of issues that are more important to U.S.-Japan bilateral relations.[131] Therefore, the North American Bureau fiercely opposed the decision to file an objection to the moratorium.[132]

Nonetheless, opinions differed on the merits of supporting whaling within the Economic Affairs Bureau, and its Fisheries Division was critical in pushing MoFA, as a whole, to endorse the Fisheries Agency's decision to oppose the IWC moratorium. Like officials in the Fisheries Agency, these fisheries officials in MoFA recognized how the moratorium could imperil Japanese fishing interests in the long term and adversely affect the development of common resource regimes.

They also recognized that Japan would lose most of its fishing allocations in the U.S. and elsewhere regardless of whaling. As more nations ratified the United Nations Convention for the Law of the Sea, the number of EEZs would increase, and with it the introduction of protectionist measures to exclude foreign fisheries interests. This knowledge enabled them to separate fishing from whaling and still appreciate their connections in decision making. Consequently, lobbying from the Japanese fishing industry did not dissuade them from supporting an objection to the IWC moratorium.[133] In fact, these fishing officials believed that trading whaling for fishing rights in the United States would not be a rational choice because fishing has only a "short life expectancy" before it would be completely phased out.[134]

The severe U.S. reaction and escalated pressure from the Japanese fishing industry forced the Japanese government to withdraw its objection, and MoFA's North American bureau officials had to sign in 1984 the Murazumi-Baldrige Agreement to recover Japan's fishing rights in U.S. waters. Nevertheless, MoFA's Fisheries Division has continued to share the basic position of their colleagues responsible for whaling in the Fisheries Agency, including support for the research whaling program. Similar education backgrounds and outlook towards fisheries and resource use have united these policy actors across ministerial lines.

In contrast, MoFA officials in general, and those in the North American bureau, in particular, continue to regard whaling an irritation. They have to defend the pro-whaling position and work to minimize damage to other national and bureaucratic concerns.

Japanese politicians.

When the IWC moratorium was passed in 1982, most Japanese politicians resisted involvement in the issue, except for a few representatives having STCW communities in their constituencies.[135] For the majority, protecting Japan's fishing rights in U.S. waters and elsewhere was more important and many were apprehensive of adverse impacts on U.S.-Japan relations.[136]

The signing of the Murazumi-Baldrige agreement in 1984 was a turning point. It marked the end of Japanese whaling so that supporting whaling from this time on would no longer be deleterious to Japanese fisheries interests overseas. In addition, the end of fishing rights in the United States and many other places was also not far away so there was little danger that more damage could be done. Finally, there were some political points to be gained. In domestic politics, supporting Japan's right to whale had evolved into a defense of national pride and culture, as well as a battle against Western oppression.[137]

As a consequence, the Liberal Democratic Party formed the Parliamentary League in Support of Whaling in May 1985.[138] It was the first open declaration of support by a group of national politicians. Other political parties followed in creating their own committees to support whaling. Yet, whaling has remained a minor political and economic issue, useful only in stirring nationalist sentiments. Japanese legislators have done little to persuade legislators in anti-whaling countries to soften their governments' anti-whaling policies or to strengthen alliances with their counterparts in countries that also favor whaling. Active intervention by Prime Minister Nakasone was the only notable exception.

The Prime Minister: Yasuhiro Nakasone.

To Prime Minister Nakasone, the Fisheries Agency's decision to oppose the 1982 IWC moratorium brought the country much unwanted publicity. There were especially deep anxieties over its negative effects on U.S.-Japan relations. With rapidly mounting U.S. pressure to address bilateral trade imbalances, Japan could not afford other confrontations with the United States. In addition, Nakasone saw how whaling could be linked to many other Japanese interests that he deemed were more important to the country and his own political ambitions. Thus, Nakasone loathed the notoriety that Japanese whaling generated and was wary of its potential harm to Japan's image and interests.[139]

Since Nakasone did not care for whaling or fisheries, he never mobilized his administration or the Liberal Democratic Party (to which he was also the head) to save the whaling industry or to protect Japan's fisheries interests. In 1984, a Diet bill to continue whaling was aborted. Two years later, a bill to create a law with retaliatory powers to respond to the drastic cuts

Whaling

in fisheries allocations in U.S. waters was also blocked. Since Nakasone could see that the U.S. was determined to expel all foreign fisheries interests in its EEZ, he knew that any measure to counter this move would only exacerbate U.S. threats of economic sanctions.[140]

Thus, Nakasone basically chose to sacrifice Japanese whaling to avoid worsening tensions in U.S.-Japan relations and to minimize damage to Japan's international image or his own. Japanese prime ministers have generally refrained from active involvement in policy making. However, in a rare move, Nakasone used his executive powers to override the powerful bureaucracy and acted personally to produce a policy decision he considered more favorable to his own political agenda.[141]

Nakasone's independent and public proposal to remove sperm whales from the research whaling program as well as to reduce the number of minke whale catches forced the Fisheries Agency to modify its plans. This was something that he was unable to achieve through closed-door talks with the Fisheries Agency. Nakasone knew he could not please both the foreign critics and the Fisheries Agency, and he chose to present himself as a forceful and international-minded chief executive. Canceling the program, on the other hand, could have incurred the wrath of the entire bureaucracy for his heavy-handedness. Hence, he considered his proposal a compromise to make this politically sensitive issue more palatable to the U.S. (and other anti-whaling countries) without completely denying the Fisheries Agency of what it wants. Although neither side would be entirely pleased, it was an outcome that all three parties (including Nakasone himself) could at least tolerate.

The non-governmental actors.

Two groups of non-governmental actors have also labored to influence Japan's whaling policy, namely, the anti-whaling conservation groups and the Japanese fishing and whaling industry. Anti-whaling groups, on the whole, have had minimal success in directly affecting Japanese policy makers. Industry groups were influential in pressing the government to protect fisheries interests. The end of commercial whaling changed the political and economic equation, making them more willing supporters of Fisheries Agency policy prescriptions.

Anti-whaling conservation groups.
Anti-whaling groups, both inside Japan and overseas, had labored against Japanese whaling. However, penetrating the domestic policy making process had been extremely difficult for groups in Japan primarily because of the Fisheries Agency's firm grip on the issue.

In comparison, groups working outside of Japan have had greater influence on the Japanese government. The most active groups have been Greenpeace International, the World Wide Fund for Nature (WWF),[142] Friends of the Earth (FoE), and the International Fund for Animal Welfare

(IFAW). Their success can be attributed to four main thrusts in their activities. First, they exerted indirect pressure on the Japanese government through the U.S. and other countries that are strong opponents of whaling. Second, they worked to produce an anti-whaling majority within IWC, which was crucial to adoption of the ban on commercial whaling in 1982. Third, they used the courts to challenge Japanese whaling. For instance, the American Cetacean Society, representing 18 anti-whaling groups sued the U.S. government for concluding with Japan the Murazumi-Baldrige Agreement, which granted Japan extra whaling seasons after the ban came into effect in 1986.[143] They also used this to pressure Japan to withdraw its objection to the IWC ban and to cease its research whaling activities. Finally, they exploited Japan's sensitivity to outside criticisms. Moderate groups chastised Japan in their publications and public announcements. Radical advocates condemned Japanese whaling in high profile activities that made international news headlines. For example, anti-whaling demonstrations at IWC meetings told graphic stories of Japanese whaling and whale eating practices.[144]

Although these tactics were useful in international campaigns against whaling, they discouraged informed and objective public discussions of the issue in Japan. First, attacks on Japanese whaling and whale meat consumption by anti-whaling groups made Japanese government claims of racism and cultural imperialism more persuasive to the public.[145] Since anti-whaling activities were seen as anti-Japan and anti-Japanese, it was very difficult to build a broad-based popular movement against whaling in Japan. Japanese offices of the major anti-whaling groups even had difficulty raising membership in Japan.

Second, the first full-scale campaign in Japan began only after the moratorium was passed in 1982. By this time, public opinion was already largely sympathetic to pro-whaling arguments. Prior to this, Western anti-whaling activists only made sporadic visits to document Japanese whaling activities for their audience in the West.[146] The "Greenpeace Japan mission" in 1976 attracted a small number of young people who became anti-whaling activists on their own or were employed as representatives of these foreign groups in Japan.[147] However, there was no significant follow up efforts by these international groups in Japan until the whaling ban was already put in place.

Third, Japanese offices of international conservation groups could not build a popular anti-whaling movement in Japan because their international headquarters controlled planning and execution of campaigns worldwide, including those in Japan. These activists did not consider their unflattering depiction of Japanese whaling and culture insensitive. Although the images they showed attracted substantial financial support and membership in North America and Western Europe, Japanese people often found these images offensive. Seeing how international anti-whaling

Whaling

campaigns hurt their efforts to raise membership in Japan, Japanese branches of the major anti-whaling groups have moved away from the whaling issue and focus instead on issues that evoke greater Japanese sympathy. For instance, both FoE (Japan) and WWF (Japan) had shifted to campaign against the tropical timber trade by the mid-1980s.[148]

Finally, apart from all the flaws and weaknesses summarized above, bad timing hurt efforts by anti-whaling groups in presenting their case to the Japanese public. Worsening U.S.-Japan trade friction during this period dominated domestic news headlines. Most Japanese were naturally more drawn to issues that had a direct and vital bearing on their lives than whaling.[149]

As for the domestic anti-whaling groups, that is, those that have their roots in Japan, their push to end whaling began after the Stockholm Conference in 1972.[150] However, many obstacles limited their influence. First, there were the usual problems associated with being small and short of funds and staff that is common to most non-governmental organizations (NGOs) in Japan. Second, the national media were largely unsympathetic and uninterested in reporting their perspectives and activities. Third, NGOs in Japan did not gain legitimacy in domestic political discussions until recently.

Fourth, the inability to reach a national consensus on whaling weakened the anti-whaling cause in the domestic debate. The proposal for a resolution to support the IWC moratorium at a meeting of the National Nature Protection Federation (*Zenkoku Jizen Hogo Rengo*) in 1982 was defeated for fear of its adverse effects on fishing.[151] Fifth, the personal background of many of activists compromised their credibility and effectiveness in the Japanese political rivalries. For example, many of the activists did not have formal education in the environmental sciences. This was a serious handicap in a culture that greatly values knowledge and in a policy setting where the most powerful policy actors frame the issue in a highly scientific and technical context. Many of these activists also trace their ideological roots and public activism to the anti-Vietnam War, anti-U.S., and anti-establishment protests of the 1960s and 1970s.[152] This again made it easy for the government and the pro-whaling lobby to cast them as radicals and traitors. Modern Japanese society emphasizes conformity, and support for whaling had, by this time, become an expression of patriotism.

The fact that many of the activists were women also weakened the credibility of these NGO groups. Given Japanese society's biases against women, the seriousness of their commitment and professionalism were often questioned. Since activists in Japan were not well paid—if at all— they were dismissed as simple-minded housewives or young women who took up the anti-whaling activities simply to escape boredom.

Finally, Japanese activists were quite vulnerable to misperceptions or allegations of being lackeys of the West. These activists did not have a message that was clearly distinct from the Japan-bashing rhetoric of Western activists in an issue that had become tainted with strong political and emotional overtones of racism and patriotism.

Cooperation between the anti-whaling groups working overseas and in Japan has been rare because an equal and respectful relationship never truly developed. A few long-time anti-whaling Japanese activists complained of exploitation by their foreign counterparts. A common grievance is that foreign activists treated them as subordinates and free help in executing their mission in Japan. Another is that foreign groups are generally ignorant of and uninterested in the objectives and work of the Japanese activists.[153]

Since Japanese commercial whaling ended in 1987, stopping Japanese research whaling has become the main goal of anti-whaling advocates. Research whaling, they charge, is a guise for commercial whaling and an obstacle to terminating the illegal trade of whale meat.[154] As the Greenpeace (Japan) campaigner for whaling had said, "the best way to prevent the smuggling of whale meat is to stop research whaling and terminate domestic meat distribution."[155] However, most Japanese offices of international groups working in Japan have ceased their anti-whaling activities.[156] Only the Japanese liaison for IFAW has continued to actively campaign against Japanese research whaling. She launched *Kujira Tsushin* (Whale Bulletin) in 1995 and puts it out each year around the time of IWC annual meetings to inform Japanese NGOs and the public of the views of the anti-whaling lobby.[157]

Japanese offices of the international conservation groups generally attribute the end of their anti-whaling activities to the passing of the moratorium. Nonetheless, staff members also indicated that the anti-whaling campaigns of their international offices have left such negative impressions on the Japanese public that continuing involvement could only deter their mission to raise funds and membership in Japan. For instance, Greenpeace (Japan) had to struggle to convince the Japanese public that it is not anti-Japanese and has concerns other than whaling.[158]

As for the domestic anti-whaling groups, they are still plagued by lack of resources and a difficult relationship with the government. The two sides have remained guarded in their infrequent encounters and meetings still have to reach higher levels of government. Many of the Japanese groups have also shifted their focus to other issues, while those who choose to continue now protest against research whaling, illegal coastal catches, and the illegal trade of whale meat. Many also support whale watching as an alternative for STCW communities. Whale-watching tours can now be found in Koichi and Ogasawara.[159] However, it is not clear all STCW communities in Japan would welcome whale watching as a replacement for whaling due to regulatory, logistical, and practical reasons.[160]

Whaling 125

Elsa, the oldest of these domestic groups to embrace the anti-whaling cause, still publishes a newsletter, and the Japan Wildlife Conservation Philosophy Group occasionally publishes on the whale-related subjects. A *Kijira Mondai Network* (Whale Problem Network) was formed in 1988 as a loose link for groups and individuals sharing interest in whaling.

Apart from the anti-whaling groups, there are also several pro-whaling ones, including the Japan Whaling Association, Japan Fisheries Association, All Japan Seamen's Union, Japan Small-Type Whaling Association, Riches of the Sea, and the Global Guardian Trust. Most of them have some economic interest in resuming commercial whaling and share the Japanese government's views on sustainable use. Many also receive support from MAFF, particularly the Fisheries Agency, and host retired officials from the ministry. They help to publicize the official views at home and provide token civilian support to the Japanese government (or specifically the Fisheries Agency) in IWC and other international forums.

However, without the kind of propaganda machine that Western anti-whaling groups have, their reach is very limited. Their ties to the government and industry also affect their credibility as independent organizations and weaken their ability to form alliances at home or overseas, except with those that share their goal to reopen whaling. For these reasons, they have been rather ineffective in advancing Japan's objectives and perspectives on whaling at home and overseas.

Japanese fishing and whaling industries.
Both the Japanese fishing and whaling industries have been involved in this issue, but only the former has any real leverage because it owns the whaling industry. Hence, the whaling industry has had to rely on its supporters within the Fisheries Agency to fight for its survival.

Until Japan lost all its fishing rights in the U.S., the primary concern for Japanese fishing companies had been their fishing rights, especially those for their deep-sea trawlers in the Bering Aleutian Straits. It was easy to choose fishing over whaling because Japanese fisheries in the U.S. were worth hundreds of millions of dollars annually, while the entire whaling industry was worth less than one-tenth of this sum. Thus, when the United States threatened to remove Japan's fishing rights in U.S. waters in reaction to Japan's objection to the IWC moratorium in 1982, the fishing industry exerted strong pressure on officials in the Fisheries Agency and MoFA to reach a compromise with the U.S. government.[161] According to a former MoFA official who led negotiations for a solution to this crisis, the Japanese fishing industry begged him and his team to "give in at any expense." He also added that that since Japanese fishing was "held hostage of the Packwood-Magnuson Amendment" the negotiators were "obliged to give in to the U.S. government" and to give up whaling. Therefore, domestic pressure forced Japanese officials to conclude the

Murazumi-Baldrige Agreement in 1984, which restored Japan's fishing rights but ended whaling for Japan under IWC.[162]

As fisheries management regulations have tightened worldwide, the Japanese fishing industry has become more supportive of the Fisheries Agency's arguments for legal principles and sustainable use. After Japan lost its fishing rights in U.S. waters, Japanese fisheries and the Fisheries Agency have found a new ally in the U.S. fishing industry. Many Japanese and U.S. fishing companies have entered into joint ventures and former Japanese deep-sea trawlers are now part of the U.S. fleet. Since annual U.S. fisheries exports to Japan is worth hundreds of millions of dollars, the U.S. fishing industry now speaks for the interests of their business partners and buyers in Japan before U.S. legislators. Japanese officials, partly driven by their sense of obligation, labored to respond to requests from the whaling industry to obtain extra whaling seasons in negotiations for the Murazumi-Baldrige Agreement. The whaling industry wanted the extra seasons to help prepare for its own demise, including arrangements for retirement and new employment for the whaling crews.[163]

Seeing that an end to Japanese whaling was inevitable, the whaling industry knew that its only clients would be the Fisheries Agency and the Institute for Cetacean Research following the end of commercial whaling. Hence, Kyodo Senpaku and the Seamen's Union pushed for a catch quota of 1,200 to 1,500 minke whales per year for the research whaling program (the scientists only sought 825) because more catches would mean a longer charter and more work for the crew. However, Fisheries Agency officials and scientists rejected these requests to protect the scientific and political credibility of the program.

In summary, the Fisheries Agency, specifically its officials for whaling, has been able to exercise a firm hold over the nation's whaling policy mainly because of its official powers over the issue. However, this monopoly may be possible only as long as no major crisis erupts. The linkage of whaling to other policy issues, particularly those outside of the Fisheries Agency's jurisdiction, could draw pressure and intervention from other domestic policy actors. The most influential include the prime minister, MITI, and, MoFA's North American Bureau.

CHAPTER CONCLUSION

Japan's policy on whaling has been most strongly determined by the perspectives of the Fisheries Agency, its chief policy maker. The two policy decisions examined here demonstrated that although other interested policy actors and changes in the international regime for whaling could have some impact, they have been unable to fundamentally challenge the Fisheries Agency's hold on the issue or alter its views. Even U.S. pressure on Japan (or specifically the Fisheries Agency) was effective only because of vulnerabilities caused by other important issues in their bilateral rela-

Whaling

tionship and the linkage of Japanese whaling to Japanese fishing rights in U.S. waters.

The change in membership within the IWC in the 1970s was reflective of developments in international discussions on the relationship between nature and human beings. Whales and nature, on the whole, would not only be valued only for their economic importance to human beings. The new perspective holds that nature has an intrinsic value independent of human needs. Animals have a right to exist and live freely as human beings do and whales became the first and one of the greatest symbols of this new thinking. Most countries have not found it difficult to embrace this new perspective of whales since these marine mammals never had or no longer held any economic value to them.

However, the Japanese government has found this perspective both alien and dangerous to its interests. As a nation with great anxiety over resource security, any proposal that bars human use of natural resources is objectionable. Suggestions that whales deserve special treatment or protection from human use on the grounds of animal rights are also incomprehensible to most Japanese. This difference in how whales (or nature) are valued by anti-whaling supporters and Japan (and a few other countries and peoples that wish to whale) has divided the two sides. Hence, while the former has continued to advocate an end to all forms of whaling, the latter has remained equally insistent on applying science and sustainable use principles in addressing whale conservation.

Japan's perspectives and policies towards whaling and related issues in this debate also highlight differences in approaches to nature conservation, the place of commerce, culture, traditions and equity as well as the effectiveness of international organizations and regimes in environmental conservation. Another important question is whether or not membership in resource management organizations should be qualified or open to all.

The history of IWC presents an argument that a management body cannot work well without a reasonable balance between different interests. Open membership without qualification of a serious interest in the objective of the organization does not encourage compromise. Within the IWC, it is evident that countries which do not see benefits for themselves in reopening commercial whaling and allowing consumptive use of whales have little interest in allowing others to do so. Therefore, those wishing to access and use this resource are denied access today.

Within IWC, in particular, Japanese actions have sustained debates on protection, sustainable use, and the place of commerce in natural resource use. Since Japan's official objection to the moratorium and research whaling program are legitimate under the International Convention for the Regulation of Whaling, pressures on Japan from inside and outside of the IWC to end all forms of whaling undermine the integrity of the international whaling regime under this agreement.

As for the making of Japan's policy towards whaling, bureaucratic dominance has clearly prevailed and the Fisheries Agency has been the strongest actor because it has uncontested control of the issue. The Fisheries Agency has also added informal authority to its formal powers by setting the issue in a context and language that serve its organizational goals and capabilities to minimize intervention by other actors.

Nonetheless, outside pressure can be effective if properly targeted. A good example was the linkage of Japanese fishing rights in the United States to force a withdrawal of Japan's formal objection to the 1982 IWC moratorium. Outside pressure also need not be directly targeted at Japan or the Fisheries Agency to be effective. Anti-whaling groups have been more successful in pressuring Japan through their lobbying of governments in the U.S., Australia, New Zealand, and most European countries, where public sentiments are on their side, to produce anti-whaling legislation and policies.

This study on Japan's whaling policy has also revealed that differences and alliances among the main policy actors are rooted in their particularistic goals and interests. Loyalties do not always form along ministerial lines. The shared perspectives of fisheries officials in MoFA and the Fisheries Agency attest to this. Thus, how an issue is defined and situated in the government bureaucracy becomes highly significant and what is national policy may be no more than the preference of those with the official power or influence to assert themselves in the policy process.

The interests and goals of a policy actor also affect his/her perception of an issue, especially in how national interest is interpreted. MAFF officials regard resource security as a national priority. Since the whaling ban affects resource use, the moratorium is seen and presented as a threat to Japanese national interests. MoFA officials, as the country's chief foreign liaison, are more concerned about how whaling affects Japan's international image and status as well as bilateral relations with the United States. Nakasone, as the chief executive, saw whaling as a liability for Japan and his own political agenda.

Changes to the Pelly and Packwood-Magnuson Amendments in 1988 and 1992 could be most effective in reducing the leverage of the Fisheries Agency and MoFA over Japan's whaling policy. The tying of non-marine agricultural and industrial products to whaling would pressure the Fisheries Agency to expand intra-ministerial negotiations with other agencies within MAFF, as well as inter-ministerial talks with the Ministry of International Trade and Industry, which is responsible for Japan's international trade interests. Pressure from non-fisheries private interests would also grow. Furthermore, recognition of whales and whaling as biodiversity conservation issues by the Basic Environmental Law of 1993 has given the Environment Agency of Japan a formal voice in this matter. All this could dilute the formal and informal powers of the Fisheries Agency.

Whaling   129

Nonetheless, it is also interesting to see how this protracted battle has cultivated a generation of Fisheries Agency officials, who matured professionally in the darkest period for Japanese whaling. These officials are quite devoted to their beliefs and outspoken about their cause. Holding post-graduate degrees from major U.S. and European universities, proficient in fisheries and legal matters, and with great fluency in English, these middle-ranking officials are critical to continuing the long-term battle to end the moratorium.

As for other government policy actors, namely, the Japanese prime minister and politicians, whaling remains a minor concern at best and an irritation when it affects (or when it is perceived to have the potential to affect) other more important policy and political concerns. Therefore, none of Nakasone's successors have spoken out for whaling.[164] Japanese politicians, too, have not devoted much attention to whaling because of their preoccupation with domestic economic problems and the biggest post-war political shake-up in Japan.

On inter-level dynamics in making Japan's whaling policy, policy actors who have to bridge domestic interests and demands in the international environment are more sensitive to the give-and-take that is required for successful negotiations. They are also more driven to seek acceptable compromises for the parties involved, instead of defending or advancing particular institutional interests. Japanese negotiators for the Baldrige-Murazumi Agreement knew that a formal withdrawal of Japan's objection to the moratorium was inevitable. Enormous pressure came domestically from the Japanese fishing industry and externally from the U.S. government. Obtaining a few extra seasons for Japanese whaling gave them a small diplomatic victory to satisfy whaling and fisheries interests at home.[165] In another example, Fisheries Agency and MoFA officials, who worked primarily in the international arena, saw merit in dropping sperm whales from the research whaling program. Seeing that sperm whales are more politically controversial than minke whales, dropping them might make the program more acceptable to IWC and the United States.[166] For Prime Minister Nakasone, his action to cut back, but not eliminate, the research whaling program was done to simultaneously appease foreign critics and domestic advocates.

In conclusion, the bureaucratic model helps to identify the Fisheries Agency as the chief bureaucratic actor in Japan's whaling policy. It explains why the Fisheries Agency has been able to maintain dominance in the domestic policy process and exposes its vulnerability when linkages occur. However, the bureaucratic model is insufficient in explaining gaps between Japan's whaling policy and the international whaling regime.

This case of whaling shows that concepts and elements in complex interdependence, regime theory, and the two-level games model can be more effective in explaining these gaps. Theories of complex interdependence and regimes demonstrate how regimes can change as a result of economic and political pressures. Within the international whaling regime, power shifted from a majority of whaling interests to a majority of conservation advocates as whaling lost its economic value to most nations. Increasing influence of conservation groups in many Western countries, in particular, fundamentally altered the policies of many governments towards whaling. Hence, a gap occured between Japanese whaling policy, which has remained basically unchanged in the last several decades, and the international whaling regime, which now emphasizes protection over the use of whale resources. Moreover, apprehensions about linkages across different resource regimes explained why Japanese fisheries officials objected to the IWC ban on commercial whaling. Complex interdependence and the two-level games model also explained how the United States exploited Japanese sensitivities and vulnerabilities. By tying Japanese whaling to Japanese fishing rights in the United States and setting Japanese whaling within the context of U.S.-Japan trade relations, the United States used synergistic linkages to challenge the dominance of the Fisheries Agency. Nonetheless, even in a situation of opposing interests, transgovernmental cooperation can occur. In negotiations for the Murazumi-Baldrige Agreement, U.S. officials readily accepted the Japanese request for extra whaling seasons. Since this was a meaningful concession to the Japanese negotiators, U.S. officials could better count on the Japanese negotiators to seek acceptance of this agreement in their domestic political setting.

The Fisheries Agency's redefinition of whaling into a policy issue that is bigger, more inclusive, and pertinent to national interest demonstrates a strategy used by policy actors in two-level games to protect themselves from outside pressure. By expanding the issue of Japanese whaling into one of national culture, pride, and sovereignty, the Fisheries Agency has made it more difficult for conservation advocates to garner public support (or establish reverberations) within Japan. Therefore, seeing how whaling is situated as an issue in the Japanese government policy structure helps to explain why economic interest is not the sole or key driver in Japan's whaling policy.

Notes

[1] Anthropologist Arne Kalland calls this the "Super Whale" phenomenon. See his article, "Super Whale: The Use of Myths and Symbols in Environmentalism" in *11 Essays on Whales and Man*, 2nd ed., Reine: High North Alliance, 1994, pp.5-11.

Whaling

131

[2] The Basques hunted right whales because they are a fairly slow-swimming species and their bodies float after they are killed. This made them easier to handle; hence, the "right" whales to catch.

[3] Bjorn L. Basberg et al., *Whaling and History: Perspectives on the Evolution of the Industry,* Sandefjord: Sandefjordmuseene, 1993, pp.55-7.

[4] The north Atlantic was the prime hunting ground for the blue, fin and sei whales in the 1920s. See Kara Zohn, *Whales*, London: Headline Books, 1988, p.125.

[5] Steinar Andersen, "Science and Politics in the International Management of Whales," *Marine Policy*, April 1989, p.101.

[6] The English ended whaling in 1963, followed by the Dutch in 1964. The height of American whaling was in the 1860s, but some U.S. commercial whaling continued until the early 1970s for pet food. See Stephen S. Boynton, "'Whaling Policy' of the United States: Yesterday, Today and Tomorrow," *Isana*, November 1994, pp.20-25.

[7] While the Japanese people eat whale meat and blubber, the Soviet catches were consumed by some aboriginal peoples and used substantially as animal feed in farms for producing fur.

[8] Shigeko Misaki, "Whaling Controversy is the Name of the Game," in *Public Perception of Whaling*, Tokyo: Institute of Cetacean Research, 1994, p.30.

[9] No species of whales has become extinct as a result of commercial exploitation. Among the 80 species of whales identified, only 20 have been commercially hunted. Industrial whaling has, however, seriously diminished specific whale stocks—or populations—in various regions.

[10] Scientific studies have not shown whales to be exceptionally intelligent. See Margaret Klinowska, "Are Cetaceans Especially Smart?" *New Scientist*, Vol.29, October 1988, p.46.

[11] Popular opposition to whaling has been strongest in many former whaling nations, including the U.S., Britain, Australia, and the Netherlands, where anti-whaling campaigns are often built on public guilt for past excesses. Anti-whaling sentiments have also been strong in New Zealand and Germany, where conservation and animals rights groups are influential in domestic politics.

[12] Although a few biologists, most notably John Lilly, have promoted the idea that marine mammals possess a high level of "non-human intelligence," no research has lent direct support to this belief. See Margaret Klinowska, "Brains, Behavior and Intelligence in Cetaceans" in *Whales and Ethics*, ed. by Orn D. Jonsson, Iceland: Fisheries Research Institute, University of Iceland, University Press, 1992, pp.23-38; and M.M. Bryden and P. Corkeron, "Intelligence," in *Whales, Dolphins and Porpoises*, ed. by R. Harrison and M.M. Bryden, New York and Oxford: Facts on File, 1982, p.160, and Milton Freeman, "Japanese Community-based Whaling, International Protest, and the New Environmentalism" in *Japan at the*

Crossroads: Hot Issues for the 21st Century, ed. by David Myers and Kotaku Ishido, Tokyo: Seibundo Publishing Co., 1998, p.16.

[13] National efforts to regulate whaling also grew. In 1929 the Norwegian Whaling Act was passed and in 1931 the Committee of International Whaling Statistics was formed. The latter is often mistakenly called the International Bureau of Whaling Statistics. The Committee was appointed by the Norwegian Government and had Norwegian members only. From Andersen, *op cit.*, p.102, taken from J.Tonnesen and A. Johnsen, *The History of Modern Whaling* (a shortened translation of *Den moderne hvalfangsts historie: Opprinnelse og utvikling*, Vol.I-IV, Sandefjord, 1959-1970), London: C. Hurst & Co., 1982.

[14] The U.S. wrote the final draft of the International Convention for the Regulation of Whaling. Although Britain and the Netherlands were the biggest whaling nations prior to the war, the U.S. was the clear leader in the new post-war world. Thus, the U.S. took leadership even as its own whaling industry was coming to an end. Junichi Takahashi, *Kujira no Nihon Bunka Shi—Hogei Bunka no Hoseki o Tadoru* (Japan's Cultural History of Whales: Tracing the Death of a Whaling Culture), Tokyo: Tankousha, 1992.

[15] Peter J. Stoett, *The International Politics of Whaling*, Vancouver: University of British Columbia Press, 1997, p.144.

[16] *International Convention on the Regulation of Whaling*, Washington, D.C., 2 December 1946.

[17] *Ibid.*

[18] *Ibid.*

[19] Scientific Committee meetings are held two weeks before the main IWC annual meeting. Special meetings may be held during the year to consider specific subjects.

[20] Contracting governments of ICRW can have any number of representatives in these two committees, but each nation has only one vote.

[21] Andersen, *op cit.*, pp.101-2.

[22] The concept was first proposed in 1944—two years before ICRW was signed, but it was later adopted by ICRW. *Ibid.*, p.101.

[23] One BWU equals one blue whale, two fin whales, two-and-a-half humpback whales, six sei whales, or 30 minke whales.

[24] Stoett, *op cit.*, p.62.

[25] See Eiichi Eguchi, "Memory of the Blue Whale," *Isana*, March 1994, p.25.

[26] Zohn, *op cit.*, pp.125-6.

[27] Hardin, *op cit.*, pp.1243-8.

[28] Whaling by non-IWC members was also called "illegal" and "pirate" whaling, but these catches were not technically illegal since these countries were not bound by ICRW.

Whaling

133

[29] David Andrew Price, "Save the Whalers," *The American Spectator*, February 1995, pp.48-9.

[30] For example, Dutch scientists used scientific uncertainty to resist reductions in fin whale catches in the Southern Oceans in the 1950s. See Tore Schweder, "Intransigence, incompetence or political expediency? Dutch scientists in the International Whaling Commission in the 1950s: Injection of Uncertainty," SC/44/O, 1/6 1992, pp.13-38.

[31] In the 1962-63 whaling season, for instance, whaling nations used less then three-quarters of that year's IWC quota.

[32] Greenpeace International was founded in 1971. Today it has over 6 million members worldwide and over US$100 million in annual income.

[33] J. Takahashi, *op cit.*

[34] IWC had already banned the killing of the Antarctic blue whales in 1964 and the North Pacific blue whales in 1965. The fin whale came under protection in 1976 and the Antarctic sei and sperm whales in 1978. See William Aron, "The Commons Revisited: Thoughts on Marine Mammal Management," *Coastal Management*, Vol.16, 1988, p.100; and David Day, *The Whale War*, Vancouver and Toronto: Douglas and McIntyre, 1987.

[35] CITES prohibits the commercial trade of endangered species and restricts and monitors trade in other threatened species listed in its appendices. The Convention came into force in 1975 and today it has over 120 contracting parties. Species under Appendix I are considered endangered and all international trade of the species or its products is banned. By 1983 CITES had put all species of baleen whales under Appendix I. The blue whale and several other species have been placed in Appendix I since CITES' adoption in 1973. See Chikao Kimura, "Whaling and Trade," in *Public Perception of Whaling*, Tokyo: Institute of Cetacean Research, 1994, pp.40-2.

[36] The MSY formula is based on the population level at which the most effective reproductive condition can be achieved. If 100% is the unexploited level when there was no contact with man, 60% of that unexploited level is the MSY, and 4% of that is the allowable catch under NMP. All stocks were divided into three categories under NMP: Sustained Management Stocks (SMS), Initial Management Stocks (IMS) and Protection Stocks (PS). Commercial whaling would be permitted for SMS and IMS. Stocks with PS status would receive complete protection from commercial whaling until they recovered to near MSY stock levels and receive reclassification as SMS. See Andersen, *op cit.*, p.106.

[37] Misaki, *op cit.*, p.26.

[38] Sumi, *op cit.*, p.322.

[39] Bruce Cumings, "Japan's position in the world system," in *Postwar Japan as History*, ed. by Andrew Gordon, Berkeley, Los Angeles, Oxford: University of California Press, 1993, p.31.

[40] Greenpeace, the most prominent among them, helped many countries to prepare their application papers and paid their annual fees as well as travel, hotel and other expenses for the IWC annual meetings. Expert advisers from Greenpeace even sat on national delegations as official representatives for the governments of Antigua and the Seychelles. For these small island states, membership in IWC meant a cheap and high profile forum for international presence. See Leslie Spencer *et al.*, "The Not So Peaceful World of Greenpeace," *Forbes Magazine*, 11 November 1991, p.177; and Alf Hakon Hoel, *The International Whaling Commission, 1972-1984: New Members, New Concerns*, 2nd ed., Lysaker: The Fridtjof Nansen Institute, 1986, p.76.

[41] Arne Kalland and Brian Moeran, *Japanese Whaling: End of an Era?* Surrey: Curzon Press, 1992, pp.12-3.

[42] On the one hand, Article 62 of UNCLOS authorizes optimum utilization of living resources in the EEZ; on the other, Article 65 recognizes marine mammals as belonging to a special regime. Later discussion shows how the U.S. used this concept of EEZ to strengthen its domestic legislation on fisheries in order to compel other nations to give up commercial whaling. See the *United Nations Convention on Law of the Sea*, 1982.

[43] At that time, the Scientific Committee objected to the ASW allocation and recommended a zero quota since the stock was considered endangered. Bowhead quotas for Alaskan Inuit have risen over time. The ASW quota began with 12 animals landed (or 18 struck, whichever came first) in 1979. Today, there is an annual quota of 51 bowhead whales, or 68 strikes, whichever comes first. Present-day whalers in Greenland, too, qualify for minke and fin whale quotas under the ASW category. See "IWC Raises Whale Quota for North Alaskan Natives," *The Japan Times*, 28 May 1994; and U.S. Dept. of Commerce, National Oceanic and Atmospheric Administration, "The Marine Mammal Protection Act of 1972: Annual Report, 1 April 1977 to 31 March 1978," p.5.

[44] See Milton M.R. Freeman, "Economy, Equity and Ethics: Current Perspectives on Wildlife Management in the North," *Human Ecology: Issues in the North*, ed. Jill Oakes, Edmonton, Alberta: Canadian Circumpolar Institute and University of Alberta, 1995, p.9.

[45] Neither did the United Nations Food and Agriculture Organization support it for lack of scientific justification. See Andersen, *op cit.*, p.110.

[46] The Canadian government did not want to face another battle that could compromise the interests of its peoples whose livelihood depends on hunting wildlife. In the 1970s, its harp seal industry, which supported thousands of families, was crushed by conservationist campaigns that destroyed the market in Europe. The European Economic Community officially banned the import of white-coat pelts in 1983. The subsequent increase in the harp seal population also had some adverse effects on these animals and the region's ecology. See Janice Scott Henke, *Seal Wars: An American*

Viewpoint, Newfoundland: Breakwater, 1985; and Alan Herscovci, *Second Nature: The Animal Rights Controversy*, Montreal: CBC Enterprise, 1987, pp.21-23.

[47] The Norwegian government can legally set its own quotas since IWC now allocates a zero quota under the moratorium and Norway had filed a reservation. See "A Misguided Policy on Whaling," *The Chicago Tribune*, 24 May 1993.

[48] See Oran R. Young *et al.*, "Global Environmental Change and International Governance—Summary and Recommendations," New Hampshire: Darthmouth College, 1991, p.118.

[49] "One Man's Sacred Cow is Another's Big Mac: Does America's Policy Depend on Whose Whale is Gored?" *The New York Times*, 9 April 1985; and Price, *op cit.*

[50] See Alexander Gillespie, "The Ethical Question in the Whaling Debate," *The Georgetown International Environmental Law Review*, Vol.9, 1997, pp.359-360.

[51] Other reasons given were the lack of guidelines for surveys and analysis, an absence of a perfectly effective inspection and observer scheme, and the lack of a guarantee that all catch limits will not exceed the range specified by RMS.

[52] Fisheries Agency of Japan, "Summary of the Results of the 44th IWC," *Isana*, November 1992, pp.3-5; and *WWF (Japan) Monthly Magazine*, May 1995, p.7.

[53] "Review of the Moratorium," *Isabiri*, May 1995, pp.1-5.

[54] However, the Commission granted permission for the Makah tribe in the U.S. to hunt up to four gray whales annually under the aboriginal subsistence whaling category. See "A-whaling they will go," *The Economist*, 1 November 1997, p.28; and <<www.ourworld.compuserve.com/home-pages/iwcoffice/press98. htm>> Viewed on 3 June 1998.

[55] For instance, see Oran Young *et al.*, "Commentary: Subsistence, Sustainability, and Sea Mammals: Reconstructing the International Whaling Regime," *Ocean & Coastal Management*, No.23, 1994, pp.117-127; Arne Kalland, "Aboriginal Subsistence Whaling: A Concept in the Service of Imperialism?" *11 Essays on Whales and Man*, 2nd ed., Reine: High North Alliance, 1994, pp.5-11; and Milton M.R. Freeman, "The International Whaling Commission, Small-type Whaling and Coming to Terms with Subsistence," *Human Organization*, Vol.52, 1993, pp.243-51.

[56] Of course, there are also those who are against all "uses" of whales, including whale watching. See Milton M.R. Freeman, "Economy, Equity and Ethics: Current Perspectives on Wildlife Management in the North," in *Human Ecology: Issues in the North*, Jill Oakes, ed., Edmonton, Alberta: Canadian Circumpolar Institute and University of Alberta, 1995, p.6.

[57] The true size of this industry is in dispute. Conservationists estimated that it generated over US$300 million in income worldwide in 1992, but many tourism experts questioned its reliability because of complexities in calculation throughout the industry and in different parts of the world. See Elizabeth Kemf and Cassandra Phillips, "1995 WWF Species Status Report: Whales in the Wild," Gland: WWF International, May 1995, p.13.

[58] See Christine Ingebritsen, "Whales, or Save the Whales?" *Isana*, No.18, May 1998, pp.11-16.

[59] Japanese literature documented coastal whaling as early as 230 B.C. but it remained unorganized until the 1600s. See Gresser *et al.*, *op cit.*, p.371.

[60] Kalland and Moeran, *op cit.*, pp.65-66.

[61] See Sachiko Iwasaki, "*Kujira niku shoku wa Nihon no Dento Bunka ka?*" (Is eating whale meat traditional Japanese culture?"), Tokyo: Greenpeace (Japan), 1992, pp.3-4; and "Small-type coastal whaling in Japan: Report of an International Workshop," Alberta, Canada: Japan Social Sciences Association of Canada and Fund to Promote International Educational Exchange and Boreal Institute for Northern Studies, 1988, pp.10-17.

[62] U.S. whaling was at its height between 1820 and 1860, accounting for 80% of the world's total catch between 1840 and 1860.

[63] Kalland and Moeran, *op cit.*, p.71.

[64] John Manjiro, one of the first Japanese to be educated in the U.S. before the approval of overseas study by the Tokugawa shogunate, was rescued and taken to America by a U.S. whaling ship. After he returned to Japan, the Japanese government hired him to instruct Japanese whalers on modern whaling techniques used by the Americans.

[65] Kalland and Moeran, *op cit.*, p.76.

[66] Japanese whalers who had worked on Russian whaling ships using the Norwegian method were hired as gunners. *Ibid.*

[67] Toshio Takahashi, "Nihon no Hogei" (Japanese Whaling), Tokyo: Greenpeace (Japan), 31 March 1994, p.14.

[68] Toyo Gyogyo was first named Japan Oceanic Fishing Company. It became Toyo Hogei in 1909 after its merger with other whaling companies. See Sumi, *op cit.*, pp.356-7.

[69] See Kalland and Moeran, *op cit.*, p.78; T. Takahashi, *op cit.*, p.14; and Gresser *et al.*, *op cit.*, p.371.

[70] The number of licenses was reduced to 25 in 1938. See Kalland and Moeran, *op cit.*, pp.78-79; and Gresser *et al.*, *op cit.*, p.371.

[71] While new technologies have been adopted, the social and economic structure, religious rites and ideological beliefs associated with STCW whaling have not changed much over time. For a detailed study, read Kalland and Moeran, *ibid.*

Whaling

[72] Japanese industrial whaling was less dependent on the world market for whale oil and spermaceti because it had a domestic market for whale meat. Meanwhile, discoveries of crude oil and other substitutes made whaling no longer profitable for Western whalers.

[73] S. Iwasaki, *op cit.*, p.7.

[74] Simba Chan *et al.*, "Observations on the Whale Meat Trade in East Asia," *TRAFFIC East Asia*, May 1995, pp.3-4.

[75] Kalland and Moeran, *op cit.*, pp.89-90. For more on the importance of whale meat as a source of protein to Japan, see Yutaka Hirasawa, "The Whaling Industry in Japan's Economy," in *The Whaling Issue in U.S.-Japan Relations*, ed. John R. Schmidhauser and George O. Totten III, Boulder: Westview Press, 1978, pp.82-114.

[76] The high price of whale meat today is due mainly to supply shortages, and not because of its appeal as a delicacy as many anti-whaling activists have claimed.

[77] Importing beef and raising cattle were both too expensive for Japan in those years.

[78] See S. Iwasaki, *op cit.*, p.8. Whale fat, too, was added to milk served in public schools as a dietary supplement until about the same time. Some critics had alleged that the Japanese government promoted whale meat consumption to foster nationalism, but there is no substantive evidence to support this claim.

[79] The leading pre-war whaling companies, Nihon Suisan (or Nissui), Taiyo and Kyokuyo, quickly re-established and became the only companies licensed by the Japanese government to hunt whales in the Antarctic. Simon Ward, *Biological Samples and Balance Sheets*, Tokyo: Institute of Cetacean Research, 1990, p.10.

[80] This was the time of "Olympic whaling" when quotas were not stocks, species or country specific. A single annual quota in volume was given and the whaling season ended when the volume was reached. Hence, it was logical to have as much tonnage as possible to maximize catch in the face of intensive competition.

[81] Ward, *op cit.*

[82] Around 15,000 more were employed in STCW. Interview with Misaki, December 1994.

[83] The moratorium has been applied to minke whales since they fall under the auspices of IWC, but STCW hunts of small cetaceans not protected by IWC, such as Baird's beaked whales, continue and are regulated by the Japanese government. See "WWF Slams Whaling," *The Japan Times*, 16 April 1995, p.2.

[84] ICR was formed as a non-profit organization in 1987 specifically to oversee Japan's research whaling program. Start-up funding for ICR came from Kyodo Senpaku, the Fisheries Agency, and private donations. Since then support mainly depends on annual grants from the Fisheries Agency

138   *The Roots of Japan's Environmental Policy*

and proceeds from the sale of by-products from Japanese research whaling. ICR also carries out the annual sighting surveys—the Southern Minke Whale Assessment Cruises—that Japan has conducted since 1987 as one of its contributions to IWC for the International Decade of Cetacean Research. See Ward, *op cit.*, pp.10, 14, 16 and 30; and "The Research on the Whale Stock in the Antarctic: The Result of the Preliminary Study in 1987/88," Tokyo: Institute of Cetacean Research, 1989.

[85] "Whale sanctuary is approved," *The Japan Times*, 28 May 1994.

[86] In the first year, 21 minke whales were caught and 100 animals in 1995. See "Review of the Moratorium," *Isabiri*, May 1995, pp.1-5.

[87] Between 1986 and 1994, Japan presented 33 papers to IWC. These were written by 23 social scientists from 8 countries to document the cultural aspects of Japanese STCW. See Kalland, "Facing the `World': Japan...," *op cit.*

[88] Arne Kalland, "Some Reflections after the Sendai `Workshop'," *Isana*, No.16, June 1997, p.12.

[89] *Ibid.*

[90] Japan officially banned import of whale meat from non-IWC countries as of 6 July 1979. Whale meat imports from Korea, Peru, Spain and Brazil stopped in 1986, followed by imports from Russia and Norway in 1989 and finally, from Iceland in 1991. See "Nihon ni ogeru kujira niku ryuutsuu kanri ni tsuite" (Managing the Import of Whale Meat to Japan), Tokyo: Institute of Cetacean Research, n.d.; and Day, *op cit.*, p.62.

[91] Anti-whaling groups have repeatedly alleged the presence of illegally imported whale meat in the Japanese market. The Japanese government has confiscated some illegal whale meat imports over the years but denies that the problem is rampant. See Chan *et al.*, *op cit.*

[92] At the same meeting, Norway proposed a downlisting of the Northeastern and North Atlantic Central stocks of minke whales from Appendix I to Appendix II. Although the motion was defeated, the number of affirmative votes has increased significantly with the introduction of secret ballots. When open ballots were used in the 1994 CITES meeting, there were only 16 yes votes against 48 no votes and 52 abstentions. At the Zimbabwe meeting, there were 57 votes in favor of the Norwegian proposal, 51 against and only 6 abstentions.

[93] It has also been suggested that the U.S. government chose to support the anti-whaling cause at this time in order to deflect international criticisms for its use of chemical defoliants and other actions in Vietnam. See for example, J. Takahashi, *op cit.*, p.147.

[94] Many old treaties with native Americans require the U.S. government to respect their right to hunt for traditional or nutritional needs, but the Secretary of Commerce can end this native exemption if taking animals "endangers, depletes, or inhibits the restoration of depleted or endangered

Whaling

stocks." See U.S. Department of Commerce, "The Marine Mammal Protection Act of 1972...," *op cit.*, pp.2 and 30.

[95] Boynton, *op cit.*

[96] Actually, the Act covered not just endangered species, but all species of whales.

[97] U.S. Department of Commerce, "The Marine Mammal Protection Act of 1972...," *op cit.*, p.30.

[98] The Pelly Amendment was initially enacted by Congress in 1971 following unsuccessful U.S. efforts to persuade Denmark, Norway, and West Germany to comply with the ban on high seas salmon fishing decided by the International Commission for the Northwest Atlantic Fisheries. All three countries agreed to phase out their salmon fishing after the Amendment became law. See Steven Charnovitz, "Environmental trade sanctions and the GATT" in *11 Additional Essays...*, *op cit.*, p.30.

[99] Boynton, *op cit.*

[100] Dean M. Wilkinson, "The Use of Domestic Measures to Enforce International Whaling Agreements: A Critical Perspective," *Denver Journal of International Law and Policy*, Vol.17, No.2, 1989, pp.282-3.

[101] The Magnuson Fishery Conservation and Management Act was passed in 1976 to protect U.S. fisheries interests. See Charnovitz, *op cit.*, p.31.

[102] Gene S.Martin, Jr. and James W. Brennan, "Enforcing the International Convention for the Regulation of Whaling: The Pelly and Packwood-Magnuson Amendment," *Denver Journal of International Law and Policy*, Vol.17, No.2, 1989, pp.294-298.

[103] *Ibid.*, pp.293-315.

[104] See Wilkinson, *op cit.*, pp.281-2.

[105] The Icelandic government tried to use the North Atlantic Treaty Organization's base in Keflavik to bargain with the U.S. See Wilkinson, *op cit.*, p.288; and C. Kimura, *op cit.*

[106] Since Alaskan Inuit receive an annual IWC quota of 51 bowhead whales for the same reason, Canada indicated that if sanctions were applied, it would challenge the U.S. decision before the World Trade Organization. See *Isabiri*, October 1993, pp.7-10; and INWR Digest, No.12, January 1997, p.2.

[107] Charnovitz, *op cit.*, p.31.

[108] Charnovitz, *ibid.*, p.31; Young *et al.*, "Commentary...," *op cit.*, pp.125-127; and "Review of the Moratorium," *op cit.*

[109] Interview at the Japan Whaling Association.

[110] Interview with Iino.

[111] As expected, U.S. fisheries exports to Japan grew exponentially after Japanese fishing stopped in the U.S. EEZ in 1988. For example, U.S. exports of *surimi* (minced fish meat for fish cake production) alone leaped

from 66,000 tons in 1982 to 340,000 tons in 1983, 430,000 tons in 1984 and 740,000 tons in 1986.

[112] The Agreement was signed between U.S. Secretary of Commerce Malcolm Baldrige and Charge d'Affairs Yasushi Murazumi of the Japanese Embassy in Washington, D.C.

[113] U.S. environmental groups challenged the legality of the agreement in a suit against the U.S. government that went all the way to the Supreme Court. Though the plaintiffs won in the district and appellate courts, they were defeated in the Supreme Court. See Martin and Brennan, *op cit.*, p.287; and Sumi, *op cit.*, pp.356-7.

[114] The entire Japanese whaling industry was worth barely one billion yen annually. IWC quota cuts throughout the 1960s and 1970s had already greatly diminished the size of the industry. Domestic economic prosperity, too, had reduced the importance of whale meat as a cheap source of animal protein.

[115] Per capita consumption of fish and marine products in Japan is the second highest in the world after Iceland. "Marine Products," *Japan Almanac 1995*, Tokyo: Asahi Shimbun, 1996, p.137.

[116] In the early 1990s, even after Japan lost its fishing rights in U.S. waters, Japanese fisheries satisfied two-thirds of the national demand for fish and other marine products and the rest was imported. *Ibid.*

[117] *Ibid.*, p.139.

[118] Interviews with Yonezawa, Iino, Shima and Komatsu.

[119] Asako Murakami, "Whale Sanctuary Fight Looms," *The Japan . Times*, 6 April 1994.

[120] Interview with Yonezawa.

[121] *Ibid.*

[122] In fact, the Japanese ideograph for whale "kujira" contains the radical for fish. So even if people are conscious of whales being marine mammals, whales are conventionally perceived as another fish from the ocean, though a much bigger one.

[123] IWC was one of the first multilateral organizations to admit NGOs as observers. In 1965 there were only 5 groups. By 1978 there were observers from 24 international organizations and most were anti-whaling conservationist groups. The number grew to 30 groups in 1980. From then on, some 50 NGOs have sat as observers in each year's IWC meeting, with the majority coming from the U.S. and Britain. See Andersen, *op cit.*, p.109.

[124] These groups lobbied national governments, like those of the U.S., Britain and the Netherlands, to embrace anti-whaling policies internationally and domestically, and to use bilateral economic sanctions and other forms of leverage to force other countries to give up whaling. For example, U.S. domestic legislation was used against Japan, Norway, Iceland, Canada and the former Soviet Union. Britain also threatened Norway with trade

Whaling

141

sanctions when the latter announced that it would resume commercial whaling in 1993.

[125] The law also requires the MAFF minister to consider the conservation of whale stocks. Japan is not alone in having this kind of arrangement. Since the history of whale fisheries preceded whale conservation, most other governments of countries that practiced commercial whaling had also placed whaling and whale conservation under the control of their fisheries departments. The end of whaling has not always shifted responsibilities for whales to environment ministries.

[126] Interview with Sano.

[127] Interview with Wada.

[128] Takeshi Hara, *Za Kujira: Umi ni Utsutta Nihonjin* (Whales! Japanese People Reflected in the Sea), new ed., Tokyo: Bunshindo, 1987, p.367; and Shiba, *op cit.*, p.23.

[129] Shiba, *ibid.*, p.29.

[130] Based on personal interviews in 1995 with several officials in the Fisheries Agency and the MoFA who had worked closely on this issue at the time. The same was reported in many Japan and English language publications. See for instance, see Shiba, *ibid.*; and Sumi, *op cit.*

[131] Interview with Iino.

[132] Interview with Sano.

[133] Interview with Iino.

[134] The Fisheries Agency was right. In 1984 when the Murazumi-Baldrige Agreement was made, Japan's fishing quota in the U.S. EEZ was 1.15 million tons. Drastic cuts reduced it to 900,000 tons in 1995, then 470,000 tons in 1986 and only 75,000 tons in 1987. By 1988 Japanese fishing terminated in U.S. waters. Interview with Sano; and Shiba, *op cit.*, p.10.

[135] It is interesting to note that no Japanese politician has explicitly spoken out against whaling. This phenomenon may be explained by the fact that whale conservation, like most other international environmental issues, had little importance in the political agendas of national politicians. Unlike politicians in countries having strong anti-whaling sentiment, opposing whaling would not earn them "green points" from their constituents.

[136] The first call to establish The Parliamentary League in Support of Whaling came from LDP Diet members from the traditional STCW towns of Taiji and Wakayama. Interview with Wada.

[137] After all, the biggest anti-whaling nations and the strongest anti-whaling conservationist groups were from the West.

[138] Following this, Diet members from other political parties also formed their own study groups and individuals declared their support for whaling. Their reasons and background were largely similar to those in the LDP League.

[139] Interview with Sano.

142   *The Roots of Japan's Environmental Policy*

[140] Shiba, *op cit.*, pp.24-25.

[141] Interview with Wada.

[142] In the United States, WWF uses the name World Wildlife Fund for Nature.

[143] The plaintiff won at the district and appellate court levels, but lost in a 5-4 decision at the Supreme Court in June 1986. This came to be known as the "whale war." See Martin and Brennan, *op cit.*, pp.287-290.

[144] Accusations of barbarism, cruelty and selfishness were common. On a few occasions, official Japanese delegates to IWC meetings were even pelted with rotten foods and spit on.

[145] Interview with Sakurai of Greenpeace (Japan).

[146] For instance, none of these foreign campaigners spoke Japanese. No Japanese language materials were ever prepared for distribution, nor did they investigate how to build popular support in Japan by working with Japanese conservationist groups. Interviews with Kamei and Sakurai of Greenpeace.

[147] The Greenpeace Japan Mission lasted six months, during which activists for walrus and dolphin protection gave public speeches and a rock concert was held. Several of the anti-whaling Japanese campaigners interviewed shared this background.

[148] Interviews with Sakurai of WWF (Japan) and Kamei.

[149] Interview with Obara.

[150] A televised debate was held between the head of the Japanese delegation to the IWC at the time and a conservation advocate.

[151] Interview with Akasaka.

[152] Interview with Kamei.

[153] Interviews with Kamei and Sakurai of Greenpeace (Japan).

[154] For instance, see Chan, *op cit.*

[155] Interview with Sakurai of Greenpeace (Japan).

[156] For instance, FoE (Japan) and WWF (Japan) made their last public statements on whaling in 1993 when the IWC meeting was held in Kyoto, while Greenpeace (Japan) carried out *Kujira Kaiyu* (Whale Migration), its only major anti-whaling campaign, in 1988 to protest the launching of Japanese research whaling. Interviews with Kamei and Sakurai of WWF (Japan).

[157] Interview with Funahashi.

[158] Its campaigner for whaling saw this as a key reason for difficulties in recruiting members in Japan. The Greenpeace (Japan) office opened in 1989 and only had around 2,300 members by 1995. To remedy this, all whaling-related activities are now set within the context of ecosystem protection and the office has shifted to focus on issues that would have greater appeal to the Japanese public, such as nuclear energy. Interview with Sakurai of Greenpeace (Japan).

[159] Interview with Akasaka.

Whaling   143

[160] For instance, whale-watching operators often come from outside the community so that the whale-watching does not always create jobs for former whalers and their families. Furthermore, not all types of whales are suitable for whale-watching. Most coastal whaling communities are small, remote, and lack infrastructure to develop tourism. Some may not even want to depend on visitors to sustain their local economy. Finally, whaling may help to perpetuate certain traditions and social, cultural and ideological values that money income alone cannot provide.

[161] Interview with Iino.

[162] Interview with Sano.

[163] Japanese whaling companies, with a paternalistic management philosophy like most Japanese businesses, could not simply dismiss their employees.

[164] For instance, see K. Bradsher, "Japan won't hunt whales, Miyazawa says," *The New York Times*, 3 July 1992.

[165] U.S. negotiators knew the same and were not unsympathetic to the plight of the Japanese negotiators or the frustrations of the Japanese fishing and whaling industries. As a result, they did not demand a complete capitulation for the Japanese who negotiated under such difficult circumstances.

[166] Interviews with Iino and Saito.

CHAPTER 5

Deforestation in the Tropics

Tropical forests have always served to satisfy human needs for timber, land, and other resources, but their rapid destruction in the last several decades and the adverse effects on ecology and human communities have become too glaring to ignore. The United Nations Food and Agriculture Organization (FAO) in 1990 estimated that only 1,700 million hectares (ha) of tropical forests remains worldwide, and annual deforestation since 1980 is 17 million ha.[1] Yet, this is a conservative figure because it does not include forest degradation, which is estimated to be an additional 4.3 million hectares of previously undisturbed forests each year. If these rates continue, there may be no tropical forests left in another 30 to 40 years.[2]

This alarming scenario catalyzed conservationists in many parts of the world to push this problem to the fore of the international environmental agenda. International campaigns to halt the destruction of tropical forests began full force in the mid-1980s. The long battle to end commercial whaling and the passing of the International Whaling Commission (IWC) moratorium a few years earlier gave confidence to those behind this cause.

TROPICAL FORESTS: TIMBER SOURCE, BIODIVERSITY STOREHOUSE, CARBON SINK AND A HOME TO MANY

Timber has long been the principal reason for the exploitation of forests. Although all forests throughout the world face various threats of destruction, those in the tropics, in particular, are disappearing at alarmingly high rates as a consequence of rapid and systematic destruction. Timber logging is one of the main causes and forest lands devoid of commercial timber are often transformed into plantation estates. In Indonesia, more than 17 million hectares of forests have been cleared since 1985. In Malaysia, oil palm plantation area grew from 600,000 ha in 1985 to over 2.2 million ha by the mid-1990s; and another 3.3 million ha will be developed in the next two to three years. Logging also opens forests to shifting agriculture, and

145

slash-and-burn farming can produce huge forest fires, such as those that burned for months and destroyed around 3 million ha in Kalimantan in 1997.[3] Smoke from the fires blanketed Singapore and parts of peninsular Malaysia, affecting human health and local atmospheric conditions.

Although the tropical timber trade represents only approximately 4 percent of all timber cuts, these are the most commercially valuable logs and they drive the industry's growth.[4] Exports of tropical hardwood from the principal producing countries grew from an annual average of 2.8 million cubic meters during the period from 1946 to 1950 to 66.6 million cubic meters during 1976 to 1980, or by a factor of 24. Global demand for tropical hardwood was driven primarily by post-World War II economic expansion in the United States, Japan, and Western Europe.

The introduction of new mechanized logging and timber transport technology has exacerbated the pace of forest destruction. Species and areas that are previously considered untenable are now exploited. Improvements in plywood manufacturing and pulping technology also allow a larger variety of tropical hardwoods to be used.[5]

Tropical forests are the richest banks of biological diversity. Covering about 5 percent of the earth's surface, they contain at least 50 percent of all plant and animal species.[6] They also play an important role in the regulation of climatic and hydrological cycles. Water-shed degradation, including loss of soil cover and water in catchment areas, flooding, and siltation of dams and irrigation systems, can all result from deforestation.

Tropical forests are also nature's sinks for carbon dioxide (CO_2), a greenhouse gas that contributes to global warming. The clearing and burning of forests have significant effects on CO_2 levels in the atmosphere. An FAO report estimated that forest destruction represents about 25 percent of global CO_2 emission. The table below shows that forest destruction in Asia is responsible for releasing an estimated 621 million tons of CO_2 into the atmosphere in 1980, or 37 percent of global carbon emissions.[7]

Deforestation in the Tropics

Table 6. Estimated net release of carbon to the atmosphere by tropical deforestation, by region, 1980

Region	Forest Cover	Estimated Net Carbon Release	Share of Total Carbon Release
	(million hectares)	(million tons)	(percent)
Tropical America	1,212	665	40
Tropical Asia	445	321	37
Tropical Africa	2,969	1,659	100

Notes: Releases from tropical Asia are nearly as high as from tropical America (despite a much smaller forest area) not because of a higher deforestation rate but because a hectare of moist tropical forest in Asia contains more carbon than a hectare of tropical forest in Latin America.
Sources: R.A. Houghton *et al.,* "The flux of Carbon from Terrestrial Ecosystems to the Atmosphere in 1980 Due to Changes inLand Use: Geographic Distribution of the Global Flux," Tellus, February/April 1987; Tropical Forest Resources, Forestry Paper 30, 1982.

Finally, deforestation affects forest communities, indigenous cultures, migration patterns and poverty. Between 50 to 140 million people live within or on the margins of forests and rely on them for fuel, food, and raw materials for clothing, buildings, and medicines. Of this population, approximately one million are hunter-gatherers who have a vast and irreplaceable knowledge of the forests in which they live.[8]

Tropical deforestation and Japan's policy responses.

Japan's connection to the tropical deforestation problem can basically be summed up in one fact: it is the world's single largest importer of tropical hardwood. Its demand for this resource drives commercial logging; hence, the destruction of tropical forest. Although Japanese consumption of this tropical timber has fallen in volume and as a share of the world's total, it still consumes a third of all raw logs, a fifth of the plywood and nearly three quarters of the wood chips traded internationally.[9] Also important to understanding the ramifications of Japan's place in this issue is that until recently Southeast Asia supplied nearly all of Japan's tropical hardwood imports.

While Southeast Asia contains only about a quarter of the world's tropical forests, it is the source of two-thirds of all tropical timber and wood products traded in the world market.[10] The international trade in tropical timber is valued at more than US$8 billion per year.[11] Today Malaysia is the world's top exporter of tropical hardwood logs and veneer, and Indonesia accounts for over half of the world's export of veneer and plywood.

Japan's involvement in tropical forest destruction goes beyond its role as a consumer. Japanese money and technology from government and private sources funded the rapid expansion of commercial logging throughout Southeast Asia in the last 50 years. While Japan reforested its own barren hills to recover from a century of extensive domestic logging, the forests of neighboring countries became its chief source for timber and other wood products. The comparative advantages in cost and quality—and considerations of environmental impact—simply made it more sensible to buy logs from Southeast Asia than to tap its own domestic timber resources.[12] Hence, as Japan's forests recovered, its domestic self-sufficiency rate in timber actually declined, dropping to only 25 percent in 1992. This trend is reflected in the figure below.

Figure 6. Shifts in Japan's consumption of domestic and imported timber and wood materials, 1986-1992

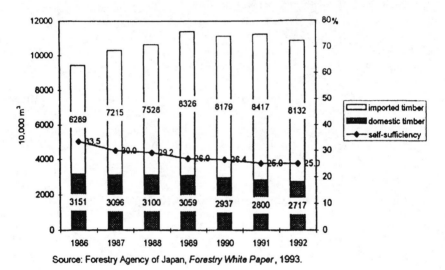

Source: *Forestry White Paper of Japan 1993.*

Japan is not the first or only country to exploit foreign resources and inflict environmental damage overseas. However, how Japan exploits and uses timber resource have drawn attacks from many critics. Tropical hardwood were wastefully used as *konpane* or wood molds/forms, logging and reforestation projects produced wood chips and pulp to feed Japanese paper mills, and Japanese general trading companies (GTCs), or *sogo sosha*, have played a big role in commercial logging throughout the region.

Konpane is the largest end-product issue for most conservation groups in their criticisms of Japan. Around 84 percent of all tropical timber imported by Japan is turned into plywood, and 50 percent of this is used as *konpane* for concrete molds in construction.[13] *Konpane* in Japan also has a much lower recycling rate than in other countries for reasons of architectural style and costs. In large and regular structures, plywood can be reused five to seven times, but wood forms can only be used once for the small and irregular structures that are common in Japan. Furthermore, most wood forms end up in furnaces or landfills because of high storage and transportation costs. Japanese demand for cosmetic quality also discourages reuse and practical difficulties deter recycling of wood forms into paper and pasteboards.[14]

As for wood chips and pulp, Japan is the world's second largest consumer of pulp and paper after the United States and it ranks fourth in terms of per capita paper consumption.[15] Japanese consumption of wood pulp and paper first soared in the 1960s and again in the 1980s due to rapid domestic economic expansion. To diversify their sources of wood chips and pulp, Japanese companies buy mangrove chips from Southeast Asia and have introduced in reforestation projects fast-growing non-indigenous species that are favored by the paper industry. This exploitation of wetlands and its consequent ecological damage have also provoked outcries from conservation groups.[16] Forest protection activists also complain about the preference for commercially valuable species that favored by the pulp and paper industry over indigenous ones in Japanese reforestation projects. Furthermore, the Japanese government has emphasized paper recycling over consumption reduction in the domestic market.[17] Critics consider this inadequate in working to Japanese demand for wood chips and paper pulp.

Japanese GTCs control virtually the entire timber import trade, including tropical timber and all other kinds of wood-related products. Their investments were critical to building commercial logging in Southeast Asia. As timber resources in one country diminish, Japanese capital moves elsewhere. This pattern has repeated itself several times over. The Philippines, for instance, was Japan's largest tropical timber source until the 1960s when decimation of its forests by logging had reduced its potential as a long-term supplier of logs. At this point, Japanese capital shifted to Indonesia. Today, the Philippines is a net timber importer, and it may never fully recover from the environmental, social, and economic effects of a century of indiscriminate logging.[18]

Therefore, conservationists hold Japan significantly responsible for deforestation in the tropics, most especially in Southeast Asia, and they want Japan to assume a major role in responding to this problem. Although both whaling and logging are resource issues for Japan, deforestation in the tropics is a more multifaceted issue and involves several large bureaucratic actors as well as big Japanese businesses. No single policy actor dominates and there is no truly united and coherent policy or guideline. Therefore, this case study focuses on two key areas in Japanese policy responses. The first is Japan's ODA for forest conservation in the tropics; and second, Japan's decision to host ITTO. They are indicative of the growing importance of international environmental issues in Japanese diplomacy and Japan's basic position and approach to the problem of deforestation in the tropics (and elsewhere). Furthermore, these decisions look like the advent of new thinking and policies; in reality, they perpetuate traditional perspectives towards resource use and conservation.

THE INTERNATIONAL REGIME FOR THE CONSERVATION OF FORESTS IN THE TROPICS

Tropical forest destruction made its way up the international environmental agenda as understanding deepened on the severity of the problem and its linkages to other environmental and development issues. Ascertaining the scale of the problem was the first critical task. An FAO and United Nations Environment Program (UNEP) tropical forest report in 1982 estimated that 7.5 million ha of tropical moist forest and 3.8 million ha of open forests are cleared annually. FAO estimated in 1985 that 11.3 million ha of tropical forest is lost annually. Refinement in information and estimating techniques prompted FAO to raise the figure in 1990 to 17 million ha for the 1981-1990 period.

Many conservationists consider these numbers too low if forest degradation is fully accounted for, but these figures were alarming enough to raise international awareness of the problem and to persuade national governments and international organizations of the need for immediate action. International concern for the future of tropical forests also intensified during the 1980s because of deeper understanding of the linkages of this issue to other international environmental and development issues, including biological diversity, the rights of indigenous and forest peoples, global warming, and economics and politics of the environment.

The evolution of an international regime in response to deforestation in the tropics thus began with this first step of worldwide recognition of tropical forest destruction as an international environmental issue. The next task was to define the causes of the problem and to set it in a framework or context for discussion.

The causes of tropical forest destruction are manifold and vary from region to region. Shifting agriculture, logging, and plantation agriculture are those most often blamed but opinions differ among the various interest groups and policy actors. Conservation groups point to commercial logging, large-scale infrastructure and industrial projects, and socio-economic inequities. For them it is ultimately the failure to manage forest effectively at local, national, and international levels that produces the many negative social and environmental effects of tropical forest destruction.[19] These include national policies on forestry, population growth, migration, and economic development, as well as changes in international trade consumption patterns.[20]

Deforestation in the Tropics

Governments in the tropics, in contrast, generally identify poverty as the main cause of forest destruction. From their perspective, commercial logging can degrade a forest, but lack of national economic development is the true cause of forest destruction. Destitution drives migration into forest land, encourages shifting agriculture, and the conversion of forest land for food production. Poverty also forces people to depend on wood as fuel since they cannot afford alternative energy sources—as in the developed countries. Hence, from their perspective, commercial logging and converting forests to other economic uses are inevitable evils. These activities are expected to produce jobs, income, and revenue for the state to pursue development goals that aim to improve the quality of life and benefit the environment in the long-term.

This difference in perception of the problem is largely responsible for different policy orientations and preferred responses. Conservation proponents agree that any true solution would rely on mediating competing economic, social, and environmental demands in addressing the issue, particularly with shifts in the development paradigm. For governments in the tropics—most of them developing nations—priority lies in defending national sovereign rights to access and exploit forests in order to realize their national development agendas. This is why some governments have questioned calls for sustainable management and conservation of tropical forests by international organizations, industrialized nations, and conservation groups. They consider these calls as disguises to undermine the sovereignty and development goals of developing nations. Others allege that this is a tactic used by softwood timber exporting countries to suppress the tropical timber trade. Since softwood timber exports are from temperate and boreal forests that are found mainly in the industrial economies and tropical timber are mainly in developing countries, debates about tropical forest conservation has a strong North-South overtone.[21]

For example, many developing countries supported Malaysia's demand for compensation from developed countries for losses that tropical forest countries might suffer from compliance with any convention that would restrict their sovereign rights to forest and resources at a preparatory meeting for the United Nations Conference on Environment and Development (UNCED) in March 1991. Malaysia also called on the UNCED secretariat to provide more information on the importance and rate of loss of both tropical and temperate forests in an attempt to thwart the adoption of any agreement that would bias against the interests of tropical forest countries.[22]

Conflicts persist over definition of the problem and the appropriate policy responses, but at least the broad consensus today is that saving forests in the tropics means more than declaring nature reserves. Tropical forests are a home for many people. They cannot be thrown out of the forests and their needs cannot be denied. Neither can the timber trade simply be stopped (as in whaling) because the consumptive need for timber and non-wood products from forests cannot be extinguished or be fully replaced. Moreover, unlike whales, tropical forests are not global commons.

Therefore, the general consensus among producers, consumers, and conservationists is to achieve, at least, sustainable management and use of tropical timber. This could be realized by a variety of measures, including greater attention to sustainability concerns in national forest and forestry policies, improvements in forestry techniques, and greater efficiency in timber processing, use and recycling. Implementing certification and eco-labeling schemes, adding economic value to non-timber forest products, and correcting barriers and flaws in international trade regimes, including the General Agreement on Tariffs and Trade and the World Trade Organization, could also benefit forest conservation.

No single institution resembling IWC, the international organ chiefly responsible for whaling, oversees the conservation and exploitation of tropical timber until the establishment of ITTO. Other major responses are FAO's Tropical Forest Action Plan, certification and eco-labeling schemes, and the UNCED Forest Principles.

The International Tropical Timber Organization (ITTO).

The International Tropical Timber Agreement (ITTA) was conceived as a commodity agreement by the United Nations Conference on Trade and Development (UNCTAD) and ITTO was established to implement the agreement, which came into force on 1 April 1985.[23] ITTA is the only major international commodity agreement that includes conservation as a main objective, noting in its preamble that it

> Recogniz[es] the importance of, and the need for, proper and effective conservation and development of tropical timber forests with a view to ensuring their optimum utilization while maintaining the ecological balance of the regions concerned and of the biosphere [and that the ITTA should] encourage the development of national policies aimed at sustainable utilization and conservation of tropical forests and their genetic resources at maintaining ecological balance in the regions concerned.[24]

Today the organization's 53 member states include both producer and consumer countries. Together they represent 75 percent of tropical forests worldwide and 90 percent of the legal international trade in tropical timber.[25] ITTO was intended by its creators to provide structural equality for North-South dialogue between tropical timber producer and consumer countries for the sustainable management and conservation of tropical

Deforestation in the Tropics

forests. It was also to be a forum for direct interaction among foresters, government officials responsible for forest policies and trade, as well as business and the conservation community.[26]

The 8th Council Meeting of ITTO in 1990 adopted a set of guidelines for sustainable tropical forest management and decided that all internationally traded timber should come from sustainably managed forest by the year 2000. This means that the international timber trade should not produce net deforestation in the tropics by the year 2000. This "Target 2000" was later renamed "Objective 2000" in the 1994 ITTA because of objection from tropical timber producer countries. The tropical forest countries, which are mainly developing ones, felt discriminated against because measures towards achieving this goal only targeted them. They point out that temperate forest countries, mainly developed ones and consumers of tropical timber, are not subjected to similar standards in their forest management practices.[27]

In fact, competition from softwood exporters was a major point of contention in negotiations for a new ITTA in 1991. Tropical forest countries wanted the new ITTA to cover all kinds of timber, but the temperate forest countries strongly opposed it.[28] Most conservation groups supported this demand by tropical forest countries because use of temperate softwoods as substitutes for tropical hardwoods was increasing rapidly. They also believed that deforestation in the tropics could not be isolated from destruction of other types of forests. Hence, a proposal was made to expand ITTO's coverage to all types of forests, thus, becoming an International Timber Organization (ITO).[29] This proposal exacerbated tensions between tropical forest countries and temperate forest countries.

Conclusion of the new ITTA was possible in 1994 only after tropical forest countries dropped this proposal and pledged to adopt specific policies by the year 2000 to better conserve their forest resources. In exchange for this concession from tropical forest countries, temperate forest countries pledged that they, too, would adopt appropriate guidelines and criteria for sustainable forest management of their forests. Developed countries also agreed to provide financial assistance to developing countries, including appropriate resources for forest conservation programs.[30]

Critics of ITTO see many problems with the organization. First, ITTO appears more focused on timber trade issues and on the quantities of standing stocks than on the qualitative aspects of forests and forest management. Second, ITTO's impact on the tropical timber trade and sustainable forest management may be too narrow when only 1 percent to 4 percent of all timber from tropical forests is traded internationally.[31] Third, emphasis on the timber trade makes ITTO more concerned about national than global (such as global warming and biological diversity) and local interests (such as forest peoples and local small-scale farmers) in forest conservation. Fourth, ITTO has failed to implement its own guidelines for sustainable management in tropical forests at the domestic level.[32] This is evident in Sarawak, Malaysia, where ITTO has made great efforts to improve forest management practices, but logging there proceeds at a far higher rate than ITTO's recommended limits.[33]

ITTO failure to compel broad-scale translation of Council-level decisions in the national forest management, trade, and official development assistance policies of its member states, significantly hampers the organization's ability to demonstrate progress that its members might have made in moving towards sustainable forest management in the tropics. This failure has also denied ITTO an effective basis for a greater mobilization of international resources to advance sustainable forest management and conservation practices in its producer member countries.[34]

Conservation groups have also attacked ITTO for over emphasizing projects at the expense of policy debate. For example, insufficient attention has been given to issues such as market transparency, internalization of costs, the illegal timber trade, and pricing in trade-related matters. Closer cooperation between ITTO and other international organizations is also recommended to address the many facets of sustainable forest management and conservation. This includes working with FAO, UNEP, and the World Bank on forest management projects; collaborating with the World Bank, the International Monetary Fund, the European Community, and the Global Environment Facility to mobilize funding; coordinating with the Biodiversity Convention and the Convention on the International Trade of Endangered Species of Fauna and Flora (CITES) to protect endangered species; and consulting the Forest Stewardship Council on eco-labeling.[35]

Finally, ITTO's voting system has been faulted for encouraging tropical forest destruction. Since vote allocation depends on the amount of timber traded, the biggest producers and consumers have the greatest leverage in the organization. This crowds out minority voices that may favor greater attention to conservation issues over mere improvements in logging techniques and terms of trade.[36]

The root of many of these weaknesses can be traced to the origin of ITTA as a commodity agreement. When it was conceptualized in the 1970s, the development paradigm reigned supreme in the minds of most policy makers in developing and developed countries alike. Nature was a commodity, or at least the source of commodities, and it was valued for the ways it serves economic activities. As a result, price stabilization and free trade of key commodities, such as energy, minerals, and timber, were the top concerns. Changes in international perspectives towards the environment and the development paradigm in the 1980s made the *raison d'etre* and work of ITTA and ITTO appear unprogressive and contradictory to the goals of conservation in the 1990s. (Like the International Convention on the Regulation of Whaling (ICRW) and the International Whaling Commission (IWC) today.)

Deforestation in the Tropics

Tropical Forestry Action Plan (TFAP).

FAO launched TFAP in 1985 to mobilize international action to protect tropical forest and as a coordinating mechanism for the funding process.[37] Nearly a hundred countries, representing 85 percent of the world's moist tropical forest area, have joined the procedures to formulate National Forestry Action Plans.[38]

TFAP received broad endorsement and some US$8 billion in contributions from national governments and the international donor community. Although the Plan succeeded in making improvements in coordinating the funding of forestry projects by governments of tropical countries and development aid agencies, it has been also severely criticized for its many shortcomings.[39] For instance, the greatest sums have been allocated for commercial forestry and wood-based industries, while conservation and protected areas management received barely 9 percent of total disbursements. This has prompted many non-governmental groups to call for a moratorium on all funding through TFAP mechanisms because they see the Plan behind the increase of unsustainable forest projects.[40]

Again the problem lies in the difference in what TFAP is and what it was envisioned to accomplish by its creators in contrast to what conservation advocates want and expect it to do. TFAP was conceptualized primarily as a technical planning exercise within the forestry sector so that forest conservation itself is not a priority. Furthermore, the complex causes of deforestation were largely ignored and the Plan did not stress the rights and needs of forest dwellers. Another problem is its top-down prescriptive nature, which did not provide consistent guidance and leadership to national governments in developing plans for the rational management and conservation of their tropical forests. Since TFAP is heavily donor driven and tightly controlled by FAO, there was little consultation with forest peoples and conservation groups, who were supposed to play a key role in drawing up and implementing the national TFAP plans. As a result, TFAP failed to recognize the need to reform existing political and economic processes in order to balance conflicting demands on tropical forests and their resources.

Finally, TFAP, like ITTA and ITTO (and ICRW and IWC), became overtaken by events. The importance of tropical forests in forestalling global climate change and protecting the world's biological diversity was not as fully appreciated then as they are now, so that some of these concerns might have been better integrated or coordinated in the TFAP planning process.[41]

Tropical timber ban in the European Community.

International conservation groups were crucial in bringing the issue of deforestation in the tropics and all its adverse human and ecological effects to the attention to the governments and people of Western Europe. Political lobbying and public campaigns by these groups eventually compelled the European Parliament to approve a motion in 1990 to stop tropical timber imports from countries that refuse to adopt or comply with sustainable management plans. In addition, the resolution calls for the creation of a European Community Tropical Forest Management Fund.[42]

Individual national and local governments later adopted even stricter measures than those endorsed by the European Community. For instance, the Dutch Parliament adopted a new policy in 1991 to allow the import of tropical timber only from sustainably managed forest areas by 1995. The Austrian parliament declared its intention to ban all tropical timber products from countries that do not practice sustainable timber management, while many local governments throughout Germany boycotted the use of tropical timber in public projects.[43]

These actions exerted substantial pressure on producer countries to accept at least sustainable forestry and timber management because, as a whole, the European Community is the largest importer of tropical timber after Japan. Their individual and united stance on this matter also helped to push for the adoption of "Objective 2000" in ITTO.

Towards a global forest convention.

Disappointed with the shortcomings of TFAP and ITTO in advancing sustainable forestry and tropical forest protection, the conservation community proposed a new alternative—a global forest convention.

There were other reasons for it. By the late 1980s, there was a deeper understanding of the ecological, economic, social importance of all types of forests, their linkages, and their role in regulating regional and global climate and hydrological conditions. There was also an emerging consensus that effective coordination of international and national actions on all aspects of forest management, conservation, and development is essential to achieve sustainability in timber management and forest conservation. Moreover, existing agreements were either too specific, such as ITTA, or too broad, as in general nature conservation. Finally, new data showed that not only are tropical forests threatened but so are the temperate and boreal forests in North America, Siberia, and elsewhere. Therefore, a global forest convention was deemed necessary to deal with all aspects of forest management, conservation, and development for all types of forests through a common code of practice. This code was expected to be applicable to both developed and developing countries in harmonizing their ecological and economic approaches to forest resources use.[44]

The United States made the first proposal for a global forest convention at the intergovernmental level at the G-7 summit in Houston in 1990. However, many officials from European and developing counties regarded this a tactic to delay negotiations for a climate change agreement as new information was emerging on the correlation between forests—particularly

Deforestation in the Tropics

tropical forest destruction—and global warming.[45] As a result, most European nations and tropical forest countries argued for a global forest agreement that would be part of a protocol to the framework convention on climate change.

There were some hopes that a global forest convention might be concluded at UNCED in 1992, but strong objections came from developing countries. Apart from their forestry and timber concerns, these governments were apprehensive of the potential implications of such a convention on their sovereign rights over access, development, and use of their natural resources. Some governments saw the rise of environmental conservation in the international agenda as just another cover for industrialized countries to expand their control over economic resources around the world and to subvert the national sovereignty of smaller and less powerful developing countries.

This view of a North-South conflict is well illustrated by Malaysia's proposal at the first official meeting for a global climate change agreement in February 1991. Malaysia, a leading tropical timber exporter and a frequent critic of the Western industrialized countries, opposed a global forest convention. With support from the Group of 77,[46] Malaysia declared that tropical forest countries would oppose negotiation for a global forest convention until developed countries commit themselves to reduce energy consumption and to provide funding and technology transfer to developing countries to control their emissions. A month later at the UNCED Preparatory Meeting, Malaysia insisted, with strong support from the Group of 77, on vetoing any intergovernmental negotiation for a global forest agreement outside the UNCED process to ensure that tropical forest countries will have a voice in the matter. Malaysia also demanded that developed countries must compensate tropical forest countries for all direct and lost opportunity costs of compliance with any convention that would commit them to halt or substantially slow deforestation by foregoing timber extraction, agricultural development projects, or converting forest for subsistence farming.[47] The deadlocks were so great that the delegates at this meeting decided that no legally binding global forest convention will be signed at UNCED, but a general and non-binding "Statement of Forest Principles" would be adopted to avoid the appearance of a complete failure for these negotiators.[48]

"Non-binding Statement of Forest Principles."

Although adoption of the "Statement of Principles on the Management, Conservation and Sustainable Development of All Types of Forests" (hereafter, Forest Principles) disappointed those who had hoped for a global forest convention, the statement at least expanded forest conservation to cover all types of forests. Learning from the shortcomings of previous efforts, such as the TFAP, the Forest Principles underlines the significance of local, national and international connections and multilevel coordination as essential for the success of any forestry management and conservation policy.

The Forest Principles has other important implications. First, to encourage its acceptance by developing countries, in particular, the sovereign right of states to utilize, manage, and develop their forests was fully acknowledged. Hence, forests, unlike whales, would not be treated as common resource properties. National governments and their policy preferences would significantly affect development of the international regime on timber and forest conservation.

Second, the Forest Principles explicitly declared that forests are not only to be valued for their timber resources. Since forests are also a source of fuel, food, medicine, places of shelter, employment, recreation, habitats for wildlife and they function as carbon sinks, they should be sustainably managed to meet the social, economic, ecological, cultural, and spiritual needs of present and future generations.

Third, the Forest Principles recommended that governments should promote and provide opportunities for participation by all interested parties in the development, implementation, and planning of national forest policies. This provides the legal basis for participation by local communities and indigenous people, industries, labor, non-governmental organizations, forest dwellers, and women in an issue that is often dominated by national governments and industry.[49]

Certification and eco-labeling schemes.

Yet conservationists were still dissatisfied with the inability of international programs and organizations to tackle the fundamental causes of forest destruction. Many agreed that TFAP's donor-led and project-oriented approach has done more harm than good to forest conservation. Many also gave up on ITTO because they consider it too dominated by business interests to go beyond technical projects in conservation, and few ITTO projects have achieved any real success.[50]

Hence, several conservation groups see market instruments, such as timber certification and eco-labeling schemes, as a new approach towards sustainable management and trade of forest products. Instead of waiting for national governments and international organizations to pass laws and issue directives, these schemes would use consumer power to demand sustainable practices in timber production and trade. Their lobbying of national governments helped to put these schemes on the official agenda of a CITES meeting in Kyoto in 1992.[51] A year later, the Forest Stewardship Council was established to function as an international non-profit and non-governmental agency to evaluate, accredit, and monitor certification organizations.[52]

Deforestation in the Tropics

However, the promotion and implementation of these schemes have faced considerable hurdles. A major one has been the international trade regime, which does not encourage sustainability. The General Agreement on Tariffs and Trade (GATT) prohibits any discrimination between "like products" on the basis of production. In other words, whether the timber or wood-based product was produced in a sustainable or non-sustainable manner should not affect its status in international trade.[53]

Moreover, the Uruguay Round was concluded in April 1994 with scant support for sustainable timber production and trade. The Uruguay Round provisions gave no clear indication on how GATT will rule on actions that limit trade based on environmental grounds. There was also a lack of clarity on unilaterally imposed import restrictions, which discriminate on the basis of the methods used for processing the product. In the case of forestry, this means forestry management or harvesting systems. Such ambiguity also affects whether or not products made from sustainably produced timber and those made from non-sustainably produced timber would be treated as "like" or different products. The only clear statement made on certification covering environmental standards was that new obligations are imposed on voluntary standard setting and the old ones are tightened to ensure technical regulations and conformity assessment procedures do not create barriers to trade.[54]

A second major hurdle has been the voluntary nature of these schemes and the presence of powerful political and economic interests in tropical timber producing and consuming countries. They have kept many efforts, such as the Forest Stewardship Council, from achieving their full potential. Only about 0.5 percent of all internationally traded forest products are certified.[55]

Finally, many tropical timber producing countries still hesitate to accept independent and third party certification and labeling of tropical timber and products. Some governments and industry groups have begun to develop their own certification and labeling schemes. Many insist that that any international scheme must be based on internationally agreed guidelines, which critics fear may be built on the lowest standards for agreement to occur. As a result, there are currently no internationally accepted standards to guide the development of these schemes or international organizations to enforce them.

Furthermore, many conservation groups also question the credibility of certification and labeling schemes developed by hardwood producing countries and industry organizations.[56] Mostly created in response to consumer demand, especially from European countries, critics fear that these schemes may serve more as marketing tools than genuine ways to encourage sustainable forestry policies and practices.

The Commission on Sustainable Development and beyond.

Although disappointed by the failure to reach a global forest convention at UNCED, some of its advocates were hopeful that one could be adopted before the year 2000. The Intergovernmental Panel on Forests (IPF) was set up under the United Nations Commission on Sustainable Development (CSD) to continue the intergovernmental forest policy dialogue, including the task of finding a consensus on whether or not to push for a global forest convention. IPF was also to implement forest-related decisions of the UNCED at the national and international levels and to promote international cooperation in financial assistance and scientific and trade issues among others.

However, difficulty in bridging differences between the North and South, producer and consumer countries, and tropical and non-tropical forest countries were quickly made obvious at the first session of the IPF in September 1995. Governments refused to negotiate until their concerns were adequately addressed, and none could be given the complexity of these issues.[57] The G-77 countries and China basically rejected any proposal that would diminish national control over forests and forest products. Developed countries were wary of requests for financial assistance and technological transfer. Developing countries wanted anti-poverty programs for local communities and forest dwellers and asked for environmentally sound technology on affordable terms and without intellectual property rights restrictions.[58]

With no agreement on major issues, including financial assistance, trade-related matters, or whether or not to begin negotiations for a global forest convention, the fourth and final session of the IPF in February 1997 could only recommend to the CSD that the intergovernmental forest policy dialogue be continued. There were expectations that the work of the IPF would help to launch an Intergovernmental Negotiating Committee (INC) at the fifth session of the CSD in April 1997. However, all countries, except the European Union, opposed any move to initiate negotiations for a global forest convention.

Hence, governments would only agree to create the Intergovernmental Forum on Forests (IFF) at the 19th Special Session of the United Nations General Assembly (UNGASS) on the Environment and Sustainable Development in June 1997. Formally created in July 1997, IFF was to promote and facilitate implementation of the proposals for action of the IPF and to continue discussions on issues left pending by the IPF.

Four years of further discussions under IFF did not bring governments (or environmental NGOs) any closer to settling their differences. At the fourth and final session of the IFF in February 2000, proponents and opponents of a global forest convention continued to fight hard to maintain their respective positions. In the end, they agreed only to recommend to the 8th session of the CSD in April 2000 that a United Nations Forum on

Deforestation in the Tropics 161

Forests be created, and that "within five years, on the basis of an assessment, consider with a view to recommend the parameters of a mandate for developing a legal framework on all types of forests."

The forest debate has become more complex today than before the Rio Earth Summit in 1992. Countries that were for or against a global forest convention were then more clearly identifiable. Those of the North were generally in favor of it, while those in the South were usually against it. Today this North-South divide no longer holds true. Canada, the European Union, Malaysia, and Costa Rica are leading voices for a global forest convention, while the United States, Brazil, India, and Australia oppose it. Opinions are also divided among conservation groups and private industry in developed and developing countries.[59]

In fact, conservation groups, which were the early supporters of a global forest convention, are now generally opposed to it. They fear that such an agreement would only advance the interests of timber trade advocates and hasten the destruction of all types of forests around the world. Therefore, many conservation groups have been working to block decisions that could lead towards a global forest convention. Many have also turned to existing mechanisms and legal instruments, including the biodiversity convention, CITES, and the climate change convention, to find ways to protest forests worldwide.[60]

While debates will continue over the conclusion of a global forest convention, there is little support for an International Timber Organization that covers all types of forests. Conservation groups and industry consider it a waste of resources to create another intergovernmental organization. National governments, too, are wary of any entity that might turn their forests into common resource properties or encroach on their sovereignty.

In summary, the evolution of an international regime for sustainable timber production and forest conservation (in the tropics and elsewhere) has been closely tied to the development paradigm and the North-South debate. Since timber is the most commercially valuable resource of forests, it is often the main cause for forest destruction. Today most international agencies, national governments, and many conservation groups concur that achieving sustainable timber production is an important first step towards halting further tropical and non-tropical forest destruction.

Yet, great differences divide the parties interested in this issue and their focus on commercial logging only addresses one facet of this complex problem. Responses by international agencies and national governments have not kept pace with changes in discussions on environment and development. Most producer countries have not moved much closer to sustainable timber production since the major factors hindering it persist and the international trade regime does not support sustainable timber production. Real improvements in forest management as well as economic and social policies at local, national, and international levels to tackle the root causes

The Roots of Japan's Environmental Policy

of deforestation have also been inadequate.[61] The inept handling of the great forest fires in Indonesia in 1997 by the Indonesian government and regional and international bodies is reflective of these weaknesses.[62]

JAPAN AND FOREST DESTRUCTION IN SOUTHEAST ASIA

Southeast Asia's primary rainforest area, estimated at 250 million ha in 1900, was reduced to only 60 million ha in 1989.[63] Deforestation rate in the tropical Asia-Pacific region is 1.2 percent per annum, which is the highest compared to other regions.[64] Land conversion, infrastructure building, public colonization programs, shifting agriculture, and intense commercial logging and fuel wood gathering have destroyed or seriously degraded these tropical forests.[65]

One of the most severe cases of rapid forest destruction is Thailand. Forests cover only 26 percent of the country in 1988, a drop from 70 percent in 1950. Less conservative estimates put it at 15 percent and natural forests are mainly contained in national parks and wildlife sanctuaries. Another severe case is Vietnam, where forest cover today is less than 20 percent compared to some 42 percent of its national territory in 1950. This loss has often been attributed to wartime destruction, but more rapid destruction began after 1975 as the result of a combination of logging, shifting agriculture, and the clearing of forest lands for state farms.[66]

Although there are many causes of forest destruction in Southeast Asia, none perhaps has greater impact than commercial logging. By opening access to natural forests, it paves way for their complete destruction by migrant settlers who cut the remaining trees for fuel wood and clear land for shifting cultivation. The transfer of new technologies in logging and wood processing over the last several decades has also greatly hastened deforestation. Japanese actions have a large role in this destructive process because Southeast Asia has been its largest supplier of tropical hardwood and Japanese domestic demand and capital have driven the expansion of this industry in the region.[67]

Japan's import of tropical hardwood from Southeast Asia.

Japan's import of tropical hardwood from Southeast Asia goes back some 80 years. Small- and medium-sized Japanese companies (except for Mitsui) began logging in southern Philippines in the 1920s. Most of this was *lauan* (or mahogany), and the Philippines was Japan's main tropical hardwood supplier until the late 1960s. For example, 90 percent of Japanese tropical hardwood imports came from the Philippines in 1955.[68]

Since timber production in Japan met the bulk of its domestic demand, most of the logs imported during this period and in the first decade after World War II were primarily for re-export and value-added processing to sell to U.S. and European markets.[69] However, Japan's forest resource was fast depleting. Although fuel wood consumption had dropped sharply with

Deforestation in the Tropics

the shift to fossil fuel for energy production, the housing and industrial construction boom quickly exhausted natural forests in various parts of Japan. In addition, rising labor costs and rapid economic growth beginning the mid-1950s were changing Japan from a processor to a consumer of tropical hardwoods.[70]

The Japanese government finally lifted all controls on timber imports in August 1961 by its introduction of the "Emergency Measures for Timber Price Stabilization."[71] Rapid domestic economic growth had greatly increased the demand for timber. This decision was the watershed in transforming Japan's domestic forestry sector and moving the country to look overseas for this commodity. Southeast Asia, being the closest source of supply, was the natural choice. Tropical forests in Southeast Asia—and later, timber resources elsewhere—thus became inextricably tied to Japan's economic fortunes.[72]

Japan quickly became a major investor in Southeast Asia's forestry sector.[73] Unlike the pre-war years, this time the large general trading companies established firm control of the timber import trade. GTCs also built domestic plywood and sawnwood manufacturing to add to the distribution of raw logs. At one time, over 90 Japanese companies were active in importing logs from Southeast Asia, but the "Big Six" that dominated were Mitsui, Marubeni, Itochu, Nissho Iwai, Mitsubishi, and Sumitomo.[74]

These large companies have clear advantages over smaller Japanese and native logging firms. First, they have the capital to construct infrastructure like roads, bridges, and ports, and to procure heavy machinery to access timber resources. Second, they have ships and control of timber processing facilities in Japan. Third, their extensive business network aids the financing, acquisition, transport, distribution, and sales of imported timber at home and overseas.[75]

Although Japanese private capital controlled many logging operations overseas and processing and sales in Japan, the Japanese government, through its ODA program, also had an important role in developing the timber industry in Southeast Asia from the 1950s to the 1980s. Loans from the Overseas Economic Cooperation Fund (OECF) and technical aid from the Foreign Ministry's Japan International Cooperation Agency (JICA), in particular, were critical because of their role in natural resource development. Intergovernmental loans by OECF funded infrastructure projects (roads and ports) that are essential for timber extraction and transport. OECF loans to Japanese companies also offset risks in overseas timber investments. In the 1950s and 1970s, Indonesia received 70 percent of all OECD forestry loans when it was the top supplier of tropical hardwood logs to Japan. Technical aid transferred through JICA also supported the inventory of forest resources for logging and transferred knowledge and technology that enabled more rapid and massive logging—or destruction—in the forests of Southeast Asia.[76]

The Roots of Japan's Environmental Policy

Japan's tropical hardwood import grew at exponential rates within a very short span. Between 1950 and 1960, Japan's tropical hardwood imports grew by a factor of 23. The housing boom and overall rapid economic growth sustained a high demand for tropical timber. Between 1960 and 1963, Japan's total log imports more than doubled as its economy boomed, and imports from Southeast Asia rose by 70 percent. By 1970 its imports had quadrupled to 20 million cubic meters in round wood equivalent (rwe). Until the oil shocks of the early 1970s, tropical timber ranked third in Japan's imports after crude oil and petroleum. The year 1973 was the peak of Japan's tropical log imports when consumption hit 27 million cubic meters.

Changes in the domestic demand and foreign supply structure have dictated the shifts in Japan's forestry investment in Southeast Asia. Signs of depletion in the Philippines in the 1960s prompted Japanese investment to move to the forests of Kalimantan and southern Sumatra in Indonesia. Many of these private business ventures benefited from Japanese government assistance and loans.[77] By the 1970s, the number of Japanese companies active in Indonesia had grown to over 200 (from just nine a decade earlier). At the same time, Indonesia replaced the Philippines as the leading supplier of tropical hardwood logs to Japan.

Table 7. Japanese log imports from Southeast Asia, 1970-87
(million cubic meters)

Year	Total	Phil.	Malaysia				Indonesia				Others
			Sabah	Sara.	Penin.	Total	Kali.	Suma.	Others	Total	
1970	20.29	7.5	4.0	1.9	0.188	6.09	4.9	0.8	0.4	6.1	0.6
1971	20.15	5.7	4.1	1.5	0.148	5.75	5.9	1.3	0.9	8.1	0.6
1972	21.69	5.1	5.4	1.4	0.088	6.89	6.2	1.7	1.1	9.0	0.7
1973	26.79	5.9	7.3	1.3	0.094	8.69	8.1	2.1	1.0	11.2	1.0
1974	24.23	3.9	7.0	1.0	0.033	8.03	7.9	2.4	1.1	11.4	0.9
1975	17.40	2.9	6.0	0.7	0.000	6.70	5.4	1.3	0.6	7.3	0.5
1976	22.21	1.7	8.5	1.7	0.006	10.21	7.2	1.6	0.9	9.7	0.6
1977	20.80	1.5	8.1	1.5	0.003	9.60	6.8	1.5	0.9	9.2	0.5
1978	21.81	1.6	9.2	1.5	0.007	10.71	7.0	1.1	0.9	9.0	0.5
1979	22.10	1.3	8.2	2.3	0.000	10.50	7.0	1.5	1.2	9.7	0.6
1980	19.01	1.1	6.3	2.3	0.014	8.61	5.4	1.6	1.6	8.6	0.7
1981	14.70	1.4	5.5	2.9	0.000	8.40	2.4	0.6	1.1	4.1	0.8
1982	15.00	1.3	6.4	4.0	0.000	10.40	1.5	0.4	0.5	2.4	0.9
1983	13.80	0.6	6.2	4.1	0.000	10.30	1.5	0.2	0.4	2.1	0.8
1984	11.97	0.9	5.5	4.3	0.000	9.80	0.07	0.2	0.1	0.4	0.9
1985	12.97	0.5	5.9	5.4	0.006	11.31	0.01	0.01	0.05	0.1	1.1
1986	12.21	0.3	6.0	4.8	0.013	10.81	0.0	0.0	0.0	0.0	1.1
1987	13.76	0.03	7.0	5.5	0.032	12.53	0.0	0.0	0.0	0.0	1.2

Note: "Phil." = Philippines, "Sara." = Sarawak, "Penin." = Peninsular, "Kali." = Kalimantan, and "Suma." = Sumatra. Original table from source reported figures in thousand cubic meters.

Source: F. Nectoux and Y. Kuroda, *Timber from the South Seas: An Analysis of Japan's Tropical Timber Trade and Its Environmental Impact*, Gland: World Wide Fund for Nature International, 1989, p.118.

Deforestation in the Tropics

By the mid-1970s, in anticipation of decline in Indonesian timber resource, Japanese GTCs began to look for a new source of tropical hardwood logs. A decision by the Indonesian government in 1978 to impose an export tax on raw logs expedited the shift of Japanese logging investment to Sabah and Sarawak in East Malaysia, where raw log exports were still permitted.[78] In that same year, Sabah became Japan's top source for tropical hardwood logs until Sarawak overtook it in the late 1980s.[79] The fact that 96 percent of Japan's tropical timber imports in 1987 came from just three sources: Sarawak, Sabah, and Papua New Guinea, underlines the importance of Southeast Asia as key supplier for Japan as well as Japan's role in the region's forestry sector.[80]

Japanese GTCs prefer to import raw logs over processed timber and wood products. A common explanation given by industry is the higher standards required to satisfy the special requirements of the top Japanese customers, namely, the construction industry and furniture manufacturers.[81] Japan produces panels in the sizes of 3' x 6' and 3' x 8', while most other countries produce 4' x 8' panels. Foreign manufacturers must have machines with these size capabilities to export to Japan.[82] Another reason for this preference clearly lies in the fact that it is more profitable for Japanese GTCs to import raw logs than processed timber and wood products because they own or finance the operation of timber mills and plywood manufacturers in Japan.

Hence, Japanese GTCs have always resisted the import of processed tropical hardwood. Imports of processed hardwood have increased only under pressure from tropical hardwood producing countries, such as Indonesia, which are eager to develop their own value-added timber industry. The table below compares the volume and types of tropical hardwood imports consumed by Japan, the European Union, and the United States.

Table 8. Trends in tropical hardwood imports 1950-1987
(Million m^3 roundwood equivalent volume)

	1950	%	1960	%	1970	%	1980	%	1987	%
Total imports	4.36		15.76		48.83		61.23		62.82	
Logs	2.45	56%	10.67	68%	36.72	75%	38.48	63%	28.69	46%
Sawnwood	1.79	41%	3.74	24%	6.72	14%	13.86	23%	17.16	27%
Plywood/veneers	0.13	3%	1.35	9%	5.39	11%	8.89	15%	16.98	27%
Japan	0.21	5%	4.74	30%	20.65	42%	19.30	32%	19.21	31%
Logs	0.10	47%	4.73	100%	19.88	96%	18.37	95%	14.24	74%
Sawnwood	0.11	53%	0.02	0%	0.43	2%	0.78	4%	1.58	8%
Plywood/veneers	0.00	0%	0.00	0%	0.44	2%	0.16	1%	3.39	18%
EC	1.66	38%	5.29	34%	8.55	18%	10.28	17%	8.17	13%
Logs	0.84	51%	3.64	69%	5.44	64%	4.30	42%	1.56	19%
Sawnwood	0.79	47%	1.43	27%	2.34	27%	4.69	46%	4.70	57%
Plywood/veneers	0.04	2%	0.22	4%	0.76	9%	1.29	13%	1.92	23%
U.S.A.	0.68	16%	1.99	13%	3.14	6%	2.68	4%	3.46	6%
Logs	0.43	63%	0.33	16%	0.17	6%	--	--	0.00	0%
Sawnwood	0.24	35%	0.70	35%	0.69	22%	0.60	22%	0.53	15%
Plywood/veneers	0.01	2%	0.97	49%	2.28	73%	2.08	78%	2.94	85%
Persian Gulf	n.a.	--	n.a.	--	n.a.	--	0.37	1%	0.73	1%
Other Asia	n.a.	--	n.a.	--	6.66	13%	13.57	22%	12.18	19%
Japan/EC/USA	2.55	59%	12.03	76%	32.35	65%	32.26	53%	30.84	49%
TOTAL	2.55	59%	12.03	76%	39.00	78%	46.20	75%	43.75	70%

Note: EC = European Community. Totals are all exports of a product. Percentages refer to national percentages of all imports/exports of a product. Plywood/veneers imports for 1950 and 1960 refer only to plywood imports; EC log imports for 1950 and 1960 exclude Greece. Source: Alan Grainger, *Controlling Tropical Deforestation*, London: Earthscan, 1993, p.74.

Apart from logging for timber, GTCs have also exploited forests in Southeast Asia for wood chips and pulp. The Japanese government and Japanese paper companies began funding wood chipping and pulping projects in the region in the early 1970s. For instance, OECF provided equity finance to Marubeni, Nippon Paper, and their Indonesian partner to construct a paper pulp mill at a 300,000 ha plantation scheme in south Sumatra that is funded by JICA.

Deforestation in the Tropics

However, important changes began in the early 1980s. Southeast Asia was Japan's main supplier of tropical hardwood logs and other wood products, but depleting supplies, rising prices, cheaper softwood substitutes, and new policies in tropical timber exporting countries were dramatically reducing Japan's imports of tropical timber and other wood products. International concern for deforestation in the tropics, too, was rising fast. There was increasing international awareness of the negative ecological and human effects of deforestation and the importance of tropical forests to global ecology. Finally, the Indonesian ban on raw log exports in 1985 decisively changed Japanese forestry investments in Southeast Asia and elsewhere.

The Indonesian log export ban and Japan's tropical timber trade.

Determined to promote its own value-added timber processing, the Indonesian government decided to impose a ban on log exports in 1985.[33] Despite shifts in Japanese logging investments to East Malaysia, Indonesia still supplied nearly half of Japan's total raw log imports. This ban led to several fundamental changes in Japan's tropical timber trade.[84] First of all, Japanese GTCs diversified their sources to Oceania and South America and increased their purchase of temperate softwoods from North America. The Indonesian government's decision was drastic, but it would not be exceptional. Japanese GTCs were aware that other tropical timber producing countries also have ambitions to develop their own timber processing industry.[85]

Second, the new business strategy initiated in the late 1970s was for GTCs to link with native firms to export logs, as well as to expand into other areas of business.[86] Mitsubishi held controlling shares in 11 Indonesian companies. By 1980, Mitsui held interests in 28 Indonesian companies that were involved in a wide range of products, including agricultural estates, pesticides, automobiles, shipping companies, and timber.[87] The move to increase valued-added production in the tropical hardwood producing countries also signaled the rise of native firms. Japanese GTCs lost their competitiveness to native firms in obtaining concessions and other privileges because the latter grew in strength and have important ties to their own power elites in government, the military, and business.

The new strategy has the Japanese side providing finance for equipment and transport and handling the distribution of logs and processed products in Japan. The more visibly controversial aspects of the business, including concessions and timber extraction, would be left to their native partners. These changes have helped to minimize Japanese GTC's exposure to criticisms from conservation groups; thereby, protect their public image and business interests worldwide. They have also protected them from liability when legal violations occur. For instance, in 1989 Marubeni invested US$3 billion in P.T. Bintuni Utama Murni Wood Industries as financing in return for a 10-year contract for 300,000 tons of woodchips annually.[88] P.T. Bintuni did not carry out the required environment impact assessment study and illegally cut 300 ha of mangrove forests from Irian Jaya's Bintuni Bay. As a result, P.T. Bintuni's logging license was suspended in October 1990 and was fined Rp1.2 billion (at the time equivalent to US$631,246) for violating the terms of the logging permit. Such joint venture arrangements conveniently allow foreign firms to distance themselves when wrongdoing is exposed. In this case, Marubeni denied any responsibility and apologized only for the inappropriate logging operations carried out by its Indonesian partner.[89]

Third, Japan's imports of sawnwood and plywood have increased substantially as tropical forest countries develop their own timber processing industries. In fact, Indonesia overtook Japan to become the world's largest plywood manufacturer in a matter of years and it has held about 50 percent of the world plywood market.[90] By 1992, there was around 2,700 sawmills with the capacity to produce 15.8 million cubic meter of sawnwood annually in Indonesia. Finally, Japanese GTCs also lost control over the import and domestic sales of Indonesian plywood. Apkindo, the Indonesian plywood maker association, set up its own company, Nippindo, in Japan as the sole agent for the direct import of Indonesian-made plywood.[91] By selling below world prices, Nippindo came to dominate Japan's tropical plywood import trade.

A new emphasis on reforestation and sustainable tropical timber.

International concerns, declining tropical hardwood stands, and shifts in Japanese private logging investments also ushered a change in Japan's official assistance for forestry development in the region. Beginning the mid-1980s, bilateral technical cooperation emphasized reforestation and afforestation. By the early 1990s, it expanded to include forest conservation, management, and agroforestry projects. In addition, Japan gave significant sums to environment and forestry programs of the World Bank, FAO, UNEP, the International Center for Agroforestry Research, and the Center for International Forestry Research (CIFOR).[92]

The other major statement of Japanese response to tropical forest destruction was its decision to host the ITTO secretariat in the city of Yokohama. ITTO would be the chief international body responsible for the promotion of sustainable forestry and timber production in the tropics. Since its establishment in 1985, Japan has been the largest contributor, with donations covering about half of its annual administrative expenses. In 1994, its assessed contribution was 93 million yen (based on the volume of tropical timber imports) and voluntary contribution was 1.652 billion yen (to support ITTO projects).[93]

Other government responses also include an industry guideline issued by the Ministry of Construction calling builders to reduce wastes of tropical timber and a set of modified building codes encouraging builders to substitute new materials for tropical timber. Since 1991, the Forestry Agency has required tropical timber traders to provide data and submit five-year import plans.[94]

Japanese businesses, too, took interest in research, reforestation, and sustainable management and production practices by the early 1990s. Before this time there was practically no interest in these activities because the primary objective was to access cheap and readily available timber resources. However, supply was declining and international criticisms threatened their corporate image. The Research Association for Reforestation of Tropical Forest (RETROF) was established in 1991 to transfer Japanese knowledge and technology to tropical reforestation projects, especially for developing mixed-species plantations. Some companies announced that they would reduce tropical timber consumption or only purchase timber from sustainable sources. For example, Obayashi, a major construction firm, announced in 1990 that it would cut its tropical timber use to 35 percent. The Japan Building Contractors' Society also introduced a non-binding target in 1992 to reduce tropical *konpane* consumption by 35 percent over the next five years and the Japan Lumber Importers' Association issued import guidelines to its members to improve forest management.[95]

Achieving sustainable tropical timber production has become the new guiding principle in Japanese ODA for forestry and the stated goal of the Japanese government and general trading companies. However, the fall in Japan's tropical hardwood imports in the last decade has had more to do with other changes in the domestic and external settings than policy changes. Within Japan, slowdown in economic and population growth has reduced the number of housing starts. In addition, non-wood housing has increased in the Japanese housing market.[96] Outside of Japan, the supply of tropical hardwoods has continued to decline, prices of temperate softwood have become more competitive, and international censure of Japan's role in tropical forest destruction has grown.

The cut in Japanese hardwood imports has also been less substantial than it appears because there has been a sharp increase in Indonesian plywood imports when Apkindo introduced severe price cuts to maintain its competitiveness in the Japanese market.[97] The volume of Indonesian plywood imports is shown in Figures 7 and 8 below.

Figure 7. Supply of domestic and imported timber and wood materials, 1992, by area

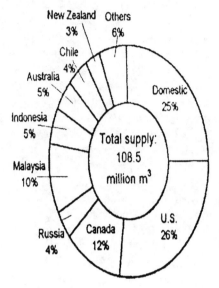

Source: *Forestry White Paper*, 1993.

Figure 8. Supply of domestic and imported timber and wood materials, 1992, by type

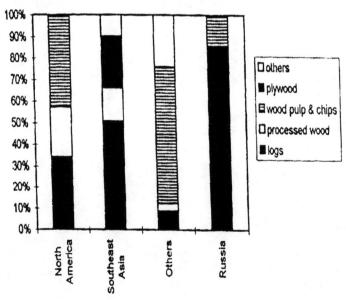

Source: *Forestry White Paper*, 1993.

Deforestation in the Tropics 171

Indeed Japan has continued to be the world's single largest importer of timber and it still consumes about 30 percent of all tropical timber traded in the world market.[98] Figure 9 shows that the main difference is that North America has replaced Southeast Asia as Japan's main source of imported timber in the 1990s. For instance, the top three sources of timber for Japan in 1996 were the U.S. (31.9%), Canada (23.2%), and Malaysia (12.1%).[99]

Figure 9. International trade of wood, 1994

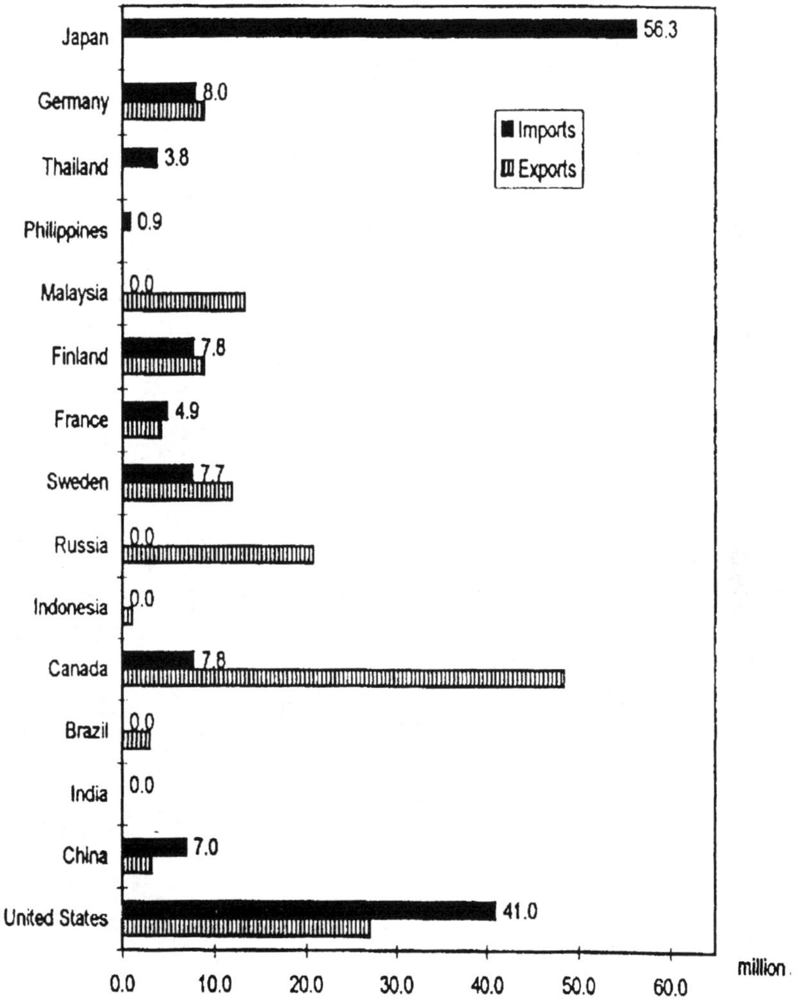

Note: China includes Taiwan. World total imports = 228.9 million m^3; exports = 222.9 million m^3.
Source: *Japan 1998: An International Comparison*, Tokyo: Keizai Koho Center, 1998, p.72.

Japanese GTCs also continue to have a large role in destroying forest in the tropics (and elsewhere). The top eleven GTCs still control 60 percent of the country's tropical timber trade.[100] In the past, they were directly involved in logging and focused in Southeast Asia. Their new strategy is to work with local firms in producer countries, diversify sources of tropical hardwood, and increase purchases of other kinds of timber and wood products. Thus, timber and other wood imports now come from Russia, the U.S., Brazil, Canada, Australia, Cambodia, Chile, New Zealand, Central America, Laos, Myanmar (Burma), Papua New Guinea, and Vietnam.[101]

The Japanese pulp and paper industry also has been diversifying its sources of raw materials since the 1980s to protect itself from price shocks and shortages.[102] Although North America and Oceania remain the chief suppliers of wood pulp and chips to Japan, smaller quantities have come from Russia, Southeast Asia, Africa, and Brazil in recent years. In fact, the involvement of Japanese pulp and paper companies in overseas reforestation and afforestation projects have helped them to develop new supply sources in Southeast Asia, Australia, and Papua New Guinea.

Thus, forest protection advocates have questioned the credibility and effectiveness of Japanese governmental and business activities in reforestation, afforestation, and sustainable tropical timber production. Among their major criticisms are that assistance given by the Japanese government and private industry has been largely limited to piece-meal efforts involving ODA loans and technology transfers. They have also charged that efforts to rehabilitate damaged land and create "sustainable timber estates" are really producing "factory forests."[103] Usually land stripped of commercially valuable timber is cleared and replaced with fast-growing and non-native species, such as eucalyptus and acacia, which are favored by the pulp and paper industry for wood chipping.

Industry experts and Japanese government officials who were interviewed in this study gave three major reasons for selecting these fast-growing species over indigenous ones. First, the former has more reliable source of seedlings and has higher survival rates. Second, the land where these seedlings are planted is so poor that only hardy species like these would survive. Third, these species are only meant to rehabilitate the land at initial stages and will be replaced by native species. However, these plantations have yet to develop beyond the initial stages and some of these reforestation and afforestation activities have been in progress for over two decades.

Many conservation groups and forestry experts have openly questioned the efficacy of this approach for the recovery and conservation of tropical forests. They cautioned that alien species could introduce pests and diseases that are harmful to the local environment and thus complete the destruction of a tropical forest. Achieving reforestation or sustainable forestry in

Deforestation in the Tropics

this manner could mean the replacement of native forests by non-native species.[104]

Moreover, the expansion of bilateral assistance from its traditional hardwood suppliers in Southeast Asia to countries in Central and South America, Africa, and the Pacific Islands (Japan's new sources of tropical hardwood) have raised concern as to whether Japanese aid could actually hasten or dampen deforestation. Other criticisms are of weaknesses in Japan's ODA program. One is that the request-based nature of Japanese ODA program relieves Japan of responsibility to actively promote sustainable forest management. Until initiatives come from recipient countries, Japan does not need to do anything. Japanese assistance, critics charged, also suffers from insufficient planning and environmental safeguards and Japanese aid officials are seen to have inadequate experience when it comes to tropical forests and forestry practices.[105]

Finally, there is the issue of illegal log imports. For example, the volume of Japanese tropical hardwood imports surpassed the total volume reported as sold to Japan in 1995 by producer countries. Mitsui, a major company in Japan's timber trade, has been caught smuggling logs out of Cambodia.[106] Since Japan's demand for tropical hardwood, through reduced and apparently stable, is still substantial, meeting this demand could continue to reduce forest resource around the world and Japanese policies have yet to show that they can help to stop deforestation in the tropics.

JAPAN'S POLICY RESPONSES TO DEFORESTATION IN THE TROPICS

Although international concern and pressure have compelled the Japanese government to respond to deforestation in the tropics with official declarations and substantial donations, they have not moved the Japanese government to honestly abandon its dominant view of forests as a source of timber. In fact, Japanese government efforts continue to focus on maintaining commercial access to timber resources worldwide and promoting sustainable forestry production over biodiversity conservation and most other non-economic aspects of forest conservation.

Two policy responses have been particularly demonstrative of this Japanese government attitude. The first is that official policies on development assistance towards the forestry sector have only shifted their emphasis from "forestry *development*" to "forestry *conservation*" (and not "*forest* conservation") for the explicit goal of sustainable timber production. In other words, commercial exploitation of forests is still the priority. The second is Japan's decision to host ITTO, the organization chiefly responsible for promoting sustainable forestry in the tropics and overseeing the tropical timber trade.

Objectives and rationale.

Until 10 to 20 years ago, a view of forests as a resource for economic development was not uncommon. Policies to protect any type of forest were largely missing in most governments and international institutions. Time and new knowledge, however, have slowly changed international opinion. Nonetheless, the Japanese government has continued to view forests primarily as sources of raw materials.

Japan's policy towards forests in the tropics (and other regions) is basically driven by concerns for resource security and demands of the domestic market. At an earlier time, Japan had to turn to outside sources because domestic timber supply was severely exhausted by industry and wartime needs. Yet, even after domestic timber supply has replenished, domestic demand still depends on timber imports because they are cheaper than domestic timber. Thus, forests overseas have continued as timber yards for Japan and Japanese government responses to foreign pressure have largely been new in form, but not in essence.

How are these two specific policy responses representative of Japanese government objectives and rationale? First, as explained above, the Japanese government values nature mainly as a resource for consumption. Thus, guaranteeing human (or more specifically, Japanese) access and use has been its priority. Japan has given generously to ITTO and the Tropical Forest Action Plan. Both efforts emphasize forestry management to satisfy production and consumption demands over conservation and other measures that address the underlying root causes of tropical forest destruction, such as economic and migration policies in tropical timber producing countries.

Second, the Japanese government has not endorsed any measure that would curtail the consumption of timber and other wood products from the tropics. Although Japan's consumption of tropical timber and plywood is much lower today than its peak in the 1970s, importing tropical hardwood is still cheaper than exploiting domestic tree stands.

Third, as a resource deficient country, the Japanese government prefers an international trade regime that allows access to all commodities. For this reason, the Japanese government has given greatest support to ITTO, TFAP, and other schemes that promote sustainable forestry management and timber production. Even criticisms of ITTO have not dampened Japanese governmental support. For instance, Japan pledged to strengthen its support for ITTO at UNGASS in June 1997. This promise is one of three major actions in nature conservation under its new "Initiatives for Sustainable Development toward the 21st Century."[107] In contrast, it has not endorsed any change in the current international trade regime to encourage a positive discrimination of sustainable timber and other wood and non-wood products from the tropics. The Japanese government also has not exercised Japan's leverage as the world's largest importer of tropi-

Deforestation in the Tropics

cal hardwoods to promote sustainable forestry and timber logging practices in producer countries through market mechanisms such as voluntary certification and labeling schemes.

Fourth, a shift to emphasize reforestation and sustainable timber production in its bilateral and multilateral assistance could help the Japanese government to achieve multiple goals. For one, the Japanese government can subsidize Japanese business responses. One example is the Research Association for Reforestation of Tropical Forest, which receives half of its budget from the Forestry Agency (the other half from the private sector).

It would also allow the Japanese government to use its sizable ODA budget as leverage to affect international responses or approaches to the problem. In this connection, the Japanese government values the presence of the ITTO secretariat in Japan because it is the chief international agency responsible for attaining the goal of sustainable timber production and overseeing the international trade of tropical timber and other wood products. By doing so, the Japanese government hopes to deflect some international criticisms for past excesses and make a prominent public statement of its commitment to the problem of deforestation in the tropics.

The Japanese government considers its hosting and funding of ITTO as important to carrying out the mandate of this organization under the International Tropical Timber Agreement. The Agreement specifically says that tropical forest conservation would be within the context of resource use and supports the access and commercial use of forests in the tropics. Japan was afraid that locating ITTO in North America or Western Europe would make the organization more vulnerable to pressure from international conservation groups. The distance, language barrier, and high expense of operating in Japan also could make it more difficult for the anti-tropical timber lobby to be effective in Japan. Their anti-whaling campaigns and influence in the International Whaling Commission have shown the Japanese government and big business the leverage of these non-governmental organizations in international politics. Therefore, the Japanese government wanted to minimize any possibility for ITTO to be turned into a platform for forest protection advocates to preach against the cutting and trading of tropical timber.

The Japanese government worked vigorously to bring the ITTO headquarters to Japan. It surpassed other bidders in promises for materials support, including generous funding for administrative staff and activities as well as free office and facilities.[108] The Japanese government also lobbied for support from developing, tropical timber producing countries, which shared the Japanese concern that locating ITTO in North America and Western Europe could make the organization more vulnerable to lobbying by environmental NGOs. The Netherlands, for example, was a strong contender, but the Dutch government was considered too friendly to the powerful international environmental NGOs.

Locating the ITTO secretariat in tropical hardwood producing countries also had its opponents. Many environmental NGOs were concerned that conservation voices would not be heard. Consumer country governments were also wary that producer country governments would dominate. As for the tropical hardwood producing countries, most are developing economies, which did not have adequate resources to host the organization. Therefore, in the end, Japan became the choice of compromise.

ITTO has been a priority for the Japanese government in the international forestry sector. It wants to keep this organization, which has a mandate to develop forestry and timber use, the leading intergovernmental organization for tropical timber and forest conservation discussions. Criticisms of ITTO, its activities, and Japan's role in it do not greatly disturb the Japanese government. It is more concerned about protecting its interests by maintaining a middle course between contending viewpoints and interests within ITTO.

This was why Japan did not oppose a proposal by conservation groups to expand ITTA to cover all types of forests in negotiations for a new ITTA in 1991. The original ITTA, conceived in the 1970s, is a commodity agreement that supports conservation. An entirely new global forest convention in the 1990s would likely emphasize protection over use. Japan also supported the proposal because it appealed to many tropical hardwood producing countries, which felt that they were unfairly targeted by the developed, temperate forest countries in forest conservation. The impasse between protection and pro-use advocates almost caused the organization to collapse.

A new agreement was finally reached in 1994 after tropical forest countries dropped their demand to expand ITTO to cover non-tropical timber. They felt that a collapse of ITTO would not be in their interest. In exchange for their concession, developed countries promised financial contributions to ITTO, including significant sums from Japan. Although most ITTO members wanted the Japanese funds, they were wary that this would increase the already large number of votes held by Japan. To diffuse the crisis, Japan had to agree to put its extra donations in special programs, which would not translate into new votes.

Fifth, the Japanese government considered hosting the ITTO secretariat a diplomatic trophy that would increase the country's international prestige and win political support from Japanese citizens. As a major economy, Japan is home few intergovernmental organizations. ITTO was thought to be the last United Nations organization to be created before the end of the twentieth century, and Japanese people have a fairly positive opinion of the international body.

Finally, the Japanese government believed it could use its financial resources, technical expertise, and economic ties with both developing and developed countries to help mediate differences in the organization. Of par-

Deforestation in the Tropics

ticular importance is that the Japanese government considers itself a consumer country that is sympathetic to the perspectives of developing countries.

The Japanese government's views and objectives towards forests (or deforestation) in the tropics has remained basically unchanged and tied to its narrowly defined national goals and interests. Sustainable timber production is emphasized in forest conservation because it accommodates the Japanese government's main interest in protecting resource security and satisfying domestic demand for timber and wood products.

POLICY ACTORS IN JAPAN'S POLICY ON DEFORESTATION IN THE TROPICS

As in whaling, the government bureaucracy was the most influential in deciding national responses to deforestation in the tropics. However, unlike whaling, no single bureaucratic actor had predominant control because it issue was seen as a matter in natural resource management, international trade, and diplomacy within the bureaucratic policy framework. For these reasons, too, the Environment Agency had no real influence. Neither were national politicians a significant voice since international environmental issues do not rank high on their list of concerns. Only a few local politicians from timber producing areas were concerned about implications of international forest trade for their constituents. As for non-governmental actors, Japanese GTCs and conservation groups were the most important.

The governmental actors.

Four large ministries have been most involved in deciding policy responses to the problem of deforestation in the tropics, including the shift in ODA emphasis and hosting of the International Tropical Timber Organization in Japan. They are the ministries of Agriculture, Forestry and Fisheries (MAFF), Construction (MoC), International Trade and Industry (MITI), and Foreign Affairs (MoFA).

The Japanese bureaucracy.
The different facets of this issue reveal how each of the four ministries was involved and what their interests were. MoFA and MITI were the most influential because they are the main actors in setting Japan's ODA policy and in representing Japan in ITTO. Without bureaucratic leadership in ODA, international trade, and diplomacy, MAFF and MoC had limited influence. Nonetheless, their involvement was important to MITI and MoFA to implement technical cooperation and to alter the domestic demand structure for all types of timber and wood products.

Ministry of Foreign Affairs.
Among the bureaucratic actors, MoFA was the strongest advocate for international cooperation and changes in Japan's policies on deforestation

178 *The Roots of Japan's Environmental Policy*

in the tropics. It especially welcomed increases in ODA funding for forestry conservation and the hosting of ITTO in Japan because it expected multiple benefit from these actions.

First, as Japan's primary liaison with the outside world, these actions would help MoFA to better deal with outside criticisms of Japan's role and responsibilities in this issue. For example, during the 1980s when Japan's large trade surplus with the U.S. and Canada was a source of diplomatic tension, MoFA favored increasing North American softwood imports as a way to alleviate some U.S. and Canadian demands on Japan.[109] MoFA also wanted Japan's ODA program to be viewed favorably by other industrialized countries.

Second, both actions could increase MoFA's resources and leverage within the government. MoFA is one of the main bureaucratic actors (others being MITI, the Ministry of Finance and the Economic Agency) responsible for setting the country's ODA policy. Its official role in this matter enables it to allocate assistance for activities that could improve its bargaining position with other policy actors inside and outside of Japan on deforestation and other related matters.

MoFA especially favored hosting the ITTO secretariat in Japan because it would have a larger voice in representing Japan in this organization. Also, as mentioned earlier, ITTO was thought to be the last United Nations agency to be established before the end of the 20th century and United Nations agencies are quite highly regarded by the Japanese public. Thus, MoFA was confident that there would be support from other key policy actors and funding from the Ministry of Finance. MoFA would also gain prestige before the domestic audience and obtain their support for other MoFA initiatives. Since MoFA has no domestic constituency, public support could give it some leverage in negotiations with other bureaucratic actors as well as private industry.

Third, these two policy responses have support from other main policy actors within the government. This convergence of interests would not only minimizes conflicts among them, but would also help them to better resist intervention by other policy actors inside and outside the Japanese government.

Fourth, having ITTO in Japan could make life easier for MoFA officials. Since MoFA is Japan's chief liaison with the world, regardless of the ministry's own policy preferences, its officials have the duty to defend their country's views and policies. Hosting ITTO in Japan would allow MoFA to demonstrate a substantial national commitment in material and goodwill. Having the ITTO secretariat in Japan, in particular, could help MoFA officials in the North American and European bureaus to respond to criticisms from governments and public in the United States, Germany, the Netherlands, and Britain, which are among the most vociferous critics of Japan's tropical timber trade. Therefore, MoFA worked vigorously to bring

Deforestation in the Tropics 179

ITTO to Japan and did so with generous offers of funding, facilities, and personnel.

Apart from agreeing to shifts in the country's ODA policy and hosting ITTO in Japan, MoFA had to adopt a new relationship with NGOs. The broad acceptance of NGOs in Western democracies and multilateral organizations as a legitimate voice and partner in tropical forest conservation put pressure on MoFA to do the same. MoFA also realized that having no strong domestic constituency, a positive relationship with NGOs increases its influence in intra-governmental negotiations and international forums. Therefore, among other activities, MoFA set up a 50 million yen funding scheme in 1994 to support Japanese NGO proposals for sustainable forestry projects. Many MoFA officials responsible for this issue also participated in NGO-organized events and engaged in formal and informal meetings with NGO representatives.

The Forestry Agency.

Strictly speaking, MAFF's Forestry Agency had not been involved in the country's tropical timber trade (and its impact on forests in Southeast Asia) because ODA and international trade lie in the official domain of MoFA and MITI. As the chief bureaucratic body responsible for Japan's domestic forestry sector, the Forestry Agency has been more concerned about the negative effects of timber imports, hardwood and softwood, on the domestic forestry sector, specifically the traditional timber producers and the domestic plywood manufacturing industry.

The depletion of domestic timber supply in the natural forest areas in the inland mountain regions and the subsequent switch to tropical timber gave rise to a modern timber processing industry, including plywood manufacturing, in the coastal areas where logs are unloaded and stored.[110] The Agency has carried out extensive and expensive afforestation programs to help traditional timber producing communities, but these secondary forests of mainly *karamatsu* (larch) and *akamatsu* (Japanese red pine) have low commercial value.[111] High labor and transport costs, superior quality of foreign timber, as well as a domestic consumption and supply structure that favors imported timber, together make it practically impossible for the domestic timber industry to be competitive.[112] The local economies of many traditional forest communities have collapsed and many are physically disappearing as younger generations leave to find work in the cities. To keep this declining industry alive, the Forestry Agency annually injects billions of yen into local forest communities in the form of loans, subsidies, and training programs.[113] More recently, incentive schemes were used to train urban youths into foresters in order to reinvigorate these aging communities.

As for the domestic plywood manufacturing industry, it grew as a result of Japan's tropical timber trade. For years, MAFF protected this industry from foreign competition by imposing severe standards to qualify for its

Japan Agricultural Standard (JAS) mark for sawnwood, plywood, and other structural wood products. Without this stamp, foreign timber products cannot be competitive in the domestic market because construction companies can rarely obtain government-subsidized loans for projects if they use non-JAS products.[114] For construction companies this makes a big difference because of enormous government spending on public projects each year. For example, in 1993, 31.8 trillion yen or 43 percent of the entire national budget of 73 trillion yen went to construction. This sum compared with the equivalent of 54 trillion yen spent by the U.S. government in the same year, although the United States is about 25 times larger than Japan in size.[115]

The change in Indonesian policy on raw log export in 1987 forced many Japanese plywood manufacturers to close down because Indonesian plywood was cheaper.[116] There were 142 plywood factories in Japan in 1985, but the number fell to 120 within three years after the log export ban was instituted.[117] The Japan Plywood Manufacturers' Association also projected that another 40 of the remaining 100 Japanese plywood mills will close by the year 2000.[118] Japanese plywood manufacturers tried to switch to softwood from North America as a substitute for tropical hardwood in response to declining tropical timber supply and rising prices.[119] However, Indonesia's aggressive marketing of its plywood dampened Japanese consumption of softwood plywood.[120] The rise of the yen in the mid- to late 1980s dealt the final blow when cost and price disadvantages became too much for Japanese plywood manufacturers to bear.

As Japan's policy towards deforestation changed in the mid-1980s, the Forestry Agency discovered many reasons to take interest in the issue. First, a reduction of tropical hardwood imports could make way for increased sales of Japanese domestic timber. For this reason, the Forestry Agency supported local governments' decision to stop using tropical timber in publicly funded projects. Second, an active role in the issue could justify the Agency's request for a larger budget. Despite cuts in the national budget, Japan's ODA had continued to grow, particularly in environment-related areas. The Agency has used the new funds to support activities that are important to its constituents. They included subsidies for the traditional timber industry, a special fund to help Japanese plywood manufacturers to survive the Indonesian log export ban and the subsequent influx of cheap Indonesian tropical plywood in the Japanese market, and research funding for RETROF.

Third, the Forestry Agency was aware that its expertise was needed to carry out technical cooperation projects overseas. This would allow the Forestry Agency a greater voice in policy discussions on international forestry cooperation and fortifies its position in inter-ministerial negotiations. The Forestry Agency's International Forestry Cooperation Office has launched several bilateral technical forestry cooperation projects since the

Deforestation in the Tropics

mid-1980s—though on a much smaller scale than JICA's because the ministry is heavily debt-ridden—and has an official presence in the International Tropical Timber Organization.

However, the Agency's greater prominence has also increased its exposure to criticism from conservation groups. Recognizing the influence of conservation groups in international politics, the Forestry Agency, like MoFA, has become more open to interaction with non-governmental organizations.[121]

Ministry of International Trade and Industry and the Ministry of Construction.

These two ministries are examined together in this section because they share a basic concern in this issue, which is to have a cheap and reliable supply of raw materials for their powerful domestic constituents. For MITI, it is the general trading companies, which profit from the tropical timber trade; for MoC, it is the 520,000 big and small construction companies, which are the biggest consumers of timber in Japan.[122]

For this reason, both ministries have supported policy responses, including the change in Japan's ODA policy and the hosting of ITTO. They knew new strategies and policies were needed to respond to declining hardwood supply. Japanese GTCs entered into new business arrangements with native firms and diversified sources for timber to ensure a stable supply of competitively priced hardwood and softwood timber. The only real sore point for Japanese GTCs was Nippindo's success in breaking their monopoly on plywood imports. Apart from financial losses, it was a significant challenge to their dominant position in the Japanese economy.

MITI saw other potential gains from these policy responses. Using ODA funds to support reforestation and afforestation could ease attacks from the conservation lobby inside and outside of the country. Japanese industry, an important client of the ministry, would benefit from ODA-supported forestry projects, many of which involve fast-growing commercial species.

The non-governmental policy actors.

Among the interested non-governmental policy actors, the general trading companies and conservation groups have stood out as the most important non-governmental policy actors. Japanese GTCs knew by the late 1970s that forests in Southeast Asia were rapidly disappearing and alternative timber sources were needed. With adequate adjustments made by the early-1980s, Japanese GTCs were not only prepared for these policy changes, they were quite supportive of them. For conservation groups, their campaigns against the tropical timber trade inside and outside of Japan forced responses from the Japanese government and Japanese GTCs, but they did not fundamentally alter the views and goals of these influential policy actors.

The general trading companies.

For Japanese GTCs, the problem of deforestation in the tropics is really a problem of depleting tropical hardwood supply. Consequently, their primary concern has been to maintain access to this commodity and its substitutes, as well as securing long-term supplies and positive terms of trade. Over the years, Japanese business have been careful to anticipate and respond to developments in the supply and pricing of tropical hardwoods, as well as changes in the policy and business environments in tropical timber producing countries. Japanese forestry investments have moved from one producer country to another as supply diminished.

The decision by Japanese GTCs to reduce hardwood imports from Southeast Asia and to withdraw from direct involvement in extraction activities since the late 1970s was mainly driven by changes in the domestic demand structure and economic factors in the external environment. Negative publicity generated by anti-tropical timber campaigns in the early and mid-1980s did cause some concern, but worries of any serious impact on their business activities were minimal. These companies have been quite invulnerable to pressure from domestic and foreign conservation groups, as well as national governments and international organizations. Their enormous size, diversified structure, and an international trade regime that biases towards free trade have provided them substantial leverage.[123] Moreover, partnership arrangements with native firms in producer countries since the late 1970s have gven them extra protection against liability and scrutiny from governmental and non-governmental organizations.

Thus, Japanese GTCs were supportive of the new Japanese government policies towards the tropical timber trade and the hosting of ITTO since they help to maintain the international trade of timber and provide new Japanese ODA funds to subsidize their own reforestation activities in Southeast Asia. An example was the formation of the Research Association for Reforestation of Tropical Forest in 1991 as the major industry response to deforestation in Southeast Asia and Oceania.[124] The Japan International Forestry Promotion and Cooperation Center (JIFPRO), an organization sponsored by the Forestry Agency, launched RETROF to engage private businesses in tree planting and research activities.[125]

This project has involved many of Japan's top players in the tropical timber import trade and pulp and paper industry, including Nissho Iwai, Oji Paper, Sumitomo Forestry, Ishinomaki Plywood Manufacturing, Mitsui, Komatsu and Toyota. Reforestation activities have concentrated in Malaysia, Indonesia, Thailand, Vietnam, and Papua New Guinea. As mentioned earlier, RETROF's use of non-indigenous commercial species to rehabilitate severely degraded lands has yet to produce results other than raw materials for the Japanese pulp and paper industry. Therefore, conservationists consider RETROF and other Japanese private efforts wholly

Deforestation in the Tropics

inadequate, largely disingenuous, and self-serving as commercial exploitation of forests in the tropics and elsewhere continue in more discreet ways.

Conservation groups.

Conservation groups critical of Japan's involvement in destroying tropical forests can be broadly classified into three groups: the northern, the southern, and the Japanese ones. The northern conservation non-governmental organizations (NGOs) are those of North America and Europe, the tropical timber consuming countries. The southern ones are those of the tropical timber producing countries. Finally, Japanese ones were formed in the late 1980s specifically to carry out an anti-tropical timber campaign in Japan in order to bring the issue to Japan and before the Japanese public.

Both northern and southern conservation NGOs worked to increase international concern for deforestation. For instance, the International Union for the Conservation of Nature and Natural Resources (IUCN) influenced the creation of ITTO and development of its biodiversity guidelines, while the World Wide Fund for Nature (WWF) played an important role in pushing for timber certification and labeling.[126] NGO criticisms of Japanese GTCs activities and the destructive effects of Japan's ODA program were especially useful in highlighting Japan's role and responsibilities in this issue. The Japanese government and industry were pressed to respond. Large companies, in particular, supported the use of ODA funds for reforestation and sustainable forest management and the hosting of ITTO in Japan.

Interestingly, however, both northern and southern groups chose only to pressure Japan from the outside. The Japanese offices of these northern groups did not engage in any high profile campaigns on this issue within Japan. They were not part of the worldwide campaigns waged by their organizations in North America, Western Europe, and the tropical timber producer countries. Even during the height of their worldwide campaigns to save tropical forests in the 1980s, their offices in Japan were not mobilized to collect data or information from within Japan.[127] This situation could possibly be attributed to their ignorance about Japan, as well as their belief in the impotence of Japanese civil society and the impenetrable triangle of Japanese politics, bureaucracy, and big business.

Nonetheless, an indigenous Japanese anti-tropical timber campaign was launched in 1987. Tropical deforestation and Japan's role in it were largely unknown or not talked about in Japan—even by its conservation groups—until 1986.[128] Two important events happened that year awoke Japanese conservation activists to their paucity of knowledge and activities on this problem. The first was the Japanese media report on the Polonoroeste project in Brazil, which was funded by Japan's ODA program. The second was their participation in an NGO meeting on tropical timber in Penang, Malaysia.[129] A year later, Friends of the Earth (FoE) International helped to set up the Japan Tropical Forest Action Network (JATAN) to coordinate the anti-tropical timber campaign in Japan and to have a Japanese NGO present at the first ITTO Council Session in Japan that year.

Right from the start, JATAN was an independent organization. Only start-up funding came from FoE International and Japanese led and staffed the organization. Its board of directors, too, would make up of respected leaders in the country's social and environmental movements. The first task for JATAN, and later the Sarawak Campaign Committee (SCC), were educating the Japanese public about deforestation and accessing the bureaucratic policy machine.[130]

The anti-tropical timber campaign had a narrow focus: logging in Sarawak.[131] Petitions to government offices protested against the Malaysian government's suppression of forest peoples in Sarawak and asked for reductions in tropical timber consumption. Foreign NGO activists and forest peoples from Papua New Guinea and Sarawak were brought to Japan to speak in public forums. An intensive campaign targeted Japanese GTCs. Protesters staged live dramas in front of GTC offices and the "Destruction Award," a card board cut-out in the shape of a chain saw, was given to these companies. The novelty of these demonstrations—in contrast to conventional practices of waving banners and shouting campaign cries—attracted national and international media coverage; thus, causing considerable embarrassment for the GTCs.[132]

After a successful launch of the campaign, JATAN shifted attention to research and dissemination of its findings. It published in 1988 "Timber from the South Seas," which is a comprehensive study of tropical timber trade in Southeast Asia.[133] SCC began a "*genchi no shien*" (support for the land) project in Sarawak to protect forest land, animals, and resources and staged a campaign in 1990 against Mitsubishi for alleged illegal logging.

This campaign ended in 1990. The campaign did not basically alter Japanese government and business perspectives or reduced Japanese hardwood imports—and activists would acknowledge this. However, unlike the anti-whaling campaign, the anti-tropical timber campaign improved the prominence and credibility of NGOs in Japanese society. NGO dialogues with the government and private industry broadened and deepened at both personal and institutional levels. It also raised popular awareness of how Japanese consumption can impact on the external environment.

This was no small achievement in view of the many difficulties NGOs face in Japan. Reasons for the success of the anti-tropical timber campaign (compared to the anti-whaling campaign) are summarized in the following:

(1) Its strategy did not alienate Japanese people. Instead of faulting Japanese people for consuming tropical timber, JATAN targeted the GTCs. The movement evoked Japanese sentiments for nature and reminded the Japanese people of their own history of industrial pollution tragedies and deforestation disasters in Japan;

Deforestation in the Tropics

(2) A non-confrontation approach towards the Japanese government helped to open contact with the relevant government policy actors;

(3) Since Japanese were the masters and executors of the anti-tropical deforestation campaign, the movement did not appear as a mere extension of white environmentalism and foreign pressure. Their sensitivity to Japanese communication style, culture, and norms was also highly significant;

(4) Evidence of tropical forest destruction was indisputable. (In contrast, both proponents and opponents of whaling exploited scientific uncertainties in the whaling and acid rain debates.) Meetings with NGOs and forest peoples from Southeast Asia and the Pacific Islands also gave the Japanese public a stronger sense of the problem;

(5) Unbiased Japanese media coverage of public protests against Japanese GTC and other activities of the campaign gave unprecedented nationwide exposure to NGOs and the tropical deforestation problem;

(6) The Japanese government could not deny Japan's responsibility. In the face of severe international criticisms, MoFA and the Forestry Agency, in particular, became less resistant to interactions with NGOs;

(7) ITTO's location exposed Japan to greater international publicity and pressure. Although nearly all NGOs had lost faith in ITTO, the Council Sessions were a useful venue for meeting and exchanges among themselves and between them and government officials, foresters, and industry representatives. Media coverage of ITTO meetings also gave NGOs opportunities to underscore weaknesses of the organization and criticize the Japanese government; and

(8) The acceptance of NGOs in Western democracies and international organizations worldwide pressured the Japanese government, big business and society to do the same. The movement also won public approval by ceasing high profile activities after the main objectives were achieved. Continuing public protests would make activists appear as uncompro-

mising troublemakers in a society where NGOs were still struggling to gain public trust and respect.[134]

Since the campaign ended, JATAN has concentrated its efforts on research, building organizational membership, improving ties and exchanges with environmental NGOs in the producer countries, and broadening public education in Japan.[135] New understanding of global forest issues has also expanded its work to include the conservation of boreal and temperate forests and the push toward a global forest convention. JATAN and SCC's last major effort to reduce tropical hardwood use in Japan was a petition to the Tokyo metropolitan government and local governments throughout the country. By August 1995, 66 local governments have agreed not to use tropical timber in public projects.[136]

In recent years, JATAN and SCC have suffered from organizational, financial, and leadership crises. There has been a steep decline in institutional support for and popular interest in international environmental activities following UNCED. Relations between Japanese NGOs and their northern and southern counterparts have also been strained by their different approaches to the problem. Foreign groups generally prefer a combination of direct political lobbying and outside pressure on the Japanese government and general trading companies. In contrast, Japanese groups consider dialogues with the government and public education as more effective ways to reduce tropical hardwood consumption in Japan. For example, JATAN and most other Japanese NGOs decided not to join a boycott against Mitsubishi initiated by the U.S.-based Rainforest Action Network.[137] They felt that the boycott would have negligible impact on Mitsubishi and other Japanese GTCs. They were also anxious that endorsing the boycott could hurt their hard-earned credibility in Japanese society, as well as their budding relations with the bureaucracy. This decision disappointed many overseas groups and even raised suspicions that Japanese groups have been co-opted by the government.[138]

Lack of funding also affected cooperation between Japanese NGOs and their foreign counterparts. Before and during the anti-tropical timber campaign, Japanese NGOs received financial assistance from WWF, the Rainforest Action Network (RAN), the National Wildlife Federation, and Greenpeace to carry out joint activities.[139] These foreign groups hoped that these joint activities would help them to raise funds and recruit members in Japan. However, charitable giving was (and still is) not quite popular among Japanese people and companies. Foreign NGOs thus lost interest in supporting Japanese NGO activities and Japanese NGOs themselves did not have sufficient financial means to carry out major or extended campaigns.[140]

Other factors that made the first anti-tropical timber campaign successful have also largely disappeared. The prominence of deforestation as a

Deforestation in the Tropics

global environmental problem has declined. The media and Japanese people in general became more concerned about their country's economic problems and political scandals. Japanese NGOs also continued to be saddled by legal, organizational, financial, and leadership problems. Some activists shifted their work to other areas, thus losing valuable expertise and scarce staff familiar with forest issues. Finally, there has been no consensus for another campaign. Some activists were wary of adverse impacts on their public image and their relations with the government bureaucracy. Compared to Western society, confrontation is more carefully avoided in Japan after a relationship is established.[141]

However, apart from increased funding for NGO activities, the government bureaucracy has continued to block NGO penetration in the policy process. At the United Nations Commission on Sustainable Development meeting in April 1995, the Japanese government did not want NGOs to sit in the sessions when talks touched upon criteria for sustainable forest management. MoFA, too, has ceased to invite several advocacy groups to its scheduled official briefings with NGOs.

CHAPTER CONCLUSION

While conservation advocates worry about loss of biological diversity as a result of forest destruction in the tropics, the Japanese government has been more concerned about deforestation as a threat to timber supply. Japanese government policy responses emphasize *forestry* conservation rather than *forest* conservation. Its policy responses have focused primarily on promoting sustainable timber production and protecting access to timber resource.

As a major consumer of all kinds of timber and wood products and a top donor of environmental assistance, Japanese actions have had a profound impact on the international regime for forests. Its emphasis on sustainable forestry and other timber use issues has impeded the development of an international regime that has a better balance between economic and other values of forests. Neither do these priorities adequately address the underlying causes of deforestation in the tropics, including mass poverty and political corruption. Furthermore, these Japanese policy responses have impacts beyond the forest issue. Linkages among regimes could cause developments within the international regime for forests to affect other regimes, particularly those on resource use.

As a host and a top donor to ITTO, Japanese leadership has been limited to mediating differences between producer and consumer countries, and Japan has offered financial incentives rather than ideas and initiatives. Japan's failure to provide responsible leadership, critics say, renders ITTO more meaningless as time goes by. However, MoFA, as Japan's chief representative in ITTO, has been unable to undertake more pro-active diplomacy because it has limited bargaining leverage *vis-a-vis* other relevant bureaucratic actors in this matter.

Each of the major governmental actors, as well as Japanese industry, had its own reasons for supporting these policy responses. Conflicts were minimal mainly because their respective interests basically converged and complemented each other. Even when they were not shared, adequate resources were available to help smooth differences and silent opposition. This situation produced two outcomes. First, there was relative ease and success in inter- and intra-ministerial negotiations, despite the absence of national guidelines or policy leadership. Second, official assistance was unfocused, driven more by bureaucratic interests than any overall government policy or vision.

MITI and MoFA had superior influence in the policy process because deforestation in the tropics was mainly treated as a commodity trade and foreign affairs issue within the domestic policy framework. Yet, they could not dominate as the Fisheries Agency could in whaling. The multifarious nature of this issue deprived chief authority for any single ministry or agency. Interested policy actors had to negotiate to find support for their own preferences. For example, for Japan to agree to an international timber certification or eco-labeling scheme, the Ministry of Foreign Affairs had to consult with MITI (which oversees Japan's international trade), the Forestry Agency (which would implements the schemes domestically), and the Ministry of Construction (to enforce compliance by the financially and politically powerful construction industry).

As long as the major policy actors consider tropical timber and deforestation in the tropics strictly as a trade and diplomatic affair, the Environment Agency will not have a meaningful voice in domestic policy discussions. Conservation also could not become a real priority in policies or an objective without economic justifications.

The bureaucratic politics model helped to identify the major policy actors involved in this issue, the sources of their power, and their relative strength in the bargaining process. Compared to the case study on whaling, no single actor dominated the bureaucratic policy process in the country's policy towards deforestation in the tropics. While there were potentials for conflict among the bureaucratic actors as each worked to advance its own objectives, sufficient resources (in the form of official development aid) prevented competition. Moreover, decisions to host ITTO and support sustainable forestry were compatible with their respective goals and interests.

While the bureaucratic politics approach aided investigation of intra-governmental bargaining in policy making process, complex interdependence, regime theory, and the two-level game model offered insights into why Japan was not highly vulnerable to outside pressure and how Japanese government actions affected the international regime for forests. First, absence of linkages between its tropical hardwood trade and other impor-

Deforestation in the Tropics

tant policy issues meant that reverberations in domestic opinion created by conservation groups could only exploit Japanese government and industry sensitivity to criticisms. However, these actors were not vulnerable to pressure (unlike in whaling where pressure came from the United States and the Japanese fishing industry). As a result, there has been no fundamental change in Japanese government policy or industry investment strategies and business practices.

Second, forest protection proponents could not advocate an end to consumptive use of forests and forces supportive of forestry development (sustainable or otherwise) were active in shaping the international regime for forests. Hence, conservation groups had less influence in affecting development of the international regime for forests and Japanese policy responses in this issue. Furthermore, this broad consensus in recognizing consumptive use of forests meant that Japanese policy preferences were not contradictory to majority opinion (as in the case of whaling).

Third, there were substitutes for tropical hardwood and Japanese big business had already instituted new investment strategies to maintain access to topical and non-tropical timber products and with a minimum of legal and economic risks. Fourth, governments and their sub-national actors had a more powerful presence in building the international regime for forests than they did in whaling. Although both whaling and forest conservation (as environmental issues) may be categorized as issues of complex interdependence, the international regime for forests did not treat forests as commons. Thus, state sovereignty over forests as territories, resources, nature reserves, and welfare for citizens was explicitly underscored or implicitly accepted in all discussions.

This case study suggests another way to redefine an issue. Instead of internationalizing it, making it bigger or more inclusive, or tying it to an important bilateral relationship, the strategy employed by Japanese conservation groups redefined this issue within the context of a domestic experience and sentiments to raise public awareness for deforestation in the tropics. By emphasizing the destructive role played by Japanese development assistance and Japanese big business in the tropical timber trade, the Japanese anti-tropical timber campaign stirred public memory of Japan's own deforestation and their anger towards the Japanese government and big business for their poor handling of domestic industrial pollution. The anti-tropical timber campaign, thus, succeeded in pressing Japanese government and big business to increase funding for reforestation activities through bilateral and multilateral channels, as well as allocating funds for NGO activities in reforestation, biodiversity conservation, and community assistance in tropical forest countries. As Schoppa concluded in his 1993 article, outside pressure may produce the most positive results when the strategies resonate with domestic politics.[142]

Notes

[1] Deforestation is defined as a complete clearance of the forest and conversion to another land use.

[2] See "Tropical Forests Conservation," Gland: WWF International, September 1991, p.5.

[3] In addition, forest fires in 1983, 1986 and 1994 also resulted in enormous loss of plant and animal life. The 1983 fire alone destroyed about 3 million ha of tropical forest with greatest damage in previously logged areas. See F. Nectoux and Y. Kuroda, *Timber from the South Seas: An Analysis of Japan's Tropical Timber Trade and its Environmental Impact*, Gland: WWF, 1989, p.15; and John McBeth, "El Nino Gets Blamed," *Far Eastern Economic Review*, 9 October 1997, pp.80-82.

[4] Ko Shioya, "The Forest Beyond the Trees," *Asia, Inc.*, April 1993, p.30.

[5] Traditionally teak was the most commercially valuable species. Technological innovations in plywood manufacturing enabled the use of mahogany (popularly known as *lauan* in Southeast Asia) and other dipterocarp species. Jan G. Laarman, "Linkages: The Global Timber Trade," in *World Deforestation in the Twentieth Century*, ed. by John F. Richards and Richard P. Tucker, London and Durham: Duke University Press, 1988, pp.151 and 159.

[6] Jacqueline Sawyer, "Tropical Forests," Gland: WWF International, 1990, p.3.

[7] Tunya Sukpanich, "Forest Management Plan Supports Logging Industry," *Bangkok Post*, 14 November 1990.

[8] Estimates differ widely. The World Rainforest Movement estimated that 50 million tribal people live within the tropical rainforests, while Poffenberger cites data from the Independent Commission on International Humanitarian issues suggesting a figure between 140 and 200 million. See World Rainforest Movement, *Rainforest Destruction: Causes, Effects, and False Solutions*, Penang: World Rainforest Movement, 1990; and M. Poffenberger, ed., *Keepers of the Forest: Land Management Alternatives in Southeast Asia*, West Hartford: Kumarian Press, 1990.

[9] Shioya, *op cit.*, p.30; and Jane N. Abramovitz, "Taking a Stand: Cultivating a New Relationship with the World's Forests," *World Watch Papers*, No.140, April 1998, p.55.

[10] Africa has about one-fifth of the total tropical forests and Latin America contains more than one half.

[11] "Tropical forest Conservation," *op cit.*, p.3.

[12] It is surprising for many people to learn that up to 67% of Japan is forested today, or some 25 million hectares. This is the second highest

Deforestation in the Tropics

among developed countries. Masaaki Imanaga, "The Japanese View of Nature from a Comparative Viewpoint," *Japan Foundation Newsletter*, July 1996, pp.5-6; and Noriyuki Kobayashi, "Tonan Ajia no Shinrin Shigen to Mokusai Boeki" (Timber Resource in Southeast Asia and the Timber Trade), *Journal of Forest Economics*, No.127, 1995, p.41.

[13] Tropical hardwoods are ideal for concrete mold application due to their strength. They are also preferred for their cosmetic feature since they usually contain fewer knots than softwood timber from North America. Of the remaining 50% of plywood, 30% is used for furniture making and 20% for miscellaneous items, including fittings for houses, packing material, musical instruments and disposable panels for fairs and exhibitions. See Japan Forest Technical Association, ed., *Forestry Technology in Japan*, Tokyo: Japan Forest Technical Association, 1981, pp.162-3.

[14] Jeremy Abrams, "Logging—The Unkindest Cut of All," *Ecotimes*, November 1992, p.7.

[15] The U.S. leads in per capita paper consumption in 1992 at 308.7 kilogram (kg). Japan is second at 228.4 kg; followed by Singapore at 217.4 kg. The global average is 45.3 kg. In addition, Japan is the world's second largest paper and paperboard maker, and the third largest pulp producer and importer of market pulp. The country purchases over 80% of the world's internationally traded wood chips. From *Japan Economic Almanac*, Tokyo: The Nikkei Weekly, 1995, p.15; and *Japan Environment Monitor*, April 1992, p.13.

[16] Land erosion and loss of habitats for fauna and flora are among the more severe ecological consequences.

[17] Both the collection and utilization rate of used paper in Japan reaches over 50%, which is the highest in the world. Paper recycling was at a high level even before the enactment of the Packaging Waste Recycling Law in April 1997. <<www.mofa.go.jp/policy/global/environment/pamph/199706/develop.html>>. Viewed on 9 May 1998.

[18] For more on this, read Peter Dauvergne, *Shadows in the Forest: Japan and the Politics of Timber in Southeast Asia*, Cambridge and London: Massachusetts Institute of Technology Press, 1997.

[19] The case of the Penan, a hunter-gathering tribe in Sarawak and Kalimantan, is perhaps best known. The Malaysian government wanted to "resettle" them elsewhere in order to take their land for logging. The Penan battled with the government and hundreds have been arrested under a federal law that makes it a crime to interfere with logging operations. Jacqueline Vaugh Switzer, *Environmental Politics: Domestic and Global Dimensions*, New York: St. Martin's Press, 1994, p.291.

[20] Larry Fisher, "Global solutions, local realities: the Tropical Forestry Action Plan," in *Management of Tropical Forests: Towards and Integrated Perspective*, ed. Oyvind Sandbukt, Oslo: Center for Development and the Environment, University of Oslo, 1995, pp.308-9.

[21] See "ASEAN to combat West's anti-tropical wood policy," *The Indonesian Times*, 14 October 1992; "Malaysia, Indonesia to push for expansion of Timber Pact," *ibid.*, 4 December 1992; and "RI-Malaysia join to face anti-tropical timber campaign," *Ibid.*, 5 December 1992.

[22] Gareth Porter and Janet Welsh Brown, *Global Environmental Politics: Dilemmas in World Politics*, Boulder: Westview Press, 1991, pp.99-103; and various papers and abstracts in *Proceedings of the Technical Workshop to Explore Options for Global Forestry Management*, ed. by David Howlett and Caroline Sargent, Bangkok: no publisher given, 1991.

[23] UNCTAD Resolution 93 (IX) of 30 May 1976 on the Integrated Program of Commodities initiated international commodity negotiations on individual products under the auspices of UNCTAD, and tropical timber is one of them. ITTO, *ITTO Manual for Project Formulation*, Yokohama: International Tropical Timber Organization, November 1992, p.14.

[24] UNCTAD, "International Tropical Timber Agreement 1983," TD/timber/11/Rev.1.

[25] G. Kristin Rosendal, "The forest issue in post-UNCED international negotiations: conflicting interests and fora for reconciliation" in Sandbukt, ed., *op cit.*, pp.341-356.

[26] Philip Hurst, *Rainforest Politics: Ecological Destruction in South East Asia*, London and New Jersey: Zed Books, 1990, p.267.

[27] See Rosendal, *op cit.*, pp.349 and 351.

[28] "Malaysia, Indonesia to push for expansion of Timber Pact," *The Indonesia Times*, 4 December 1992; and "ASEAN to combat West's Anti-Tropical Wood Policy," *op cit.*

[29] "Non-Paper on ITTA Renegotiations," November 1992, p.4.

[30] David S. Cassells, "Considerations for Effective Inter-national Cooperation in Tropical Forest Conservation and Management" in Sandbukt, ed., *op cit.*, p.369.

[31] Rosendal, *op cit.*, p.349.

[32] For example, the *ITTO Guidelines for the Sustainable Management of Natural Tropical Forests*, *ITTO Guidelines for Sustainable Forest Industries*, *ITTO Guidelines for the Sustainable Management of Planted Tropical Forests*, *ITTO Guidelines on the Conservation of Biological Diversity in Tropical Production Forests*. See Nigel Dudley, "Forest Targets," Gland: WWF, 1995, p.11.

[33] "Incentives and Sustainability - Where is ITTO Going?" Gland: WWF International, November 1991, p.6.

[34] Cassells, *op cit.*, p.369.

[35] "Non-Paper on ITTA Renegotiations," *op cit.*, pp.1-4.

[36] Nonetheless, it can also be argued that having a large number of votes does not usually mean relatively greater power in decision making but only a greater liability to fund the organization since ITTO traditionally makes

Deforestation in the Tropics

consensus decision and have only voted three times in its history. See Rosendal, *op cit.*, p.350; and Lachlan Hunter, "Financing an International Organization (Part 1)," *Tropical Forest Update*, Vol.5, No.4, December 1995, pp.17-18.

[37] Fisher, *op cit.*, pp.307 and 313.

[38] Switzer, *op cit.*, p.286.

[39] Larry Lohmann and Marcus Colchester, "Paved with Good Intentions: TFAP's Road to Oblivion," *The Ecologist*, Vol.20, No.3, May/June 1990, p.720.

[40] Marcus Colchester and Larry Lohmann, *The Tropical Forestry Action Plan: What Progress?* Penang and England: World Rainforest Movement and The Ecologist, 1990, p.2.

[41] Colchester and Lohmann, *op cit.*, p.92; Fisher, *op cit.*, pp.308, 313-314; Robert Winterbottom, *Taking Stock: The Tropical Forestry Action Plan: After Five Years*, Washington, D.C.: World Resource Institute, 1990, pp.15 and 25; and Omar Sattaur, "Last Chance for the Rainforest Plan?" *New Scientist*, 2 March 1991, p.729.

[42] "Tropical Forest Conservation," *op cit.*, pp.14-15.

[43] "Incentives and Sustainability...," *op cit.*, p.6.

[44] "Tropical Forest Conservation," *op cit.*, p.3.

[45] The United States was strongly resistant to any international calls to cut emissions or raise energy prices. Being the largest producer of greenhouse gases, there were deep domestic anxieties of the costs for compliance. Only Canada and Japan joined the U.S. in supporting a separate global forest convention. At this time, these two countries also held positions on global warming that were similar to that of the United States. See Porter and Brown, *op cit.*, pp.101-103.

[46] The term is the name of the group formed originally by 77 developing countries to counter the weight of the developed countries in talks on creating a New International Economic Order in 1976. Membership has since expanded to over a hundred countries but the name remains the same.

[47] Porter and Brown, *op cit.*, pp.99-101.

[48] The formal title is the "Authoritative Statement of Principles for a Global Agreement on the Management, Conservation and Sustainable Development of all Types of Forests." See David Humphreys, "Regime Theory and Non-Governmental Organizations: The Case of Forest Conservation," in Potter, ed., *op cit.*, p.97.

[49] Chapter 11 and 27 of Agenda 21, respectively, provide more specific guidelines on tackling deforestation, including human resource training and technology transfer, and recognition of NGOs as partners for sustainable development.

[50] One prominent exception is WWF, which supports ITTO projects that can demonstrate sustainable logging techniques and trade.

[51] However, CITES controls apply only to international trade so that the felling and domestic trade of listed species are not prohibited, and this makes up the vast majority of the total volume consumed in the world. CITES also does not provide an adequate framework for protecting tropical timber species. In tropical forest protection, CITES—not being a habitat protection treaty—only protects individual species threatened by trade because forests are not considered endangered as a whole. See Heather Wolf, "Deforestation in Cambodia and Malaysia: The Case for an International Legal Solution," *Pacific Rim Law and Policy Journal*, Vol.5, No.2, March 1996, pp.447-448.

[52] "A WWF Guide to Forest Certification," Surrey: WWF, 1995, p.15.

[53] WWF, "Tropical Forest Conservation," op cit., pp.2 and 18; and please see Baharuddin Hj. Ghazali and Markku Simula, "Report of the Working Party on Certification of All timber and Timber Products," Yokohama: International Tropical Timber Organization, May 1994 for a detail report on the many issues and aspects on certification.

[54] Chris Elliott, "Timber certification and the Forest Stewardship Council," in Sandbukt, ed., op cit., pp.322-323; "Forest Certification: An SAF Study Group Report," *Journal of Forestry*, Vol.93, No.4, April 1995, p.10; Markku Simula and Baharuddin Hj. Ghazali, "Timber Certification in Transition," *Tropical Forest Update*, Vol.6, No.4, 1996, pp.20-22; and I.J. Bourke, "The Uruguay Round Results: An Overview," *ITTO Tropical Forest Update*, Vol.6, No.2, 1996, p.15.

[55] For more on timber certification and the Forest Stewardship Council, see Chris Elliott, "Timber Certification and the Forest Stewardship Council," in Sandbukt, ed., *op cit.*, pp.319-340.

[56] Her Suharyanto, "Big Forest, Small Ministry," Indonesia Business Weekly, Vol.11, No.10, 18 February 1994, p.16; and Bruce Cabarle *et al.*, "Certification Accreditation: The Need for Credible Claims," *Journal of Forestry*, Vol.93, No.4, April 1995, pp.12-17.

[57] The first session was from 11 to 15 September 1995 in New York. The second, third and fourth sessions were, respectively, from 11 to 22 March 1996 in Geneva, 9 to 20 September in Geneva, and 11 to 21 February 1997 in New York. Roslan bin Ismail, "Disappointment at UNGASS," *ITTO Tropical Forest Update*, Vol.17, No.3, 1997, p.18.

[58] See <<www.iisd.ca/linkages/forestry/forest.html>>. Viewed on 2 May 1998.

[59] Ismail, *op cit.*, p.18.

[60] Abramovitz, *op cit.*, p.63.

[61] See Norman Myers, "The World's Forests: Need for a Policy Appraisal," *Science*, Vol.268, 12 May 1995, pp.823 and 824.

[62] Smoke from the fires moved from Kalimantan in Indonesia to the Malaysian peninsular and Singapore. Several people died and many more were hospitalized. Although the problem became a major bilateral and

Deforestation in the Tropics

regional issue, political sensitivities obstructed cooperation to address these problems. In the end, the environment ministers of these countries were only able to produce a "regional haze action plan" in December 1997. The plan committed Malaysia to study ways to help combat the fires, Singapore to monitor them, and Indonesia to agree to improve its fire-fighting capacity. "The Fires Next Time," *The Economist*, 28 February 1998, p.44.

[63] Fisher, *op cit.*, p.308.

[64] Sawyer, *op cit.*, p.4.

[65] Cattle ranching is a main cause for the loss of tropical forests in Latin America, whereas commercial logging is more significant in Southeast Asia, and the spread of subsistence agriculture is important in East Africa. See WWF, "Tropical Forest Conservation," *op cit.*, p.5.

[66] John Terborgh, Diversity and the Tropical Rain Forest, New York: Scientific American Library, 1992, p.197; and P. Hirsh, "Deforestation and Development in Comparative Perspective: Thailand, Laos, and Vietnam," in Sandbukt, ed., *op cit.*, pp.40-42.

[67] The European Community (EC) and Japan have similar levels of tropical timber imports, but until recently Japan's imports consisted almost entirely of hardwood logs. The value of tropical timber imports by EC is also higher than Japan's because EC purchases more value-added wood products. EC also has more diverse sources: tropical logs come mainly from West Africa, tropical sawnwood from Southeast Asia and West and Central Africa and plywood from Indonesia. See Nectoux and Kuroda, *op cit.*, pp.25 and 27.

[68] See Nihon Bengoshi Rengo Kai, *Nihon no Kaigai Yushyuu to Kankyo Hakai* (Japan's overseas exports and environmental destruction), Tokyo: Heibunsha, 1991, pp.24 and 26.

[69] Japan Forest Technical Association, ed., "Forestry technology in Japan," *op cit.*, p.160.

[70] A detail study of the decline of Japan's domestic timber industry can be found in Minoru Kumazaki "Japanese Economic Development and Forestry" in *Forest policy in Japan*, ed. by Ryoichi Handa, Tokyo: Nippon Ringyo Chosakai, 1988, pp.1-15.

[71] Some government ministries opposed this new law because the re-export of processed tropical hardwood was a dollar-earner for the national treasury. A shift to domestic consumption, they feared, could eliminate this revenue and require expenditure of valuable foreign exchange. Nextoux and Kuroda, *op cit.*, p.32.

[72] Kumazaki, *op cit.*, and Ryuchi Handa, "Timber Economy and Forest Policy after the [sic] World War II," *ibid.*, pp.22-36.

[73] The other top investors, also foreign firms, were the U.S. companies Weyerhauser and Georgia Pacific.

[74] Jonathan Holliman, "Japan's Trade in Tropical Timber with Southeast Asia," in Sahabat Forest Resource Crisis in the Third World, Penang:

Sahabat Alam Malaysia, 1987, pp.250-259; Nihon Bengoshi Rengo Kai, *op cit.*, p.37.

[75] Richards and Tucker, eds., *op cit.*, p.156.

[76] Examples are projects on forestry development in the Pantabangan area in the Philippines (June 1976 to July 1992); mountain logging practices in Java (December 1977 to April 1982); trial plantation in Benakat, South Sumatra; and logging and log transport training in Thailand (October 1983 to September 1988). See Forestry Agency of Japan, "Forestry White Paper, Summary," 1994; also Dauvergne, *op cit.*, pp.24 and 25.

[77] Yoichi Kuroda, "Japan's Consumption of Tropical Timber and Effects on Tropical Forests," n.d.

[78] Logging, mining and plantation agriculture had already decimated most of peninsular Malaysia's forests so that the export of raw logs from this part of the country was prohibited—or rather no longer possible.

[79] Nihon Bengoshi Rengo Kai, *op cit.*, p.29.

[80] Nectoux and Kuroda, *op cit.*, p.36.

[81] Japan produces panels in the sizes of 3' x 6' and 3' x 8', while most other countries produce 4' x 8' panels. The Japanese construction companies do not import plywood themselves; instead, GTCs are subcontracted to provide *konpane* and often to dispose of the forms after use. See Abrams, *op cit.*

[82] Hayden Stewart, "JAS Standard, North American Plywood Makers target Japan," *The Japan Times*, 19 September 1994, p.14.

[83] In line with international trade agreements, Indonesia later converted the ban into a tariff, but log imports are discouraged by the high export tax. See Stewart, *op cit.*

[84] Alan Grainger, *Controlling Tropical Deforestation*, London: Earthscan, 1993, p.73.

[85] "Proposal for a Pacific Rim Forests International Forum," Tokyo: JATAN, November 1993.

[86] While in North America, it is more common for Japanese firms to purchase a local company or to set up a buyer company under a different name.

[87] Hurst, *op cit.*, p.17.

[88] Nihon Bengoshi Rengo Kai, *op cit.*, p.29.

[89] Debra Callister, "Illegal tropical timber trade: Asia-Pacific," *A Traffic Network Report*, 1992, p.7; and Joe Rinkevich, "A Situational Overview of Bintuni Bay: Destruction of an Internationally Important Wetland in Irian Jaya, Indonesia, for wood chipping exports to Japan," *Japan Environment Monitor*, June 1990, p.16-18.

[90] Seeing that the change was irreversible, many Japanese GTCs provided financing, machinery and technology to help build the Indonesian plywood industry.

Deforestation in the Tropics

[91] "Mistaking Plantations for Indonesia's Tropical Forests." Jakarta: Wahana Lingkungan Hidup Indonesia, 1992, pp.17-8.

[92] CIFOR was one of Indonesia's concrete follow-up measures for implementing the Forest Principles and Agenda 21 in the country. See Sandra Moniaga, "CIFOR Establishment: Consistent with Conservation?" *Environesia*, Vol.7, No.1, January-March 1993, pp.10-11.

[93] Japan agreed to provide for rent, maintenance, equipment and furnishings of the ITTO offices in Yokohama, as well as the initial recruitment costs of professional staff. Japan also funds the biannual Council Sessions, including venue, equipment, Secretariat travel, and interpreters, translators and local support staff. Under both 1983 and 1994 ITTA, the extra costs of holding a Council Session away from the ITTO head-quarters must be borne by the host country, but Japan agreed to shoulder these costs as well when it is held in a producer member country. The Kanagawa Prefectural government, where Yokohama is situated, also assumes some of ITTO's expenses. See Hunter, *op cit.*, pp.17-18.

[94] Dauvergne, *op cit.*, p.38.

[95] These reduction targets may sound impressive but are very difficult to attain because smaller subcontractors are responsible for actual construction and they may have little commitment to the target. Obayashi's decision also angered the Indonesian government and Bob Hasan, that country's "plywood king" and head of Apkindo (Indonesia's plywood manufacturers' association) and Nippindo (sole distributor of Indonesian plywood in Japan). Hasan urged Indonesian companies not to award contracts to Obayashi. See Gavan McCormack, "Growth, Construction, and the Environment: Japan's Construction State," Japan Studies, Vol.15, No.1, May 1995, p.27.

[96] Nectoux and Kuroda, *op cit.*, p.30.

[97] Apkindo was responding to increasing softwood imports by the Japanese plywood industry. Apkindo not only succeeded in dampening Japanese demand for softwood, it also further depressed the price of tropical hardwood. See Gary Nageri Munthe and Rin Hindryati, "Apkindo under Fire," *Indonesia Business Weekly*, Vol.3, No.12, 6 March 1995, pp.4-7; and Rin Hindryati, "Apkindo's all-encompassing role," *Ibid.*, p.8.

[98] *Ibid.*, pp.37-39.

[99] In addition, Canada supplied 40% of Japan's total paper pulp imports, following by the U.S. with 31.4% and Brazil with 9.1% See "Concentrated Origin of Main Resources Imported (1996)," *Japan 1998: An International Comparison*, Tokyo: Keizai Koho Center, 1998, p.72.

[100] Nectoux and Kuroda, *op cit.*, pp.37-39.

[101] N. Kobayashi, *op cit.*, pp.41-46.

[102] A shortage of wood chips in the U.S. gave rise to a rapid price increases of over 138% in a six-month period in 1979 and 1980. See Natasha Davis, "Paperpower: The Japanese paper industry and the envi-

ronment in Australia and Japan," in *Japanese Studies Bulletin*, Vol.15, No.1, 1995, p.11.

[103] For discussions on this, see Richard Forrest and Yuta Harago, "Japan's Official Development Assistance (ODA) and Tropical Forests," Gland: World Wide Fund for Nature, 1990; Forestry Agency, "Forestry White Paper, Summary," Tokyo: Government of Japan, 1994, p.29-30; and "Mistaking plantations...," *op cit.*, pp.29-41.

[104] Interview with Kumazaki. See also Charles Arden-Clarke, "Conservation and Sustainable Management of Tropical Forests: The Role of ITTO and GATT," Gland: World Wide Fund for Nature International, November 1990.

[105] Forrest and Harago, *op cit.*

[106] Dauvergne, *op cit.*, pp.174 and 175.

[107] "Japan's Official Development Assistance Summary 1997," *op cit.*, p.7.

[108] The Yokohama City government gave the ITTO secretariat free office space in a new building for international activities in its bay area development zone in Saguragicho.

[109] See Holliman, *op cit.*, pp.250-259.

[110] Abrams, *op cit.*, p.7.

[111] Industry does not like them because they seldom have broad and straight trunks.

[112] Access to timber resource is difficult and costly because Japanese forests are generally in mountainous areas, requiring considerable manpower, special skills and machinery to handle on such terrain.

[113] Thomas R. Cox, "The North American-Japanese Timber Trade: A Survey of its Social, Economic and Environmental Impact" in Richards and Tucker, eds., *op cit.*, p.171.

[114] Stewart, *op cit.*

[115] McCormack, *op cit.*

[116] The same was true for wood-processing industries in other tropical timber-importers like Taiwan and South Korea.

[117] K. Matsuki, "The Current and Future Timber Demand and supply in Japan and the Prospects of Japanese Timber Industry," in Draft Report on Timber Project PD 57/89 (F,I), November 1989, p.16; and Hurst, *op cit.*, p.15.

[118] Dauvergne, *op cit.*, p.175.

[119] By the mid-1980s, tropical timber made up only 10 percent of the total requirement for housing construction compared to 30 percent a decade earlier.

[120] Munthe and Hindryati, *op cit.*; and Hindryati, *ibid.*

[121] Interview with MoFA officials.

Deforestation in the Tropics 199

[122] The construction industry employs some 6.2 million people, nearly 10% of the entire workforce, making it by far the largest industry in Japan. See McCormack, *op cit.*

[123] Interviews Kuroda and with staff at Keidanren and Sumitomo.

[124] JIFPRO, "Japan's International Cooperation," Tokyo: Japan International Forestry Promotion and Cooperation Center, n.d., pp.9-11. Also interviews with staff at Sumitomo and RETROF.

[125] JIFPRO receives half of its funding from the Forestry Agency and makes grants to Japanese and foreign NGOs.

[126] Humphreys, *op cit.*, p.110.

[127] Only Friends of the Earth (Japan) organized a few public seminars and WWF-Japan urged the Japanese government to accept a timber certification scheme.

[128] Prior to this, there were few small Japanese NGOs, such as Nettai Rin no Mamoru Kai (Organization for the Conservation of Tropical Forests), but their disparate efforts had little impact in raising public awareness and official attention. Interviews with Forrest, Kamei and Helten.

[129] Interview with Kamei.

[130] JATAN created the Sarawak Campaign Committee to work specifically on the Sarawak timber and forest people issues. Differences between the leadership of the two groups led to the Committee's departure from JATAN.

[131] Interview with Forrest.

[132] Interviews with Kuroda and Kamei.

[133] The 1988 publication is in Japanese and was later published by WWF in English in 1989.

[134] Interview with Kuroda.

[135] JATAN also shares its experience and knowledge with South Korean environmental groups. South Korea is another major buyer of tropical timber, but its nascent environmental movement has barely any knowledge on Southeast Asia.

[136] This act has more symbolic than practical value because together they only consume a minute amount of Japan's total tropical timber imports. Interview with Uramoto.

[137] The boycott was initiated in reaction to allegations that Mitsubishi ships large volume of timber, raw logs, and wood chips from the U.S. northwest and Canada to Japan.

[138] Interview with Kuroda.

[139] Interview with Forrest.

[140] Based on interviews with leaders, staff, and representatives of Japanese and international NGOs in Japan.

[141] Schoppa, *op cit.*

CHAPTER 6

Acid Deposition in Asia

Fossil fuel consumption creates many environmental problems. Among them is acid rain which first became a major environmental concern in Europe, then North America, and in Asia today. Acid rain, along with global warming, is recognized today as one of the most serious international environmental problems associated with fossil fuel combustion.

The first scientific observation of the ecological and health dangers of acid rain was made in 1852 by Robert Angus Smith, a Scottish chemist studying the quality of air in Manchester. Smith found local rainfall to be unusually acidic and suspected a connection between acid precipitation and the sulfur dioxide given off when coal was burned by local factories. Following 20 years of fieldwork in England, Scotland, and Germany, Smith published the seminal work on the subject, *Acid and Rain: The Beginnings of a Chemical Climatology*. In it, he demonstrated the linkage between sulfur pollution, producing what he named "acid rain."

Yet, it was not until a century later that people began to pay serious attention to acid rain. The Scandinavian countries, as net importers of acid pollution from other parts of Europe, alerted the world to the dangers of acidification. Norway was the first to notice fish deaths in its lakes in the early 1950s. By the mid-1950s, strong acid rain was observed in southeastern England, northern France, and the Benelux countries. In the next two decades, increasing evidence of acid rain was found in western and northern Europe and in parts of North America.[1] In 1983, the United Nations Environment Program identified acid rain as one of three key international environmental issues in its annual report, *State of the World Environment*.[2]

Although technological solutions are available, they are not cheap. There is also a lack of complete understanding on how chemicals transform to produce acid rain, the transport of acid pollutants, and the impact of acid pollution on ecology and human health. Complexity of this problem

201

requires investigations under several scientific disciplines.[3] This has made it extremely difficult to establish clear costs and benefits in proposing regulatory actions and other responses. Policy uncertainly is further complicated by the fact that acid rain is a transboundary pollution problem, making international cooperation essential to its solution. Since a polluter country is not always affected by its own actions, persuading polluter countries to control sulfur dioxide (SO_2) and nitrogen oxide (NO_x) emissions, the main acid pollutants, has not generally been easy.

This is why it took several decades of scientific study and intense political negotiations to reach agreements and implement measures to control SO_2 and NO_x emissions in Europe in the late 1970s and in North America in the 1980s.[4] Since governments, industry, and the public have to recognize existence of the problem, its severity, as well as the high costs in control, curbing acid rain is fundamentally a question of how much a society values material wealth, economic growth, health, and the environment.[5]

ACID RAIN: DEFINITION, DANGERS AND CHARACTERISTICS

Acid rain generally describes the deposition of all atmospheric pollutants of an acidic, or potentially acidic nature, whether they are deposited in wet (rain or snow) or in the dry (gases and small particles) state.[6] Since acid pollution is mainly caused by the SO_2 produced in fossil fuels combustion, this problem is closely tied to industrial development.[7] Scientific evidence shows that since the 1960s, the area affected by acid rain in northeastern United States, in northern Europe, and in Scandinavia has more than triple. In the last two decades, SO_2 emissions have risen rapidly in the Asia-Pacific region.[8] Coal, a widely used source of energy, is among the heaviest producers of SO_2.

Acid pollution is not entirely anthropogenic in origin, but human activities have made it an environmental problem of global proportions.[9] Although recent estimates of annual global sulfur emissions range from 50 to 100 Mt S (megatons of sulfur), estimates of human caused emissions alone range from 60 to 80 Mt S. About 35 Mt S (or 40 percent) of artificial emissions originates from Europe, 19 Mt S (24 percent) from North America, and about 18 Mt S (23 percent) from Asia. Although emissions have fallen substantially in Western Europe in the last two decades, it is still increasing at a global level, and its growth has been particularly high in Asia.[10]

Like many other environmental problems, acid pollution is multifaceted. SO_x and NO_x rank among the most dangerous chemical air pollutants, and acid rain affects air, water, soil, and biota. Although scientific studies disagree on the severity of acid rain damage, there is consensus that the harmful effects are real and long-term. For instance, research suggests that acid rain can destroy aquatic ecosystems by liberating minerals in watersheds.[11]

Acid Deposition in Asia

In Ontario, Canada, nearly 50,000 lakes are considered vulnerable to acid pollution. Of these, 140 have been certified as so acidic that they have no fish at all.[12] On land, acid pollution leaches aluminum from soils and destroys tree root system by depriving them of water. Trees die because a weakened root system is vulnerable to fungi and bacterial attacks. "Forest deaths" (*waldsterben*) in West Germany were so severe that they compelled the government to completely change its attitude towards acid rain.[13]

As for human health, although science does not indicate sulfur pollution as a direct cause of death or disease, studies have shown correlation between increased sulfate levels and premature death, as well as heart and respiratory diseases.[14] There have been many cases where the loss of human lives and injuries were attributed to acid pollution. The most severe occurred in the winter of 1952 in London. Acid pollution and adverse weather conditions created a "killer fog" that hung over the city for several days.[15] British authorities estimated that 4,000 persons died and another 2,000 were hospitalized as a direct result of this killer fog.[16]

Materials, too, can be affected by acid pollution. Buildings, monuments, and other points of cultural heritage throughout Europe and in many parts of North America have displayed signs of acid damage. Railroad tracks in Poland have suffered severe corrosion. Even books and paintings in libraries and museums are vulnerable. A U.S. government study in 1979 estimated that the annual cost of acid ran damage to architectural structures alone was in excess of US$2 billion.[17]

Complicating this problem is the mobile and transboundary nature of chemical pollutants. Sulfur dioxide appears able to remain in the air for up to five days and travel long distances in a weather system.[18] The longer SO_2 and NO_x remain in the air, the greater is the likelihood of chemical transformation (oxidation) to produce sulfuric acid and nitric acid. So the movement and effects of acid pollution can transcend political and natural boundaries usually within a geographical region that is governed by a common weather system.[19] Effective control of acid pollution, thus, often demands international cooperation in implementing bilateral and multilateral emissions reduction measures and targets.

ACID RAIN IN ASIA AND JAPAN'S POLICY RESPONSES

While SO_2 and NO_x emissions have declined significantly in Europe and North America as a result of multilateral agreements and unilateral reduction measures, acid pollution has reached to alarming levels in Asia's industrializing economies. Coal is the primary energy source in Asia. The region's total SO_2 emissions are expected to reach 62 million tons by the year 2010, up from 29 million in 1987.[20] Other pollutants like NO_x and carbon dioxide (CO_2) have also increased. Serious environmental damage will occur unless drastic changes are made.

Most of the region's governments are now keen to address the problem as more data have emerged on the economic and human costs of acid pollution. Public pressure for improvements, too, has increased. For example, a survey by the People's University of China between 1993 and 1994 found that 42.1 percent of the respondents replied that the "environment may be more important than economic development" and air pollution was identified as the third biggest environmental problem in China.[21]

This heightened public concern has prompted governments in the region to adopt, in the past decade, source emission standards and set ambient aid quality goals that are consistent with the World Health Organization's guidelines for particulates, sulfur dioxide, and nitrogen oxide emissions. Individual economies, including Hong Kong, Thailand, Vietnam, Taiwan, and Indonesia, have also considered an increase in natural gas use as a means to reduce SO_2 emissions at source.[22] However, emphasis on economic growth often overshadows environmental protection. The financial crisis that has swept across the Asian economies since 1997 has also significantly slowed progress in environmental protection in the region. Finally, the region has a shortage of experience and institutions for multilateral cooperation to tackle this kind of transboundary pollution problem. The Asia Pacific Economic Cooperation (APEC), for instance, promotes cooperation in coal and energy, but does not stress transboundary pollution control because it is not in its mandate.

Where SO_2 emissions are concerned, China is by far the most worrisome threat to Asia (and the world). Research suggests that China is responsible for two-thirds of the total SO_2 emissions and half of all NO_x emissions in the Asian region and some 37 percent of Japan's acid deposits are from China.[23] With some 75 percent of its energy derived from coal combustion, China is already the world's second largest emitter of SO_2 after the United States. By the early 1990s, China was producing as much as 19 million tons of SO_2 annually. This compared with less than 1 million ton for Japan and, between 22 and 23 million tons for the United States.[24] Furthermore, the spread of desulfurization equipment in power generation in the region has not grown quickly enough to cope with increases in coal use. Low efficiency in energy production and consumption is another significant problem. For instance, energy efficiencies at China's coal-fired power plants are estimated at no more than 33 percent.

Although Japan is not the main sulfur emitter, industrial growth in the Asia-Pacific region in the past two decades has been fueled substantially by Japanese investment. Japan also has the experience, financial wealth, and technological know-how to respond to this problem. An aggressive domestic acid rain control program began in Japan in the early 1970s. External pressure due to the Oil Crisis of 1973 and internal pressure due to public discontent with industrial pollution drove the Japanese government to make the country more energy efficient.[25] As Table 9 shows, Japan, on a

Acid Deposition in Asia

country basis, is the smallest producer of SO_2 and NO_x among leading industrialized economies. Between 1970 and 1975, Japan reduced its SO_2 emissions by 50 percent, while its energy production increased by 120 percent. The total volume of SO_2 emissions dropped from 6.25 million tons in 1970 to 876,000 tons in 1990.

Table 9. Comparison of SO_x and NO_x emissions, by country [1990]

Country	Sulfur oxides	Nitrogen oxides
	(tons)	(tons)
Japan	876,000	1,301,000
Canada	3,323,000	1,923,000
France	1,200,000	1,487,000
West Germany	939,000	2,605,000
Italy	1,988,000	1,996,000
United Kingdom	3,780,000	2,779,000
United States	21,060,000	19,380,000

Note: Figures for Japan and Italy are for 1989
Source: OECD, *Environment Data*; and *ECO Japan: International Comparison of Environmental Data*, Tokyo: Keizai Koho Center, 1994, p. 16-17

Several government actions that began in the early 1970s are responsible for these impressive results:

(1) A shift from coal to low-sulfur oil for energy greatly reduced the amount of SO_2 emissions and particulates. By 1992, oil constituted 57.4 percent of Japan's total primary energy consumption—the highest ratio in the world;[26]

(2) Success in developing and implementing desulfurization technology reduced the average sulfur content of the heavy oils used in Japan from 2.50 percent in 1967 to just 1.13 percent in 1992;[27]

(3) Introduction and strict enforcement of stringent air quality laws by national and local governments. The most important measure has been the pollution load levy system for SO_x emissions. It was created originally to raise funds for compensating victims of pollution, but it became an economic incentive for the industry to actively develop and introduce desulfurization technology;[28] and

(4) Government incentives and assistance helped to overcome economic concerns. The Japanese government gave low interest loans to industry for pollution control investment and over a thousand

acid scrubbers have been installed throughout the country under the Clean Coal Technologies program.[29]

Reductions in NO_x emissions, too, were achieved by the widespread use of catalytic converters in automobiles. All of this has enabled Japan to greatly reduce emissions and raise energy efficiency within a very short period of time.[30] Today the Japanese government continues to cut domestic SO_2 emission by reducing its energy dependence on coal by increasing natural gas import and making nuclear power generation a key component in its energy strategy.[31] Thus, Japan has experience and expertise that could be relevant to the developing countries in the Asia and Pacific region.

As an environmental issue, acid deposition awoke Japan to the fact that domestic clean up measures are not sufficient to protect the country's environment and its people, and that helping neighboring countries to improve efficiency in energy production and consumption would be the best way to serve Japan itself.

Japan's goal is to build a regional acid rain control regime and reducing emissions in China is a priority. Hence, the two key Japanese policy initiatives examined in this case study are (1) its decision to build an acid rain monitoring network in East Asia and (2) its active extension of bilateral assistance to help improve the Chinese energy sector as well as other means to engage Chinese cooperation.

The Japanese government knows that building a regional acid rain control regime would not be easy. China and the majority of the developing economies in the region depend heavily on coal for energy production because it is cheap and plentiful. However, its high mineral content makes it the worst fossil fuel for energy production and a switch to cleaner alternatives and implementation of pollution control technology are impeded by insufficient financial resources. In addition, gaps in economic development have hampered international cooperation in responding to this transboundary pollution problem. Some economies, such as Japan, Singapore, and Hong Kong, have the means and the interest to control emissions, but many others do not.

Political differences have been another great obstacle to international cooperation. For instance, a regional inter-governmental sampling network or agreement for acid rain control in Northeast Asia is not likely to include Taiwan and North Korea. These two countries contribute significantly to the problem in the region but Beijing and Seoul would likely object to their participation as long as the political feuds remain unsettled.

Since acid rain is basically a regional pollution problem, there is no international regime for acid rain control. The dangers of acid rain and its damage in Europe two decades ago motivated European policy makers and public to cooperate. Policy makers in Japan, looked to the European experience for guidance in approaching the problem in Asia. At the same time,

Acid Deposition in Asia

Japanese policy makers learn from the North American experience also showed the Japanese government that diplomatic rigor and delicacy are critical when a single polluter has enough leverage to make or break the success international negotiations.

Therefore, the European and U.S. experience represent the international level forces that were most influential in shaping Japan's policies and approaches in responding to acid deposition in Asia. Other international forces were the state of the energy sector in China and other economies in the region and the political and economic complexities in Sino-Japanese relations. Finally, it should be noted that transboundary acid deposition is one of few international environmental issues in which Japan takes a pro-active approach to the problem. It is also one in which the Environment Agency of Japan is a major policy actor.

ACID RAIN CONTROL IN EUROPE AND NORTH AMERICA

Although scientists have long suspected connections between acid rain and ecological damages and have documented evidence of their findings, it was not until the issue was set within in the context of political discussions that governments began to contemplate policy responses. It took many more years before policy makers truly accepted the severity of the problem and enacted policies and regulations to address it. Considerations of the high costs of emissions controls as well as the potential political implications have kept many governments, industry, and the public from accepting pro-posed solutions to acid pollution.

While science and technology are critical to meeting the environmental challenges of the problem, they can also encourage new perspectives on costs and benefits, which are often the strongest arguments used against emissions control. This is important because political conflicts and eco-nomic anxieties often take precedence over environmental concerns in the minds of government policy makers, businessmen, and the public.

The building of a regional regime for acid rain control has gone the fur-thest in Europe, where the problem was first identified and its effects stud-ied. The Scandinavian countries, among the most severely affected, have been the strongest advocates for emission controls. Their situation demon-strated to Japanese policy makers the economic costs and ecological and health hazards of acid pollution, and helped to persuade them to reduce domestic sulfur emissions by the early 1970s. Their vociferous push for multilateral responses also alerted Japanese policy makers the need for a regional acid rain control regime in Asia.

North America's experience in acid rain control, too, offered some important lessons for Japan. In this case, only two countries were involved, and one was the net importer (Canada) and the other was the net exporter (the United States) of acid pollution. As long as the United States was unwilling to address the problem, neither Canada nor international pressure could influence the U.S. government. A similar situation exists in Asia, where China is a net exporter of acid pollutants and Japan is a net importer. The Japanese government could see that unless China decides to reduce emissions, outside requests for reductions and offers of assistance would not make any significant difference.

The North American case also made the Japanese government more aware of how unmet expectations and frustrations in joint efforts to address the problem could affect other aspects of Sino-Japanese relations. Historical wounds, political sensitivities, and economic ties between the two countries make any potential conflict highly unwelcome.

Therefore, in addition to understanding the scientific aspects of the acid rain problem, the European and North American experiences taught Japanese policy makers about the political conditions necessary for success in emissions control and limits to what is practically achievable.

The European experience.

Establishing the presence of acid pollution and its harmful effects was the first critical step towards building a control regime. The world's first acid scientific monitoring programs and networks began in Europe after World War II. These efforts enabled scientists to document this problem and their work was an important base for future research.

Identifying acid rain and the European Air Chemistry Network.
In the mid-1940s, Hans Egner, a Swedish soil scientist, conceived of a rain monitoring program in Scandinavia to study the new concept of rain fertilization of crops. By 1955, his observed that acid rain was affecting large parts of Europe. This prompted the International Meteorological Institute to expand the sampling network into the European Air Chemistry Network (EACN) in 1956. EACN's main duty was to systematically collect data on precipitation throughout Scandinavia and in most parts of Western and Central Europe, including the former Soviet Union and Poland.[32] This network became the earliest basis for scientific study of acid rain across Europe.

EACN's major contribution is its demonstration that acid rain is not a local problem, but a transboundary one. EACN's broad geographical coverage increased understanding of the long-range transport patterns, which are key to debates about the causes and effects of acid pollution. This network is still operating today, making it the oldest continuous rain sampling program in the world.[33]

Turning acid rain into a policy debate.
Scientific knowledge about acid rain and its connection to atmospheric changes increased. The work of Swedish agriculture scientist Svante Oden was particularly important. In 1961, Oden began collecting samples from Scandinavian lakes and rivers as part of an effort to establish a surface

Acid Deposition in Asia

water monitoring network. EACN data helped him to show that acid rain could travel great distances and could be affected by atmospheric conditions. He also observed that acidity of precipitation over northern Europe had increased over time. Rising acidity, he cautioned, could have serious environmental impact, including destruction of fish populations, leaching of toxic metals from soils damaging land and water life, removal of essential plant nutrients thus exposing plants and trees to diseases, and even damage to man-made structures of marble and limestone.[34]

Oden also brought the acid rain problem into the policy arena. By publishing his findings on 24 October 1967 in a Swedish newspaper—instead of a scientific journal—he spurred scientific and political communities to respond to this problem.[35] A year later, establishing links between massive fish death in southern Scandinavia to acid pollution from East and West Germany and Britain, Oden provided the first tangible proof of acid rain and its international reach and impact.[36] This finding pushed governments in Scandinavian countries to initiate serious diplomatic and scientific efforts to tackle acid pollution.

Preparations for international negotiations.

Although at this time only governments in the Scandinavian countries openly acknowledged the problem, concern for acid rain moved the United Nations Economic Commission for Europe (UNECE) to form a working party to study air pollution in 1969. The year 1972 marked a critical change in the attitude of many West European governments. In April that year, the Organization for Economic Cooperation and Development (OECD) launched a four-year study (the Cooperative Technical Program to Measure the Long-range Transport of Air Pollutants or CTP) in 11 European member countries. About 80 observation stations were set up to monitor sulfur content in air and precipitation.[37] This program was vital to finding diplomatic and scientific solutions to the problem. International negotiations were impossible without knowing the causes and effects of sulfur emissions and their transport within Europe, and a commonly accepted scientific base was essential to setting reduction targets. Scientific data were also essential to prevent economic and political arguments from hijacking the debate and obstructing efforts to address the problem.

The other important event was the Stockholm Conference in June 1972. The Swedish government used this high-profile event to highlight acid rain as an international environmental problem and to emphasize its call for the control of long-range sulfur pollution. The meeting also brought acid rain, as an environmental and policy issue, to North America. A Swedish government report underlined the urgent need to investigate acid pollution in certain regions of Canada and the northeastern part of the United States. However, this warning did not precipitate serious responses from those identified as the major emitters of SO_2 and NO_x, including West Germany, Britain, and the United States.[38] Only one significant statement was made on transboundary pollution. Number 21 of the 26 general principles adopted by the participating governments at this United Nations forum states that,

> States have, in accordance with the Charter of the United Nations and the principles of international law, the sovereign right to exploit their resources pursuant of their own environmental policies and the responsibility to ensure that activities within their jurisdiction or control do not cause damage to the environment of other states or of areas beyond the limits of national jurisdiction.[39]

Witnessing overwhelming evidence of ecological damage by acid rain, the Scandinavian countries knew that international cooperation was necessary even if the polluter countries were not responsive to their calls for action. Norway, Sweden, Finland, and Denmark signed the Nordic Convention on the Protection of the Environment in 1974. The agreement technically eliminated international boundaries with respect to pollution and the environment among the Nordic countries and provided reciprocal environmental protection to all citizens of the four nations from threats within. Similarities in their domestic legal structures and approaches enabled a high degree of integration and coordination, and ensured a strong regional response to external environmental threats.[40]

The Watershed: Conference on Security and Cooperation, 1975.
The watershed development came in 1975 at the Conference on Security and Cooperation in Helsinki. For the first time, countries from both Eastern and Western Europe met to discuss the problem of transboundary pollution. A relaxation of tensions in East-West relations prompted the Soviet leader Leonid Brezhnev to suggest an attempt to reach agreement on three pan-European problems, namely, energy, transportation, and the environment. Despite the thaw in East-West relations, security concerns disabled talks on energy and transportation. This left environment, the least politically charged issue among the three, for discussion.

Norway and Sweden seized this opportunity to propose pollution as the main agenda item, and they chose UNECE as the forum for talks because it brought together both countries producing acid rain and those affected by it.[41] Negotiations began in 1977 to produce a convention on long-range transboundary air pollution to be signed by all European countries, the United States, and Canada.

Norway and Sweden, victims of acid pollution from foreign sources, wanted tough emission controls, but strong opposition came from Britain and West Germany, which were the major producers of sulfur dioxide in Europe. Without their participation, any convention concluded would be meaningless. Nonetheless, Britain would not commit to any action until it saw potential in reducing sulfur emissions through its nuclear power pro-

Acid Deposition in Asia

gram, and West Germany entered the talks as a result of diplomatic pressure from France, Sweden, and Norway.[42]

Responding to long-range transboundary air pollution.

By the mid-1970s, most governments in Europe could no longer ignore acid rain. OECD research results published in 1977 provided convincing evidence of the chemistry and transport of acid pollution, supporting many of the assertions made by Scandinavian scientists. There was also evidence of acid rain damage in European countries north of the Alps.[43]

This persuaded European governments to establish in 1978 the Cooperative Program for Monitoring and Evaluation of Long-Range Transmission of Air Pollutants in Europe (EMEP). The program would provide information on the deposition and concentration of air pollutants, as well as the quantity and significance of long-range transmission of pollutants and fluxes across boundaries. Sixty monitoring stations were set up in 20 countries in Eastern and Western Europe. The World Meteorological Organization (WMO) also provided meteorological data and served as an independent forum for evaluation. By this time, sufficient data on acid pollutants and their transport had gathered to develop models to assess long-range movement of pollutants.[44] UNECE also formed a Special Group on Long-Range Transboundary Air Pollution in 1978 to support talks for an agreement to control long-range acid pollution.[45]

After three years of negotiations, the Convention on Long-range Transboundary Air Pollution (CLRTAP) was signed in Geneva in November 1979. The Convention was placed within the framework of UNECE in order to include all European countries on both sides of the iron curtain, as well as the European Economic Community, Canada, and the United States.[46] Although a landmark achievement, critics charged that the convention was much watered down by requiring contracting parties only to "endeavor to limit and, as far as possible, gradually reduce and prevent air pollution including long-range transboundary air pollution." They also stressed that allowing the use of "best available technology, which is economically feasible in new and retrofitted plants," would leave room for wide and loose interpretations that allow financial costs to take precedence over environmental protection.[47] Nonetheless, apart from its symbolic significance of having signatories from both sides of the iron curtain, the convention committed pollution exporting and importing countries to work together.[48] Moreover, by targeting emissions control for SO_2, NO_x, and other chemical pollutants, as well as heavy metals, the convention had long-run significance in reducing air pollution in general. The convention also helped EMEP to garner resources to continue its monitoring work.[49]

Conclusion of the convention represented consensus on the presence of acid rain and the need for more national and international responses. However, political and economic arguments against implementing new laws and technologies were significant obstacles to actual reductions in emissions.[50]

Stockholm Acid Conference 1982.
This was why Sweden hosted the Conference on Acidification of the Environment in June 1982 to encourage ratification of CLRTAP in order to bring it into force. James MacNeill, environment director of OECD, observed that "the principal issue and the main source of controversy is who should bear the costs, how should the costs be borne, and when." Towards this end, Sweden organized a ministerial meeting, in addition to scientific and technical ones, to find political commitment to implement the convention. [51]

However, a resurgence of Cold War tensions kept most Communist bloc countries away. East Germany was the only major East European polluter present. Bulgaria, Poland, Czechoslovakia, and the Soviet Union boycotted the meeting.[52] To prevent this reduced participation from Eastern Communist countries from becoming a setback to the process, the Nordic proposed for a mutual 30 percent reduction in SO_2 emissions from 1983 to 1993.

The "30 percent Club."
This Nordic proposal was supported by Canada, Austria, Switzerland, and West Germany, but was rejected by Britain, U.S., France, and the East European countries. Britain, the United States, and France were worried about the high costs they would have to bear as major polluters and how the large cut might compromise their national economic competitiveness. East European countries opposed on the basis that the proposal violates their national sovereignty. Setting aside their political rhetoric, it was clear that they did not want to expose their economic frailty and further weaken their industrial base as their economies continued to falter.

Despite these objections, 10 countries agreed to a unilateral 30 percent cut in SO_2 emissions and signed an agreement in Ottawa in March 1984.[53] A 30 percent reduction was not an arbitrary or unrealistic target. A German report from 1979 had shown that desulfurization in renovated power plants could reduce emissions by 30 percent. For this reason, France, West Germany, Canada, and Norway unilaterally committed themselves to a 50 percent reduction, and Denmark and the Netherlands agreed to a 40 percent reduction.[54]

These countries wanted to show that large emission cuts were technically possible and anxieties about high costs should not discourage ambitious reduction targets. Their commitment put more pressure on the United States, Britain, and the Soviet Union to respond to the problem. This "30 percent Club" grew to 18 nations at the International Conference on Environmental Protection in Munich in June 1984.[55] Having a significant number of acid pollution exporting and importing countries accepting a fixed percentage reduction, the drafting of a protocol commenced.

Acid Deposition in Asia

Table 10. Original Members of the 30% Club

Date of accession	Reducing 30% by 1993	Reducing more than 30%
March 1984	Finland	
March 1984	Sweden	
March 1984	Switzerland	
June 1984	Belgium	
June 1984	Bulgaria	
June 1984	Byelorussia	
June 1984	East Germany	
June 1984	Liechtenstein	
June 1984	Luxembourg	
June 1984	Soviet Union	
June 1984	Ukraine	
September 1984	Czechoslovakia	
September 1984	Italy	
April 1985	Hungary	
March 1984		Austria (50% by 1993)
March 1984		Canada (50% by 1994)
March 1984		Denmark (40% by 1995)
March 1984		West Germany (50% by 1993)
March 1984		Norway (50% by 1994)
March 1984		France (50% by 1990)
March 1984		Netherlands (40% by 1995)

Source: John McCormick, *Acid Earth: The Global Threat of Acid Pollution*, London: International Institute for Environment and Development, 1985, p.81.

The first and second sulfur protocols.

The signing of CLRTAP in 1979 made way for international agreements to reduce acid pollution. For SO_2 emissions, two protocols were concluded in 1985 and 1994, respectively. The First Sulfur Protocol, signed in Helsinki, required all parties to reduce their annual sulfur emissions or transboundary fluxes by at least 30 percent as soon as possible or at the latest by 1993 (using 1980 as a baseline year for calculating reductions).

Most signatories to CLRTAP accepted the protocol, except Britain, Poland, and the United States, which were the major SO_2 producers. Britain objected on the basis of uncertainties about SO_2 emission levels in the next decade. Britain also charged that the baseline year and reduction level chosen were arbitrary, making no correlation between acid deposition and environmental impacts.[56] Poland refused to sign the protocol because it was highly dependent on domestic coal, which has high sulfur content, and the country did not have the means to acquire emissions control technologies.[57] In the United States, the Reagan administration did not consider acid pollution a high priority policy issue and was basically hostile to most multilateral undertakings.[58]

The second protocol was signed in Oslo 26 parties (including the European Community) in 1994.[59] The goal was to reduce emissions to a level that would not exceed the critical load level (the level of annual deposits, which are deemed sustainable without adverse effects). Unlike the Helsinki Protocol, the same percentage cut was not demanded of all parties, and each could set its own deadline for meeting its national target.[60] This allowed for a more flexible joint implementation system to encourage greater acceptance.[61]

Controlling NOx emissions.

Following significant progress in international reductions of SO_2 emissions, attention turned to nitrogen oxides, the other major acid pollutant. In May 1986, the International Conference on Acidification and its Policy Implications was held in Amsterdam to push for international emissions standards for nitrogen oxides. Two years later, 24 countries signed the Protocol on the Control of Emissions from Nitrogen Oxides Emissions or their Transboundary Fluxes on 1 November 1988 in Sofia. This agreement aimed to freeze NO_x emissions at 1987 levels by 1994. Since the United States was the biggest producer of nitrogen oxides, its acceptance of the treaty greatly bolstered the credibility of this protocol, which came into effect in 1991.

The European Union's Council of Environment Ministers also agreed to a binding directive to restrict SO_2, NO_x and dust emissions from large combustion plants. This is by far the most important legislation for emissions reduction in Europe.[62] The directive commits European Union countries to reduce SO_2 emissions by 58 percent by 2003, and NO_x and particulate emissions by 40 percent by 1998. Strict emission limits are also placed on all power plants approved after July 1987.[63] Finally, 21 members of UNECE signed the Protocol Concerning the Control of Emissions from Volatile Organic Compounds or Their Transboundary Fluxes in Geneva in November 1991. Using 1988 as the base year, volatile organic compounds were to reduce by at least 30 percent by 1999.[64]

In summary, Europe's success in acid pollution control was made possible by several factors. They included rigorous scientific research, commitment by policy makers, scientists and the public, presence of regional frameworks for multilateral cooperation in scientific research, policy coordination and implementation, and availability of financial and technologi-

Acid Deposition in Asia

cal resources. The absence or shortage of these attributes in North America and Asia has decisively deterred effective responses to acid pollution.

The North American experience.

Scientific interest and policy response to acid pollution came much slower in North America. To begin with, continuous records on sulfur emission in the U.S. did not exist until the late 1970s. Hence, the U.S. government refused to accept that the U.S. was a leading exporter of acid pollution despite pleas for action from Canada and Western Europe.

In addition, there was weak domestic demand to address the problem. Most affected areas within U.S. territory were sparsely populated and public awareness of the destructive effects of acid pollution was very limited. U.S. industry also fiercely opposed emissions control because of the high costs involved in switching to low-sulfur fuels and installing desulfurization technology. Oil price hikes and domestic economic slowdown made the U.S. government and industry less willing to risk invest in expensive technologies that have uncertain payoffs.

The Canadian government, on the other hand, was forced to confront the problem at central and provincial levels by the early 1970s. Canadian forests and lakes were dying from acid pollution, and two-thirds of all sulfuric acid in Canada came from the United States. Canada was keenly aware of the economic consequences of acid pollution. Forestry provided thousands of jobs in the timber and pulp industries and fishing communities depended on fish populations in lakes throughout southern Ontario and Nova Scotia.[65]

U.S. policy took a major turn in 1978. Acid rain had become a major priority concern for many conservation groups.[66] Their campaigns raised public awareness, and state government support from affected areas, such as New York, Vermont, and Maine, supported their efforts to pressure the Congress and the president. In 1978, President Jimmy Carter announced the Initiative on Acid Precipitation and launched the National Acid Deposition Program.[67]

Shortly after, the first U.S.-Canadian acid rain research program commenced its work. Research showed 11 times more NO_x and two to four times more SO_2 were transported from the U.S. to Canada than *vice versa*. These findings forced the United States to be more responsive to the problem, which had, by this time, grown into a major sore point between the two countries. Subsequently, the U.S. Congress passed a resolution calling for bilateral discussions with Canada, and a Joint Statement on Transboundary Air Quality issued in 1979 stated that the two countries were united by "common determination to reduce or prevent transboundary air pollution, which injures health or property."[68]

The momentum for cooperation continued. In 1980, a Memorandum of Intent (MOI) on Transboundary Air Pollution was signed. This MOI emphasized the need for domestic pollution control policies to tackle the "already serious problem of acid rain."[69] On the Canadian side, laws were amended to give the parliament authority to control sources that contribute to cross-border pollution to better enable high level discussions with the U.S. government.[70]

All progress came to a halt when the Reagan administration took over in 1981. Bilateral talks during the Carter presidency had led scientists from Canada and the U.S. to agree on a target loading level. However, the new U.S. working group under the Reagan administration refused to accept the target loading figure and downgraded the problem and level of discussions with Canada despite criticisms from environmental groups, scientists and the Canadian government. Citing scientific uncertainties, the U.S. government called for more information and research to delay implementation of regulatory measures.[71] Canada signed the first sulfur protocol in 1985 to put pressure on the United States. However, Canada and other countries had very little leverage over the United States because, unlike in Europe, the power asymmetry was much greater in North America.[72]

No breakthrough occurred until 1988. The Bush administration had a more positive attitude towards environmental concerns. At the same time, global environmental issues had gained prominence in international affairs so that refusing to address the problem would be a diplomatic embarrassment. Talks with Canada resumed and the president outlined a strong domestic acid pollution control program in June 1989. Bush also asked the Congress to amend the 1970 Clean Air Act. As a result, an acid rain program was initiated under the 1990 Clean Air Act Amendment to reduce annual SO_2 emissions by 10 million tons below 1980 levels by the year 2000.[73] Market-based mechanisms, such as tradable pollution permits, would be main tool in inducing emission cuts by industry.[74] Emissions are expected to be down by 40 percent when the program is fully implemented by 2010.[75]

Phase One of the U.S. Environment Protection Agency's Acid Rain Program targeted SO_x emissions reduction at 445 mostly coal-burning electric utility plants across the country. Emissions data indicated that SO_2 emissions at these units in 1995 were reduced by almost 40 percent below their required level. Phase Two of the program begins in 2000 to tighten the annual limits for large, higher emitting plants, and to set restrictions for smaller, cleaner plants fired by coal, oil, and gas. This will affect over 2,000 power plants, including all new ones and those having an output capacity of greater than 25 megawatts.[76] Nonetheless, U.S. emissions would still be five times greater than Canada's, and more than half of all acid deposition in eastern Canada would come from the United States.[77]

The North American experience again underscored the importance of political leadership and a government's commitment to finding solutions. It showed Japan that even scientific evidence and public demand are insuffi-

Acid Deposition in Asia

cient to persuade a polluter in a dominant position—like the United States in North America and China in Asia—to accept unilateral changes or multilateral cooperation. International censure through governmental and non-governmental channels would also be quite useless unless a polluter country is willing and able to act, whether on it own or with foreign assistance. Finally, a strategy that engages a polluter country to act can be more constructive than one that condemns and alienates it.

CHINA: NUMBER ONE POLLUTION SOURCE IN ASIA

While pollution control agreements in Europe and North America have significantly reduced SO_2 and NO_x emissions, no similar effective regional efforts exist in Asia where its industrializing economies have been among the fastest growing ones in the world.[78] In addition to high economic growth rates, the region has the highest share of coal in total primary energy consumption and the highest growth rate in electricity generation capacity. The Intergovernmental Panel on Climate Change projected energy demand in Asia will grow on average by 5.6 percent per year between 1990 and 2025, and by an average of 2.9 percent per year between 2025 and 2100. Coal, considered the most significant resource affecting global climate change and the biggest source of anthropogenic acid pollution, will play a large role in fueling this growth.

Table 11. Coal consumption in Asia, 1990-2010

Economy	1990	2000	2010	Increase, 1990-2010
China	1,063	1,365	1,655	592
India	205	360	575	370
Japan	113	142	151	38
Australia	57	66	85	28
Korea (North)	52	65	75	23
Korea (South)	43	56	60	17
Taiwan	19	35	57	38
Hong Kong	10	13	16	6
Indonesia	7	25	45	38
Vietnam	4	8	17	13
Philippines	3	13	22	19
Thailand	1	6	25	24
Other	10	16	22	12
Total	1,587	2,170	2,805	1,218

Note: Asia includes the SW Pacific but excludes the Russia; 1990 figures do not include stock adjustments; excludes lignite. Source: EWC Coal Project projections, Program on Resources: Energy and Minerals, East-West Center, Honolulu, 1992.

The Roots of Japan's Environmental Policy

Table 12. Average annual electricity growth rates (in percentages)

	1980-1990	1990-2000	2000-2010
Indonesia	14.2	10.0	7.2
Pakistan	11.9	8.8	6.0
South Korea	11.1	8.0	6.0
Thailand	10.8	9.5	6.0
India	9.1	6.0	5.0
Malaysia	8.6	7.7	6.0
Hong Kong	8.5	5.5	6.0
Taiwan	8.3	7.0.	5.0
China	7.7	8.1	6.5
Philippines	4.3	5.2	5.0
Japan	3.7	3.3	2.6

Source: *Coal Information, 1991*; International Financial Statistics; and East-West Center Coal Project estimates.

In fact, Asia leads the world in dependence on coal. Almost half of Asia's energy is supplied by coal. This compares to an average of 25 percent for the rest of the world. Exacerbating this are weaknesses in applying technologies and regulations to control emissions. Although most Asian economies have plans to install clean coal technologies (CCTs) in future power plants, Japan is the only country currently having widespread use of CCTs in Asia.[79] Recent recognition that deteriorating air quality in Asia will have wide-ranging consequences for the region and the world, governments in the region have begun efforts to control transboundary acid pollution and its effects.

The Chinese environment juggernaut.

While acid pollution elsewhere in Asia is also serious, China is the biggest concern for Japan—and the world—because of its physical size, population, rapid economic growth, and energy demands. Today China is the third largest energy consumer in the world, using more than one billion tons of coal each year and producing 19 million tons of SO_2 annually since the early 1990s.[80]

Acid Deposition in Asia

Table 13. Electric power production, 1994
(billion kwh)

	Total	Hydro	Thermal	Nuclear
World	12,680.8	2,402.5	8,074.8	2,203.5
United States	3,268.3	281.6	2,346.2	640.5
Japan	964.3	75.7	619.5	269.1
China	928.1	168.1	745.9	14.0
Russia	875.9	177.0	601.1	97.8
Canada	554.2	328.1	118.2	107.8
Germany	528.2	22.5	354.6	151.2
France	475.6	81.0	34.6	360.0
India	384.4	71.1	307.8	5.6
United Kingdom	325.4	6.5	230.6	88.3

Note: Thermal power includes geothermal power generation.
Source: *Japan 1998: An International Comparison*, Tokyo: Keisai
Koho Center, 1998, p.75.

This compares with less than 1 million tons of SO_2 for Japan, between 22 and 23 million tons for the United States, and 40 tons for Europe (excluding the former Soviet Union).

In 1986, China replaced the United States as the largest producer and consumer of coal in the world.[81] In 1997, China produced two-thirds of the total SO_2 and half of NO_x and CO_2 in Asia in 1997.[82] China's coal consumption is so massive that Asia, including China, has a 48 percent dependence on coal; excluding China, it is closer to the world's average of 25 percent. With continuing industrial expansion, China will be the world's largest producer of greenhouse gas and sulfur dioxide in another decade unless drastic changes are made.[83]

The Roots of Japan's Environmental Policy

Figure 10. World CO_2 emissions, 1994

U.S.A.	22.4
China	13.4
Russia	7.1
Japan	4.9
India	3.8
Germany	3.5
Africa	3.4
South Am	3.1
U.K.	2.4
Canada	2.0
Italy	1.7
Oceania	1.4
Others	30.9

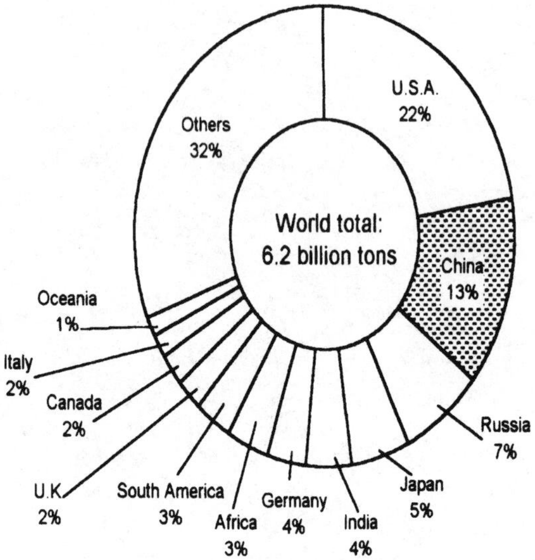

Source: *Japan 1998: An International Comparison*, Tokyo: Keizai Koho Center, 1998 p.78.

Yet, reducing energy demand in China is difficult for a country with 1.3 billion people.[84] Although energy consumption on a per capita basis is low in China by world standards, total electric consumption in China in 1995 reached 748 billion kilowatt-hours (kwh). Driven by average annual growth around 6 percent, that number is forecast to reach 2,457 billion kwh by 2015.[85] Chinese power plants work virtually non-stop, but still cannot satisfy the country's energy demand.[86] A 1992 estimate suggested that eliminating power shortages would require a 20 percent to 30 percent increase in the national power supply. Moreover, energy consumption is concentrated in the cities.[87] Six major urban industrial centers consume nearly 40 percent of China's total energy.[88] Addressing this imbalance and producing sufficient energy to support industrial growth are top priorities for the Chinese government.

China's dependence on coal, which already supplies three-quarters of its energy, will not likely fall in the near future.[89] The country's heavy reliance on coal will persist for economic and practical reasons even with the introduction of alternative energy sources, including nuclear power, natural gas,

Acid Deposition in Asia

and hydroelectricity.[90] Furthermore, wind, solar, tidal, geothermal, and bio-mass energy sources are at early stages of study, and none is expected to substantially reduce national coal consumption.[91] Although China has the largest proven recoverable coal reserves (730,000 million tons) in the world, as well as sizable deposits of oil and minerals, they cannot significantly reduce the country's reliance on coal.[92] In fact, China is now a net importer of energy.[93] Coal imports will increase from 178 million tons to about 350 million tons by 2010, even if Chinese coal production and consumption will increase by more than 1.1 billion tons per year.[94]

China still has a long way to go towards reducing air pollution. Fossil fuel consumption continues to increase and energy efficiency remains low. Widespread application of technology is necessary to realize significant gains. For instance, China converts just 30 percent of its fuel into useful energy, compared to 40 percent to 55 percent in North America and Europe, and 60 percent in Japan. Large industrial boilers in China operate at 55 percent to 60 percent efficiency compared to 75 percent to 80 percent or higher in Japan, North American, and Western Europe. For China's 300,000 small industrial boilers, efficiency is even lower at 50 percent to 60 percent compared to an average of 80 percent for OECD countries.[95]

Serious health, environmental, and economic effects of acid pollution are already evident. For this reason, controlling air pollution is a top concern for China's environmental authorities.[96] Coal combustion is responsible for most of the atmospheric pollution in China, especially in the big cities. Every year over 23 million tons of SO_2 is emitted in China. Most of this is produced by coal burning boilers and the region's weather system carries acid pollutants to Japan and the Korean peninsula, damaging forests, crops, and water systems.[97]

Statistics help to illustrate the severity of air pollution in China today. A study by the Chinese Research Academy of Environmental Sciences conducted in the early 1990s concluded that acid rain affects 40 percent of the country's land territory.[98] This is a very serious problem since only about 10 percent of China's land are arable, and one-third of its cropland is already degraded because of over-farming in the past 50 years.[99] The situation is even worse in provinces south of the Yangtze River where soil and surface waters are already more acidic; thus, more vulnerable to human-caused acidification.[100] The economic costs of acid rain damage are enormous. The World Bank estimated that losses for farming and forestry reached US$4.36 billion in 1995, and total economic loss that year was US$32 billion, or almost 5 percent of China's gross domestic product.[101]

Acid rain also threatens public health. For example, deaths from lung cancer rose sharply to 18.5 percent from 1988 to 1993 in major Chinese cities. The Chinese National Environment Agency reported that lung cancer is now a leading cause of death. Air pollution-related illnesses were responsible for 1.9 million deaths in 1990, or 21.2 percent of the Chinese total. In 1995 alone, air pollution caused 178,000 premature deaths among city dwellers and 1.7 million cases of chronic bronchitis. Women—the homemakers—are at even greater risk because many Chinese homes in rural and urban areas use low-quality coking coal for cooking and heating.[102]

Such figures are not entirely surprising. Average daily concentrations of SO_2 and suspended particulates in most Chinese cities exceed the World Health Organization (WHO) guidelines of 100 to 150 micrograms per cubic meter of air for SO_2 and 150 to 230 micrograms per cubic meter of air for total suspended particulates. Increasing vehicular traffic has also increased acid pollution in urban China. For instance, there were about 200,000 vehicles in Beijing in the 1980s, but recent estimates put the number around one million units. Smog has become so bad in some areas that satellites have failed to pick up entire Chinese cities. Localized acid precipitation and subsidence inversion (that produced the killer smog of London in 1952) could occur in areas where atmospheric dispersion capacity is low. Chongqing city, Guizhou province, and the eastern Sichuan province are potential disaster areas because of their location and meteorological conditions.[103]

Introducing unleaded gasoline, low-sulfur diesel, low-sulfur coal, and catalytic converters has improved the situation in some major cities. By 1995, SO_2 concentration in Beijing, Shanghai, and Tianjin had dropped to 90, 53, and 82 micrograms, respectively. In the same year, total suspended particulates in these cities had also fallen to 377, 246 and 306 micrograms, respectively. In Guangdong, the provincial government decided in May 1995 that no new coal-fired power plants would be built in the Pearl River Delta area.[104] However, similar achievements are rare in most Chinese cities due to lack of resources and weaknesses in implementation.[105]

Although the above are positive developments, two important factors can hinder success in tackling transboundary air pollution in Asia. First, the Chinese government considers acid rain primarily a domestic pollution issue. Second, the region lacks multilateral forums to provide framework for international cooperation. Since China is a major political and economic power as well as environmental juggernaut in Asia, engaging Chinese cooperation requires diplomatic skill and sensitivity.

Japan and acid rain control in China.

Japan has good reasons to worry about chemical air pollution from China because common weather systems govern the Northeast Asian region. A survey conducted in the early 1990s reported that half of the acid rain recorded in Japan's Shimane and Tottori prefectures came from China, one-third from Japan, and one-sixth from the Korean peninsula.[106] In 1994, the Environment Agency of Japan (JEA) announced that a study by University of Tokyo researchers indicated that Japan is exposed to transboundary air

Acid Deposition in Asia

pollution from mainland Asia, and 20 percent of the SO_x was from China and half of that produced by coal-fired power plants.[107] Other studies also showed higher acidity in precipitation (two to three times the average annual level) during winter and spring in areas on the inland side of Japan facing mainland Asia.[108]

Since domestic remedies for acid rain damage (and some are irreversible) would cost hundreds of billions of dollars, assisting China to produce cleaner energy is a cheaper and more effective way to protect Japan's environment and public health interests. Japanese bilateral aid to China has financed the building of new power plants and installation of scrubbers in old ones. Japan has also simultaneously worked to engage China and other Asian countries in building a regional precipitation monitoring network, which would be the first step towards a multilateral emissions control regime in Asia.

Japanese bilateral cooperation with China.

Deepening knowledge of the Chinese situation caused Japan to give higher priority to the environment in its policies towards China, and 1994 was a particularly important year. A MoFA report on bilateral environmental and economic cooperation with China released in March identified acid rain as one of the top four issues for Japanese-Chinese environmental cooperation. Warning of the potential impact of transboundary acid deposition on Japan, this report stressed the need for technology transfer and personnel training.[109] This partly explains why China has become not only the second largest country-recipient of Japanese Official Development Assistance (ODA), but is by far the largest recipient of technical assistance from Japan.

Table 14. Major recipients of Japan's bilateral assistance by aid type, 1996 (net disburstment: US $ million, %)

	Technical cooperations		
Rank	Country/Territory	Amount	Share
1	China	303.73	9.55
2	Indonesia	163.31	5.13
3	Thailand	135.41	4.26
4	Republic of Korea	95.00	2.99
5	Philippines	94.34	2.97
6	Malaysia	69.91	2.20
7	Brazil	51.99	1.63
8	Viet Nam	46.67	1.47
9	Mexico	37.71	1.19
10	Kenya	35.18	1.11
Total aid for top 10 countries		1,033.25	32.50
Total aid for all developing countries		3,180.92	100.00

	ODA loans		
Rank	Country/Territory	Amount	Share
1	Indonesia	737.81	26.54
2	China	533.01	19.17
3	Thailand	526.73	18.95
4	India	522.26	18.79
5	Philippines	228.96	8.24
6	Pakistan	192.83	6.94
7	Mexico	174.24	6.27
8	Sri Lanka	87.39	3.14
9	Jordan	77.34	2.78
10	Ghana	73.03	2.63
Total aid for top 10 countries		3,153.60	113.45
Total aid for all developing countries		2,779.84	100.00

	Total of bilateral aid		
Rank	Country/Territory	Amount	Share
1	Indonesia	965.53	11.55
2	China	861.73	10.31
3	Thailand	664.00	7.95
4	India	579.26	6.93
5	Philippines	414.45	4.96
6	Pakistan	282.20	3.38
7	Mexico	212.84	2.55
8	Egypt	201.32	2.41
9	Bangladesh	174.03	2.08
10	Sri Lanka	173.94	2.08
Total aid for top 10 countries		4,529.30	54.20
Total aid for all developing countries		8,356.26	100.00

Note: Grant aid is not shown because China is not among the top 30 recipients in this category.

Total aid for developing countries includes aid for Eastern Europe and advanced developing countries.

Source: Ministry of Foreign Affairs, "Japan's Official Development Assistance Summary 1997," n.d., p.42.

Acid Deposition in Asia

Another important milestone was the signing of the Sino-Japanese Environmental Protection Cooperation Agreement in March 1994 during a visit to Beijing by Japanese Prime Minister Morihiro Hosokawa. This was the first of such agreement between Japan and a developing country in Asia. Later that year, the Green Aid Plan of the Ministry of International Trade and Industry (MITI) added the transfer of clean coal technologies as a priority in bilateral assistance to China and 580 billion yen in low-interest development loans was extended to China. The loans covered 40 infrastructure projects for the 1996-1998 period, and 15 of them were environment-related.[110]

The Center for Sino-Japanese Friendship and Environmental Protection, which opened in Beijing in May 1996, is another key symbol of bilateral cooperation in environmental conservation. The Center, built with an ODA grant of 10.5 billion yen, serves to coordinate environmental research and monitoring activities between the two countries. It also hosts a number of Chinese and foreign organizations (some of them recipients of Japanese funds) that work on environment-related activities in China.[111]

The Japan International Cooperation Agency (JICA) sends experts to China to help China to develop independent capability in environmental research. Many of these JICA efforts emphasize cooperation with local governmental and non-governmental bodies to strengthen monitoring and quality control systems.[112] For example, a JICA study mission visited Beijing, Dalien, Chongqing, Chengdu, Gweizhou, Yunnan, and other cities and provinces in November and December 1995 to formulate environment cooperation projects, and Szechuan and Gweizhou were picked as key areas for air pollution and acid rain monitoring and control projects. This particular JICA mission also included representatives from the local and city governments of Hiroshima and Kitakyushu, both cities with a history of severe industrial air pollution and successful clean up and both interested in strengthening economic ties with China and other Northeast Asian countries.[113]

In May 1996, the first Integrated Forum for Environmental Cooperation was held in Beijing for talks between Japanese and Chinese officials, and a second meeting in Tokyo followed in November 1997. In both meetings, air pollution and acid rain were identified as priority areas for bilateral cooperation.[114] Numerous high-level visits by Japanese politicians, government officials, researchers, businessmen, and non-governmental organizations (NGOs) also underscored the importance of environmental cooperation in Sino-Japanese relations. By 1995 over 30 Japanese delegations had visited Chongqing, where air pollution is severe. In June 1995, Hiroshi Hashimoto, a former Japanese ambassador to China, led a mission of government and private experts to Beijing and other cities for policy talks with Chinese officials about medium- and long-term strategies for bilateral environmental cooperation.[115] The agenda emphasized closer cooperation in air pollution and acid rain control and the transfer of Japanese technology and know-how.[116]

These Japanese dialogue missions to China grew into the Japan-China Comprehensive Forum on Environmental Cooperation for high-level exchanges. The first and second meetings were held in 1996 and 1997. Conclusion of an agreement on "Japan-China Environmental Cooperation towards the 21st Century" at a Sino-Japanese summit meeting in September 1997 is expected to further bilateral cooperation. At the core of this bilateral agreement is a proposal by Prime Minister Ryutaro Hashimoto to establish an environmental information network and to create environmental model cities.

In the first project under this bilateral agreement, Japan will supply computers for processing environmental information in 100 major Chinese cities and help to train personnel to run this network. In the second project, the model cities will carry out environmental programs with the aid of Japanese ODA loans and technical cooperation. In this connection, Hashimoto announced a lowering of interest rates to 0.75 percent and extended the repayment period to 40 years (with a grace period of 10 years) on loans for projects that aim to improve the global environment and promote transfer of anti-pollution technology.[117]

Building an East Asia Monitoring Network.

JEA launched the first national acid rain survey to measure the presence and severity of acid pollution from mainland Asia.[118] The project lasted from 1983 to 1987 and precipitation samples were collected by thousands of school children throughout Japan.[119] The results confirmed suspicions of acid pollution from foreign sources and found that it was increasing in many parts of the country.[120]

These findings paved way for the second national acid rain survey in 1988 to deepen understanding of the problem. This time 23 national meteorological institutes were involved in the five-year project to collect data for building medium- and long-range transmission models of air pollutants. Water surveys were also conducted: covering snow from 1988 to 1990, groundwater since 1991, surface waters since 1989, and acidified lakes since 1992. For the terrestrial ecosystem, monitoring of soil quality and acid rain effects began in 1988, studies of forests commenced in 1991, and an integrated study of the biological and ecological effects of acid rain started in 1990.[121]

A third national survey lasted from 1993 to 1998 to conduct integrated monitoring of aquatic, terrestrial, and atmospheric ecosystems as well as to gather information on the effects of acid precipitation on biota.[122] Computer models for acid precipitation forecasts and transport patterns were constructed and officials stressed public education on the transboundary air pollution.[123] The objective of these activities was to harness sufficient scientific data to demonstrate to other Japanese policymakers

Acid Deposition in Asia

and the public that a problem exists and that actions and resources are urgently needed to address the situation.

In additions to broadening environmental cooperation with China, JEA initiated efforts to inform neighbor countries of its survey findings and to invite them to participate in similar monitoring activities and information exchange in order to broaden sources of outside pressure on China. The "Environment Congress for Asia and the Pacific" was started in 1991 as a forum for high-level exchanges by environmental ministries and departments in the region. Soon after United Nations Conference on Environment and Development (UNCED) in June 1992, Japan proposed a new regional forum for high-level government exchanges on the environment. The Environment Congress for Asia and the Pacific (ECO ASIA) thus began in 1992 to build an Asia-Pacific environment information network by 1996. JEA hoped that this would increase confidence in multilateral processes and create a forum for high level policy making by the region's environment ministers. However, ECO ASIA has no mechanism for action so Japan could only urge China to investigate its pollution problems.[124]

In 1993, JEA began a series of expert meetings to increase regional support for an acid deposition monitoring network in Asia. The first acid rain symposium was held that year in Toyama prefecture. Japan invited government officials and experts from China, South Korea, Indonesia, among others.[125] International organizations, with relevant expertise, were also invited, including the World Bank, UNECE, the United Nations Environment Program (UNEP) and RAINS-ASIA (Regional Air Pollution INformation and Simulation-Asia).[126] The main objectives of this first meeting were to alert countries in the region to the presence of transboundary air pollution in Asia, to point out that the situation would worsen unless treated, and to suggest that common criteria and methodology in research and monitoring are necessary for international cooperation.[127]

The second symposium was held in March 1995 in Tokyo.[128] A larger number of foreign government representatives and international organizations was invited. Japanese officials from several ministries and agencies, as well as more than a hundred observers from NGOs and universities, also came, reflecting growing interest in the issue. Technical meetings were also added to host discussions on approaches to emissions control in Asia. As a result, a set of monitoring guidelines was produced.

To sustain the momentum, the third acid rain symposium was held in November 1995 in Niigata. Experts from 10 Asian countries agreed to create the Acid Deposition Monitoring Network in East Asia and adopted a conceptual design for its construction. A fourth expert meeting in Hiroshima in February 1997 continued discussions on the design and construction of this network. The goal was to have it fully operational by 2000, and an international center for coordination and information exchange would be located in Niigata city. Participants also adopted the

"Guidelines for Monitoring Acid Deposition in the East Asia Region" as well as technical manuals for monitoring wet deposition, soil and vegetation, and inland aquatic environments. These guidelines and manuals were to help build national capacities in monitoring and data collection in order to foster a common understanding of the problem.[129]

Consequently, the First Intergovernmental Meeting on the Acid Deposition Network in East Asia, sponsored by JEA and the Ministry of Foreign Affairs, was held in Yokohama in March 1998. Participants agreed to begin implementation of preparatory phrase activities in April 1998.[130] These include monitoring of wet and dry deposition in selected sites, in soil and vegetation, and in inland aquatic environment. China's decision to join the monitoring network gave a great boost to this Japanese initiative and moved the region another step forward in establishing a multilateral regime for transboundary air pollution.

In summary, China and Japan are the two most important countries in tackling acid pollution in Asia. Although their perspectives and interests differ, they are not incompatible. Japan, much like the Scandinavian countries, took proactive responses to the problem because of its vulnerability to long-range acid pollution from mainland Asia. The costs of damage to human health and the natural environment in the Japanese islands could be extremely high if China fails to improve its energy sector. For China, improving its energy sector to meet the country's rapidly expanding energy needs was the primary motivation for cooperation with Japan. Growing public concern about the human health and environmental impacts would also benefit from transfers of Japanese capital and pollution abatement technology. Therefore, despite different motivations, the two governments chose to cooperate to achieve their respective goals.

JAPAN'S POLICY ON ACID RAIN CONTROL IN ASIA

For Japan, acid rain is foremost a transboundary air pollution problem. The country's domestic cleanup and even the movement of energy intensive and polluting industries overseas cannot fully protect Japan from the influx of air pollutants from foreign sources. Hence, building a regional acid deposition monitoring network is the first concrete step towards a multilateral framework for emissions control. In this endeavor, engaging Chinese cooperation, through bilateral and multilateral channels, is critical because China is the biggest producer of SO_x and NO_x and air pollutants from China pose the greatest potential threat to Japan.

Objectives and rationale.

Although Japan has a clear interest in tackling acid pollution in Asia, there were no concrete plans or commitment of resources to undertake a leadership role until quite recently.[131] Nonetheless, two priorities were clear to government offices concerned about this problem. The first was to estab-

Acid Deposition in Asia

lish a common scientific understanding of the state of acid deposition in Asia, and the second was to involve China in curbing transboundary air pollution.

The first goal was pursued by Japanese initiatives to create a region-wide precipitation sampling network by the year 2000.[132] This network would have common and standardized methods in data analysis and evaluation to create a common understanding of the state of acid deposition in Asia, and all information would be open and shared. Acid rain, as a transboundary pollution problem, requires a multilateral response, but no framework exists to facilitate this in Asia. Since independent country efforts to produce scientific data might not encourage a consensus on the state of the problem and its treatment, building a regional acid deposition monitoring network was an essential first step.[133] The European experience, particularly the European Community's EMEP program, served as the key model for the Japanese government's push for this initiative.[134]

The second goal would use diplomacy to bring China into multilateral discussions as well as bilateral assistance to improve China's energy sector. China's energy needs and their environmental effects have to be addressed to achieve substantive cuts in SO_2 emissions. Unless China is committed to proactively reduce emissions, no amount of outside pressure and assistance could make a real and lasting difference.[135]

Science played a central role in both endeavors. The European experience showed that an emphasis on science was most effective for overcoming political differences. EMEP's emphasis on scientific data and its use of the critical load concept and computer models to determine levels of reduction managed to minimize domestic or international political entanglements that could otherwise complicate the search for solutions. Few other international conventions have such close links between science and policy.

Containing political difference in responding to the acid rain problem is especially critical in Asia, where a multitude of political entities exists and historical conflicts and present-day tensions are smoothed over only by a common desire for regional peace, domestic stability, and economic development. Enmity on the Korean peninsula and between China and Taiwan, in particular, have been the most intractable political obstacles in the region for multilateral cooperation in many issues. Using science to build a multilateral consensus on the sources and transport of acid rain could help to alleviate potential political sensitivities when identifying pollution exporters. In the case of China, the country is enormous and wields tremendous leverage as a net exporter of acid pollutants. Hence, an accusatory approach could discourage Chinese cooperation and adversely affect the credibility and effectiveness of any multilateral regime for air pollution control in the region.

Engaging China in a multilateral enterprise to monitor and survey acid pollution and using these scientific results might be a better way to induce

Chinese cooperation. Since Asia does not have any international institutions that are sufficiently strong and encompassing to bring together the region's countries for international discussions or to enforce multilateral agreements, approaches that promote voluntary cooperation would be more conducive to productive outcomes.

Assisting China also makes good economic sense for Japan, apart from minimizing the costs of potential acid damage to Japan's environment and human health. Japan has already completed several rounds of investment in energy-saving projects domestically so that any further improvement would require an exponential rise in funding. There was also enormous business potential in the sale of power generation equipment, desulfurization technologies, and other kinds of energy and environment-related goods and services.[136] In fact, China could be the single biggest market in Asia, although sales to other regional economies were expected to increase because they had all adopted new air quality standards in the last decade. Achieving these targets will require technology and scientific know-how to upgrade fuel efficiency in power generation and energy consumption.

Figure 11. Projected new CCT capacity in Asia, 1990-2000

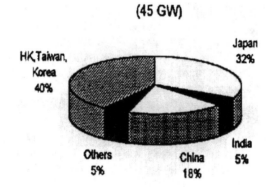

Source: East-West Center Coal Project, Program on Resource, Energy and Minerals, East-West Center, Honolulu, 1992.

Japanese industry expected an added advantage against its competitors in the United States and Western Europe in selling pollution abatement technologies to developing countries. Japan's substantial official development aid loans and grants would provide informal support to help win business contracts from governments receiving Japanese assistance.

POLICY ACTORS IN JAPAN'S ACID RAIN POLICY

In the two previous case studies on whaling and forests, JEA did not have a major role in the policy process. In the matter of acid rain control, however, JEA was the leading advocate for a national response to acid deposition in Asia. Although JEA was small and limited in its powers, it managed to establish a stronghold over this issue by taking advantage of its position as a policy coordinating body in the Japanese government. This is not to say that JEA had dominant influence in the policy process. It did not and could not because cooperation from other bureaucratic actors was essential to achieving JEA's goals.

Although Japanese policy makers looked to the European experience for guidance, there were virtually no important policy actors outside of the bureaucracy in shaping Japan's national response to acid pollution in Asia in the 1990s. The main reason was that severe and visible environmental damage in Japan (and other parts of Asia) was not yet evident. Moreover, acid rain and transboundary chemical air pollution did not have dramatic or charismatic appeal like whaling and deforestation in the tropics, which had helped conservation groups and the media to engage the Japanese public. Other practical barriers for both governmental and non-governmental actors included the scientific complexity of the problem.[137] Not having adequate scientific data and technical expertise, they could not effectively participate in the heavily science-based policy discussions sponsored by JEA to define this problem and propose responses to it.

The governmental actors.

Japan's response to the problem of transboundary acid pollution in Asia in the 1990s was basically in the hands of one governmental actor, that is, the central government bureaucracy.

The Japanese bureaucracy.
Within the Japanese bureaucracy, JEA was the key force in shaping national responses to the problem of transboundary air pollution in Asia. JEA's leadership was established through creative approaches to the problem itself and endeavors to define its role in the policy process. Checking challenges from MITI, its biggest potential rival, and making MoFA an ally were among its first tasks.

Acid rain, as a transboundary air pollution problem, was a relatively new issue to the Japanese bureaucracy. Since no single ministry or agency had established clear authority over the matter, it was an issue or an area of jurisdiction open to bureaucratic competition for resources. Due to severe domestic economic problems and national deficits, budget cuts and hiring moratoriums had become commonplace in most government ministries and agencies. However, ODA allocations for international development and environmental activities had continued to grow despite these economic constraints. As a result, seizing control of such a new, cash-rich and politically non-controversial (even popular) issue could expand a government body's bureaucratic powers and new government resources with which to strengthen itself and bolster its position in intra-governmental negotiations over a variety of issues. Profits from potential sales of pollution abatement technology and devices could also garner support from the powerful business sector and incur other important benefits, such as *amakudari* positions for retiring officials.[138]

Since fossil fuel combustion is the main source of SO_2 and controlling acid rain is primarily a matter of improving energy production and consumption, MITI attempted to assert control on the basis that it is the most powerful bureaucratic actor in energy matters.[139] JEA challenged this claim by asserting its leadership on the basis of its official mandate and history. The Agency was created in 1971 as a policy coordinating agency in response to domestic industrial pollution problems, and it had played a major role in overseeing domestic acid rain control in the 1970s. By defining transboundary acid deposition as a pollution problem, JEA made a strong case for its involvement and effectively separated the issue from global warming (which was under MITI's control).

In addition, JEA managed to establish bureaucratic leadership in this issue by taking initiative to draft a national response to this issue. As a result, Japan has a "dual track" policy response to these two closely connected issues: JEA is the chief actor in tackling acid rain, while MITI is the lead bureaucratic actor in responding to global warming.

The agency also knew that as a small bureaucratic actor with severely limited human and material resources it could not independently attain its objectives. It was also a policy coordinating body, not an implementing one. By emphasizing the human health and environmental impacts of acid pollution, JEA was able to make the Ministry of Agriculture, Forestry and Fisheries (MAFF), the Ministry of Health and Welfare (MHW) and the Meteorological Agency useful allies in intra-governmental debates with MITI. These ministries cooperated with JEA because they, too, would have great difficulty asserting their voices in national policy discussions.

For MAFF, its biggest worries were the effects of transboundary air pollution on Japan's inland aquatic ecosystems and land conditions, especially its forests, as these are matters that lie within its jurisdiction. MAFF, however, would have to wait until damage was done to justify its initiatives for action. By then, the costs of damage and repair would be too high, and some consequences could even be irreversible. MHW, with its responsibility for public health, faced a similar predicament as MAFF. As for the Meteorological Agency, its technical expertise and facilities would be indispensable to data collection and surveys, including monitoring stations set up under WMO. However, the Meteorological Agency was too small and restricted in its capacity to independently launch and carry out policy pref-

Acid Deposition in Asia

erences. Prefectural governments and local authorities in areas vulnerable to transboundary chemical air pollution came behind JEA's initiatives. The prospects of costly damage motivated them to support preventive measures, such as ODA assistance to China's energy sector. The magnitude and foreign origin of the problem also required the central government to work with foreign governments and multilateral organizations to find solutions.

Securing cooperation from MITI and MoFA was not as easy for JEA. These large and traditional ministries are strongly protective of their regulatory powers and bureaucratic jurisdictions. Being older and more powerful, they control a broad range of issues and the enthusiasm or ambition of small smaller bureaucratic offices like JEA was considered by some officials an encroachment on their powers.

JEA, MITI, and MoFA each organized its own activities on acid rain, and participation was largely limited to their own officials, researchers, and supporters from inside and outside of the government. For MITI and MoFA, bigger and more powerful ministries than JEA, they generally disregarded invitations to JEA-sponsored activities or only sent low-level representation.[140] This shows that having bureaucratic leadership is not sufficient for a small policy actor like JEA to independently achieve its objectives. It must work to cultivate support—or at least non-opposition—from other interested policy actors, particularly the stronger ones, while simultaneously defending its position and preferences.

The Environment Agency of Japan.

JEA has the greatest interest in the environmental effects of acid rain among the governmental actors involved because of its position as the government's coordinating agency for environment-related policies. And its approach to the acid rain problem was strongly affected by two historical experiences. The first is Japan's own history of industrial air pollution and its ecological and health effects. The passing of strict air pollution laws and the installation of CCTs in power plants throughout the country since the 1970s have dramatically reduced SO_2 emissions. The second are the European and North American experiences in transboundary air pollution. JEA officials were afraid of a similar ecological nightmare in Asia, with Japan as the net importer of acid rain. The European approach to multilateral emissions control was considered a useful model for Japan. Thus, Japanese initiatives during much of the 1990s pushed to standardize survey and modeling techniques in order to build a common scientific data base that would serve as a basis for a future multilateral emissions reduction agreement.

Although JEA managed to obtain a government consensus on its initiative for an Acid Deposition Monitoring Network in East Asia and on making emissions control a priority concern in Sino-Japanese environmental cooperation, it had to guard against intervention by other policy actors. In this regard, JEA, or specifically its Global Environment Department (which is responsible for overseeing transboundary pollution problems) learned from the European experience the usefulness of a science-based approach. Utilizing the expertise of its officials and researchers in the environmental sciences, JEA protected itself from intervention by other interested policy actors, just as Fisheries Agency officials did in whaling.

Another way JEA used to gain leverage in inter-ministerial talks was to obtain public support for its initiatives. By involving school children across the country in its precipitation surveys and reporting its findings in the Japanese media, JEA raised public awareness of the dangers of transboundary air pollution and acid deposition. Industrial pollution, such as acid rain, can strike a particularly sensitive nerve among the Japanese people because of the industrial pollution tragedies that stuck the country all through the 1950s to the 1970s. Public support generated by these activities helped JEA to assert its initiatives and to harness government funds for scientific surveys and studies. Since most surveys and research were carried out by JEA facilities, the funds and information gathered also fortified the Agency and strengthened its grip on an issue that favors those with scientific knowledge.

Finally, JEA's sponsorship and organization of ECO Asia and international acid rain meetings help to reduce its reliance on MoFA. For example, JEA consulted with MoFA, the ministry chiefly responsible for the country's external affairs, before proposing to neighbor countries its series of acid rain symposia and expert meetings. However, as JEA affirmed its position as the lead government agency for tackling transboundary air pollution, these activities made JEA more independent of MoFA.

Ministry of International Trade and Industry.
Although MITI lost control of the acid rain issue to JEA, it still has a major role in government policy discussions. This is because greenhouse gas emission and acid rain are related problems and MITI has decisive influence over capital and technologies that are needed to improve energy infrastructure in the region's developing economies. For one, MITI is one of the key ministries in shaping the country's ODA policy. Another reason is that Japanese industry, MITI's chief constituent, owns and produces the technologies for emissions control. Hence, it was necessary to invite MITI participation in JEA activities.

MITI also has its own acid rain control initiatives. Its Green Aid Plan was conceived originally for greenhouse gases but was expanded to cover acid pollutants. The Clean Coal Technology Model Project, one of the main thrusts of this plan, promotes environmental-friendly coal utilization technologies in developing countries, and special emphasis is placed on transfers to China.

Acid Deposition in Asia

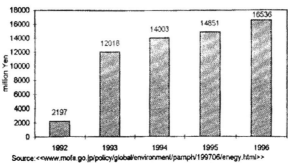

Figure 12. The trends of Green Aid Plan-related budget

Source:<<www.mofa.go.jp/policy/global/environment/pamph/199706/enegy.html>>
Viewed on 11 May 1998.

Table 15. Coal-related projects supported by the Green Aid Plan

Project name	Term of Project	Country concerned/ Candidate site
Development of simplified desulfurizer for coal boiler	1991-1993	Indonesia
Cooperation in coal thermal power plant desulfurization technology (No.1, No.2)	1992-2000	China
Simplified Desulfurization equipment model project (3 units)	1993-1995	China
Circulating fluidized bed boiler model project (3 units)	1993-1994	China/Philippines
Briquette manufacturing facility model project (2 units)	1993-1995	China/Indonesia
Water-saving coal washing system model project (2 units)	1994-1997	China

Source:<<www.mofa.go.jp/policy/global/environment/pamph/199706/energy.html>>
viewed on 11 May 1998.

These initiatives are important to MITI because they could generate substantial profits for Japanese industry, MITI's powerful constituent. The RAINS-Asia model estimated that full application of advanced emissions control technologies in the region would require US$90 billion annually by the year 2020.[141] China would be the largest market, followed by India, Thailand, and others. Although purchases so far have been limited and have been slowed by the Asian financial crisis since the second half of 1997, they will expand in the long-run because energy demands will continue to grow in the region. Financing some of these purchases will be money from Japan's ODA program, as well as multilateral development banks and agencies. For instance, the World Bank provided nearly US$1 billion to China for energy projects in 1992, and the Asian Development

236   *The Roots of Japan's Environmental Policy*

Bank approved a US$17 million loan to improve energy efficiency in Chinese fertilizers, cement, and steel production. Between 1986 and 1990 alone, China's energy sector had received more than US$7 billion in foreign bilateral and multilateral assistance.

Ministry of Foreign Affairs.

MoFA could benefit in many ways as a key player in deciding the country's policy responses to transboundary acid pollution in Asia. First, should Japan succeed in persuading China and other countries in the region to conclude a multilateral agreement on emissions control, Japan—and MoFA—could get a boost in international image. Second, as the Japanese government's primary liaison for international affairs, MoFA could gain leverage in intra-ministerial negotiations over this and other issues related to China. Third, helping China to meet its needs for energy and domestic environmental cleanup would win Chinese government goodwill. Finally, MoFA would find gratitude from JEA, MITI, the business sector, and Japanese political leaders who could boast of their country's commitment to the environment and Chinese development.

Since MoFA was responsible for communicating Japan's concerns to China, it did so with delicacy to avoid Chinese impressions of Japanese accusations. This task was made easier because Chinese authorities wanted Japanese assistance. Top Chinese leaders, most importantly the energy and economic czars, as well as its Environment Ministry—explicitly or quietly recognized that urgent actions were needed to address severe air pollution in China.[142] For example, new central government directives ordered all power plants to be equipped with acid scrubbers after the year 2000.[143] Systematic acid rain monitoring was introduced in many Chinese cities, including nationwide acid precipitation surveys, and a new law was passed in 1995 specifically to control air pollution.[144]

Without scientific expertise of its own, MoFA knew that its role in ODA policy making would be the best way for it to influence China and other interested parties. China has been the second largest recipient of Japan's bilateral aid in the last decade. By the end of 1995, Japan has given over US$10.6 billion in official assistance to China, including US$8.2 billion in loans, US$678 million in grants, and US$1.7 billion for technical cooperation. Japan also led OECD countries in bilateral aid transfer to China. Net OECD disbursements to China was US$2.38 billion in 1994, of which Japan contributed US$1.47 billion.[145] Air pollution control is now a top priority in Japan's environmental assistance to China, equal to Japanese aid for disaster relief and exceeded only by its support for energy saving and substitution activities in China.

In addition, under Japan's ODA program, JICA is MoFA's chief agent for environmental cooperation with China.[146] JICA sends technical experts to China for surveys, exchanges, and project implementation. Critics have charged that there have yet to be meaningful missions and projects because

Acid Deposition in Asia

JICA does not possess sufficient independent expertise or scientific data (as JEA and MITI does) to effectively address the problem. MoFA tried to remedy this weakness by working with international bodies and Chinese state agencies, local authorities, and non-governmental groups. MoFA also emphasized data collection and information sharing in the work of the Sino-Japanese environmental cooperation center in Beijing, which is mainly supported by ODA funds.[147]

The non-governmental actors.

Although some non-governmental actors were interested in this issue, the problem's scientific complexity and a closed government policy process obstructed their ability to influence decision making.

For conservation groups, having limited ability to collect and evaluate their own scientific data and propose policy input, their participation in national policy making was mainly restricted to two options. The first was to support government initiatives, and the second was to remain silent until enough scientific data become publicly available to allow them assess the issue and advocate their policy preferences. For most conservation groups, the latter was more common.

Japanese industry, as a non-governmental actor interested in selling its products and services to China (and other countries), had MITI as its chief promoter. Other government agencies also recognized that industry involvement would be crucial to the success of their initiatives. Scientists represented the third group of non-governmental actors in this issue. Although their expertise played a crucial role in shaping the issue and its policy discussion, scientists (and scientific organizations) were not independent policy actors.

Conservation groups.

Citizen-based conservation groups, both at the international and domestic levels, were largely unable to actively influence national policy responses for several reasons. First, the issue is highly technical, particularly in the early stages when data collection, technical analysis, and modeling are crucial to establishing the problem and its severity. Most conservation groups do not have such expertise. At the same time, leading governmental actors often used science as a barrier to more extensive participation in the policy process.[148] Third, unlike whaling, tropical deforestation, or acid rain damage in Europe and North America, physical evidence of acid pollution damage was not yet widely visible in Asia. This made it difficult for conservation groups to politicize the problem to generate public pressure on Japanese or foreign governments and industry to accept stricter domestic air quality laws and international agreements.[149] Finally, many conservation groups were busy with other more urgent issues, including social and ecological impacts of the international trade regime emerging under the World Trade Organization (WTO), equity issues in greenhouse gas emissions control, quality of Japanese ODA, and negative effects of structural adjustment loans by multilateral development banks.

Nonetheless, citizens groups assisted in JEA's precipitation sampling surveys. Many groups, including school children, in areas vulnerable to foreign acid pollution collected daily pH readings for government researchers. Their efforts helped JEA to establish scientifically and politically the problem of foreign acid pollution.

Japanese industry.

Industry, on the whole, supported initiatives launched by JEA and MITI. The Asian region was seen as a highly lucrative market for Japanese energy and environment industries.[150] These industrializing economies had passed new and stricter air quality laws since the early 1990s and most were just beginning to implement CCTs. Their demand for efficient power plants and desulfurization technologies would increase in the decades ahead in order to raise economic competitiveness and to respond to public pressure for higher environmental quality standards.

Nonetheless, resources are essential to finance the purchase and operation of pollution abatement equipment. Several Asian countries, including China and Indonesia, were top beneficiaries of Japanese bilateral assistance. Japanese companies expected such official largess, and the new stress on environmental cooperation, would give them a competitive advantage over their Western counterparts in these Asian markets.

Scientists.

Complexity of the issue and lack of basic data on the scale of the problem made science a highly influential instrument in articulating appropriate policy responses and for those in positions of power. However, scientists were not independent or influential policy actors. Most scientific research in Japan is financed either by the government or private industry. Those who work outside the national universities and industry laboratories are vulnerable to attacks as radicals and doubts are cast on the credibility of their work. Furthermore, scientists in Japan and elsewhere usually are not assertive policy advocates. While they provide a scientific basis for policies, most leave the task of policy articulation to government bureaucrats, politicians, and other policy professionals.

Transboundary air pollution is also a complex scientific problem and uncertainties abound. Government officials in JEA and MITI, many with scientific training, stressed the importance of science as a means to deter intervention by most citizens groups and other government actors who did not possess this capacity. Scientists in Japan and elsewhere rarely work to communicate to public audiences because messages that are adequately simple and direct for the non-scientifically trained usually lack the depth that these experts deem essential. Since conservation NGOs in Japan had extremely limited ability to give independent assessment of the problem,

Acid Deposition in Asia

they could not challenge government policy proposals or significantly increase public knowledge about the problem.

In short, the national bureaucracy, the most powerful policy actor in Japan, used its superior position in scientific information and knowledge to block challenges to its authority and influence. As explained in Chapter 3, the majority of academics and researchers in Japan are employed in national universities, government research institutes, and the private sector. Consequently, their employers or patrons consider them more as employees than as independent thinkers. They are expected to serve the interests of their supervising ministries or sponsors, and those who do not could jeopardize their own careers.

The influence of foreign scientists and international scientific organizations was circumscribed by similar restrictions. Although they were not supervised or controlled by Japanese government ministries and agencies, their link to and leverage in the Japanese foreign policy process were affected by their relationship with individual ministries and agencies. In other words, their influence was determined by the strict demarcations of bureaucratic authority and complex inter- and intra-ministerial relationships within the Japanese government policy structure. For example, the United Nations Environment Program and the International Institute for Applied Systems Analysis (IIASA) have principal ties to JEA, while the World Meteorological Organization works most closely with Japan's Meteorological Agency.

Although JEA was small and resource poor compared to other government actors, its official role as a coordinating agency for pollution issues under the Prime Minister's Office helped it to establish bureaucratic leadership in formulating national policy responses to acid pollution in East Asia. JEA's leverage in intra-governmental negotiations was built on its superior command of scientific information and national research facilities, as well its success in mobilizing public opinion and support of local governments in regions vulnerable to foreign air pollution for its initiatives.

However, JEA knew it could not pursue its objectives without support from the bigger and more powerful ministries, which held important influence over official aid and loans to China and other foreign countries. As a result, JEA chose to engage them (instead of isolating them) in executing its policy initiatives.

CHAPTER CONCLUSION

Controlling emissions involves the interplay of science, politics, and economics. Since humans cannot currently relinquish dependence on fossil fuels, technologies are applied to improve fuel efficiency and reduce emissions. Finding technological solutions is not a serious obstacle to emissions control. The greater obstacles, in most cases, are political difficulties due to high the economic costs and uncertainties involved in addressing this problem.

While scientific knowledge and economics have helped to clarify the potential costs and consequences of emissions control, they are not immune to exploitation. Science can be used to further the goals of parties-at-interest by targeting specific substantive areas, but neglecting others. For example, an emphasis on particular technological alternatives or specific hazards or risks over others can affect the definition of an issue, its discussion, and the actors that would be involved in the policy process.[151]

In the case of Japan's domestic cleanup in the 1970s, the Japanese government decided to implement strict air quality standards despite scientific uncertainties and high economic costs. Health hazards, environmental damages and policy debates in Europe were enough to convince the Japanese government of the greater costs of procrastination. There were also substantial domestic economic and political pressures for change.

Consequently, the Japanese government emphasized the use of "best available technologies based on present knowledge" to spur immediate actions and preempt opposition based on arguments of high costs and uncertainties. Low interest government loans were also extended to private industry to invest in pollution abatement technologies. Finally, there was heavy government investment in environment-related scientific research and development. The outcome was a dramatic improvement in Japan's domestic air quality and the country's emergence as a world leader in emissions control technology, particularly in coal-fired power plants.

Reducing Japan's reliance on coal and other fossil fuels would cut domestic SO_2 emissions, but the Japanese government knew that unilateral actions would not be enough to protect Japan. Acid rain as a transboundary pollution problem underscored to Japan that its domestic well being is connected with the rest of the world. Domestic cleanup and export of energy-intensive industries overseas cannot alone stop the influx of chemical air pollutants from foreign sources. A real solution requires pollution control overseas through bilateral and multilateral cooperation.

Countries in the region generally welcome the Japanese initiatives to create an Acid Deposition Monitoring Network in East Asia as a foundation for multilateral emissions reduction negotiations. They also support the use of Japanese ODA to assist transfers of desulfurization technologies. However, even with financial resources and leadership from Japan, building a multilateral emissions control regime in Asia is still extremely difficult. The following is a list of the major obstacles:

> (1) An abundance of political barriers are found in Asia. At the international level, hostility among some governments in the region will make it quite impossible to produce a truly comprehensive regional emissions control regime. For instance, the Japanese government could not invite Taiwan, inarguably an

Acid Deposition in Asia

industrial power in Asia, to participate in official activities because formal recognition is due to China. Involving Taiwan in government-level activities will incite Chinese opposition or even cause Chinese withdrawal. North Korea is another problem. Animosity between the two Korean governments also renders impossible their simultaneous involvement in multilateral forums. In Southeast Asia, the practice of mutual non-interference in domestic affairs by members of the Association of Southeast Asian Nations inhibits the use of bilateral and collective pressure through the organization to improve energy use and emissions control;

(2) At a national level, some governments could refuse to announce their monitoring results and energy data (or make public honest and reliable ones) because they fear to reveal the true state of their economy. This was Western Europe's experience with many East European governments during the Cold War years. There is also the equity argument, which basically asserts the right to develop (or pollute) by latecomers of industrialization as advanced industrial economies had done before them;[152]

(3) The region has multiple handicaps in multilateral cooperation. Asia lacks experience, faith, and institutions to promote international cooperation. Countries in Asia also differ significantly in physical size, power, political and economic systems, and level of development. These disparities can complicate consensus-building for agreements and actions;

(4) Japan could have a hard time pursuading China and other countries to reduce their emissions when Japan produces four times as much CO_2 as China. By tying together emissions control for SO_2 with CO_2 (acid rain and global warming, respectively), Japan's neighbors can weaken Japanese leverage by pointing out that Japan cannot press others to reduce SO_2 emissions while ignoring its own CO_2 emissions. Japan's calls for SO_2 reduction may be castigated as a self-centered motivation to protect itself from transboundary air pollution and an opportunistic tactic to sell desulfurization devices;

(5) Acid deposition differs in importance as a policy matter among nations. For Japan, Malaysia, and Singapore, acid rain is seen mainly as a transboundary air pollution problem, while China and Indonesia place greater weight on reducing localized dep-

osition and suspended particles. Hence, China had to first become aware of the domestic damages (cost of pollution) in order to push China to recognize the problem and be proactive in controlling it;

(6) Disparities in economic development can affect a government's commitment to emissions control. Research has shown positive correlation between per capita income levels and environmental protection. Hence, Japan, the most advance economy in Asia, leads the region in emissions control, while Taiwan, Singapore, South Korea, and Hong Kong, the next tier of Asian economies, are following with plans to install advanced clean coal technologies. In comparison, China, India, Indonesia, and the Philippines are more interested in lower cost options for emission control.[153] Stress on economic growth also outweighs environmental protection in many developing countries. Where development is interpreted as synonymous to industrial growth and vital for social stability, environmental degradation is rationalized as an inevitable cost to realize economic growth and future employment;

(7) In building a monitoring network, each nation must be able to handle the technical aspects of environmental protection, such as carrying out scientific observations and computer simulation. Bridging current disparities will require substantial investments in equipment and training;[154]

(8) There is a general lack of data on acid deposition in much of Asia so that it will take many years before scientifically (and politically) acceptable data will be available for a multilateral convention.[155] In tropical Asia, presence of volcanic dust makes it harder to identify causes of SO_x and the setting of reduction targets.[156] Widespread bush and grass fires are also important sources of trace gases in the atmosphere. Thus, the experiences of Europe and North America are not always appropriate to Asia (or *vice versa*). The difference in temperature, wind, and climatic conditions in the tropics can also have different effects on chemical processes and the movement of air pollutants. Again, the experiences of Europe, North America, and Japan may not be fully relevant;[157]

(9) China and other developing countries need financial support and technical assistance to acquire appropriate emission control systems and expertise. Although Japanese industry was keen to

Acid Deposition in Asia

sell its latest desulfurization equipment, they are very expensive and cutting edge technology is generally not the most pressing need in China and most other developing economies. What they require are simplified desulfurization devices for their coal-fired power plants; and

(10) In the case of China, although its leadership and environmental authorities have a sincere commitment to address the problem, there are serious weaknesses in its energy sector. For one, China's heavy reliance on coal will remain inflexible for many years to come and coal combustion is generally inefficient in China.[158] China's coal deposits are unevenly distributed and the great distances separating energy reserves, processing facilities, and end users hamper exploitation. Poor energy management, too, exacerbates energy waste.[159] The Chinese administrative structure also has weaknesses in its top-down enforcement of environmental laws by government agencies. Lax and inconsistent enforcement of air quality standards is especially bad outside the major urban and industrial centers.[160] Furthermore, Chinese authorities stress responses to local acid damage over long-range transboundary movements.[161]

Finally, when a multilateral framework is formed, the institution needs independent assessment of findings and a handling of sensitive data in a manner that is acceptable to all parties concerned. Verification is a necessary adjunct to the implementation process, while negotiation and dispute resolution mechanisms must be in place. Setting environmental standards is difficult in a multilateral regime because they must be explicit and flexible to accommodate domestic political, economic, and social conditions in a wide range of locations. Funding for research and technologies must also be available and accessible to enable implementation for actual improvements.

Nonetheless, Japanese actions to control acid deposition in Asia make a positive push towards a multilateral response to this transboundary pollution problem. Seeing how the Environment Agency of Japan has drawn lessons from the experience of European countries and North America to build a regional acid rain control regime in Asia shows linkages between these regimes. In this case, the acid rain control regime in Western Europe, in particular, influenced Japanese approaches to the problem in Asia. Japanese initiatives, based on the European experience, are giving rise to a new acid rain control regime in East Asia.

In conclusion, this case study of Japan's policies towards acid rain in Asia recognizes that the bureaucratic politics model is central to understanding Japan's foreign policy decision making process for international environmental issues. At the same time, the other theories used in this research supplement to provide important insights into dynamics within this process. It was through issue redefinition that the Environment Agency was able to assert a place for itself in this policy issue. This redefinition also expanded participation in the foreign policy process. It brought into it other weak and small government ministries and agencies, as well as public opinion, to bolster the Environment Agency in intra-government negotiations against the powerful Ministry of International Trade and Industry.

Complex interdependence shows how the problem of transboundary acid pollution in Asia encourages the formation of transgovernmental coalitions among the region's ministries and agencies for environmental affairs. How the Environment Agency looked to regimes for acid rain control in Europe and North America confirms linkages among regimes and shows how the fabric of one can give rise to another. Furthermore, the Environment Agency's proposal for an East Asia Acid Monitoring Network acknowledged the importance of shared knowledge and values in building regimes.

Realism may sufficiently account for the Japanese government's proactive approach to the problem of transboundary acid pollution (Japan's vulnerability to acid pollution from China and the Japanese public's sensitivity to industrial pollution issues). However, complex interdependence and two-level games theory explained how China exploited this Japanese sensitivity and vulnerability to obtain Japanese technology transfer and financial assistance to meet Chinese priorities in energy development and air pollution control. This asymmetrical interdependence grants China additional leverage in other negotiations with Japan. This insight is important because of disparities in Chinese and Japanese views of and responses to the problem: the Chinese government gives priority to local air pollution, while the Japanese government emphasizes its transboundary movement and impact on Japanese human and ecological health.

At the same time, Japan also worked to improve its bargaining position vis-a-vis China by redefining the problem. Being a potential net importer of acid pollution, it did not have much bargaining leverage against China. Limiting discussions within the context of Japan-China relations may also be undesirable because complexities in their bilateral relationship could open opportunities for China to tie its actions to demands on Japan. Hence, by internationalizing the problem (emphasizing a multilateral framework for regional acid control in its policy response), Japan could recruit other voices to press China to deal with the transboundary aspects of this problem.

Notes

[1] Hirotaka Hirose, *Sanseikasuru Chikyu* (The Acidifying Earth), Tokyo: NHK Books, 1990, pp.23-24.

[2] Chris C. Park, *Acid Rain: Rhetoric and Reality*, London and New York: Methuen, 1987, p.174.

[3] The acidity (and alkalinity) of a substance is measured by the pH scale. On the pH scale, 7 is perfectly neutral, that is, neither acidic nor alkaline. Numbers greater than 7 indicate increasing alkalinity, while numbers lower than 7 indicate increasing acidity. Each whole number increase or decrease on the pH scale indicates a tenfold increase or decrease in alkalinity and acidity. See Jon R. Luoma, *Troubled Skies, Troubled Waters: The Story of Acid Rain*, New York: The Viking Press, 1984, p.29.

[4] James L. Regens and Robert W. Rycroft, *The Acid Rain Controversy*, Pittsburgh: University of Pittsburgh Press, 1988, p.4.

[5] Peter S. Gold, ed., *Acid Rain: A Transjurisdictional Problem in Search of Solution*, New York: Canadian-American Center, State University of New York at Buffalo, 1982, p.187.

[6] The pollution itself may not always be "acid" but may trigger acidification in soils, lakes and rivers. See B.J. Mason, *Acid Rain: Its causes and its effects on inland waters*, Oxford: Clarendon Press, 1992, p.1; and John McCormick, *Acid Earth: The Global Threat of Acid Pollution*, London: International Institute for Environment and Development, 1985, p.3.

[7] Once SO_2 is oxidized, it dissolves readily in water to form sulfuric acid. See Luoma, *op cit.*, p.33.

[8] Park, *op cit.*, pp.19-20.

[9] Rain is slightly acidic under perfectly natural circumstances because carbon dioxide in the atmosphere combines with water to form weak carbonic acid. SO_2 also occurs naturally in volcanic eruptions and natural soil processes, while nitrogen is found in certain natural, organic decomposition processes, lightning and volcanic eruptions. See Luoma, *Ibid.*, pp.30-31 and Park, *op cit.*, pp.33-34.

[10] Mason, *op cit.*, p.7.

[11] Fred Pearce, *Acid Rain: What is it and what is it doing to us?* Middlesex: Penguin Books, 1987, pp.63-65.

[12] McCormick, *op cit.*, pp.2 and 37.

[13] In 1984, about 50% of West German forests were dying or dead. Almost every species of forest trees in Europe was affected by 1985. Evidence also shows long-term exposure to acid pollutants will reduce the growth and yield of sensitive agricultural crops. See *Ibid.*, p.30; and M.J. Chadwick and H. Hutton, eds., *Acid Depositions in Europe: Environmental effects, control strategies and policy options*, Stockholm: Stockholm Environment Institute, 1991, p.viii.

[14] Some studies now tie ozone with SO_2. See Luoma, *op cit.*, p.20; and Pearce, *op cit.*, p.47.

[15] This condition is known scientifically as subsidence inversion.

[16] Following this disaster, the British banned the use of coal in home heating and a significant drop in SO_2 level was observed. Other cases include 63 deaths in the Meuse Valley, Belgium, in 1930; 20 deaths and 14,000 ill in Donora, Pennsylvania, in 1948; 340 deaths in London in 1962; and 500 ill in Athens, Greece, in 1984. As recently as September 1997, several people in Indonesia and Malaysia died and many were ill because of severe smog from forest fires in Indonesia. The same smog was also responsible for the crash of a passenger plane in Medan that killed over 200. See John Firor, *The Changing Atmosphere: A Global Challenge*, New Haven and London: Yale University Press, 1990, p.9; McCormick, *op cit.*, pp.2 and 43; and Luoma, *op cit.*, pp.20-24.

[17] Sandstone, limestone and marble are most vulnerable to acid rain. See Park, *op cit.*, pp.40 and 117; and Luoma, *Ibid.*, p.103.

[18] The time of day, season and weather conditions all affect the transport of acid pollutants.

[19] Park, *op cit.*, p.44.

[20] Hirotoshi Kunitomo, "Japanese Policy for Cooperation with Asian economies on environmental issues," *Proceedings of APEC Fifth Technical Seminar on Clean Fossil Energy, in Reno, Nevada, 27-30 October 1997*, p.22.

[21] Over half of the respondents (58.5%) chose water pollution and forest destruction and soil erosion as the top two environmental problems in China, while air pollution ranked third (46.8%). See Liu *et al.*, *op cit.*, pp.88 and 89.

[22] Presentation by Dr. Charles Johnson on the long-term demand for coal in Asia at the 4th Asia Pacific Economic Cooperation Coal Flow Seminar, Honolulu, Hawaii, 11-13 November 1997. For more alternative scenarios for acid rain control in Asia, see G.R. Carmichael and R. Arndt, "Baseline Assessment of Acid Deposition in Northeast Asia," at <<www.nautilus.org/esena/ Paper/carmichael.html>>. Viewed on 12 May 1998.

[23] Robert Perlack *et al.*, "Energy and Environmental Policy in China," *Annual Review of Energy Environment*, Vol.16, 1991, p.207; and web site at <<http:www.nautilus.org/esena/choice.html>>. Viewed on 12 May 1998.

[24] China is also the second largest producer of carbon dioxide (CO_2) after the U.S. China releases some 2.97 billion tons of CO_2 every year compared to 5.4 billion tons for the U.S., and China is expected to reach the U.S. level within 25 years. See A. Terry Rambo, "The Fallacy of Global Sustainable Development," *Asia Pacific Issues*, No.30, March 1997, p.4.

[25] There were 547 reports of acid rain damage in 1973. New awareness of the problem and monitoring in various points throughout the country raised the number of reports to a peak of 33,181 in 1974. As pollution abatement devices began operation, the number of reports fell to 244 cases in 1975, 6 in 1976, zero in 1977 and 1978 and 3 in 1981. See Hirose, *op cit.*, p.164.

[26] Coal made up only 16.6% of its primary energy; natural gas, 10.46%; nuclear energy, 15.2%; and hydroelectricity, 1.4% in 1995. International Energy Agency, *Energy Statistics and Balances: OECD Countries 1960-1995, Non-OECD Countries 1971-1995*, diskette service, May 1997, sheets for Japan.

[27]<<www.mofa.go.jp/policy/global/environment/pamph/1992/2_back.html>>. Viewed on 9 May 1998.

[28] Shun'ichi Teranishi, "A Critical Review of Pollution Issues and Environmental Policy in Japan," in Kojima *et al.*, eds., *op cit.*, pp.75 and 76.

[29] For details on the number of facilities installed and their total processing capacity, see Makoto Natori, "Japan's Pollution Control Technologies and their role in the World," *Japan Review of International Affairs*, Vol.7, No.1, Winter 1993, pp.52-54.

[30] See Hirose, *op cit.*, p.160.

[31] By the end of 1993, there were 47 nuclear power plants in operation in Japan. They accounted for 16.9% of Japan's total power generating capacity and 24.9% of its total electric power. However, high construction and production costs have been holding back the building of new nuclear power plants. Also, accidents and poor responses by the authorities in recent years have increased popular objection to nuclear power generation. Since 1991, the Japanese central government, the power industry, and citizens groups have tried to actively promote the use of solar heating equipment in homes and small businesses. The government and industry hope that this will ease the demand on electricity since it has become increasingly difficult to overcome public opposition to all kinds of power plant construction. See Barbara Litt, trans., "Citizen Power for Solar Power," orig. in Japanese in *Asahi Shimbun*, 9 June 1997, in *Japan Environment Monitor*, electronic ed., No.92, August-September 1997; and "Demand and Supply of Electric Power" and "Nuclear Power Generation," in *Japan Almanac 1995*, Tokyo: Asahi Shimbun, 1994, pp.168 and 169.

[32] Park, *op cit.*, p.158.

[33] See Luoma, *op cit.*, p.75; and Hirose, *op cit.*, p.30.

[34] Luoma, *ibid.*, p.77.

[35] *Ibid.*, p.78.

[36] Park, *op cit.*, p.158.

[37] McCormick, *op cit.*, p.74.

[38] Luoma, *op cit.*, p.78.

[39] Park, *op cit.*, pp.158-159.

[40] John E. Carroll, "Acid Rain—Acid Diplomacy," in *The Acid Rain Debate: Scientific, Economic, and Political Dimensions*, ed. by Ernest J. Yanarella and Randal H. Ihara, Boulder and London: Westview Press, 1985, p.265.

[41] The European Community was not feasible because Norway and Sweden were not members.

[42] McCormick, *op cit.*, pp.75-76.

[43] *Ibid.*, p.74.

[44] J.M. Jakobowicz, "Acid Rain: An Issue for Regional Cooperation," in *Acid Rain: Current Situation and Remedies*, ed. by J. Rose, Amsterdam: Gordon and Breach Science Publishers, 1994, pp.144-145.

[45] Carroll, *op cit.*, p.263.

[46] Roderick W. Shaw, "Acid-Rain Negotiations in North America and Europe: A Study in Contrast," in *International Environmental Negotiation*, ed. by Gunnar Sjostedt, Newbury Park: Sage, 1993, p.92.

[47] McCormick, *op cit.*, pp.75-76

[48] By 1994, 34 countries and the European Economic Community had signed the Convention. Thirty-two countries have ratified it, and it was entered into force in March 1983. See Jakobowicz, *op cit.*, p.142.

[49] EMEP, originally under the auspices of UNECE, is now run by the Executive Body of CLRTAP. See McCormick, *op cit.*, p.77.

[50] For instance, acid rain became a major political issue in domestic politics in Germany by the 1970s as the public grew to be more environmentally conscious. Membership in the Green Party rose and so did the group's influence. This "greening" of West Germany (and other European countries) helped to push for changes in government policies toward transboundary pollution in Western Europe. See Park, *op cit.*, p.170.

[51] McCormick, *op cit.*, p.52.

[52] Hungary and Romania attended, but as smaller economies their presence made little difference. See Park, *op cit.*, pp.170-171.

[53] The ten countries are Denmark, Norway, Finland, Sweden, Austria, Canada, France, West Germany, the Netherlands, and Switzerland. France came around as the country's dependency on coal dropped with the use of nuclear power. There was also pressure from West Germany and other neighbors.

[54] Ger Klaassen, *Acid Rain and Environmental Degradation: The Economics of Emission Trading*, Laxenburg: International Institute for Applied Systems Analysis, 1996, p.190.

[55] The 8 new members were Belgium, Bulgaria, Byelorussia, East Germany, Liechtenstein, Luxembourg, the Soviet Union, and the Ukraine. See McCormick, *op cit.*, p.81.

[56] Uncertainties about the level of SO_2 emissions due to the rate of economic expansion, costs and changes in clean coal technologies, the intro-

Acid Deposition in Asia 249

duction of alternative energy sources such as nuclear power, natural gas, hydroelectricity and others that are SO_2 emission-free. See Jakobowicz, *op cit.*, p.148.

[57] Klaassen, *op cit.*, p.190.

[58] By this time, acid rain had grown into a major sore point in bilateral ties with Canada. The U.S. attended the Helsinki meeting only to prevent the Soviet Union from getting all the positive publicity for appearing cooperative on pollution control. See McCormick, *op cit.*, pp.81-82.

[59] At the end of 1994, 27 parties have signed.

[60] Klaassen, *op cit.*, pp.193-197.

[61] Peter Bailey *et al.*, "Prospects for the Joint Implementation of Sulfur Emission Reductions in Europe," *Energy Policy*, June 1996, pp.507-16; and Helen ApSimon and Rachel Warren, "Trans-boundary Air Pollution in Europe," *Energy Policy*, July 1996, pp.631-40.

[62] Large combustion plants are defined as clusters of boilers with aggregate input capacity exceeding 50 megawatts (thermal). Walter Patterson, ed., *Environmental Profiles of European Business*, London: Earthscan, 1993, pp.68-69.

[63] This was based on its December 1983 proposal to cut SO_2 by 60% and NO_x and dust by 40% each. All member countries were also urged to switch to unleaded gasoline starting 1989 and to adopt the U.S.-standard catalytic converter by 1995 at the latest. McCormick, *op cit.*, p.83; and Chadwick and Hutton, eds., *op cit.*, p.331. Also <<www.soton.ac.uk/~engenvir/environment/ air/acid.laws.html>>. Viewed on 12 May 1998.

[64] Jakobowicz, *op cit.*, p.153; Klaassen, *op cit.*, p.192.

[65] Robert H. Boyle, *Acid Rain*, New York: Nick Lyons Books, 1983, p.95; McCormick, *op cit.*, p.75.

[66] This included the Sierra Club, the National Audubon Society, Friends of the Earth, the National Wildlife Federation and the Izaak Walton League. See Regens and Rycroft, *op cit.*, p.122.

[67] To this day, it maintains a nation-wide network of sampling stations. *Ibid.*, p.123.

[68] McCormick, *op cit.*, p.75.

[69] Luoma, *op cit.*, pp.125-126.

[70] Before this, provincial governments set their own emissions standards for SO_2 and NO_x.

[71] The treatment of science provides a good contrast in how the two administrations use science and their attitude toward acid pollution. While the Carter administration used science as a catalyst for action, the Reagan administration used it to justify inaction. See Regens and Rycroft, *op cit.*, p.119.

[72] See Luoma, *op cit.*, pp.125-129; Shaw, *op cit.*, p.93.

[73] The Act also calls for a reduction by 2 million tons in NO_x emissions by the year 2000.

[74] The 1990 Clean Air Act sought to reduce annual SO_2 emissions by about 10 million tons, or about a 40% reduction from the 1980 level of 25 million tons. Electric power-generating facilities that burn coal and fossil fuel are the main target. See Kent E. Portney, *Controversial Issues in Environmental Policy: Science vs. Economics vs. Politics*, Newbury Park: Sage Publications, 1992, p.94; and Masanobu Kaizu and Shigeo Hiratsuka, "Environmental Business Opportunities in Japan," *NRI Quarterly*, Vol.1, Summer 1992, p.25. For more on the U.S.-Canadian acid rain conflict, read Archie M. Kahan, *Acid Rain: Reign of Controversy*, Golden: Fulcrum, Inc., 1986; Jurgen Schmandt *et al.*, eds., *Acid Rain and Friendly Neighbors: The Policy Dispute between Canada and the United States*, rev. ed., Durham: Duke University Press, 1988; Gold, ed., *op cit.*; McCormick, *op cit.*, pp.159-163; and Shaw, *op cit.*, pp.84-109.

[75] "Canada `still has a long way to go' in effective control of acid rain," *Nature*, Vol.390, 6 November 1997, p.6.

[76] <<www.epa.gov/acidrain/overview.html>> Viewed on 12 May 1998.

[77] "Canada `still has a long way to go'...," *op cit.*

[78] Although a joint action plan exists under UNEP, it is not implemented because of complex political relations in the region

[79] Charles Johnson and Binsheng Li, "Asia's Coal and Clean Coal Technology Market Potential," The East-West Center, September 1992, p.1.

[80] By 1995, Chinese coal consumption was up to 1.3 billion tons. See Todd Johnson *et al.*, *Clear Water, Blue Skies: China's Environment in the New Century*, Washington, D.C.: The World Bank, China 2020 Series, 1997, p.8.

[81] Perlack *et al.*, *op cit.*, p.207.

[82] China's share of SO_2 emissions in Asia in 1997 was 63% to 70% of the total. India's share was 14% and the rest belonged to other Asian countries. Interview with Charles Johnson.

[83] N. Kata *et al.*, "Analysis of the Structure of Energy Consumption and the Dynamics of Emissions of Atmospheric Species related to Global Environment: China SO_2, NO_x and CO_2 in Asia," Tokyo: National Institute of Science and Technology Policy and the Science and Technology Agency, 1991, Report No.21, n.p. For more on China as a source of pollution and environment legislation in China, see Hailin Zhou, "Environmental Law and Administration: The Case of China," and Reeitsu Kojima, "Mainland China grows into the World's Largest Source of Environmental Pollution," in Kojima *et al.*, eds., *op cit.*, pp.176-192 and pp.193-211, respectively.

[84] This represents a fifth of the world's population, and it expands by 16 million annually. See Liu *et al.*, *op cit.*, p.61.

[85] Chinese per capita electricity consumption was 780 kwh in 1994. This compares with 3,405 kwh for Venezuela, 5,805 kwh for Russia and 12,711

Acid Deposition in Asia 251

kwh for the U.S. See Arthur Zich, "China's Three Gorges: Before the Flood," in *National Geographic*, Vol.192, No.3, September 1997, p.11; and Trish Saywell, "Power to the People," *Far Eastern Economic Review*, 29 January 1998, p.36.

[86] Chinese power plants have the world's highest equipment usage rates, averaging more than 7,000 hours per year. The optimal rate for most coal and oil-fired generating equipment is about 4,000 hours annually. See Carl Goldstein, "China's generation gap," *Far Eastern Economic Review*, 11 June 1992, p.45. For more on China's energy sector, see T. Johnson *et al.*, *op cit.*, pp.45-56.

[87] *Ibid.*; and J.P. Dorian, *Minerals, Mining and Economic Development in China*, Oxford: Clarendon Press, 1994, p.232.

[88] Liaoning province; the Beijing-Tianjin-Tangshan area; Jiaodong area; Changjiang Triangle; Zhuojiang Triangle; and Wuhan area. See Binsheng Li and Charles J. Johnson, "The booming electricity sector of China - Its opportunities and challenges," East-West Center, Program on Energy and Minerals, China Energy Project Series Paper CEP-94-1, 1994, p.6.

[89] Dependency on coal declined through the 1960s and up to the mid-1970s with the discovery and development of new oil reserves. The maturation of the country's major oil fields and lack of new oil discoveries renewed its reliance on coal. Coal's share began to rise after 1976 and has been around 75% since then. Apart from coal, China's primary energy sources consisted of petroleum (18%), natural gas (2%), and hydroelectricity (5.1%). From Program on Resources: Energy and Minerals, The East-West Center, *Energy Advisory*, No.121, 16 February 1994, p.3; Program on Resources, Energy and Minerals, the East-West Center, *China Energy Update, op cit.*, p.1.

[90] Nuclear power generation has not proven to be economically competitive. There are also waste disposal problems and technical and safety concerns. China has enormous hydro-power potential. However, this energy source is not generally close to the industrial centers and a lack of infrastructure hampers energy transport. There are also serious adverse effects. The hydroelectric station at the Three Gorges area of the Yangtze is highly controversial for its mass displacement of people (at least 1.2 million people along the river) and its potential damage on the environment and historical artifacts. Development of offshore natural gas fields and the giant Shan-Gan-Ning gas field in northwest China is in progress. Natural gas at present is only 2% of primary energy consumption. Increased usage depends on the building of infrastructure, but its share will remain small compared to coal. See Program on Resources: Energy and Minerals, *China Energy Update*, 2nd quarter, 1994, p.1; and Richard Louis Edmonds, *Patterns of China's Lost Harmony: A Survey of the Country's Environmental Degradation and Protection*, London and New York: Routledge, 1994, pp.79-86.

252   *The Roots of Japan's Environmental Policy*

[91] Edmonds, *ibid.*, p.249.

[92] This is nearly half of the 1,597,980 worldwide total. See Program on Resources: Energy and Minerals, *China Energy Update, op cit.*, p.1.

[93] China is the sixth largest oil producer, but domestic demand surpasses output. In 1993 China, for the first time since the 1960s, became a net importer of oil. *Ibid.*

[94] Johnson and Li, *op cit.*, p.2.

[95] Nicholas Lenssen, "All the Coal in China," World Watch, April 1993,p.25.

[96] See Soichiro Seki, "Kaihatsutojokoku no Kankyo Osen" (Environmental Pollution in Developing Countries), *Kankyo Kenkyu*, No.76, 1989, pp.72-76. For more on the Chinese government's efforts to address the country's environmental problems, see also T. Johnson *et al.*, *op cit.*

[97] Lenssen, *op cit.*

[98] See <<www.nautilus.org/esena/Papers/carmichael.html>>. Searched on 12 May 1998.

[99] Higher soil alkalinity in the north helps to offset some of the effects of acid rain. However, soil and river acidification is a threat to most provinces south of the Yangtze River where soil and surface waters are generally acidic and the soil is poorly buffered.

[100] Higher alkalinity in soils and surfaces in the north offers some protection from acid rain. However, there are more heavy industries in the north and low-sulfur coal is less commonly used.

[101] See T. Johnson *et al.*, *op cit.*, p.27; and "Survey on Development and the Environment," *The Economist*, 21 March 1998, p.8.

[102] T. Johnson *et al.*, *op cit.*, pp.8, 18 and 21-22.

[103] "Chyugokku kogai ga shinkoku ka" (Worsening pollution in China), *Yomiuri Shimbun*, 23 April 1994; "Rich is glorious," *The Ecologist*, January/February 1995, pp.14-15; and "Survey on Development and the Environment," *op cit.*

[104] "APEC, "Study on Atmospheric Emissions...," *op cit.*, p.29.

[105] Transboundary air pollution from South Korea, Indonesia, and other Asian countries are less urgent because the threat is at a much smaller scale. Weather systems in Southeast Asia also localize chemical air pollution in the region, and the Association of Southeast Asian Nations (ASEAN) offers a forum to coordinate regional responses. See "Environment: Air Pollution,"*1998 World Development Indicators*, Washington, D.C.: The World Bank, 1998, p.162; and McCormick, *op cit.*, p.203.

[106] In response, the Environment Agency set up 10 monitoring stations on the inland side of Japan to add to those already operating in 29 locations throughout the country. See Hideki Asai, "Pollution Problems in China Already Raining down on Japan," *Tokyo Business Today*, December

Acid Deposition in Asia   253

1993, pp.44-47; and OECD, *OECD Environmental Performance Review of Japan*, November 1993, p.128.

[107] See Liu *et al.*, *op cit.*, p.204.

[108] In November 1992, very high concentrations of SO_2 were observed west of the Oki islands in the Sea of Japan. Wind directions strongly indicate that the emissions came from the Asian mainland. See <<www.nies.go.jp:8092/web-doc/e/text5.html>>. Viewed on 11 May 1998; and Michio Kato *et al.*, "*Higashi Ajia no Sanseiu Mondai to Nihon no Ya.kuwari*" (Acid rain problem in East Asia and the Role of Japan), *Kankyo Kenkyu*, No.99, September 1995, p.96.

[109] Kato, *ibid.*

[110] China is now the single largest recipient of Japanese ODA. See Hisane Misaki, "China sinks deeper into ecological cesspool," *The Japan Times*, 23 July 1995; and Liu *et al.*, *op cit.*, p.195.

[111] Prime Minister Noboru Takeshita proposed the creation of this Center to commemorate the first decade of Sino-Japanese Friendship Treaty in 1988 and he officially opened it. See "China opens environmental center," *The Japan Times*, 6 May 1996, p.2.

[112] Interview with Yamauchi.

[113] Yokkaichi City, too, has established its own International Center for Environmental Technology Transfer for interchange with researchers from China and other countries on air pollution prevention activities. See Liu *et al.*, *op cit.*, p.198; and JICA, "*Chyugokku ni taisuru JICA no kankyo kyoryoku*" (JICA's Environmental Cooperation with China), Draft, 29 July 1997, p.2.

[114] *Ibid.*

[115] These cities included Shenyang, Benxi, Chongqing, Chengdu and Guiyang, which also suffer severe air pollution. See M. Kato *et al.*, *op cit.*, p.103.

[116] JICA, "Chyukokku ni taisuru...," *op cit.*

[117] <<www.mofa.go.jp/policy/oda/summary/1998/8.html>>. Viewed on 10 March 2000.

[118] Prior to this, the first chemical study of precipitation was conducted in 1973 and limited to the Marunouchi area of Tokyo. Systemic monitoring of precipitation throughout the country began after the mid-1970s as the emissions controls came underway. See Hirose, *op cit.*, p.164.

[119] M. Kato *et al.*, *op cit.*, p.88.

[120] Final results released in 1989 reported a national average of 4.4 to 5.5 pH level. See Hirose, *op cit.*, p.163.

[121] "Sanseiu o kangaeru" (Thinking about Acid Rain), Tokyo: Nihon Kankyo Kyokai, October 1991, pp.2-3. For more on the history of acid deposition monitoring in Japan and the results, see H. Hara, "Acid Deposition Chemistry in Asia," *Bulletin of the Institute for Public Health*, Vol.42, 1993, pp.426-437 and K. Murano, "Activity of JEA for East Asian

254   *The Roots of Japan's Environmental Policy*

Acid Precipitation Monitoring Network." Presented at Workshop in Acid Rain Network in South, East and Southeast Asia, Malaysia, 17-19 May 1994.

[122] Tadashi Takeuchi, "Kankyocho ni yoru Sanseiu Mondai e no tori gumi" (The Environment Agency's Initiative for the Acid Rain Problem), *Kankyo Kenkyu*, No.99, September 1995, pp.143-146.

[123] Early results in 1994 reported that an average 4.8 pH level nation-wide produced no obvious damage, but the inland side of the islands has received higher acidity readings in the fall and winter months. See M. Kato *et al.*, *op cit.*, p.96.

[124] Another major ECO ASIA undertaking is the Long-term Perspective Project, proposed at the ECO ASIA in 1993, to provide decision-makers in the Asia-Pacific with a scientific basis for policy formulation to achieve sustainable development for the period until the year 2025. Interview with Y. Natori.

[125] Other countries invited were Malaysia, Mongolia, the Philippines, Russia, Singapore, Thailand, and Vietnam.

[126] The RAINS model estimates regional impacts of acid deposition and evaluates costs and effectiveness of specific technologies and measures. UNECE was first to use it to develop new protocols for sulfur and nitrogen oxides emissions. See <<www.iiasa.ac.at/~heyes/docs/rains.asia.html>>. Viewed on 11 May 1998.

[127] Speech by Mr. Kazumi Kishibe of the Environment Agency at the Third Acid Rain Symposium in Niigata in November 1995.

[128] The conference was originally scheduled to take place in Kobe but the Great Hanshin earthquake in January 1995 forced the event to move to Tokyo in March.

[129] Interview with Yamauchi.

[130] <<www.eic.or.jp/eanet/e/jeq/v003-01.html#7>>. Viewed on 9 May 1998.

[131] "Stress Environmental Aid to China, Panel Urges," *The Japan Times*, 23 May 1996, p.2.

[132] Interview with Kishibe.

[133] M. Kato *et al.*, *op cit.*, p.101.

[134] The North American experience was not considered useful as a model. Interview with Wilkening.

[135] Liu *et al.*, *op cit.*, p.189.

[136] See Patterson, ed., *op cit.*, p.78.

[137] Interview with Kawashima.

[138] *Amakudari* or "the descent from heaven" describes the placement of ex-government officials, often in the private sector, following their departure from government. The ex-bureaucrat transforms his role from a regulator of an industry or business into an advisor and liaison with his former employer. This practice is regarded as highly significant to the close ties

Acid Deposition in Asia

between government and big business in Japan and a reason for MITI's enormous influence. A survey conducted in October 1993 found that among the 217 *amakudari* executives interviewed, 34 came from MITI, 32 from MAFF and 25 from MoF. See "'Amakudari' positions widespread," *op cit.*

[139] This same argument was used by MITI to establish bureaucratic leadership over the Japanese government's policy toward global warming, another international environmental problem that is rooted in fossil fuel combustion.

[140] Interview with Otsuka.

[141] Wes Foell *et al.*, eds., "RAINS-ASIA: An Assessment Model for Air Pollution in Asia, *Report on the World Bank-sponsored project "Acid Rain and Emissions in Asia*," December 1995, p.VII-14.

[142] See Liu *et al.*, *op cit.*, pp.189-191.

[143] "A matter of priorities," *Far Eastern Economic Review*, 16 November 1995, p.70; and Asai, *op cit.*, p.46.

[144] D. Zhao and J. Xiong, "Acidification in Southwestern China" in *Acidification in Tropical Countries*, ed. by Henning Rodhe and Rafael Herrera, Chichester and New York: John Wiley & Sons, 1988, p.317; and interview with Wang.

[145] Germany follows with US$300 million and Spain with US$153 million.

[146] The JICA Environment Office in China opened in 1988. See Liu *et al.*, *op cit.*, p.188.

[147] Interview with Yamauchi.

[148] Interview with Kawashima.

[149] See Shaw, *op cit.*, p.98.

[150] See Masanobu Kaizu and Shigeo Hiratsuka, "Environmental Business Opportunities in Japan," *NRI Quarterly*, Vol.1, Summer 1992, p.25.

[151] Regens and Rycroft, *op cit.*, p.119; and Tom Albin and Steve Paulson, "Environmental and Economic Interests in Canada and the United States," in Schmandt *et al.*, eds., *op cit.*, pp.110-111.

[152] Interview with Tian; see also Liu *et al.*, *op cit.*, pp.66-67 and 84.

[153] Johnson and Li, *op cit.*, pp.5 and 6.

[154] Shohei Yonemoto, "Tokyo should take lead on environment," *The Nikkei Weekly*, 27 June 1994, p.6.

[155] Rodhe and Herrera, eds., *op cit.*, p.12.

[156] Hiroshi Hara of the Institute of Public Health, panelist at the Third Acid Rain Symposium in Niigata, 13 November 1995.

[157] For more on acid rain in the tropics, see Rodhe and Herrera, eds., *op cit.*

[158] Since China washes less than 20 percent of its coal before use, a large amount of heavy metals and particulates are released with SO_2 when the

coal is burned. See Sandra Burton, "Taming the River Wild," *Time*, 19 December 1994, pp.62-64.

[159] For details, see Yingzhong Lu, "Fueling One Billion: An Insider's Story of Chinese Energy Policy Development," Washington, D.C.: The Washington Institute, 1993.

[160] Interviews with Otsuka and Tian in Beijing; and Nishihira *et al.*, *op cit.*, pp.100-101.

[161] Chinese official representative at the Third Acid Rain Symposium in Niigata in November 1995.

CHAPTER 7

Conclusions

Taking a role in international environmental issues meant different things to different groups and interests in Japan. To Japan, as a whole, it was an opportunity for the country to assert itself in international affairs. To the Japanese prime minister and a few other top politicians, they supported international cooperation in environmental affairs to boost their own image and stature in international affairs. To the government ministries and agencies, it promised new powers and resources. To Japanese big business, they had to become more responsive to ecological concerns in order to maintain their competitiveness, and many saw potentials to profit in the sale of environmental technologies and services. To many Japanese people, it represented an opportunity to find common identity with other people and nations, as well as an opportunity to push for public participation in government policy making.

Although the Japanese government had committed generous funding for international environmental activities in the past decade, international opinion still largely consider Japanese government responses as inadequate. The case studies showed that Japan lacks a coherent national policy towards international environmental issues and its government bureaucracy dominates the policy process. However, these conditions are typical of most countries and governments, so they do not sufficiently explain the how the Japanese government respond to different kinds of international environmental issues or the motivations behind its policy choices and actions. They also do not adequately explain how domestic politics affects Japanese government perspectives and actions towards the global environment.

For these reasons, this study drew on concepts in complex independence, the two-level games theory, and the bureaucratic politics model to investigate the sources of perspectives, interests, goals, and dynamics that influence Japanese government policies towards international environmental issues. In addition, emphasis was placed on understanding how a problem or concern evolved into a policy issue within Japan's domestic political framework and at the international level. Doing so makes more visible the influential actors, their objectives, powers, and influence, as well as the dynamics of their interactions.

As a result, we see that governments are not internally coherent or monolithic in form. Disparities in the powers, influence, and vulnerabilities of policy actors affect intra-governmental negotiations as well as negotiations with outside groups. The policy decisions that result are usually products of such give-and-take rather than the dictate of any one entity. This is especially true in three kinds of situations. First, when the cooperation or endorsement of other interested actors are needed for one to achieve its goals. Second, when actors are bound by long existing relationships or seek to promote such relationship. Third, when linkages exist across policy issues and decision levels. Policy actors must consider calculations of opportunities, costs, strength, and benefits in the negotiations beforehand as well as those in the linked arenas and issues.

POLICY MAKING IN JAPAN AND THE INTERNATIONAL ENVIRONMENT

Policies on environmental issues, whether they are domestic or international, present challenges to policy actors because environmental issues often cut across conventional categories of jurisdictions. Increasing concern for international environmental problems in the past several decades has given rise to new perspectives on international relations, the powers of the state, the goals of development, and the voices of civil society among others.

Since Japan is a major economic power and donor of development assistance that has an immense impact on the global environment, it is important to identify the roots of Japan's international environmental policies. Whaling, deforestation in the tropics, and transboundary acid pollution represent different types of international environmental issues. Examining Japanese government policy responses to each gave insights into the determinants of perspectives and goals. It also exposed the complex power relationships in policy making.

The key findings of this study are summed up in the 10 points below. Although they are built on observations of Japanese policies towards these three issues, their relevance extend beyond international environmental issues because these case studies were vehicles to understanding foreign policy making in Japan. These findings may be particularly useful to exploring policies towards other types of issues that challenge traditional policy frameworks, such as biotechnology and telecommunication.

Conclusion 259

(1) Gaps between Japanese policies and international expectations are largely due to differences between how an issue is viewed and set within Japan's domestic policy framework and the regime that governs this issue at the international level. While differences may be present from the start, even a shared perspective can deviate over time.

For example, as whaling lost its economic significance to most nations, the issue transformed from one of resource use to conservation of commons. A change in the power structure occurred within the international regime for whaling followed. Conservation advocates became the new majority and the passing of the temporary ban against commercial whaling by the International Whaling Commission, in particular, marked a key turning point in the whaling debate. Since the Japanese domestic policy framework continued to treat whaling as a resource use matter, Japan's policies and objectives came to contrast sharply with new trends and sentiments in the international arena. As a result, Japan and a few other countries that are supportive of resuming commercial whaling became the small minority in this debate.

In the case of deforestation in the tropics, the gap between Japanese policy responses and the developing international regime for forests is small. Japan's policy emphasis on pursuing forest conservation strategies that support sustainable consumptive and commercial uses of forests is shared by most other governments, international organizations, and even conservation groups. Thus, Japanese policy preferences are not contradictory to the evolving international regime in which forests are widely recognized to have multiple values, including economic ones. Furthermore, Japan's influence in international forest policy discussions is underscored by its position as a major importer of forest products. Hence, even most critics of Japanese policies accept that to effectively address the problem of deforestation in the tropics (and other region) it would be more useful to engage Japan than to criticize or isolate it.

In responding to transboundary acid pollution, Japan's proposal for an acid pollution control regime in East Asia drew on similar experiences in other parts of the world. Since Japanese assistance and leadership in building this monitoring network would create benefits for the entire region, China and other countries have largely been supportive of this Japanese initiative. Indeed, concern for the health and ecological effects of acid pollution (as well as the costs of damages and remedy) motivated involvement and cooperation by many sub-national, national, and international actors.

(2) Most Japanese government policies towards international environmental issue have stressed defense of resource use (sustainable or otherwise) over advocacy for nature conservation. One source of this tendency is the primacy of energy and resource security as a central guideline in all

Japanese government policies. Another is the Japanese government's sensitivity to linkages among issues and the regimes that govern them.

Japan's Fisheries Agency continues to oppose in principle the moratorium on commercial whaling because it is afraid that acceptance could make way for similar biases in other international regimes for other types of fisheries and resource use. Similar concerns for resource security explain why Japan stresses sustainable forestry, such as its support for the International Tropical Timber Organization, as a priority in forest conservation.

(3) International environmental cooperation presented a safe opportunity for Japan to assert international leadership. The global environment, as an issue of complex interdependence, requires more than positive or negative sanctions by any one power find effective and acceptable solutions.

The Japanese government offered itself as a mediator or bridge between developed and developing countries in international discussions on development and the environment. Japanese leadership would rely on the country's financial and technological capabilities to provide incentives for compromise and cooperation. However, this approach still has to prove its efficacy because solutions to issues of complex interdependence require creativity and entrepreneurial skills to identify and put together mutually beneficial deals for the interests involved.

The failure of this approach is most clearly evident in Japan's response to forest destruction. In contrast, Japan's response to transboundary acid pollution in Asia included actions and resources to garner public, bureaucratic and industry support within Japan and in foreign countries. Neighboring countries could address their domestic priorities with the help of bilateral aid transfer from Japan. At the same time, Japanese leadership and resources to establish common standards in monitoring acid rain throughout the region helped to form an epistemic community and a common understanding of the problem, which are crucial to any region-wide multilateral agreement.

For many bureaucratic actors, international environmental issues held promise for expanded powers and new resources. Official development assistance, particularly for international environmental cooperation, was the only area where increases occurred in the national budget. International environmental issues are concurrently old and new issue to the domestic policy framework. It is old because many policy issues, such as whaling and tropical forestry, have long existed within Japan's domestic policy framework. In such issues, the history and power dynamics that dictate the foreign policy making process are extremely difficult to alter. For example, Fisheries Agency remains the leading voice in deciding national policies towards whaling because the legal regulatory framework continues to designate whaling as a fisheries issue. While other bureaucratic actors may not

Conclusion

support Fisheries Agency's policy choices, they have to respect jurisdictional boundaries and resist temptations to intervene. To do otherwise would incite conflicts and compromise their bargaining positions in linked issues.

Environmental issues that are new to the domestic policy framework are those that are not defined or governed by existing regulatory jurisdictions. Since clear bureaucratic control is lacking, intense bureaucratic battles often ensue to establish regulatory control and policy leadership in these matters. There are several ways to do this. Interested actors could try to establish their position and participation in the policy process by identifying elements in the issue that come under their jurisdiction. For example, the Ministry of International Trade and Industry (MITI) and the Environment Agency of Japan (JEA) competed for bureaucratic leadership in the acid rain issue. The former based its claim on its powers over energy matters. The latter stressed its mandate as the coordinating agency for all government policies on pollution matters.

JEA emphasized the domestic health and ecological effects of foreign acid pollutants in shaping the policy discussion. This helped JEA to mobilize support from other bureaucratic agencies responsible for domestic health and ecological protection, including the Ministry of Health and Welfare and the Ministry for Agriculture, Forestry and Fisheries. These bureaucratic actors could not establish policy control or leadership on the basis of their regulatory powers and they would have less influence in intragovernmental policy negotiations if a large and powerful body like MITI were the lead agency. Thus, JEA was able to win control and leadership.

Issue redefinition by expanding participation can also improve an actor's leverage in bargaining at both domestic and international levels. By defining the acid deposition in Asia as a transboundary pollution problem (in addition to emphasizing its domestic health and environmental hazards), JEA separated this issue from global warming, which had become an established issue under MITI control and leadership.

In whaling, the Fisheries Agency expanded the issue into a bigger one. Beyond the core emphasis on whaling as a resource use issue, Fisheries Agency made it more inclusive to Japanese society and significant to national core values by suggesting that foreign attacks on Japanese whaling are a form of cultural imperialism. This served the Fisheries Agency in two important ways. First, it reduced the efficacy of domestic and foreign anti-whaling messages on Japanese public opinion. Second, it allows the Fisheries Agency to pledge that its opposition to the international moratorium on commercial whaling is in defense of the interests of the nation as a whole, and not just for Japanese whaling or fisheries.

Redefinition could also constrict rather than expand the scope of an issue. In the forestry issue, the chief actors limited the parameters of policy discussions to sustainable forestry management and use. This served to advance their respective organization goals, reduced conflicts in intra-governmental negotiations, and aided consensus-building among these chief actors when dealing with outside forces. Japanese industry also benefited from this restricted definition because maintaining access to timber is their foremost priority.

(4) The government bureaucracy is the strongest domestic policy actor, but it is not a unitary one. In fact, sectionalism permeates throughout the government bureaucracy and the policy process. Each administrative body has its own goals and priorities, and its powers are determined largely by the boundaries of its statutory authority in regulation. All these affect how bureaucratic actors view issues, define their role and interests in them, and their choice of policy preferences.

Thus, acid rain is a human health threat to the Ministry of Health and Welfare, an energy issue to MITI, an air pollution problem to the Environment Agency, and an ecological threat to the Ministry of Agriculture, Forestry and Fisheries. In whaling, the Fisheries Agency opposed the moratorium because of possible implications for other fisheries regimes, but MITI did not object an end to Japanese whaling because of its linkage to non-fisheries trade issues adversely affected MITI interests. The North American Bureau of the Ministry of Foreign Affairs also preferred an end to Japanese whaling in order to remove this politically charged issue from the U.S.-Japan agenda.

However, decisions to cooperate and form alliances among policy actors are due more to convergence of views and interests than institutional boundaries because each issue has its own political structure, processes, and relationships among policy elites and constituents. For example, officials responsible for fisheries in both the Ministry of Agriculture, Forestry and Fisheries and the Ministry of Foreign Affairs considered the defense of commercial whaling important to broader Japanese interests in fisheries despite threats of sanctions from the United States. In contrast, officials responsible for North American affairs and fisheries matters within the Ministry of Foreign Affairs took opposite positions on whether Japan should accept the commercial whaling moratorium. In another instance, local governments agreed to terminate the use of tropical timber in publicly funded projects because it was beneficial to their public image as citizens became more aware of the social and environmental effects of tropical forest destruction. It also gave local authorities a reason to purchase more expensive domestic timber, thus helping ailing forestry businesses in many rural communities throughout the country.

International cooperation and alliances are also determined by similar convergence of policy views and interests. Japanese officials for whaling and fisheries found sympathy from their American counterparts in negotiations to retrieve Japanese fishing quotas in the United States. Officials of

Conclusion 263

environment ministries and agencies in Japan and other Asian countries understood that their cooperative efforts in data collection would help them to speak to their respective domestic audiences.

(5) Sectionalism within the government bureaucracy affects access to the policy process by those outside of the government. Ministries and agencies tend to consult with those deemed useful to bureaucratic consensus in decision making, essential to policy implementation, or beneficial to bolstering their bargaining leverage. As a result, consultation is largely restricted to constituents under their regulatory control, and the most powerful ones have the biggest influence.

Fisheries Agency officials had to persuade the fisheries industry to accept their opposition to the commercial whaling moratorium before filing the official objection. Forestry Agency support for forestry research by Japanese big business helped the agency to define a role (and obtain new budget allocation) in international forest policy discussions. For bureaucratic actors that have no powerful domestic constituents, such as the Environment Agency and the Ministry of Foreign Affairs, they were more open to contacts with non-governmental organizations (NGOs) and sought to mobilize public opinion to support their policy preferences. NGOs can also compensate for some of their weaknesses, such as providing labor for overseas cooperation activities.

(6) Consensus decision making marked by intense bargaining and negotiations is central to policy making in Japan because policy actors usually have long established relationships and their interests overlap over a broad range of issues. Consensus in policy choices at the outset minimizes conflicts (or political and economic costs) in policy implementation. It also encourages reciprocity within the policy issue at hand and/or in other policy issues when linkages exist (or are expected to occur).

Consensus decision making is useful especially because bureaucratic leadership or dominance over one policy issue does not guarantee a policy actor an equally advantaged position in another policy matter. Consensus is particularly important to smaller and less powerful policy actors, such as the Environment Agency, because political and material support from other policy actors could be indispensable to the execution of their policy choices.

Furthermore, consensus among major policy actors should not be interpreted as the presence of a single or integrated national policy. Rather such consensus generally implies an absence of conflict over a policy choice and an acceptance of policy leadership by a particular bureaucratic actor. For instance, sustainable forestry as the core activity in Japan's policy responses to deforestation helped to forge consensus among the major policy actors even as their motivations and goals for supporting sustainable forestry differ.

(7) The double-edged quality of consensus decision making is another reason for policy actors to limit consultation and resist outside input in the policy process. Consultation can reduce the potential for conflict, but it can also allow opportunity for opposition to delay or block actions, and conditioning consent can dilute policy measures.

For this reason, policy makers generally resist intervention in the policy process by those who are unable or unwilling to contribute to the give-and-take that occurs in a long relationship and across issue areas. Policy actors also regard unsolicited input a practical burden. They could disturb built-in or agreed consensus, thereby extending and complicating negotiations. Thus, convincing policy makers (in Japan and elsewhere) to allow greater openness and transparency in policy processes has always been a difficult task.

(8) Two-level dynamics in decision making shows that outside pressure is not unidirectional and domestic decision makers are not passive recipients. Policy actors can use outside pressure, including international agreements, public opinion, and foreign criticisms to improve their bargaining leverage in both domestic and international arenas.

For instance, the Environment Agency used international opinions to hasten the passing of a new Environment Basic Law in 1993. A scheduled review of Japan's environmental legislation by the Organization of Economic Cooperation and Development (OECD) made the Japanese government anxious to be seen in a positive light. The new law gave the Environment Agency more power and resources to increase its influence in intra-governmental negotiations.

(9) Reverberations also occur and put pressure on domestic policy actors. However, success in mobilizing reverberations is significantly determined by the choice of targets and strategy or message.

In the case of whaling, the strategy and message used by anti-whaling advocates created a backlash against them and gave credibility to Japanese government assertions. In comparison, the anti-tropical timber campaign in Japan was successful because the strategy and messages used were appropriate for the Japanese audience. Public opinion affected the actions of some Japanese big business in the tropical timber trade and encouraged more financial support for reforestation activities from governmental, quasi-governmental, and private sources.

(10) In issues of complex interdependence, which include most types of international environmental concerns, multiple channels of contact would

Conclusion

open up and the influence of non-governmental and transnational actors would expand.

In the case of Japan, NGOs have extremely small impact on government decision making because the policy process is highly impervious to outside intervention. Big business, on the other hand, finds new opportunities and increased leverage in their relationship with government regulators. Their joint ventures with native timber companies in Southeast Asia assured them access to tropical hardwood without having to deal directly with the more controversial aspects of the tropical timber trade. In fact, native firms changed from competitors into partners. For the Japanese fishing industry, too, losing its catch quotas in American waters has turned the U.S. fishing industry from a foe to a friend. Japanese investment in the U.S. fishing industry had made the two allies in lobbying the United States government.

As to the merits of the theoretic approaches used in this study, the bureaucratic politics model is most useful in explaining policy processes that are heavily dictated by domestic bureaucratic rivalries. In the case of Japan, it is especially appropriate because the policy process is—with rare exceptions—a relatively closed one. Organizational structure and setting strongly affect the power and influence that actors yield, the potential intersections of interests and conflicts, as well as their calculations of costs and benefits in making decision choices.

However, the bureaucratic politics model alone is inadequate in enabling appreciation of the rich complexity of forces and motivations in decision making, particularly in issues of complex interdependence. In a world where intersections are plentiful and increasing between domestic politics and the international system, using the bureaucratic politics model alone would fail to account for the interactive dynamics that exist between domestic politics and the international system. Drawing on concepts in complex interdependence, regime theory and two-level games approach helps to compensate these shortcomings of the bureaucratic political model.

The emphasis on energy and resource security (in addition to military defense) in the Japanese government's Comprehensive National Security Strategy agrees with a basic tenet of complex interdependence, which assumes that there is no clear hierarchy of issues. Japanese policy responses to international environmental issues are often colored by this articulation of national interests. This and other studies have shown that the Japanese state is far from being a unitary or monolithic entity. Instead, subnational actors often use Japanese national interest in energy and resource security to justify their personal and/or organizational goals and actions. In fact, assertions of energy and resource security as a national interest often function as a consensus builder for policy actors in Japan. Finally, complex interdependence helps to explain the opening of multiple channels, albeit restricted at times, for non-state actor participation in policy processes.

Concepts from these theoretic approaches also aid to shed light on how formation of international regimes, the changes that occur within it, as well as linkages across regimes, can impact national policies and the goals and actions of sub-national policy actors, and *vice versa*. The two-level games model, in particular, is critical to investigating how inter-level dynamics and the use of various bargaining strategies, including issue linkages, issue redefinition, and reverberations, can be used by policy actors to pursue personal and organizational goals and interests.

Therefore, using a combination of theoretic approaches and concepts in investigating the roots, that is, the objectives and political processes, behind policies paints a picture of superior richness and complexity.

Appendix
List of Interviewees[*]

Mr. J.E.K. Aggrey-Orleans, Assistant Director, Economic Information and Market Intelligence, International Tropical Timber Organization, Yokohama, 19 October 1995.

Mr. Kazunori Akasaka, OIKOS Magazine, Tokyo, 11 August 1995.

Mr. Tadashi Akimoto, Staff Economist, Industry and Telecommunications Department, Global Environment Office, Japan Federation of Economic Organizations (Keidanren), Tokyo, 21 September 1995.

Mr. Shinichi Arai, Deputy Director, Control and Cooperation Division, Global Environment Department, Environment Agency, Government of Japan, Tokyo, 13 September 1995.

Mr. Eriberto C. Argete, OIC Director, Planning and Policy Studies Office, Department of Environment and Natural Resources, Government of the Republic of the Philippines, Yokohama, 13 November 1995.

Mr. Shouchuan Asuka-Zhang, Research Center for Advanced Science and Technology, University of Tokyo, Tokyo, 20 November 1995.

Dr. Monica Borobia, Program Officer, Marine Mammal Action Plan and Marine Biodiversity, Oceans and Coastal Areas Program Activity Center, United Nations Environment Program, Taiji, 24 February 1995.

Mr. Richard Forrest, Eastern Asia Representative, International Program, National Wildlife Foundation, Tokyo, 15 August 1995.

Dr. Milton M.R. Freeman, Professor, Department of Anthropology, University of Alberta, Edmonton, 22 June 1996.

Mr. Shigeaki Fujisaki, Coordinator, Research Project on Development and the Environment, Development Studies Department, Institute of Developing Economies, Tokyo, 30 November 1995.

Ms. Naoko Funahashi, Liaison, International Fund for Animal Welfare (IFAW), Tokyo, 6 July 1995.

Mr. Brad Glosserman, Editorial Department, The Japan Times, Tokyo, 5 December 1995.

Mr. Takeshi Goto, Deputy Director, International Forestry Cooperation Office, Forestry Agency, Ministry of Agriculture, Forestry and Fisheries, Government of Japan, Tokyo, Japan, 17 October 1995.

Mr. Lili Hasanuddin, Forest Campaigner, Wahana Lingkungan Hidup Indonesia (WALHI), Jakarta, 10 January 1996.

Mr. Noriyoshi Hattori, Secretary, Japan Whaling Association, Tokyo, 25 April 1995.

Mr. Randal Helten, International Affairs Friend of the Earth (Japan), Tokyo, 25 August 1995.

Mr. Hidehiro Hosaka, Assistant Director, Developing Economies Division, Economic Affairs Bureau, Ministry of Foreign Affairs, Government of Japan, Tokyo, 20 October 1995.

Mr. Lachlan A.J. Hunter, Assistant Director, Management Services, International Tropical Timber Organization, Yokohama, 19 October 1995.

Mr. Kenro Iino, Director, Fishery Division, Economic Affairs Bureau, Ministry of Foreign Affairs, Government of Japan, Tokyo, 18 July 1995.

Ms. Akiko Ishihara, Program Officer, TRAFFIC (Japan), World Wide Fund for Nature (Japan), Tokyo, 20 July 1995.

Ms. Asahi Ito, Pacific-Asia Resource Center, Tokyo, 24 July 1995.

Mr. Makoto Ito, Vice-Secretary, Japan Whaling Association, Tokyo, 25 April 1995.

Ms. Misako Iwasaki, Program Officer, Environment—Thailand, Japan International Volunteer Center (JVC), Tokyo, Japan, 29 October 1995.

Mr. Shunsuke Iwasaki, Executive Director, People's Forum 2001 Japan, Tokyo, 7 September 1995.

Dr. Charles Johnson, Senior Fellow, Resource and Energy Program, The East-West Center, Honolulu, 7 and 9 October 1997.

Appendix 269

Dr. Arne Kalland, Senior Research Associate, Center for Development and the Environment, Oslo, 27 September 1996.

Ms. Nayoko Kamei, Japan Center for a Sustainable Environment and Society (JACSES), Tokyo, 24 July 1995.

Dr. Yoshio Kaneko, Director, Global Guardian Trust, Tokyo, Japan, 31 August 1995.

Mr. Hideki Kato, Director, Research Department, Institute of Fiscal and Monetary Policy, Ministry of Finance, Government of Japan, Tokyo, 24 November 1995.

Dr. Yasuko Kawashima, Researcher, Environmental Economics Section, National Institute for Environmental Studies, Tokyo, 12 December 1995.

Dr. Tsutomu Kayama, Managing Director, Research Association for Reforestation of Tropical Forest (RETROF), Tokyo, 4 October 1995.

Mr. Kazumi Kishibe, Deputy Director, Air Pollution Control Division, Air Quality Bureau, Environment Agency, Government of Japan, Tokyo, 27 November 1995.

Mr. Hikaru Kobayashi, Director, Planning Division, Global Environment Division, Environment Agency, Government of Japan, Tokyo, 27 November 1995.

Mr. Noriyuki Kobayashi, General Manager, Green Environmental Research and Development Division, Sumitomo forestry Co., Ltd., Tokyo, 4 October 1995.

Mr. Michikazu Kojima, Researcher, Development Studies Department, Institute of Developing Economies, Tokyo, 5 September 1995.

Mr. Masayuki Komatsu, Deputy Director, Far Seas Fisheries Division, Oceanic Fisheries Department, Fisheries Agency, Ministry of Agriculture, Forestry and Fisheries, Government of Japan, Tokyo, 19 June 1995.

Mr. Masashi Kotake, Acting Director, Keidanren Nature Conservation Fund, Tokyo, 7 September and 1 December 1995.

Dr. Tsutomu Koyama, Research Association for Reforestation of Tropical Forest (RETROF), Tokyo, 4 October 1995.

Dr. Minoru Kumazaki, Professor, Institute of Agriculture and Forestry, Tsukuba University, Tsukuba, 25 October 1995.

Ms. Kaori Kuroda, Program Officer, The Asia Foundation (Japan office), Tokyo, several meetings in 1995, July 1996 and December 1997.

Mr. Yoichi Kuroda, Director, Japan Tropical Forest Action Network (JATAN), Tokyo, 16 August 1995.

Ms. Faina Lucero, Assistant to the Secretary General in International Communications, Japanese NGO Center for International Cooperation (JANIC), Tokyo, 6 October 1995.

Mr. Eishi Maezawa, Conservation Division, World Wide Fund for Nature (Japan), Tokyo, 22 June 1995.

Mr. Toichi Makita, Program Officer, International Division, The Toyota Foundation, Tokyo, 28 September and 16 November 1995.

Mr. William Mankin, Coordinator, Global Forest Policy Project, Yokohama, 14 November 1995.

Mr. Kazuo Matsushita, Director General, Department of The Japan Fund for Global Environment, Japan Environment Corporation, Tokyo, 21 July 1995.

Mr. Masahiro Mikami, Assistant Director, Policy Planning Division, Foreign Policy Bureau, Ministry of Foreign Affairs, Government of Japan, Tokyo, 21 July and 20 October 1995.

Ms. Shigeko Misaki, Counselor for International Relations, The Institute of Cetacean Research, Tokyo, 26 November 1994, 8 September 1995 and 2 August 1996.

Mr. Hideki Miyakawa, Deputy Director, International Forestry Cooperation Office, Forestry Agency, Ministry of Agriculture, Forestry and Fisheries, Government of Japan, Tokyo, 17 October 1995.

Mr. Arnaldo P. Mosteiro, Department of Science and Technology, Forest Products Research and Development Institute (Philippines), Tokyo, 8 December 1995.

Dr. Fukuzo Nagasaki, Director-General, Institute of Cetaecean Research, Taiji, 25 February 1996.

Appendix 271

Dr. Yoshifumi Nakai, Senior Research Fellow, Center for Asia-Pacific Studies, The Japan Institute of International Affairs, Tokyo, 24 August and 6 December 1995.

Mr. Yasuharu Nakajima, Senior Research Fellow, Japan Association of Corporate Executives (Keizai Doyukai), Tokyo, 6 November 1995.

Mr. Hiroshi Nakata, Forestry Officer, International Forestry Cooperation Office, Ministry of Agriculture, Forestry and Fisheries, Government of Japan, Tokyo, 17 October 1995.

Mr. Yoshihiro Natori, Deputy Director of Planning Division, Global Environment Division, Environment Agency, Government of Japan, Tokyo, 27 November 1995.

Mr. John Neuffer, Senior Research Fellow, Mitsui Marine Research Institute Co., Ltd., Tokyo, 28 November 1995.

Dr. Shunsan Nishioka, Researcher, National Institute of Environmental Studies, Tsukuba, 22 November 1995.

Mr. Makoto Noda, Senior Program Officer, Japan Center for International Exchange, Tokyo, 21 May 1995.

Dr. Hideo Obara, Professor, Humanology and Zoology, Kagawa Nutrition University, Tokyo, 24 July 1995.

Dr. Seiji Ohsumi, Executive Director, The Institute of Cetacean Research, Tokyo, 15 April 1995.

Mr. Sadahiko Okano, Senior Manager, International Affairs Department, Japan Association of Corporate Executives (Keizai Doyukai), Tokyo, 6 November 1995.

Mr. Kenji Otsuka, Researcher, Development Studies Department, Institute of Developing Economies, Tokyo, 12 October 1995; in Beijing, 31 October 1997.

Dr. Luis Pastene, Chief, Ecology Section, Institute of Cetacean Research, Tokyo, 5 April 1995 and 2 August 1996.

Dr. Douglas Craig Pattie, Projects Manager, Forest Industry, International Tropical Timber Organization, Yokohama, 19 October 1995.

Mr. Tadashi Saito, Assistant Director of Asian Affairs Department and Head of Asia-Pacific Economic Cooperation (APEC) Affairs, Japan Federation of Economic Organizations (Keidanren), Tokyo, 1 November 1995.

Mr. Tatsuo Saito, Special Advisor to the Minister on International Affairs, Ministry of Agriculture, Forestry and Fisheries, Government of Japan, Tokyo, 31 August 1995.

Mr. Chikaya Sakai, Assistant to Manager, Advanced Research Lab, Research Division, Komatsu Ltd., Tokyo, 12 September 1995.

Ms. Tomoko Sakuma, Peoples' Forum 2001, Japan, Tokyo, 7 September 1995.

Ms. Junko Sakurai, Campaigner, Greenpeace (Japan), Tokyo, 24 May 1995.

Ms. Miyako Sakurai, Communication Officer, World Wild Fund for Nature (Japan), Tokyo, 22 June 1995.

Mr. Masran Md. Salleh, Director of Forest Management, Forestry Department of Peninsular Malaysia, Government of Malaysia, Yokohama, 11 November 1995.

Mr. Hiroya Sano, President, Japan, Japan Fisheries Association, Tokyo, 25 July 1995.

Ms. Akiko Sato, Secretary, The Riches of the Sea, Women's Forum Sakana, Tokyo, 5 July 1995.

Mr. Katsuo Seiki, Executive Director, Global Industrial and Social Progress Research Institute (GISPRI), Tokyo, 18 May 1995.

Mr. Sulaiman N. Sembiring, Indonesia Center for Environmental Law, Jakarta, 10 January 1996.

Mr. Hirohisa Shigemune, Vice-Secretary, Japan Whaling Association, Tokyo, 25 April 1995.

Mr. Kazuo Shima, Vice-President, Japan Fisheries Association, Tokyo, 30 June 1995.

Appendix 273

Mr. Susumu Shimoyama, Editor, Bungei Shinju, Ltd., Tokyo, 21 November 1995.

Dr. R.J. Smith, Senior Environmental Scholar, Competitive Enterprise Institute, Taiji, 25 February 1995.

Mr. Tadanori Suzuki, Deputy Director of Forestry Cooperation Division, Forestry and Fisheries Development Cooperation Department, Japan International Cooperation Agency (JICA), Government of Japan, Tokyo, 11 September 1995.

Mr. Koshiro Takada, Program Officer, The Sasakawa Peace Foundation, Tokyo, 19 September 1995.

Mr. Masaatsu Takehara, Program Officer, Keidanren Nature Conservation Fund, Tokyo, 7 November and 1 December 1995.

Dr. Dexiang Tian, Chief, Office of Environmental Protection, Peking University, Beijing, 29 October 1997.

Dr. John Tofflemire, International Service Department, Mitsubishi Research Institute, Inc., Tokyo, 7 December 1995.

Mr. Tsugio Toriu, Assistant to the Chairman, World Wide Fund for Nature (Japan), Tokyo, 22 June 1995.

Mr. S. Indro Tjahjono, Coordinator, SKEPHI (The NGO Network for Forest Conservation in Indonesia), Jakarta, 10 January 1996.

Dr. Yutaka Tsujinaka, Associate Professor, Institute of Social Sciences, Tsukuba University, Tsukuba, 3 November 1995.

Ms. Akiko Tsuru, Director, Japan-Indonesia NGO Network (JANNI), Tokyo, 5 December 1995.

Dr. Juha I. Uitto, Academic Officer, Environment and Sustainable Development, The United Nations University, Tokyo, 13 December 1995.

Ms. Miwako Uramoto, Staff, Sarawak Campaign Committee and the Mekong Watch, Tokyo, 11 November 1995.

Mr. Reynaldo B. Ureta, Executive Director, Philippine Development Assistance Program (Philippines), Tokyo, 8 December 1995.

Mr. Ichiro Wada, Deputy Researcher, Committee on Agriculture, Forestry and Marine Resources, Lower House, Diet of Japan, 16 June 1995.

Dr. Akihiro Watabe, Associate Professor, Department of Economics, Kanagawa University, Tokyo, 18 August 1995.

Dr. Kenneth Wilkening, Visiting Researcher, National Institute for Environmental Studies, Tsukuba, Japan, December 1995.

Mr. Hiroshi Yagita, Managing Director, Global Guardian Trust, Tokyo, 30 August 1995.

Dr. Taizo Yakushiji, Professor, Department of Political Science, Keio University, Tokyo, 3 May 1995.

Mr. Kunihiro Yamauchi, Deputy Director, Environment, Women in Development and other Global Issues Division, Planning Department, Japan International Cooperation Agency, Government of Japan, Tokyo, 16 December 1997.

Dr. Fumio Yanagizawa, Taiji Whale Museum and Marinarium, Taiji, 26 February 1995.

Mr. Shohei Yonemoto, Head, Program on Life Science and Society, Mitsubishi Kasei Institute of Life Sciences, Tokyo, 21 November 1995.

Mr. Kunio Yonezawa, President of Global Guardian Trust and Adviser to the Board of Directors of Nippon Suisan Co., Ltd., Tokyo, 7 August 1995.

Mr. Seiichi Yoshida, Assistant Director-General for Oceanic Fisheries, Fisheries Agency, Ministry of Agriculture, Forestry and Fisheries, Government of Japan, Taiji, 25 February 1995.

Mr. Zhongtian Zhang, Program Officer, Division of International Programs, Ministry of Forestry, Government of the People's Republic of China, Yokohama, 14 November 1995.

*Titles, offices and names of institutions were current at the time of the interview. Changes may have since occurred.

Bibliography

English Sources

11 *Essays on Whales and Man*, 2nd ed. Reine: High North Alliance, September 1994.

"A Matter of Priorities." *Far Eastern Economic Review* (16 November 1995): 70-71.

"A Misguided Policy on Whaling." *The Chicago Tribune*, 24 May 1993.

"A WWF Guide to Forest Certification." Surrey, England: World Wide Fund for Nature (United Kingdom), 1995.

Abrams, Jeremy. "Logging: The Unkindest Cut of All." *Ecotimes* (November 1992): 1, 3, 6 and 7.

Abramovitz, Jane N. "Taking a Stand: Cultivating a New Relationship with the World's Forests." *World Watch Papers* 140 (April 1998).

Adler, Emanuel and Peter H. Haas. "Conclusion: Epistemic Communities, World Order and the Creation of a Reflective Research Program." *International Organization* 46:1 (Winter 1992): 367-390.

Aita, Kaoruko. "Global Envrionmental Perspective Urged." *The Japan Times*, 7 January 1995, p.1.

Akaha, Tsuneo and Frank Langdon, eds. *Japan in the Posthegemonic World*. Boulder: Lynne Rienner Publishers, 1993.

Akao, Nobutoshi, ed. *Japan's Economic Security: Resources as a Factor of Foreign Policy*. Hampshire: Gower, 1983.

_____. "A double standard on sustainable development." *Global Guardian Trust Newsletter* 1 (February 1994): 2-3.

Akimichi, T. *et al. Small-type Coastal Whaling in Japan*. Edmonton, Canada: Boreal Institute of North Studies, 1988.

Albin, Tom and Steve Paulson. "Environmental and Economic Interests in Canada and the United States." In *Acid Rain and Friendly Neighbors: The Policy Dispute between Canada and the United States*, ed. Jurgen Schmandt *et al.*, 107-136. Durham: Duke University Press, 1988.

Allen, Scott. "Acid Rain." *The Boston Globe*, 23 December 1996.

Allinson, Gary D. and Yasunori Sone, eds. *Political Dynamics in Contemporary Japan*. Ithaca and London: Cornell University Press, 1993.

Allison, Graham T. *Essence of Decision: Explaining the Cuban Missle Crisis*. Boston: Little, Brown and Company, 1971.

Almond, Gabriel A. "The Elites and Foreign Policy." In *International Politics and Foreign Policy: A Reader in Research and Theory*, ed. James N. Rosenau, 268-272. New York: The Free Press of Glencoe, 1964.

Altman, Kristin Kyoko. "Television and Political Turmoil: Japan's Summer of 1993." In *Media and Politics in Japan*, ed. Susan J. Pharr and Ellis S. Krauss, 165-186. Honolulu: University of Hawaii Press, 1990.

"Amakudari Position Widespread." *Yomiuri Daily*, 4 November 1994.

Amemiya, Takako. "The Nonprofit Public Corporation in Japan." *Sasakawa Peace Foundation Newsletter* 2 (March 1994): 1-3.

_____. "The Nonprofit Public Corporation in Japan." *Sasakawa Peace Foundation Newsletter* 3 (July 1994): 4-5.

_____. "The Nonprofit Public Corporation in Japan, Part III." *Sasakawa Peace Foundation Newsletter* 4 (October 1994): 2-3.

_____. "Nonprofit Public-Interest Corporations in Japan, Part IV." *Sasakawa Peace Foundation Newsletter* 5 (February 1995): 3-5.

Andersen, Steinar. "Science and Politics in the International Management of Whales." *Marine Policy* (April 1989): 99-117.

_____. "The Effectivenss of the International Whaling Commission." *Artic* 46 (1993): 108-15.

Angel, Robert C. "Prime Ministerial Leadership in Japan: Recent Changes in Personal Style and Administrative Organization." *Pacific Affairs* 61:4 (Winter 1988/89): 533-602.

ApSimon, Helen and Rachel Warren. "Transboundary Air Pollution in Europe." *Energy Policy* (July 1996): 631-40.

Arden-Clarke, Charles. "Conservation and Sustainable Management of Tropical Forests: The Role of ITTO and GATT." Gland: World Wide Fund for Nature International, November 1990.

_____. "Environmental Taxes and Charges and Border Tax Adjustment - GATT Rules and Energy Taxes: A Critique for the World Wide Fund for Nature." Gland: World Wide Fund for Nature International, September 1994.

Aron, William. "The Commons Revisited: Thoughts on Marine Mammal Management." *Coastal Management* 16 (1988): 99-110.

Asai, Hideki. "Pollution Problems in China Already Raining Down on Japan." *Tokyo Business Today* (December 1993): 44-47.

"ASEAN to combat West's anti-tropical wood policy." *The Indonesia Times*, 14 October, 1992.

Bibliography

Asia Pacific Economic Cooperation, Regional Energy Cooperation Working Group, Clean Fossil Energy Experts Group. "Study on Atmospheric Emissions Regulations in APEC Economies and their Compliance at Coal-Fired Plants." January 1997.

"Asia-Pacific Forests." Tokyo: Japan Tropical Forest Action Network, November 1993.

"Asian economies exact environment toll." *The Japan Times*, 7 December 1993.

Asquith, Pamela J. and Arne Kalland, eds. *Japanese Images of Nature: Cultural Perspectives*. Surrey: Curzon, 1997.

Aufderheide, Pat and Bruce Rich. "Environmental Reform and the Multilateral Banks." *World Policy Journal* (Spring 1988): 301-321.

Axelrod, Robert. *The Evolution of Cooperation*. New York: Basic Books, 1984.

Bachler, Gunther, "The Anthropogenic Transformation of the Environment: A Source of War? Historical Background, Typology and Conclusions." In "Environmental Crisis: Regional Conflicts and Ways of Cooperation," ed. Kurt R. Spillmann and Gunther Bachler, 10-27. Occasional Paper 14. Zurich: Center for Security Studies and Conflict Research, Swiss Federal Institute of Technology, September 1995.

"Background papers of the Fourth International Whaling Symposium on Wildlife and Local Culture." Tokyo: Institute of Cetacean Research, 1994.

Baharuddin, Hj. Ghazali and Markku Simula. "Report of the Working Party on Certification of All timber and Timber Products." Yokohama: International Tropical Timber Organization, May 1994.

Baldwin, David A. and Helen V. Milner. "Economics and National Security." In *Power and Security: The United States and Japan in Focus*, ed. Henry Bienen, 29-50. Boulder: Westview Press, 1992.

Banuri, Tariq and Frederique Apffel Marglin. *Who will save the Forests? Knowledge, Power and Environmental Destruction*. London and New Jersey: Zed Books, 1993.

Barrett, Brendan F.D. and Riki Therival. *Environmental Policy and Impact Assessment in Japan*. London and New York: Routledge, 1991.

Barthelmess, Klaus. "Whaling: Con & Pro." Germany: Klauss Barthelmess, 1994.

Basberg, Bjorn L. *et al.*, eds. *Whaling and History: Perspectives on the Evolution of the Industry*. Sandefjord: Sandefjordmuseene, 1993.

Bedau, Hugo Adam. "Ethical Aspects of Environmental Decision Making." In *Environmental Decision-Making: A Multidisciplinary Perspective*, ed. Richard H. Chechile and Susan Carlisle, 176-194. New York: Van Nostrand Reinhold, 1991.

Berg, Scott and Rob Olszewski. "Certification and Labeling: A Forest Industry Perspective." *Journal of Forestry* 93:4 (April 1995): 30-32.

Berkes, Fikret, ed. *Common Property Resources: Ecology and Community-based Sustainable Development*. London: Belhaven Press, 1989.

Bernauer, Thomas. "The Effect of International Environmental Institutions: How we might learn more." *International Organization* 49:2 (Spring 1995): 351-77.

Bienen, Henry, ed. *Power, Economics and Security: The United States and Japan in Focus*. Boulder: Westview Press, 1992.

Blichfeldt, Georg. "Bigger than whales." In *11 Essays on Whales and Man*, 3-4. Reine: High North Alliance, 1994.

Boge, Voller. "Proposal for an Analytical Framework to grasp 'Environmental Conflict.'" Occasional paper of the Environment and Conflicts Project, No.1, July 1992.

Bonner, Raymond. *At the Hand of Man: Peril and Hope for Africa's Wildlife*. New York: Alfred A. Knopf, 1993.

Bloomfield, Lincoln P. "The Foreign Policy Process: Making Theory Relevant." London and Beverly Hills: Sage Professional Papers, International Studies Series, No.02-028, 1974.

Bourke, I.J. "The Uruguay Round Results: An Overview." *ITTO Tropical Forest Update* 6:2 (1996): 12-15.

Boyle, Robert H. *Acid Rain*. New York: Nick Lyons Books, 1983.

Boynton, Stephen S. "'Whaling Policy' of the United States: Yesterday, Today and Tomorrow." *Isana* (November 1994): 20-25.

Bradsher, K. "Japan won't hunt whales, Miyazawa says." *The New York Times*, 3 July 1992.

Braile, Robert. "New state survey shows lakes, ponds still hit by acid rain." *The Boston Globe*, 2 June 1996.

Broadbent, Jeffrey. *Environmental Politics in Japan: Networks of Power and Protest*. Cambridge: Cambridge University Press, 1998.

Bromley, Daniel W. *et al.*, eds. *Making the Commons Work: Theory, Practice and Policy*. San Francisco: Institute for Contemporary Studies, 1992.

Brown, Lester. *Redefining National Security*. Washington, D.C.: Worldwatch Paper 4 (October 1997).

Brown, Michael and John May. *The Greenpeace Story*. Scarborough: Prentice-Hall, Inc., 1989.

Bruun, Ole and Arne Kalland, eds. *Asian Perception of Nature: A Critical Approach*. Surrey: Curzon, 1995.

Bryden, M.M. "Marine Mammals and Conservation in the Antarctic Marine System." *Australian Zoologist* 29 (August 1993): 63-76.

Bibliography

Bryden, M.M. and P. Corkeron, "Intelligence." In *Whales, Dolphins and Porpoises*, ed. R. Harrison and M.M. Bryden, 160-165. New York and Oxford: Facts on File, 1982.

Bubenick, David V., ed. *Acid Rain Information Book*, 2nd ed. New Jersey: Noyes Publications, 1984.

Bukro, Casey. "Clean Air Act Ahead of Schedule." *The Chicago Tribune*, 27 March 1996.

Burch, Ernest S., Jr. and Linda J. Ellanna, eds. *Key Issues in Hunter-Gatherer Research*. Oxford and Providence: Berg, 1994.

"Bureaucrats dragging their feet toward administrative reform." *Daily Yomiuri*, 15 September 1994.

"Bureaucrats find more executive jobs." *The Japan Times*, 30 March 1995.

Burke, William T. "Editorial Comment: Memorandum of Opinion on the Legality of the Designation of the Southern Ocean Sanctuary by the IWC." *Ocean Development and International Law* 27 (1996): 315-326.

Burton, Sandra. "Taming the River Wild." *Time* (19 December 1994): 62-64.

Butterworth, D.S. "Commentary: Science and Sentimentality." *Nature* 357 (18 June 1992): 532-534.

Cabarle, Bruce *et al.* "Certification Accreditation: The Need for Credible Claims." *Journal of Forestry* 93:4 (April 1995): 12-17.

"Cabinet Green Panel to be formed." *The Japan Times*, 22 December 1993.

Calder, Kent. "Japanese Foreign Economic Policy Formation: Explaining the Reactive State." *World Politics* 40 (July 1988): 517-41.

Caldwell, Lynton K. *Between Two Worlds: Science, the Environmental Movement and Policy Choice*. Cambridge: Cambridge University Press, 1991.

_____. *Biocracy: Public Policy and the Life Sciences*. Boulder and London: Westview Press, 1987.

_____. *International Environmental Policy: Emergency and Dimensions*, 2nd ed. Durham and London: Duke University Press, 1990.

_____. "Environment Policy as a Catalyst of Institutional Change." *In The Politics of Environmental Policy*, ed. Lester W. Milbrath and Frederick R. Inscho, 95-114. Beverly Hills and London: Sage, Contemporary Social Science Issues 18, 1975.

Callicott, J. Baird. *Earth's Insights: A Survey of Ecological Ethics from the Mediterranean Basin to the Australian Outback*. Berkeley: University of California Press, 1994.

Callister, Debra. "Illegal Tropical Timber Trade: Asia-Pacific." A Traffic Network Report, 1992.

Cameron, James *et al.* "Sustainable Development and Integrated Dispute Settlement in GATT 1994." Gland: World Wide Fund for Nature International, June 1994.

Cameron, Owen. "Japan and South-East Asia's Environment." In *Environmental Change in South-East Asia: People, Politics and Sustainable Development*, ed. Michael J.G. Parnwell and Raymond L. Bryant, 67-93. London and New York: Routledge, 1996.

Campbell, John C. *Contemporary Japanese Budget Politics*. Berkeley: University of California Press, 1977.

_____. "Democracy and Bureaucracy in Japan." In *Democracy in Japan*, ed. Takeshi Ishida and Ellis S. Krauss, 113-137. Pittsburgh: University of Pittsburgh, 1989.

_____. "Media and Policy Change in Japan." In *Media and Politics in Japan*, ed. Susan J. Pharr and Ellis S. Krauss, 187-212. Honolulu: University of Hawaii Press, 1996.

_____. "Policy Conflict and its Resolution within the Governmental System." In *Conflict in Japan*, ed. Ellis S. Krauss, Thomas P. Rohlen and Patricia G. Steinhoff, 294-334. Honolulu: University of Hawaii Press, 1984.

"Canada 'still has a long way to go' in effective control of acid rain," *Nature* 390 (6 November 1997): 6.

Canter, L.W. *Acid Rain and Dry Deposition*. Michigan: Lewis Publishers, Inc., 1986.

Carroll, John E. "Acid Rain—Acid Diplomacy." In *The Acid Rain Debate: Scientific, Economic, and Political Dimensions*, ed. Ernest J. Yanarella and Randal H. Ihara, 261-273. Boulder and London: Westview Press, 1985.

Carson, Rachel. *Silent Spring*. Boston: Houghton Mifflin, 1962.

Carter, L.J. "Uncontrolled SO_2 Emissions Bring Acid Rain." *Science* 204:4398 (15 June 1979): 1179-1182.

Cassells, David S. "Considerations for Effective International Cooperation in Tropical Forest Conservation and Management." In *Management of Tropical Forests: Towards an Integrated Perspective*, ed. Oyvind Sandbukt, 357-376. Oslo: Center for Development and the Environment, University of Oslo, 1995.

Chadwick, M.J. and H. Hutton, eds. *Acid Depositions in Europe: Environmental effects, control strategies and policy options*. Stockholm: Stockholm Environment Institute, 1991.

Chan, Simba *et al.* "Obervations on the Whale Meat Trade in East Asia." TRAFFIC East Asia, May 1995.

Bibliography

Chan, Steve. "Humanitarianism, Mercantilism or Comprehensive Security? Disbursement Patterns of Japanese Foreign Aid." *Asian Affairs* (Spring 1992): 3-17.

Chapman, J.W.M., R. Drifte and I.T.M. Gow. *Japan's Quest for Comprehensive Security: Defense-Diplomacy-Dependence.* London: Frances Pinter, 1983.

Charnovitz, Steven. "Environmental trade sanctions and the GATT." In *11 Additional Essays on Whales and Man,* 29-37. Reine: High North Alliance, 1995.

Chechile, Richard H. and Susan Carlisle, eds. *Environmental Decision-Making: A Multidisciplinary Perspective.* New York: Van Nostrand Reinhold, 1991.

Chechile, Richard H. "Introduction to Environmental Decision Making." In *Environmental Decision-Making: A Multidisciplinary Perspective,* ed. Richard H. Chechile and Susan Carlisle, 1-13. New York: Van Nostrand Reinhold, 1991.

Chen, Yingrong. "Renewables in China: Case Study." *Energy Policy* 19:9 (November 1991): 892-896.

Cheng, Peter P. "Japanese Interest Group: An Institutional Framework." *Asian Survey* 30:3 (March 1990): 251-265.

"China opens environmental center." *The Japan Times,* 6 May 1996.

Cohen, Margot. "Cautious Cooperation." *Far Eastern Economic Review* (16 November 1995): 67.

Cohen, Raymond. *Negotiating Across Cultures: Communication Obstacles in International Diplomacy.* Washington, D.C.: U.S. Institute for Peace, 1991.

Colchester, Marcus. "The International Tropical Timber Organization: Kill or Cure for the Rainforests?" *The Ecologist* 20:5 (September/October 1990): 166-173.

Colchester, Marcus and Larry Lohmann. *The Tropical Forestry Action Plan: What Progress?* Penang and England: World Rainforest Movement and The Ecologist, 1990.

Colchester, Marcus and Larry Lohmann, eds. *The Struggle for Land and the Fate of the Forests.* London and Penang: Zed Books, The Ecologist and World Rainforest Movement, 1993.

"Collapse of Trade Barriers will be bad for Environment." *The Indonesian Times,* 15 June 1994.

Cowhey, Peter F. "Domestic Institutions and the Credibility of International Commitments: Japan and the United States." *International Organization* 47:2 (Spring 1993): 299-326.

Cox, Thomas R. "The North American-Japanese Timber Trade: A Survey of its Social, Economic and Environmental Impact." In *World Deforestation in the Twientieth Century*, ed. John F. Richards and Richard P. Tucker, 164-186. Durham and London: Duke University Press, 1988.

"Criteria for the Measurement of Sustainable Tropical Forest Management." *ITTO Policy Development Series* 3 (1992).

Cumings, Bruce. "Japan's Position in the World System." In *Postwar Japan as History*, ed. Andrew Gordon, 34-63. Berkeley, Los Angeles and Oxford: University of California Press, 1993.

Curtis, Gerald L., ed. *Japan's Foreign Policy after the Cold War: Coping with Change*. New York: M.E. Sharpe, 1993.

Dauvergne, Peter. *Shadows in the Forest: Japan and the Politics of Timber in Southeast Asia*. Cambridge and London: Massachusetts Institute of Technology Press, 1997.

Davis, David H. *How the Bureaucracy Makes Foreign Policy: An Exchange Analysis*. Massachusetts: D.C. Heath, 1972.

Davis, Natasha. "Paperpower: The Japanese Paper Industry and the Environment in Australia and Japan." *Japanese Studies Bulletin* 15:1 (1995): 1-25.

Day, David. *The Whale War*. Vancouver and Toronto: Douglas and McIntyre, 1987.

Destler, I.M. *et al. The Textile Wrangle: Conflict in Japanese-American Relations, 1969-1971*. Ithaca: Cornell University Press, 1979.

Deudney, Daniel. "The Case Against Linking Environmental Degradation and National Security." *Millenium: Journal of International Studies* 19:3 (1990): 461-476.

Dibner, Mark D. and R. Steven White. *Biotechnology Japan*. New York: McGraw-Hill Publishing Co., 1989.

Donnelly, Michael W. "Conflict over Government Authority and Markets: Japan's Rice Economy." In *Conflict in Japan*, ed. Ellis S. Krauss, Thomas P. Rohlen and Patricia Steinhoff, 355-374. Honolulu: University of Hawaii Press, 1984.

Dorian, J.P. *Minerals, Mining and Economic Development in China*. Oxford: Clarendon Press, 1994.

Dougherty, James E. and Robert L. Pfaltzgraff, Jr. *Contending Theories of International Relations: A Comprehensive Survey*, 3rd ed. New York: Harper and Row, 1990.

Dove, Michael R. "A Revisionist View of Tropical Deforestation and Development." *East-West Center Reprints, Environment Series* 19 (1994).

_____. "Foresters' Beliefs About Farmers: A Priority for Social Science Research in Social Forestry." *East-West Center Reprints: Environment Series* 12 (1992).

Bibliography

_____. "North-South Differences, Global Warming, and the Global System." *Chemosphere* 29:5 (1994): 1063-1077.

Dudley, Nigel. *Forest Targets*. Gland: World Wide Fund for Nature International, 1995.

_____. *Targets for Forest Conservation: An Assessment of a Range of Targets and Recommendations set by International Agencies contrasted with Targets set by WWF*. Gland: World Wide Fund for Nature International, April 1995.

Eccleston, Bernard. "Does North-South Collaboration Enhance NGO Influence on Deforestation Policies in Malaysia and Indonesia?" In *NGOs and Environmental Policies: Asia and Africa*, ed. David Potter, 66-89. London and Portland: Frank Cass, 1996.

Edmonds, Richard Louis. *Patterns of China's Lost Harmony: A Survey of the Country's Environmental Degradation and Protection*. London and New York: Routledge, 1994.

Eguchi, Eiichi. "Memory of the Blue Whale." *Isana* (March 1994): 25.

Ehrlich, P. and A. Ehrlich. *The Population Bomb*. New York: Ballantine, 1968.

Elliott, Chris. "Timber Certification and the Forest Stewardship Council." In *Management of Tropical Forests: Towards an Integrated Perspective*, ed. Oyvind Sandbukt, 319-340. Oslo: Center for Development and the Environment, University of Oslo, 1995.

Encarnation, Dennis and Mark Mason. "Neither MITI nor America: the Political Economy of Capital Liberalization in Japan." *International Organization* 44:1 (Winter 1990): 25-54.

"Encouraging Volunteerism." *Japan Report* 36:10 (November 1990): 6.

"Environment: Air Pollution." *1998 World Development Indicators*. Washington, D.C.: The World Bank, 1998, p.162.

"Environment: Forests." *1998 World Development Indicators*. Washington, D.C.: The World Bank, 1998, p.120.

Environment Agency, Government of Japan. "Basic Environment Plan Established." *Japan Environment Summary* 22:5 (10 January 1995): 1-3.

_____. *Quality of the Environment in Japan 1993*. n.d.

"Environment Agency Proposes Law, Getting Tough in Protecting Wildlife, Recommends Taking Global Environmental Lead." *Japan Report* 38:2 (April 1992): 1-2.

"Environmental Business, Filthy Rich." *The Economist* (21 November 1992): 80.

Evans, Peter B., Harold K. Jacobson and Robert D. Putnam, eds. *Double-Edged Diplomacy: International Bargaining and Domestic Politics*. Berkeley: University of California Press, 1993.

Falk, Richard A. "Introduction: Preserving Whales in a World of Sovereign States." *Denver Journal of International Law and Policy* 17:2 (1989): 249-253.

Farley, Maggie. "Japan's Press and the Politics of Scandal." In *Media and Politics in Japan*, ed. Susan J. Pharr and Ellis S. Krauss, 133-164. Honolulu: University of Hawaii Press, 1996.

Farrell, R. Barry, ed. *Approaches to Comparative and International Politics.* Evanston: Northwestern University, 1966.

Farrington, John *et al.*, eds. *Non-governmental Organizations and the State in Asia.* London and New York: Routledge, 1993.

Ferguson, Yale H. and Richard W. Mansbach. *The Elusive Quest: Theory and International Politics.* Columbia: University of South Carolina Press, 1988.

Firor, John. *The Changing Atmosphere: A Global Challenge.* London and New Haven: Yale   University Press, 1990.

Fisher, Larry. "Global Solutions, Local Realities: the Tropical Forestry Action Plan." In *Management of Tropical Forests: Towards an Integrated Perspective*, ed. Oyvind Sandbukt, 307-318. Oslo: Center for Development and the Environment, University of Oslo, 1995.

Fisheries Agency of Japan. "Summary of the Results of the 44th IWC." *Isana* (November 1992): 3-5.

Foell, Wes *et al.*, eds. "RAINS-ASIA: An Assessment Model for Air Pollution in Asia." *Report on the World Bank-sponsored project Acid Rain and Emissions in Asia*, December 1995.

"Foreign investment in China's power industry." *East-West Center Program on Resources, Energy and Minerals Energy Advisory* 120, 14 February 1994.

"Forest Certification: An SAF Study Group Report." *Journal of Forestry* 93:4 (April 1995): 6-11.

Forestry Agency of Japan, Ministry of Agriculture, Forestry and Fisheries, Government of Japan. "Forestry White Paper, Summary," 1994.

_____. "Forests and Forestry in Japan," 1993.

Forrest, Richard A. "Japanese Aid and the Environment." *The Ecologist* 21:1 (January/February 1991): 24-32.

Forrest, Richard A. and Yuta Harago. "Japan's Official Development Assistance (ODA) and tropical forests." Gland: World Wide Fund for Nature International, November 1990.

Fransman, Martin *et al.*, eds. *The Biotechnology Revolution?* Oxford and Cambridge: Basil Blackwell, 1995.

Freeman, Clemon Jr. "The U.S. Politics of Acid Rain." In *The Acid Rain Debate: Scientific, Economic, and Political Dimensions*, ed. Ernest J. Yanarella and Randal H. Ihara, 277-314. Boulder and London: Westview Press, 1985.

Freeman, Milton M.R. "A Commentary on Political Issues with Regard to Contemporary Whaling. *North Atlantic Studies* 2:1-2 (1990): 106-116.

———. "Economy, Equity and Ethics: Current Perspectives on Wildlife Management in the North." In *Human Ecology: Issues in the North*, ed. Jill Oakes, 3-12. Edmonton, Alberta: Canadian Circumpolar Institute and University of Alberta, 1995.

———. "Japanese Community-based Whaling, International Protest, and the New Environmentalism." In *Japan at the Crossroads: Hot Issues for the 21st Century*, ed. David Myers and Kotaku Ishido, 13-31. Tokyo: Seibundo Publishing Co., 1998.

———. "The International Whaling Commission, Small-type Whaling, and Coming to terms with Subsistence." *Human Organization* 52 (1993): 243-51.

———. "Why Whale? Do Ecology and Common Sense Provide any Answers?" In *Whales and Ethics*, ed. Orn D. Jonsson, 39-56. Iceland: Fisheries Research Institute, University of Iceland, University Press, 1992.

Freeman, Milton M.R. and Urs P. Kreuter, eds. *Elephants and Whales: Resources for Whom?* Switzerland: Gordon and Breach Science Publishers, 1994.

Friedheim, Robert L. et al., eds. *Japan and the New Ocean Regime*. Boulder and London: Westview Press, 1984.

Friedmann, John. *Empowerment: The Politics of Alternative Development*. Cambridge: Blackwell Publishers, 1992.

Friends of the Earth, Japan. "Paper Industry Report." *Japan Environment Monitor* (April 1992): 13.

Friman, Richard H. "Side-payments versus Security Cards: Domestic Bargaining Tactics in Inter-national Economic Negotiations." *International Organization* 47:3 (Summer 1993): 387-408.

Fujiaki, Shigeaki. "Environmental Issues in Developing Countries and the Role of ODA." *Japan Review of International Affairs* 7:1 (Winter 1993): 68-83.

———. "The Global Environment and North-South Relations: Considering the Future of the Earth." In *Environmental Awareness in Developing Countries: The Cases of China and Thailand*, ed. Sigeki Nishihira et al., 1-28. Tokyo: Institute of Developing Economies, 1997.

Fukai, Shigeko and Haruhiro Fukui. "Elite Recruitment and Political Leadership." *Political Science* 25 (March 1992): 25-36.

Fukui, Haruhiro. "How Japan Handled UNCLOS Issues: Does Japan have an Ocean Policy?" In *Japan and the New Ocean Regime*, ed. Robert L. Friedheim et al., 21-54. Boulder and London: Westview Press, 1984.

_____. "Studies in Policymaking: A Review of the Literature." In *Policymaking in Japan*, ed. T.J. Pempel, 22-59. Ithaca and London: Cornell University Press, 1977.

_____. "Too Many Captains in Japan's Internationalization: Travails at the Foreign Ministry." *The Journal of Japanese Studies* 13 (Summer 1987): 359-382.

Gilleland, Diane Suitt and James H. Swisher, eds. *Acid Rain Control: The Costs of Compliance*. Carbondale and Edwardsville: Southern Illinois University Press, 1985.

_____. *Acid Rain Control II: The Promise of New Technology*. Carbondale and Edwardsville: Southern Illinois University Press, 1986.

Gillespie, Alexander. "The Ethical Question in the Whaling Debate." *The Georgetown International Environmental Law Review* 9 (1997): 355-387.

Gilmour, Donald A. "Conservation and Development: Seeking the Linkages." In *Management of Tropical Forests: Towards an Integrated Perspective*, ed. Oyvind Sandbukt, 255-268. Oslo: Center for Development and the Environment, University of Oslo, 1995.

Gold, Peter S., ed. *Acid Rain: A Transjurisditional Problem in Search of Solution*. New York: Canadian-American Center, State University of New York at Buffalo, 1982.

Goldstein, Carl. "The Nuclear Option." *Far Eastern Economic Review*, 11 June 1992): 50-51.

_____. "Southern Acumen." *Far Eastern Economic Review* (11 June 1992): 47-49.

Gordon, Andrew, ed. *Postwar Japan as History*. Berkeley, Los Angeles and Oxford: University of California Press, 1993.

Gourevitch, Peter. "The Second Image Revisited: The International Sources of Domestic Politics." *International Organization* 32 (Autumn 1978): 881-911.

Gowa, Joanne. "Public Goods and Political Institutions: Trade and Monetary Policy Processes in the United States." *International Organization* 42:1 (Winter 1988): 14-32.

Grainger, Alan. *Controlling Tropical Deforestation*, London: Earthscan, 1993.

_____. "Changes in Land Use and Forest Management in Southeast Asia: An Evolutionary Perspective." In *Management of Tropical Forests: Towards an Integrated Perspective*, ed. Oyvind Sandbukt, 3-18. Oslo: Center for Development and the Environment, University of Oslo, 1995.

"Greenland's Whalers want to export whale meat." *High North Alliance* 10 (15 May 1995): 8.

Gresser, Julian, Koichiro Fujikura and Akio Morishima. *Environmental Law in Japan*. Cambridge: Masschusetts Institute of Technology Press, 1981.

Bibliography

Grieco, Joseph. *Cooperation Among Nations*. Ithaca: Cornell University Press, 1990.

Gross, Neil. "Charging Japan with Crimes against the Earth." *Business Week* (9 October 1989): 108 and 112.

Grubb, M. *et al. The Earth Summit Agreements: A Guide and Assessment*. London: Royal Institute of International Affairs, 1993.

Gunderson, Lance H., C.S. Holling and Stephen S. Light, eds. *Barriers and Bridges to the Renewal of Ecosystems and Institutions*. New York: Columbia University Press, 1995.

Haas, Peter. *Saving the Mediterranean*. New York: Columbia University Press, 1990.

_____. "Do Regimes Matter? Epistemic Communities and Mediterranean Pollution Control." *International Organization* 43:3 (Summer 1989): 378-403.

Haggard, Stephan and Beth A. Simmons. "Theories of International Relations." *International Organization* 41:3 (Summer 1987): 491-517.

Haley, John O. "Governance by Negotiation: A Reappraisal of Bureaucratic Power in Japan." *The Journal of Japanese Studies* 13 (Summer 1987): 343-58.

Hall, Ivan. *Cartels of the Mind: Japan's Intellectual Closed Shop*. New York and London: W.W. Norton, 1998.

Handa, Ryoichi. "Timber Economy and Forest Policy after the [sic] World War II." In *Forest policy in Japan*, ed. Ryoichi Handa, 22-35. Tokyo: Nippon Ringyo Chosakai, 1988.

Handa, Ryoichi, ed. *Forest Policy in Japan*. Tokyo: Nippon Ringyo Chosakai, 1988.

Hara, H. "Acid Deposition Chemistry in Asia." *Bulletin of the Institute for Public Health* 42 (1993): 426-437.

Hardin, Garret. "The Tragedy of the Commons." *Science* 162 (December 1968):1243-8.

Harrison, R. and M.M. Bryden, eds. *Whales, Dolphins and Porpoises*. New York and Oxford: Facts on File, 1982.

Hashimoto, Michio. "Some Thoughts on Japan's Role in Tackling Environmental Problems in Developing Countries." *Technology and Development*, No.3 (January 1990): 5-15.

Hayao, Kenji. *The Japanese Prime Minister and Public Policy*. Pittsburgh and london: University of Pittsburgh Press, 1993.

"Haze from forest fires add to Malaysian asthma cases." *The Japan Times*, 19 September 1993.

Bibliography

He, Bochuan. *China on the Edge: The Crisis of Ecology and Development.* San Francisco: China Books, 1991.

Heaton, George R. Jr., R. Darryl Banks and Daryl W. Ditz. "Missing Links: Technology and Environmental Improvement in the Industrializing World." World Resources Institute, October 1994.

Hellenstvedt, Elisabeth and Georg Blichfeldt, eds. *Additional Essays on Whales and Man.* Reine: High North Alliance, 1995.

Henke, Janice Scott. *Sea Wars: An American Viewpoint.* Newfoundland: Breakwater, 1985.

Hermann, Charles F. *et al. Why Nations Act: Theoretical Perspectives for Comparative Foreign Studies.* Beverly Hills: Sage, 1978.

Hermann, Margaret G. "When leader personality will affect foreign policy: Some propositions." In *In Search of Global Patterns: A Reader in Research and Theory,* ed. James N. Rosenau, 326-333. New York: The Free Press, 1976.

Herscovi, Alan. *Second Nature—The Animal Rights Controversy.* Montreal: CBC Enterprise, 1985.

Hesse, Stephen. "Japan's Timber Hunger Appears Endless." *The Japan Times,* 17 March 1994, p.17.

Higashi, Chikara and G. Peter Lauter. *The Internationalization of the Japanese Economy.* Boston: Kluwer Academic Publishers, 1987.

Hilsman, Roger. *The Politics of Policy Making in Defense and Foreign Affairs.* New York: Columbia University Press, 1971.

————. "The Foreign Policy Consensus: An Interim Research Report." *Journal of Conflict Resolution* 3 (1959): 361-82.

Hindryati, Rin. "Apkindo's All-Encompassing Role." *Indonesia Business Weekly* 3:12 (6 March 1995): 8.

Hirasawa, Yutaka. "The Whaling Industry in Japan's Economy." In *The Whaling Issue in U.S.-Japan Relations,* ed. John R. Schmidhauser and George O. Totten III, 82-114. Boulder, CO: Westview Press, 1978.

Hirsh, P. "Deforestation and Development in Comparative Perspective: Thailand, Laos, and Vietnam." In *Management of Tropical Forests: Towards an Integrated Perspective,* ed. Oyvind Sandbukt, 37-50. Oslo: Center for Development and the Environment, University of Oslo, 1995.

Hoel, Alf Hakon. *The International Whaling Commission, 1972-1984: New Members, New Concerns,* 2nd ed. Lysaker: The Fridtjof Nansen Institute, 1986.

Holliman, Jonathan. "Environmentalism with a Global Scope." *Japan Quarterly* 37:3 (July-September 1990): 284-290.

Bibliography

Holliman, Jonathan. "Japan's Trade in Tropical Timber with Southeast Asia." In *Forest Resource Crisis in the Third World*, ed. Sahabat Alam Malaysia. Penang: Sahabat Alam Malaysia, 1987.

Holsti, K.J. "National Role Conceptions in the Study of Foreign Policy," *International Studies Quarterly* 14:3 (September 1970): 233-309.

Hosoya, Chichiro. "Characteristics of the Foreign Policy Decision-Making System in Japan." *World Politics* 16:3 (April 1974): 353-369.

Howard, Michael C., ed. *Asia's Environmental Crisis*. Boulder: Westview Press, 1993.

Huang, J.P. "Fueling the Economy." *The China Business Review* (March/April 1991): 22-29.

Huddle, Norie *et al. Island of Dreams: Environmental Crisis in Japan*. New York: Autumn Press, 1975.

Humphreys, David. "Regime Theory and Non-Governmental Organizations: The Case of Forest Conservation." In *NGOs and Environmental Policies: Asia and Africa*, ed. David Potter, 90-115. London and Portand: Frank Cass, 1996.

Hunter, Lachlan. "Financing an International Organization (Part 1)." *Tropical Forest Update* 5:4 (December 1995): 17-18.

_____. "Financing an International Organization (Part 2)." *Tropical Forest Update* 6:1 (March 1996): 17-18.

Hurrell, Andrew and Benedict Kingsbury, eds. *The International Politics of the Environment: Actors, Interests and Institutions*. Oxford: Clarendon Press, 1992.

Hurst, Philip. *Rainforest Politics: Ecological Destruction in South East Asia*. London and New Jersey: Zed Books, 1990.

Ikeda, Tadashi. "Japan's International Contribution." *Japan Review of International Affairs* (Spring/Summer 1989): 3-26.

Ikenberry, G. John, David A. Lake and Michael Mastanduno. "Introduction: Approaches to explaining American Foreign Economic Policy." *International Organization* 42:1 (Winter 1988): 1-14.

Ikle, Fred Charles and Terumasa Nakanishi. "Japan's Grand Strategy." *Foreign Affairs* 69:3 (Summer 1990): 81-95.

Imanaga, Masaaki. "The Japanese View of Nature form a Comparative Standpoint." *Japan Foundation Newsletter* (July 1996): 1-3.

Imura, Hidefumi. "Japan's Environmental Balancing Act: Accommodating Sustained Development." In *Asian Survey* 3:4 (April 1994): 355-368.

Inada, Juichi. "Japan's aid diplomacy: Increasing role for global security." *Japan Review of International Affairs* 2:1 (Spring/Summer 1988): 91-112.

"Incentives and Sustainability - Where is ITTO Going?" Gland: World Wide Fund for Nature International, November 1991.

Ingebritsen, Christine. "Whales, or Save the Whales?" *Isana* 18 (May 1998): 11-16.

Inoguchi, Takashi and Daniel I. Okimoto, eds. *The Political Economy of Japan: The Changing International Context.* Stanford: Stanford University Press, 1988.

Inose, Hiroshi. "Technological Innovation and Japan's International Contribution." *Japan Review of International Affairs* 6:3 (Fall 1992): 255-274.

International Convention on the Regulation of Whaling, 10 November 1949, T.I.A.S. 1849, 161 U.N.T.S. 72.

International Union for the Conservation of Nature and Natural Resources (IUCN). *World Conservation Strategy: Living Resource Conservation for Sustainable Development.* Gland: IUCN, 1980.

International Convention on the Regulation of Whaling. Washington, D.C., 2 December 1946.

International Tropical Timber Organization. *ITTO Manual for Project Formulation.* Yokohama: ITTO, November 1992.

Ishida, Takeshi and Ellis S. Krauss, eds. *Democracy in Japan.* Pittsburgh: University of Pittsburgh, 1989.

Ismail, Roslan bin. "Disappointment at UNGASS." *ITTO Tropical Forest Update* 17: 3 (1997): 18.

IUCN/UNEP/WWF, "Caring for the Earth, A Strategy for Sustainable Living." Gland: World Wide Fund for Nature International, 1991.

Iwasaki-Goodman, Masami and Milton M.R. Freeman. "Social and Cultural Significance of Whaling in Contemporary Japan: A Case Study of Small-type Coastal Whaling." In *Key Issues in Hunter-Gatherer Research*, ed. Ernest S. Burch, Jr. and Linda J. Ellanna, 377-400. Oxford and Providence: Berg, 1994.

"IWC raises whale quota for north Alaskan natives." *The Japan Times*, 28 May 1994.

"IWC rejects minke hunting." *The Japan Times*, 29 May 1994.

Izumi, Eiji. "A Brief History of Japanese Forests and Forestry up to the 19th Century." In *Forest Policy in Japan*, ed. Ryoichi Handa, 151-160. Tokyo: Nippon Ringyo Chosakai, 1988.

Jakobowicz, J.M. "Acid Rain: An Issue for Regional Cooperation." In *Acid Rain: Current Situation and Remedies*, ed. J. Rose, 129-156. Amsterdam: Gordon and Breach Science Publishers, 1994.

"Japan feels the effects of acid fog." *Japan Report* 35:10 (October 1989): 5.

Bibliography

Japan Forest Technical Association, ed. *Forestry Technology in Japan*. Tokyo: Japan Forest Technical Association, 1981.

Japan International Cooperation Agency. *An Introduction to JICA*. September 1997.

"Japan's International Forestry Cooperation." Tokyo: Japan International Forestry Promotion and Cooperation Center, n.d.

"Japan pledges $7 to $7.7 billion in new environmental aid." *Japan Report* 38:5 (July 1992): 1.

"Japan to lead green group coalition." *The Japan Times*, 22 January 1994.

"Japan seen able to sway vote on whale santuary." *The Japan Times*, 6 February 1994.

"Japan slams IWC's whale sanctuary." *The Japan Times*, 16 April 1995.

"Japan's Next Stimulus Package to focus on Public Works." *The Nihon Keizai Shimbun*, 9 April 1998.

"Japan's ODA, The Blessings and the Bane." *Tokyo Business Today* (September 1991): 10-17.

Japanese Research on Antarctic Whale Resources, Tokyo: Institute of Cetacean Research, 1991.

Johnson, Chalmers. *MITI and the Japanese Miracle: The Growth of Industrial Policy, 1925-1975*. Tokyo: Charles E. Tuttle, 1982.

————. "Japan: Who governs? An Essay on Official Bureaucracy." *The Journal of Japanese Studies* (Autumn 1975): 21-28.

Johnson, Steven. "Production and Trade of Tropical Logs." *Tropical Forest Update* 6:1 (March 1996): 20-22.

Johnson, Todd *et al*. *Clear Water, Blue Skies: China's Environment in the New Century*. Washington, D.C.: The World Bank, China 2020 Series, 1997.

Jonsson, Orn D., ed. *Whales and Ethics*. Iceland: Fisheries Research Institute, University of Iceland, University Press, 1992.

K.S., Jomo, ed. *In the Shadow of the Rising Sun*. London: Routledge, 1994.

————. "Malaysian Forests, Japanese Wood: Japan's Role in Malaysia Deforestation." In *Japan and Malaysian Development: In the Shadow of the Rising Sun*, ed. Jomo K.S., 182-210. London: Routledge, 1994.

Kahan, Archie M. *Acid Rain: Reign of Controversy*. Golden: Fulcrum, Inc., 1986.

Kaizu, Masanobu and Shigeo Hiratsuka. "Environmental Business Opportunities in Japan." *NRI Quarterly* 1 (Summer 1992): 2-25.

Kalland, Arne and Brian Moeran. *Japanese Whaling: End of an Era?* Surrey: Curzon Press, 1992.

292 *Bibliography*

Kalland, Arne. "Aboriginal Subsistence Whaling: A Concept in the Service of Imperialism?" In *11 Essays on Whales and Man*, 2nd ed., 5-11. Reine: High North Alliance, 1994.

_____. "Culture in Japanese Nature." In *Asian Perceptions of Nature: A Critical Approach*, ed. Ole Bruun and Arne Kalland, 243-257. Surrey: Curzon, 1995.

_____. "Some Reflections after the Sendai Workshop." *Isana* 16 (June 1997): 12.

_____. "Super Whale: The Use of Myths and Symbols in Environmentalism." In *11 Essays on Whales and Man*, 2nd ed., 5-11. Reine: High North Alliance, 1994.

Kalland, Arne and Pamela J. Asquith. "Japanese Perceptions of Nature: Ideals and Illusions." In *Japanese Images of Nature: Cultural Perspectives*, ed. Pamela J. Asquith and Arne Kalland, 1-35. Surrey: Curzon, 1997.

Kambara, Tatsu. "The Energy Situation in China." *China Quarterly* 131 (September 1992): 608-636.

Kamishima, Jiro. "Society of Convergence: An Alternative for the Homogeneity Theory." *The Japan Foundation Newsletter* (January 1990): 1-6.

Kata, N. *et al.* "Analysis of the Structure of Energy Consumption and the Dynamics of Emissions of Atmospheric Species related to Global Environment: China SO_2, NO_x and CO_2 in Asia." Tokyo: National Institute of Science and Technology Policy and the Science and Technology Agency, 1991.

Kato, Junko. *The Problem of Bureaucratic Rationality: Tax Politics in Japan.* Princeton: Princeton University Press, 1994.

Katzenstein, Peter J., ed. *Between Power and Plenty: Foreign Economic Policies of Advanced Industrial States.* Madison: University of Wisconsin Press, 1978.

Kawashima, Shiro. "A Survey of Environmental Law and Policy in Japan." *North Carolina Journal of International Law and Commercial Regulations* 20:2 (1995): 232-272.

Kay, David A. and Harold K. Jacobson, eds. *Environmental Protection: The International Dimension.* New Jersey: Allanheld Osmun, 1983.

Kegley, Charles W. Jr. and Eugene R. Wittkopf. *American Foreign Policy: Pattern and Process.* New York: St. Martin's Press, 1987.

Keidanren Environment Subcommittee on Environment and Safety. "Basic Views of the Global Environmental Problem." Tokyo: Keidanren, April 1990.

Keidanren Nature Conservation Fund. "The Keidanren Nature Conservation Fund." Tokyo: KNCF, n.d.

Keizai Doyukai. "Strategies to Arrest Global Warming." Tokyo: Keizai Doyukai, October 1991.

Bibliography

Kemf, Elizabeth and Cassandra Phillips, "1995 WWF Species Status Report: Whales in the Wild." Gland: World Wide Fund for Nature International, May 1995.

Kemp, Ronald H. and Dhira Phantumvanit. "1995 Mid-Term Review of Progress towards the Achievement of the Year 2000 Objective." Yokohama: ITTO, 1995.

Keohane, Robert O. *After Hegemony: Cooperation and Discord in the World Political Economy*. Princeton: Princeton University Press, 1984.

_____. "Multilateralism: An Agenda for Research." *International Journal* 65:4 (Autumn 1990): 733-36.

Keohane, Robert O. and Joseph S. Nye, Jr. *Power and Interdependence*. Boston: Little, Brown and Co., 1977.

_____. "Power and Interdependence Revisited." *International Organization* 41 (Autumn 1987): 725-753.

Kerski, Anita. "Pulp, Paper and Power: How an Industry Reshapes its Social Environment." *The Ecologist* 25:4 (July/August 1995): 142-149.

Kimmins, Hamish. *Balancing Act: Environmental Issues in Forestry*. Vancouver: University of British Colombia Press, 1992.

Kimura, Chikao. "Whaling and Trade." In *Public Perception of Whaling*. Tokyo: Institute of Cetacean Research, 1994.

Kimura, Yo. "The Environmental Impact of Foreign Aid." Program on U.S.-Japan Relations, Harvard University, Occasional Paper, 1990.

Klassen, Ger. *Acid Rain and Environmental Degradation: The Economics of Emission Trading*. Laxenburg: International Institute for Applied Systems Analysis, 1996.

Klinowska, Margaret. "Are Cetaceans Especially Smart?" *New Scientist* 29 (October 1988): 46.

_____. "Brains, Behavior and Intelligence in Cetaceans." In *Whales and Ethics*, ed. Orn D. Jonsson, 23-38. Iceland: Fisheries Research Institute, University of Iceland, University Press, 1992.

Koh, B.C. *Japan's Administrative Elite*. Berkeley: University of California Press, 1989.

Kojima, Reeitsu. "Mainland China grows into the World's Largest Source of Environmental Pollution." In *Development and the Environment: The Experiences of Japan and Industrializing Asia*, ed. Reeitsu Kojima *et al.*, 193-211. Tokyo: Institute of Developing Economies, 1995.

Kojima, Reeitsu *et al.*, eds. *Development and the Environment: The Experiences of Japan and Industrializing Asia*. Tokyo: Institute of Developing Economies, 1995.

Krasner, Stephen. *International Regimes*. Ithaca and London: Cornell University Press, 1983.

Krauss, Ellis S. "Media Coverage of U.S.-Japanese Relations." In *Media and Politics in Japan*, ed. Susan J. Pharr and Ellis S. Krauss, 243-274. Honolulu: University of Hawaii Press, 1996.

_____, Thomas P. Rohlen and Patricia Steinhoff, eds. *Conflict in Japan*. Honolulu: University of Hawaii Press, 1984.

Kumazaki, Minoru. "Japanese Economic Development and Forestry." In *Forest Policy in Japan*, ed. Ryoichi Handa, 1-15. Tokyo: Nippon Ringyo Chosakai, 1988.

Kunitomo, Hirotoshi. "Japanese Policy for Cooperation with Asian Economies on Environmental Issues." *Proceedings of APEC Fifth Technical Seminar on Clean Fossil Energy in Reno, Nevada, 23-30 October 1997.*

Kuroda, Yoichi. "Japan's Consumption of Tropical Timber and Effects on Tropical Forests." Tokyo: Japan Tropical Forest Action Network, n.d.

Kurosaka, Miwako. "Japan and the Global Environment." *NIRA Review* (Spring 1995): 19-22.

Laarman, Jan G. "Linkages: The Global Timber Trade." In *World Deforestation in the Twientieth Century*, ed. John F. Richards and Richard P. Tucker, 147-163. Durham and London: Duke University Press, 1988.

Lamprecht, James L. *ISO 14000: Issues and Implementation: Guidelines for Responsible Environmental Management*. New York: Amacom, 1997.

Lehman, Harold P. and Jennifer L. McCoy. "The Dynamics of the Two-level Bargaining Game: The 1988 Brazilian Debt Negotiations." *World Politics* 44:4 (July 1992): 600-644.

Lenssen, Nicholas. "All the Coal in China." *World Watch* (April 1993): 22-29.

Levin, Norman D. "The Strategic Dimension of Japanese Foreign Policy." In *Japan's Foreign Policy After the Cold War*, ed. Gerald L. Curtis, 202-217. New York: M.E. Sharpe, 1993.

Levine, Mark D. *et al*. "China's energy system: Historical Evolution, Current Issues, and Prospects." *Annual Review of Energy Environment* 17 (1992):405-535.

Li, Binsheng and Charles J. Johnson. "The Booming Electricity Sector of China - Its Opportunities and Challenges." East-West Center, Program on Energy and Minerals, China Energy Project Series Paper CEP-94-1, 1994.

Libiszewski, Stephan. "What is Environmental Conflict?" Occasional paper of the Environment and Conflicts Project, No.1, July 1992.

"Limited whaling can be tolerated." *Atlanta*, 7 May 1993.

Litt, Barbara, trans. "Citizen Power for Solar Power." In *Japan Environment Monitor*, electronic ed. (August/September 1997).

Bibliography

Lohmann, Larry. "Freedom to plant; Indonesia and Thailand in a Globablizing Pulp and Paper Industry." In *Environmental Change in South-East Asia: People, Politics and Sustainable Development*, ed. Michael J.G. Parnwell and Raymond L. Bryant, 23-48. London and New York: Routledge, 1996.

Lohmann, Larry and Marcus Colchester. "Paved with Good Intentions: TFAP's Road to Oblivion." *The Ecologist* 20:3 (May/June 1990): 720-727.

Lowi, Theodore. "American Business, Public Policy, Case Studies and Political Theory. *World Politics* 16:4 (July 1964): 677-715.

Lu, Yingzhong, "Fueling One Billion: An Insider's Story of Chinese Energy Policy Development." Washington, D.C.: The Washington Institute, 1993.

Luoma, Jon R. *Troubled Skies, Troubled Waters: The Story of Acid Rain.* NY: The Viking Press, 1984.

Lynge, Finn. *Artic Wars: Animals Rights, Endangered Peoples.* Translated by Marianne Stenback, Hanover and London: Darthmouth College, University Press of New England, 1992.

_____. "Ethics of a Killer Whale." In *Whales and Ethics*, ed. Orn D. Jonsson, 11-21. Iceland: Fisheries Research Institute, University of Iceland, University Press, 1992.

MacDougall, T.E., ed. *Political Leadership in Contemporary Japan.* Ann Arbor: Center for Japanese Studies, University of Michigan Press, 1982.

McBeth, John. "El Nino Gets Blamed." *Far Eastern Economic Review* (9 October 1997): 80-82.

McCay, Bonnie J. and James M. Acheson, eds. *The Question of Commons: The Culture and Ecology of Communal Resources.* Tucson: University of Arizona Press, 1987.

McCormack, Gavan. "Growth, Construction, and the Environment: Japan's Construction State." *Japan Studies* 15:1 (May 1995): 26-35.

McCormick, John. *Acid Earth: The Global Threat of Acid Pollution.* London: International Institute for Environment and Development, 1985.

McGill, Douglas. "Japan's Pseudo-environmentalism." *The New York Times Magazine*, 4 October 1992.

McGuiness, P.P. "Lifting whaling ban a test of sentiment versus sanity." *The Weekend Australian*, 17-18 April 1993.

_____. "Maturing Japanese puts its trade partners to shame." *The Australian*, 16 April 1993.

_____. "Western arrogance leaves an Asian heritage all at sea." *The Australian*, 15 April 1993.

_____. "World whaling ban survives on myths alone." *The Australian*, 14 April 1993.

McKean, Margaret A. *Environmental Protest and Citizen Politics in Japan.* Berkeley: University of California Press, 1981.

McNeely, Jeffrey A. and Paul Spencer Sochaczewski. *Soul of the Tiger: Searching for Nature's Answers in Southeast Asia.* Honolulu: University of Hawaii Press, 1988.

McNelly, Theodore. *Politics and Government in Japan*, 3rd ed. London: University Press of America, 1984.

Mahar, Dennis J. "Government Policies and Deforestation in Brazil's Amazon Region." Washington, D.C.: The World Bank, January 1989.

"Malaysia, Indonesia to push for expansion of Timber Pact." *The Indonesia Times,* 4 December 1992.

Mansbach, Richard W., Yale H. Ferguson and Donald E. Lampert. *The Web of World Politics: Nonstate Actors in the Global System.* New Jersey: Prentice-Hall, 1976.

March, James G. and Herbert A. Simon. *Organizations.* New York and London: John Willy and Sons, 1958.

"Marine Products." *Japan Almanac 1995.* Tokyo: Asahi Shimbun, 1996.

Martin, Gene S., Jr. and James W. Brennan, "Enforcing the International Convention for the Regulation of Whaling: The Pelly and Packwood-Magnuson Amendment." *Denver Journal of International Law and Policy* 17:2 (1989): 293-315.

Masaki, Hisane. "Confidence voiced with ODA focus." *The Japan Times,* 1 January 1994.

Mason, B.J. *Acid Rain: Its causes and its effects on inland waters.* Oxford: Clarendon Press, 1992.

Mastanduno, Michael *et al.* "Toward a Realist Theory of State Action." *International Studies Quarterly* 33 (December 1989): 457-474.

Masuda, Misa. "International Cooperation in Forestry." In *Forest Policy in Japan,* ed. Ryoichi Handa, 441-457. Tokyo: Nippon Ringyo Chosakai, 1988.

Matsuki, K. "The Current and Future Timber Demand and Supply in Japan and the Prospects of Japanese Timber Industry." In *Draft Report on Timber Project PD 57/89 (F,I)*, Yokohama: International Tropical Timber Organization, November 1989.

Matthews, Jessica T. "Redefining Security." *Foreign Affairs* 68:2 (Spring 1989): 162-177.

Maull, Hanns W. "Japan's Global Environmental Policies." *Pacific Review* 4:3 (1991): 254-62.

Mayer, Frederick W. "Bargains within Bargains: Domestic Politics and International Negotiations." Ph.D. dissertation, Harvard University, 1988.

Bibliography

———. "Managing Domestic Differences in International Negotiations: The Strategic Use of Internal Side-Payments." *International Organization* 46:4 (Autumn 1992): 793-818.

Meadows, Donella H. *et al. The Limits to Growth: A Report for the Club of Rome Project on the Predicament of Mankind.* New York: Universe Books, 1972.

Mandelbaum, Paulette, ed. *Acid Rain: Economic Assessment.* New York: Plenum Press, 1985.

Menju, Toshihiro and Takako Aoki. "The Evolution of Japanese NGOs in the Asia Pacific Context." In *Emerging Civil Society in the Asia Pacific Community: Nongovernmental Underpinnings of the Emerging Asia Pacific Regional Community,* ed. Tadashi Yamamoto, 143-160. Tokyo: Japan Center for International Exchange, 1995.

Mera, Koichi. "Problems in the Aid Program." *Japan Echo* 16:1 (Spring 1989): 13-18.

Milbrath, Lester. *Envisioning a Sustainable Society: Learning our way out.* Albany: University of New York Press, 1989.

——— and Frederick R. Inscho, eds. *The Politics of Environmental Policy.* Beverly Hills and London: Sage, 1975.

Miller, Alan S. and Curtis Moore. *Japan and the Global Environment.* College Park: Center for Global Change, University of Maryland, 1991.

Miller, Alan S. "Three Reports on Japan and the Global Environment." *Environment* 31:6 (July/August 1989): 25-29.

Miller, Annetta. "Japan's Window of Opportunity." *International Wildlife* 21:1 (January/February 1991): 12-17.

Miller, Marian A.L. *The Third World in Global Environmental Politics.* Boulder: Lynne Rienner, 1995.

Milner, Helen. "International Theories of Cooperation Among Nations: Strengths and Weaknesses." *World Politics* 44:3 (April 1992): 466-496.

Ministry of Foreign Affairs, Government of Japan. "Japan's Environmental Cooperation." n.d.

———. "Japan's ODA Annual Report 1995."

———. "Japan's Official Development Assistance Summary." n.d.

———. "Japan's Official Development Assistance Summary 1997."

———. "Looking Ahead: A Foreign Policy for a Changing World." Japan's Policy Series, No.9320E, July 1993.

Misaki, Hisane. "China Sinks Deeper into Ecological Cesspool." *The Japan Times,* 23 July 1995.

Misaki, Shigeko. "Whaling Controversy is the Name of the Game." In *Public Perception of Whaling.* Tokyo: Institute of Cetacean Research, 1994.

298   *Bibliography*

"Mistaking Plantations for Indonesia's Tropical Forests." Jakarta: Wahana Lingkungan Hidup Indonesia, 1992.

Mochizuki, Katsuya. "Economic Development and Environmental Issues in Asia: Focusing on Official Development Aid." In *Development and the Environment: The Experiences of Japan and Industrializing Asia*, ed. Reeitsu Kojima *et al.*, 410-420. Tokyo: Institute of Developing Economies, 1995.

Moeran, Brian. "The Cultural Construction of Value: `Subsistence', `Commercial' and other terms in the debate about whaling." In *Report of the Symposium on Utilization of Marine Living Resources for Subsistence* 1 (March 1992): 83-104.

Moniaga, Sandra. "CIFOR Establishment: Consistent with Conservation?" *Environesia* 7:1 (January/March 1993): 10-11.

Moomaw, William R. and Judith T. Kildow. "International Environmental Decision Making: Challenges and Changes for the Old Order." In *Environmental Decision-Making: A Multidisciplinary Perspective*, ed. Richard H. Chechile and Susan Carlisle, 269-289. New York: Van Nostrand Reinhold, 1991.

Moravcsik, Andrew. "Introduction: Integrating International and Domestic Theories of International Bargaining." In *Double-Edged Diplomacy: International Bargaining and Domestic Politics*, ed. Peter B. Evans, Harold K. Jacobson and Robert D. Putnam, 3-42. Berkeley: University of California Press, 1993.

Morgan, T. Clifton. "Issue Linkages in International Crisis Bargaining." *American Journal of Political Science* 34:2 (May 1990): 311-33.

Morrisette, Peter M. and Andrew J. Plantinga. "How the CO_2 Issue is viewed in Different Countries." Washington, D.C.: Energy and Natural Resources Division, Discussion Paper ENR 91-03, December 1990.

Mott, Richard N. "Japan's Whale Hunt: A Case of Ecological Piracy." *The Los Angeles Times*, 12 February 1996, p.B5.

Munthe, Gary Nageri and Rin Hindryati. "Apkindo Under Fire." *Indonesia Business Weekly* 3:12 (6 March 1995): 4-7.

Murakami, Asako. "Whale sanctuary fight looms." *The Japan Times*, 6 April 1994.

Muramatsu, Michio and Ellis S. Krauss. "Bureaucrats and Politicians in Policymaking: The Case of Japan." *The American Political Science Review* 78:1 (March 1984): 126-146.

Murdo, Pat. "Environmental Developments Offer Opportunities for Japan." *JEI Report* 1A, 10 January 1992.

_____. "Japanese Environmental Proposals Draw Criticisms." *JEI Report* 43B (13 November 1992).

Bibliography

Murphy, R. Taggart. "Power without Purpose: The Crisis of Japan's Global Financial Dominance." *Harvard Business Review* (March/April 1989): 71-83.

Myers, David and Kotaku Ishido, eds. *Japan at the Crossroads: Hot Issues for the 21st Century*. Tokyo: Seibundo Publishing, 1998.

Myers, Norman. "Environment and Security." *Foreign Policy* 74 (1989): 23-41.

_____. "The World's Forests: Need for a Policy Appraisal." *Science* 268 (12 May 1995): 823-824.

Nagasaki, Fukuzo. "Pro- and Anti-Whaling Attitudes as Revealed in Public Opinion Polls." In *Public Perception of Whaling*, 5-20. Tokyo: ICR, 1994.

Nakajima, Ai. "Aid offered to clean environment abroad." *The Nikkei Weekly*, 27 July 1991.

Nakamura, Ritsuko. "Green Desert mirage for scientist." *The Japan Times*, 11 November 1993.

Nasu, Kenji. *Stories of Whales*. Tokyo: Japan Whaling Association, 1985.

"Nation's Agenda 21 plan finalized." *The Japan Times*, 25 December 1993.

Natori, Makoto. "Japan's Pollution Control Technologies and Their Role in the World." In *Japan Review of International Affairs* 7:1 (Winter 1993): 51-67.

Nectoux, F. and Y. Kuroda. *Timber from the South Seas: An Analysis of Japan's Tropical Timber Trade and its Environmental Impact*. Gland: World Wide Fund for Nature International, 1989.

Nishihira, Sigeki *et al.*, eds. *Environmental Awareness in Developing Countries: The Cases of China and Thailand*. Tokyo: Institute of Developing Economies, 1997.

Nomura, Yoshihiro. "History, Structure and Characteristics of Japan's Environment Law." *Development and the Environment: The Experiences of Japan and Industrializing Asia*, ed. Reeitsu Kojima *et al.*, 128-157. Tokyo: Institute of Developing Economies, 1995.

"Non-Paper on ITTA Renegotiations." Gland: World Wide Fund for Nature International, November 1992.

"Norwegian whales mad quota cut by over 20%" *The Japan Times*, 4 May 1995, p.20.

"Nuclear Power Generation." In *Japan Almanac 1995*. Tokyo: Asahi Shimbun, 1994, p.169.

Oakes, Jill, ed. *Human Ecology: Issues in the North*. Edmonton, Alberta: Canadian Circumpolar Institute and University of Alberta, 1995.

Office of Technology Assessment, Congress of the United States. *Acid Rain and Transported Air Pollutants: Implications for Public Policy*. New York: Unipub, 1985.

Bibliography

Ofreneo, Rene E. "Japan and the Environmental Degradation of the Philippines." In *Asia's Environmental Crisis*, ed. Michael C. Howard, 201-233. Boulder: Westview Press, 1993.

Okimoto, Daniel I. "Political Inclusivity: The Domestic Structure of Trade." In *The Political Economy of Japan: The Changing International Context*, ed. Takashi Inoguchi and Daniel I. Okimoto, 305-344. Stanford: Stanford University Press, 1988.

"One Man's Sacred Cow is Another's Big Mac: Does America's Policy Depend on Whose Whale is Gored?" *The New York Times*, 9 April 1985.

Organization for Economic Cooperation and Development. *OECD Environmental Performance Review of Japan*. Paris: OECD, Novermber 1993.

_____. *The OECD Environment Industry: Situation, Prospects and Government Policies*. Paris: OECD, 1992.

Orr, Robert M., Jr. *The Emergency of Japan's Foreign Aid Power*. New York: Columbia University Press, 1990.

Ostrom, Elinor. *Governing the Commons: The Evolution of Institutions for Collective Action*. Cambridge: Cambridge University Press, 1990.

Oye, Kenneth A., ed. *Cooperation under Anarchy*. Princeton: Princeton University Press, 1985.

Ozaki, Robert S. and Walter Arnolds, eds. *Japan's Foreign Relations: A Global Search for Economic Security*. Boulder: Westview Press, 1985.

"Papers on Japanese Small-Type Coastal Whaling Submited by the Government of Japan to the International Whaling Commission, 1986-1995." Tokyo: Institute of Cetacean Research, March 1996.

Park, Chris C. *Acid Rain: Rhetoric and Reality*. London and New York: Methuen, 1987.

Parnwell, Michael J.G. and Raymond L. Bryant, eds. *Environmental Change in South-East Asia: People, Politics and Sustainable Development*. London and New York: Routledge, 1996.

Patterson, Walter, ed. *Environmental Profiles of European Business*. London: Earthscan Publications, Ltd., 1993.

Pearce, Fred. *Acid Rain: What is it, and what is it doing to us?* Middlesex, England: Penguin Books, 1987.

Pempel, T.J. *Policy and Politics in Japan: Creative Conservatism*. Philadelphia: Temple University Press, 1982.

_____. *Policymaking in Contemporary Japan*. London and Ithaca: Cornell University Press, 1977.

Bibliography 301

_____. "Japanese Foreign Economic Policy: The Domestic Bases for International Behavior." In *Between Power and Plenty: Foreign Economic Policies of Advanced Industrial States*, ed. Peter J. Katzenstein, 139-90. Madison: University of Wisconsin Press, 1978.

_____. "The Unbundling of `Japan, Inc.': The Changing Dynamics of Japanese Policy Formation." *The Journal of Japanese Studies* 13 (Summer 1987): 271-306.

Pempel, T.J., ed. *Policymaking in Japan*. Ithaca and London: Cornell University Press, 1977.

Perlack, Robert D. *et al.* "Energy and Environmental Policy in China." *Annual Review of Energy Environment* 16 (1991): 205-33.

Pharr, Susan J. and Ellis S. Krauss, eds. *Media and Politics in Japan*. Honolulu: University of Hawaii Press, 1996.

Pharr, Susan J. "Media as Trickster in Japan: A Comparative Perspective." In *Media and Politics in Japan*, ed. Susan J. Pharr and Ellis S. Krauss, 19-44. Honolulu: University of Hawaii Press, 1996.

Ploman, Edward. "Global Learning: Concept and Applications." In *Environmental Change and International Law: New Challenges and Dimensions*, ed. Edith B. Weiss, 459-478. Tokyo: United Nations University Press, 1992.

Poffenberger, M., ed. *Keepers of the Forest: Land Management Alternatives in Southeast Asia*. West Hartford: Kumarian Press, 1990.

Poore, Duncan *et al*. *No Timber without Trees: Sustainability in the Tropical Forest, A Study for ITTO*. London: Earthscan, 1989.

Porter, Gareth and Janet Welsh Brown. *Global Environmental Politics: Dilemmas in World Politics*. Boulder: Westview Press, 1991.

Portney, Kent E. *Controversial Issues in Environmental Policy: Science vs. Economics vs. Politics*. Newbury Park: Sage, 1992.

"Position paper on whaling." Tokyo: World Wide Fund for Nature (Japan) 29 May 1995.

Potter, David, ed. *NGOs and Environmental Policies: Asia and Africa*. London and Portand: Frank Cass, 1996.

Price, David Andrew. "Save the Whalers." *The American Spectator* (February 1995): 48-9.

"Primary Energy Consumption by Fuel [1992]." In *ECO Japan: International Comparison of Environmental Data*. Tokyo: Keizai Koho Center, 1994, pp.16-17.

Prince, Cathryn. "As world heats up, U.S. plan would make firms pay to pollute." *Christian Science Monitor* (19 July 1996): 6.

302   *Bibliography*

Princen, Thomas and Matthias Finger. *Environmental NGOs in World Politics: Linking the Local and the Global.* London and New York: Routledge, 1994.

Program on Resources: Energy and Minerals, "Market Report: The Potential for Emulsion Fuel in the Asia-Pacific Region," Honolulu: The East-West Center, May 1996.

"Proposal for a Pacific Rim forest international forum." Tokyo: Japan Tropical Forest Action Network, November 1993.

"Pulp and Paper." *Japan Economic Almanac 1995.* Tokyo: The Nikkei Weekly, 1995, p.114.

Putnam, Robert D. "Bureaucrats and Politicians: Contending Elites in the Policy Process." *Tulane Studies in Political Science* 15 (1973): 179-202.

_____. "Diplomacy and Domestic Politics: The Logic of Two-level Games." *International Organization* 42:3 (Summer 1988): 427-460.

Putnam, Robert D. and Nicholas Bayne. *Hanging Together: The Seven-Power Summits.* Cambridge: Harvard University Press, 1984.

Raufer, Roger K. and Stephen L. Feldman. *Acid Rain and Emissions Trading: Implementing a Market Approach to Pollution Control.* New Jersey: Rowman and Littlefield, 1987.

Rambo, Terry. "The Fallacy of Global Sustainable Development." *Asia Pacific Issues* 30 (March 1997): 4.

Redclift, Michael. *Sustainable Development: Exploring the Contradictions.* London and New York: Methuen, 1987.

Redclift, Michael and Ted Benton, eds. *Social Theory and the Global Environment.* London and New York: Routledge, 1994.

Rees, William. "the Ecology of Sustainable Development." *The Ecologist* 20:1 (January/February 1990): 18-23.

Regens, James L. and Robert W. Rycroft. *The Acid Rain Controversy.* Pittsburgh: University of Pittsburgh Press, 1988.

_____. "Perspectives on Acid Deposition Control: Science, Economics, and Policymaking." In *The Acid Rain Debate: Scientific, Economic, and Political Dimensions,* ed. Ernest J. Yanarella and Randal H. Ihara, 87-106. Boulder and London: Westview Press, 1985.

Reid, L. *The Sociology of Nature.* London: Penguin Books, 1962.

"Report on Eucalyptus Plantation Schemes in Brazil and Chile by Japanese Companies." Tokyo: Japan Tropical Forest Action Network, May 1993.

Research on Whales. Tokyo: Institute of Cetacean Research, 1995.

"Review of the Moratorium." *Isabiri* (May 1995): 1-5.

"RI-Malaysia join to face Anti-Tropical Timber Campaign." *The Indonesia Times,* 5 December 1992.

Bibliography

"Rich is glorious." *The Ecologist* (January/February 1995): 14-15.

Richards, John F. and Richard P. Tucker, eds. *World Deforestation in the Twentieth Century*. Durham and London: Duke University Press, 1988.

Ridgley, Susan. "Environmental Protection Agreements in Japan and the United States." *Pacific Rim Law and Policy Journal* 5:3 (July 1996): 639-672.

Ringold, Paul, "The Evolving Science of Acid Deposition." In *Acid Rain Control II: The Promise of New Technology*, ed. Diane Suitt Gilleland and James H. Swisher, 1-18. Carbondale and Edwardsville: Southern Illinois University Press, 1986.

Rinkevich, Joe. "A Situational Overview of Bintuni Bay: Destruction of an Internationally Important Wetland in Irian Jaya, Indonesia, for wood chipping exports to Japan." *Japan Environment Monitor* (June 1990): 16-18.

Risse-Kappen, Thomas. "Ideas Do Not Float Freely: Transnational Coalitions, Domestic Structure and the End of the Cold War." *International Organization* 48:2 (Summer 1994): 185-214.

Rodhe, Henning and Rafael Herrera, eds. *Acidification in Tropical Countries*. Chichester and New York: John Wiley & Sons, 1988.

Rose, J., ed. *Acid Rain: Current Situation and Remedies*. Amsterdam: Gordon and Breach Science Publishers, 1994.

Rosecrance, Richard. "Japan and the theory of International Leadership." *World Politics* 42 (January 1990): 184-209.

Rosenau, James N. "Adaptive Polities in an Interdependent World." *Orbis* 16 (Spring 1972): 158-173.

_____. "Before Cooperation: Hegemons, Regimes, and Habit-driven Actors in World Politics." *International Organization* 40:4 (Autumn 1986): 849-894.

_____. "Capabilities and Control in an Interdependent World." *International Security* 1 (October 1976): 32-49.

_____. "International Studies in a Transnational World." *Millenium: Journal of International Studies* 5:1 (Spring 1976): 1:20.

_____. "Pre-theories and Theories of Foreign Policy." In *Approaches to Comparative and International Politics*, ed. R. Barry Farrell, 27-92. Evanston: Northwestern University, 1966.

_____. *Linkage Politics: Essays on the Convergence of National and International Systems*. New York: The Free Press, 1969.

Rosenau, James N., ed. *Domestic Sources of Foreign Policy*. New York: The Free Press, 1967.

Rosenbluth, Frances McCall. *Financial Politics in Contemporary Japan*. London and Ithaca: Cornell University Press, 1989.

Rosendal, G. Kristin. "The Forest Issue in Post-UNCED International Negotiations: Conflicting Interests and Fora for Reconciliation." In *Management of Tropical Forests: Towards an Integrated perspective*, ed. Oyvind Sandbukt, 341-356. Oslo: Center for Development and the Environment, University of Oslo, 1995.

Sahabat Alam Malaysia, ed. *Forest Resource Crisis in the Third World*. Penang: Sahabat Alam Malaysia, 1987.

Samhat, Nayef H. "International Regimes as Political Community." *Millenium: Journal of International Studies* 26:2 (1997): 349-378.

Samuels, Richard. *The Business of the Japanese State: Energy and Markets in Comparative and Historical Perspective*. Ithaca and London: Cornell University Press, 1987.

Sandbukt, Oyvind. "Decentralization and Development: Implications for Deforestation in Indonesia." In *Management of Tropical Forests: Towards an Integrated Perspective*, ed. Oyvind Sandbukt, 51-72. Oslo: Center for Development and the Environment, University of Oslo, 1995.

Sandbukt, Oyvind, ed. *Management of Tropical Forests: Towards an Integrated Perspective*. Oslo: University of Oslo, Center for Development and the Environment, 1995.

Sattaur, Omar. "Last Chance for the Rainforest Plan?" *New Scientist* (2 March 1991: 728-729.

"Saving the whale." *The Financial Times*, 17 May 1993.

Sawyer, Jacqueline. "Topical Forests." Gland: World Wide Fund for Nature International, 1990.

Saywell, Trish. "Power to the People." *Far Eastern Economic Review* (29 January 1998): 36.

Scalapino, Robert A., ed. *The Foreign Policy of Modern Japan*. Berkeley and Los Angeles: University of California Press, 1977.

Schmandt, Jurgen, Judith Clarkson and Hilliard Roderick, eds. *Acid Rain and Friendly Neighbors: The Policy Dispute between Canada and the United States*, rev. ed. Durham: Duke University Press, 1988.

Schmidhauser, John R. and George O. Totten III, eds. *The Whaling Issue in U.S.-Japan Relations*. Boulder: Westview Press, 1978.

Schmiegelow, M., ed. *Japan's Response to Crisis and Change in the World Economy*. London: M.E. Sharpe, 1986.

_____. "Cutting Across Doctrines: Positive Adjustment in Japan." *International Organization* 39:2 (Spring 1985): 261-296.

Schoppa, Leonard J. *Bargaining with Japan: What American Pressure Can and Cannot Do*. New York: Columbia University Press, 1997.

Bibliography

_____. "Two-level Games and Bargaining Outcomes: Why *Gaiatsu* succeeds in Japan in some cases but not others." *International Organization* 47:3 (Summer 1993): 353-385.

Schreurs, Miranda. "Japan's Changing Approach to Environmental Issues." *Environmental Politics* 6:2 (Summer 1997): 150-156.

Schwartz, Frank. "Advice and Consent: The Politics of Consultation in Japan." USJP Occasional Paper, No.90-11, Program on U.S.-Japan Relations, Harvard University, 1991.

Schweder, Tore. "Intransigence, incompetence or political expediency? Dutch scientists in the International Whaling Commission in the 1950s: injection of uncertainty," Scientific Committee/44/O, 1/6 1992, pp.13-38.

Shaw, Roderick W. "Acid-Rain Negotiations in North America and Europe: A Study in Contrast." In *International Environmental Negotiation*, ed. Gunnar Sjostedt, 84-109. Newbury Park: Sage, 1993.

Sheehan, James M. "Whales Rock the Trade Boat." *Journal of Commerce* (21 June 1993): 60.

Shinohara, Miyohei. "Japan's Role in a Changing World Economy." *Japan Echo* 17:1 (1990): 17-26.

Shioya, Ko. "The Forest Beyond the Trees." *Asia, Inc.* (April 1993): 30.

Shirasu, Takeshi. "In Search of Closer Collaboration between Japan and US in the Aid Sphere." Washington, D.C.: Overseas Development Council, 1990.

Shiva, V. *Staying Alive: Women, Ecology and Development.* New Delhi: Zed Books, 1988.

Sikkink, Kathryn. "Human Rights, Principled Issue-Networks, and Sovereignty in Latin America." *International Organization* 47:3 (Summer 1993): 411-42.

Silberman, Bernard. "Structural and Functional Differentiation in the Political Modernization of Japan." In *Political Development in Modern Japan*, ed. Robert E. Ward, 337-386. Princeton: Princeton University Press, 1968.

Singer, J. David. "International Conflict: Three Levels of Analysis." *World Politics* 12 (April 1960): 453-461.

_____. "The Level-of-Analysis Problem in International Relations." *World Politics* 14 (October 1961): 77-92.

Sinkule, Barbara J. and Leonard Ortolano. *Implementing Environmental Policy in China.* Westport: Praeger, 1995.

Simmons, I.G. *Environmental History: A Concise History.* Oxford and Cambridge: Blackwell, 1993.

Simon, Herbert A. *Administrative Behavior: A Study of Decision-Making Processes in Administrative Organization*, 3rd ed. New York: The Free Press, 1976.

Simula, Markku and Baharuddin Hj. Ghazali. "Timber Certification in Transition." *Tropical Forest Update* 6:4 (1996): 20-22.

Singer, J. David. "International Conflict: Three Levels of Analysis." *World Politics* 12 (April 1960): 453-461.

————. "The Level-of-Analysis Problem in International Relations." *World Politics* 14 (October 1961): 77-92.

Singer, S. Fred. "Sustainable Development vs. Global Environment: Resolving the Conflict." *Columbia Journal of World Business* (Fall/Winter 1992): 154-162.

————. "The Southern Oceans Whale Santuary: Last Gasp of the Anti-Whalers?" *Isana* (November 1994): 15-19.

Sjostedt, Gunnar, ed. *International Environmental Negotiation*. Newbury Park: Sage, 1993.

Slack, A.V., "Current Technology for SO_2 Emission Control." In *Acid Rain Control II: The Promise of New Technology*, ed. Diane Suitt Gilleland and James H. Swisher, 147-162. Carbondale and Edwardsville: Southern Illinois University Press, 1986.

"Small-type coastal whaling in Japan: Report of an International Workshop," 10-17. Alberta:Japan Social Sciences Association of Canad and Fund to Promote International Educational Exchange and Boreal Insitute for Northern Studies, 1988.

Smil, Vaclav. *China's Environmental Crisis: An Inquiry into the Limits of National Division*. Armonk: M.E. Sharpe, 1993.

————. *Energy in China's Modernization: Advances and Limitations*. London and New York: M.E. Sharpe, Inc., 1988.

Smil, Vaclav. "China's Environmental Refugees: Causes, Dimensions and Risks of an Emerging Problem." In "Environmental Crisis: Regional Conflicts and Ways of Cooperation," ed. Kurt R. Spillmann and Gunther Bachler, 75-91. Occasional Paper 14. Zurich: Center for Security Studies and Conflict Research, Swiss Federal Institute of Technology, September 1995.

Smith, Emily T. *et al*. "Growth vs. Environment." *Business Week*, 11 May 1992, p.73.

Speart, Jessica. "Pawns in the Game." *Animals* (January/February 1995): 10-14.

Spencer, Leslie *et al*. "The Not So Peaceful World of Greenpeace." *Forbes Magazine* (11 November 1991): 177.

Spillmann, Kurt R. "From Environmental Change to Environmental Conflict." In "Environmental Crisis: Regional Conflicts and Ways of Cooperation," ed. Kurt R. Spillmann and Gunther Bachler, 4-10. Occasional Paper 14. Zurich: Center for Security Studies and Conflict Research, Swiss Federal Institute of Technology, September 1995.

Bibliography

Spillmann, Kurt R. and Gunther Bachler, eds. "Environmental Crisis: Regional Conflicts and Ways of Cooperation." Occasional Paper 14. Zurich: Center for Security Studies and Conflict Research, Swiss Federal Institute of Technology, September 1995.

Sprinz, Detlef and Tapani Vaahtoranta. "The Interest-based Explanation of International Environmental Policy." *International Organization* 48:1 (Winter 1994): 77-105.

Sprout, Harold and Margaret Sprout. *Foundations of International Politics*. Princeton: Nostrand, 1962.

Steinbruner, Jonathan. *A Cybernetic Theory of Decision: New Dimensions in Political Analysis*. Princeton: Princeton University Press, 1974.

Steiner, Kurt *et al.*, eds. *Political Opposition and Local Politics in Japan*. Princeton: Princeton University Press, 1980.

Stewart, Hayden. "JAS Standard, North American Plywood Makers target Japan." *The Japan Times*, 19 September 1994.

Stockwin, J.A.A. et al. *Dynamic and Immobilist Politics in Japan*. Honolulu: University of Hawaii Press, 1988.

Stoett, Peter J. *The International Politics of Whaling*. Vancouver: University of British Columbia Press, 1997.

Stokke, Olav Schram. "Transnational Fishing: Japan's Changing Strategy." *Marine Policy* 15 (July 1991): 231-43.

"Stories of the Whale." Tokyo: Japan Whaling Association, 1985.

Strange, Susan. "Cave! hic dragones: A Critique of Regime Analysis." *International Organization* 36:2 (Spring 1982): 479-496.

"Stress Environmental Aid to China, panel Urges." *The Japan Times*, 23 May 1996.

"Study on Atmospheric Emissions Regulations in APEC Economies and their Compliance at Coal-Fired Plants," Asia-Pacific Economic Cooperation, Regional Energy Cooperation Working Group, Clean Fossil Energy Experts' Group, January 1997.

"Study urged on levies to save the environment." *The Japan Times*, 4 February 1994.

Suharyanto, Her. "Big Forest, Small Ministry." *Indonesia Business Weekly* 11:10 (18 February 1994): 16.

Sukpanich, Tunya. "Forest Management Plan Supports Logging Industry." *Bangkok Post*, 14 November 1990.

Sumi, Kazuo. "How to Strengthen Environmental Considerations in Japan's Development Assistance." Tokyo: ODA Research Group, October 1988.

Sumi, Kazuo. "The 'Whale War' between Japan and the United States: Problems and Prospects." *Denver Journal of International Law and Policy* 17:2 (1989): 317-372.

Sumitro, Achmad. "Industrial Pressures for Overexploitation of Forest: the Indonesian Experience." In *Management of Tropical Forests: Towards and Integrated Perspective*, ed. Oyvind Sandbukt, 183-188. Oslo: Center for Development and the Environment, University of Oslo, 1995.

"Survey on Development and the Environment." *The Economist* (21 March 1998): 8

Susskind, Lawrence E. *Environmental Diplomacy: Negotiating More Effective Global Agreements*. New York and Oxford: Oxford University Press, 1994.

Swap, Walter C. "Psychological Factors in Environmental Decision Making: Social Dilemmas." In *Environmental Decision-Making: A Multidisciplinary Perspective*, ed. Richard A. Chechile and Susan Carlisle, 14-37. New York: Nostrand Reinhold, 1991.

Switzer, Jacqueline Vaughn. *Environmental Politics: Domestic and Global Dimensions*. New York: St. Martin's Press, 1994.

Synder, Richard C. *et al.*, eds. *Foreign Policy Decision-Making: An Approach to the Study of International Politics*. New York: Free Press of Glencoe, 1962.

Tamamoto, Masaru. "Reflections on Japan's Postwar State." *Daedalus* 24 (Spring 1995): 1-22.

Teranishi, Shun'ichi. "A Critical Review of Pollution Issues and Environmental Policy." In *Development and the Environment: The Experiences of Japan and Industrializing Asia*, ed. Kojima Reeitsu *et al.*, 68-78. Tokyo: Institute of Developing Economies, 1995.

Terborgh, John. *Diversity and the Tropical Rain Forest*. New York: Scientific American Library, 1992.

"The Concept of Timber Estate Development: The Government Version." *Setiakawan* 8 (July-September 1992): 13-17.

"The Fifth International Whaling Symposium on Sustainable Use of Wildlife and International Regime—with special reference to cetaceans." Tokyo: Institute of Cetacean Research, 1995.

"The Fires Next Time." *The Economist* (28 May 1998): 44.

"The First Green Summit." *The Economist* (15 July 1989): 13.

The Global 2000 Report to the President. Washington, D.C.: U.S. Government Printing Office, 1980.

"The History of Timber Estate Development in Indonesia." *Setiakawan* 8 (July-September 1992): 7-12.

Bibliography

"The Keidanren Nature Conservation Fund." Tokyo: Keidanren Nature Conservation Fund, n.d.

"The Research on the Whale Stock in the Antarctic." Tokyo: Institute of Cetacean Research, 1989.

"The Role of Coal and Clean Coal Technologies in the Asia-Pacific Region." Report of the APEC Expert Group on Clean Coal Technology. October 1992.

"The Whale—Culture." Tokyo: Japan Whaling Association, 1985.

Tilton, Mark. "Informal Market Governance in Japan's Basic Materials Industries." *International Organization* 48:4 (Autumn 1994):663-85.

"Timber Estate: An Illusion of Sustainable Development Policy." *Setiakawan* 8 (July-September 1992): 18-20.

Tobayama, Teruo, Fumio Yanagisawa and Toshio Kasuya."Incidental take of Minke Whales in Japanese Trap Nets." *Report to the International Whaling Commission* 42 (1992): 433-436.

Totman, Conrad. *The Green Archipelago: Forestry in Preindustrial Japan.* Berkeley: University of California Press, 1989.

————. *The Origins of Japan's Modern Forests.* Honolulu: University of Hawaii Press, 1985.

"Tropical Forest Conservation." Gland: World Wide Fund for Nature International, September 1991.

Tsuru, Shigeto and Helmut Weidner, eds. *Environmental Policy in Japan.* Berlin: Edition Sigma, 1989.

Ui, Jun. "The Role of Citizen's Movement." *Kogai*, Special Issue, 1975.

United Nations Center for Transnational Corporations. "Environmental Aspects of the Activities of Transnational Corporations: A Survey." New York: The United Nations Press, 1985.

United Nations Conference on Trade and Development, "International Tropical Timber Agreement 1983." TD/timber/11/Rev.1.

United Nations Convention on Law of the Sea, 1982.

U.S. Department of Commerce, National Oceanic and Atmospheric Administration. "The Marine Mammal Protection Act of 1972: Annual Report, 1 April 1977 to 31 March 1978."

Van Wolferen, Karel G. *The Enigma of Japanese Power: People and Politics in a Stateless Nation.* New York: Knopf, 1989.

Vasquez, John A. "Domestic Contention on Critical foreign Policy: The Case of the United States." *International Organization* 39:4 (Autumn 1985): 643-666.

Vertzberger, Yaacov. *The World in their Minds: Information Processing, Cognition and Perception in Foreign Policy Decisionmaking.* Stanford: Stanford University Press, 1990.

Vidal, John. "Weeping and whaling." *The Guardian*, 7 May 1993.

Vogel, Ezra F., ed. *Modern Japanese Organization and Decision-Making*. Berkeley: University of California Press, 1975.

Wang, Zhiyong. "Reducing Air Pollution from Electric Power Generation in China." *Environmental Conservation* 18:3 (Autumn 1991): 243-248.

Wanner, Barbara. "Japanese Politics: On the Brink of Change or Stuck in Neutral?" *JEI Report* 31A, 14 August 1992.

Ward, Robert E., ed. *Political Development in Modern Japan*. Princeton: Princeton University Press, 1968.

Ward, Simon. *Biological Samples and Balance Sheets*. Tokyo: Institute of Cetacean Research, 1990.

Ward, Simon, ed. *Who's Afraid of Compromise*. Tokyo: Institute of Cetacean Research, 1990.

Weatherford, Stephen M. and Haruhiro Fukui. "Domestic Adjustment to International Shocks in Japan and the U.S." *International Organization* 43:4 (Autumn 1989): 585-623.

Weidner, Helmut. "Japanese Environmental Policies in an International Perspective: Lessons for a Preventure Approach." In *Environmental Policy in Japan*, ed. Shigeto Tsuru and Helmut Weidner, 479-552. Berlin: Edition Sigma, 1989.

Weiss, Edith B., ed. *Environmental Change and International Law: New Challenges and Dimensions*. Tokyo: United Nations University Press, 1992.

Westing, Arthur H. "Environmental Approaches to the Avoidance of Violent Regional Conflicts." In "Environmental Crisis: Regional Conflicts and Ways of Cooperation," ed. Kurt R. Spillmann and Gunther Bachler, 148-161. Occasional Paper 14. Zurich: Center for Security Studies and Conflict Research, Swiss Federal Institute of Technology, September 1995.

————. "The Environmental Component of Comprehensive Security." *Bulletin of Peace Proposals* 20:2 (1989): 129-134.

"Whale sanctuary is approved." *The Japan Times*, 28 May 1994.

"Whale sanctuary ok'd; Japan casts sole no vote." *The Japan Times*, 28 May 1994.

"Whale tape damages ordered." *The Japan Times*, 30 March 1996.

"Whaler returns from 'research' with 330 minkes." *The Japan Times*, 13 April 1995.

"Whalers return with catch of 440." *The Japan Times*, 20 April 1996.

"Whales—Pain and Ethics of the Kill." *Ecotimes* 2:3 (March 1993): 5.

"Whaling allies deny bribery." *New Zealand Herald*, 14 May 1993.

"Whaling for the Twenty-First Century." Tokyo: Institute of Cetacean Research, 1996.

Bibliography

"Whaling moratorium to continue for a year." *New Zealand Dominion*, 15 May 1993.

White Paper of Japan, 1981-82. Tokyo: The Japan Institute of International Affairs, 1981.

White, John. *The Politics of Foreign Aid.* London: Bodley Head, 1974.

Wilkenfeld, Jonathan, ed. *Conflict Behavior and Linkage Politics.* New York: David McKay, 1973.

Wilkinson, Dean M. "The Use of Domestic Measures to Enforce International Whaling Agreements: A Critical Perspective," *Denver Journal of International Law and Policy* 17:2 (1989): 271-291.

Winterbottom, Robert. *Taking Stock: The Tropical Forestry Action Plan: After Five Years.* Washington, D.C.: World Resource Institute, 1990.

Wolf, Heather. "Deforestation in Cambodia and Malaysia: The Case for an International Legal Solution." *Pacific Rim Law and Policy Journal* 5:2 (March 1996): 429-455.

Wolfers, Arnold. *Discord and Collaboration.* Baltimore: Johns Hopkins University Press, 1962.

World Commission on Environment and Development, *Our Common Future,* Oxford: OxfordUniversity Press, 1987.

World Rainforest Movement. *Rainforest Destruction: Causes, Effects, and False Solutions.* Penang: World Rainforest Movement, 1990.

Wu, Zongxin and Wei Zhihong. "Policies to promote energy conservation in China." *Energy Policy* 19:10 (December 1991): 934-939.

"WWF Policy Statement: Whaling and the IWC." Gland: World Wide Fund for Nature International, 1992.

"WWF Position Statement on Whaling and the IWC: 1995 IWC Annual Meeting." Gland: World Wide Fund for Nature International, March 1995.

"WWF Slams Whaling." *The Japan Times*, 16 April 1995.

Wynne, Brian. "Scientific Knowledge and the Global Environment." In *Social Theory and the Global Environment*, ed. Michael Redclift and Ted Benton, 169-189. London and New York, NY: Routledge, 1994.

Yanaga, C. *Big Business in Japanese Politics.* New Haven: Yale University Press, 1968.

Yamamoto, Tadashi, ed. *Emerging Civil Society in the Asia Pacific Community: Nongovernmental Underpinnings of the Emerging Asia Pacific Regional Community.* Tokyo: Japan Center for International Exchange, 1995.

Yanarella, Ernest J. "Environmental vs. Ecological Perspectives on Acid Rain: The American Environmental Movement and the West German Green Party." In *The Acid Rain Debate: Scientific, Economic, and Political Dimensions*, ed. Ernest J. Yanarella and Randal H. Ihara, 243-260. Boulder and London: Westview Press, 1985.

————. "The Foundations of Policy Immobilism over Acid Rain Control." In *The Acid Rain Debate: Scientific, Economic, and Political Dimensions*, ed. Ernest J. Yanarella and Randal H. Ihara, 39-56. Boulder and London: Westview Press, 1985.

Yanarella, Ernest J. and Randal H. Ihara, eds. *The Acid Rain Debate: Scientific, Economic, and Political Dimensions*. Boulder and London: Westview Press, 1985.

Yonemoto, Shohei. "Japan and the Global Environmental Crisis." *Japan Echo*, 18:3 (1991): 2100-2105.

————. "Tokyo should take lead on Environment." *The Nikkei Weekly*, 27 June 1994.

Young, Oran R. *International Cooperation: Building Regimes for National Resources and the Environment*. Ithaca: Cornell, 1989.

————. *Resource Regimes: Natural Resources and Social Institutions*. Berkeley, Los Angeles and London: University of California Press, 1982.

————. "Institutional Linkages in International Society: Polar Perspectives." Global Governance 2:1 (1996): 1-24.

———— and Konrad von Moltke. "The Consequences of International Environmental Regimes." *International Environmental Affairs* 6:4 (Fall 1994): 348-370.

Young, Oran R. "Institutional Linkages in International Society: Polar Perspectives." *Global Governance* 2:1 (1996): 1-24.

Young, Oran R. *et al.* "Commentary: Subsistence, Sustainability, and Sea Mammals: Recon-structing the International Whaling Regime." *Ocean & Coastal Management* 23 (1994): 117-127.

————. *et al.* "Global Environmental Change and International Governance—Summary and Recommendations of a Conference held at Darthmouth College, Hanover, New Hampshire, June 1991." New Hampshire: Darthmouth College, 1991.

Young, Oran R. and Gail Osherenko, eds. *Polar Politics: Creating International Environmental Regimes*. Ithaca and London: Cornell University Press, 1993.

Zingg, Elizabeth. "Illegal Commerce in Tropical Woods thriving in Asia-Pacific." *The Indonesian Times*, 16 November 1992.

Bibliography

Zhao, D. and J. Xiong, "Acidification in Southwestern China." In *Acidification in Tropical Countries*, ed. Henning Rodhe and Rafael Herrera, 317-346. Chichester and New York: John Wiley & Sons, 1988.

Zhao, Dianwu and Bozen Sun. "Atmospheric Pollution from Coal Combustion in China." *Journal of the Air Pollution Control Association* 36 (1986): 371-374.

Zhou, Hailin. "Environmental Law and Administration: The Case of China." In *Development and the Environment: The Experiences of Japan and Industrializing Asia*, ed. Kojima Reeitsu *et al.*, 176-192. Tokyo: Institute of Developing Economies, 1995.

Zich, Arthur. "China's Three Gorges: Before the Flood." In *National Geographic* 192:3 (September 1997): 2-33.

Zohn, Kara. *Whales*. London: Headline Book, 1988.

Zou, Hailin. Environmental Law and Administration: The Case of China." In *Development and the Environment: the Experiences of Japan and Industrializing Asia*, ed. Reeitsu Kojima *et al.*, 128-141. Tokyo: Institute of Developing Economies, 1995.

Non-English Sources

Akao, Nobutoshi. *Chikyu wa Utteru: Taikenteki Kankyo Gaikoron* (An Agenda for Global Survival: An Ambassador Reflects on Environmental Protection). Tokyo: Sekai no Ugokisha, 1993.

Another Voice: *Kitte Kudasai, Nihonjin mo Shogyo Hogei niwa Hantai Shitai no desu*" (Another Voice: Please listen, Japanese, too, want to oppose Commercial Whaling), Vol. 1 & 2. Tokyo: Shogyo Hogei Saikai Hantai Panfureto Hakko Iinkai, n.d.

"*Chyugokku kogai ga shinkoku ka*" (Worsening pollution in China). *Yomiuri Shimbun*, 23 April 1994.

Doi, Zenjiro. *Saikin Hogei Hakusho* (The Latest White Paper on Whaling). Tokyo: Maruzen Library, 1992.

Eguchi, Yoichiro. *Beikoku Hogei Shoshyou 1984-86* (The U.S. Whaling Suit 1984-86). Tokyo: Nihon Suisan Shigen Hogo Kyokai, 1986.

Environment Agency of Japan. *Kankyo Hakusho (Sosetsu)* (Environment White Paper (Summary)). Tokyo: Government of Japan, 1993.

Forestry Agency of Japan. *Za! Nettai Rin: Midori no Chiyu Keiei no Jitsugen ni Mukete* (Tropical Rainforest: Toward Realizing a Green Earth). Tokyo: Kenkyukai, 1990.

Freeman, Milton, ed. *Kujira no Bunka Jinruigaku: Nihon no Kogatta Engan Hogei* (The Cultural Anthropology of Whaling: Japan's Small-scale Coastal Whaling). Tokyo: Kaimeisha, 1989.

Bibliography

Fujiwara, Eiji, "*Kokusai Hogei Sukandaru*" (The Scandal of International Whaling), in *Whales*. Tokyo: Kujira Mondai Network, n.d.

Government of Japan. "*Heisei Yonendo ni oite Kojiyotosuru Kogai no Boshi ni Kansuru Shisaku*" (Measures for Pollution Prevention being implemented in 1992). Tokyo: Government of Japan, 1992.

"*Hogei zaikai wa kano*" (Restarting whaling is possible). *Yomiuri Shimbun*, 9 June 1993.

Hara, Takeshi. *Za Kujira: Umi ni Utsutta Nihonjin* (Whales! The Japanese People Reflected in the Sea), new ed. Tokyo: Bunshindo, 1987.

He, Bo Zhuan. *Chugokku: Mirai e no Sentaku* (Choices for the Future), Tokyo: Nihon Hoso Shupan Kyokai, 1988.

Hirose, Hirotada. *Sanseikasuru Chikyu* (The Acidifying Earth). Tokyo: NHK Books, 1990.

"*Hogei ni waku shima*" (Island rises for whaling). *Nikkei Shimbun*, 12 December 1993.

Inoguchi, Takashi. *Kokusai Keizai no Seiji Gaku: Nihon no Yakuwari to Senkaku* (The Politics of International Economy: Japan's Roles and Choices) Tokyo: Tokyo Daigakku Shupan Kai, 1985.

Iwasaki, Sachiko. "*Kujira niku shoku wa Nihon no Dento Bunka ka?*" (Is eating whales Japan's traditional culture?) Tokyo: Greenpeace (Japan), 1992.

Iwasaki, Shunsuke. "*NGO wa Hito to Chikyu o Musubu*" (Tying People and the Earth with NGO). Tokyo: Daisan Shokan, 1993.

Japan Fund for Global Environment. *Newsletter* 2 (20 May 1994): 2-4.

_____. *Newsletter* 3 (6 December 1994): 3.

JICA. "*Chyugokku ni taisuru JICA no kankyo kyoryoku*" (JICA's Environmental Cooperation with China). Draft. (29 uly 1997): 2.

"*Kankyo hogo ha mi kujira tatezu*" (Environmentalists examine whales). *Nikkei Shimbun*, 12 December 1993.

Kato, Michio *et al*. "*Higashi Ajia no Sanseiu Mondai to Nihon no Yakuwari*" (Acid Rain Problem in Asia and the Role of Japan). *Kankyo Kenkyu* 99 (September 1995): 96.

Kawashima, Nobuko. "*NGO no Seisakuteki Igi to Maneijimento no Kadai — NGO o `Sukeru Appusuru' tameni*" (Policy implications of NGO and the subject of management — to `scale up' NGO). Tokyo: Dentsu Soken, June 1995.

Kayama, Tsutomu. "*Nettai Rin Saisei Gijutsu Kenkyu Kumiai no Katsudo ni tsuite*" (Activities of Research Association for Reforestation of Tropical Forest). *Tropical Forestry* 27 (May 1993): 23-30.

Bibliography

Kitai, Hitoshi. "*Mushibamareta Tonan Ajia no Midori — Firipin, Indoneshia kara no Shogen*"(Losing Southeast Asia's Forests — Testimonies from the Philippines and Indonesia). *Sekai* (August 1987): 152-160.

Kobayashi, Noriyuki. "*Tonan Ajia no Shinrin Shigen to Mokusai Boeki*" (Timber resource in Southeast Asia and the Timber Trade). *Journal of Forest Economics* 127 (1995): 41-46.

Kogai Taisaku Kankyo Hozen Iinkai, Nihon Bengoshi Rengokai, ed. *Nihon no Kogai Yushutsu to Kankyo Hakai: Tonan Ajia ni okeru Kigyo Shinshutsu to ODA* (Exporting Japan's Pollution and Environmental Destruction: ODA and the Advancement of Business Enterprises into Southeast Asia). Tokyo: Nihon Hyoronsha, 1991.

"*Kujira, Kujira, Kujira*" (Whales, Whales, Whales). *Oikos Magazine* 8 (Spring 1990): 51-59.

Kumazaki, Minoru. "*Nettai Rin no Hakai to Chikyu no Ondanka*" (Tropical Deforestation and Global Warming). *Kankyo Joho Kagaku* 18:3 (1989): 29-34.

Kusachi, Kenichi. *Ajia no Kusa no Nekokusai Kouryu* (Asia's Grassroots International Exchanges). Tokyo: Akashi Shoten, 1993.

Liu, D.C. *et al. Huanjin Wenti: Cong Zhong Ri Bijiao Yu Hezuo De Guandian Kan.* (Environmental Problems: A Comparative View of Sino-Japanese Conditions and Cooperation). Beijing: People's University Press of China, 1995.

MacNeill, Jim, Pieter Winsemius and Taizo Yakushiji. *Beyond Interdependence: The Meshing of the World's Economy and the Earth's Ecology.* Translated by the Japan Committee of the Japan-U.S.-Europe Committee. Tokyo: Diamondosha, 1991.

Matsubara, Satoru. *Tokushu Hojin Kaikaku* (The Reform of Special Corporations). Tokyo: Nihon Heironsha, 1995.

Minsai Gaiko 10 Nenshi Kikaku Henshyu Iinkai, ed. *Minsai Gaiko no Chyousen* (Challenges in People's Diplomacy). Tokyo: Nihon Hyoronsha, 1990.

Miyamoto, Kenichi. *Kankyo to Kaihatsu* (The Environment and Development). Tokyo: Iwanami Shoten, 1992.

————. *Nihon no Kankyo Mondai sono Seiji Keizaiteki Kousatsu* (A Political Economic Examination of Japan's Environmental Problems). Tokyo: Yuhikakusensho, 1981.

Miyamoto, Kenichi, ed. *Ajia no Kankyo Mondai to Nihon no Sekinin* (Asia's Environmental Problems and Japan's Responsibilities). Tokyo: Kamogawa Shuppan, 1992.

Mokuzai Bichiku Kikou. *Goban Jyuyou Dokou Chosa* (A Survey of Plywood Demand Forecasting). Tokyo: Mokuzai Bichiku Kikou, 1989.

Bibliography

Nihon Bengoshi Rengo Kai. *Nihon no Kaigai Yushyuu to Kankyo Hakai* (Japan's overseas exports and environmental destruction). Tokyo: Heibunsha, 1991.

Nihon Mokuzai Gakkai, ed. *Ki to Nihon no Kurashi* (Trees and the lives of Japanese People). Tokyo: Nihon Mokuzai Gakkai, 1983.

"*Nihon ni ogeru Kujira Niku Ryuutsuu Kanri ni tsuite*" (Managing the Import of Whale Meat to Japan). Tokyo: Institute of Cetacean Research, n.d.

Nishizaki, Mariko *et al. Kokusai Kyoryoku o Shigoto toshite* (International Cooperation as Careers). Tokyo: Yayoi Shobo, 1995.

Obara, Hideo. "*Aete Nankyokukai kara no tettai*" (Dare to retreat from the Antarctic), Kujira Zoron! n.d.

———. "*Iruka no Seizon wa Jinrui no Seizon ni kakawaru*" (The existence of dolphins is tied to the existence of mankind). *Asahi Janaru* (June 1980): 90-94.

———. "*Kankyo Kagakuteki Ronri ni Mototzuku Yasei Dobutsu Hogo to Hogei o Meguru Shyomondai*" (Environment Science-based Logic in Wildlife Protection and Turning Around Whaling and Other Issues). In *Keirui Shigen no Kenkyu to Kanri* (The Study and Management of Whales), ed. Kazumi Sakuramoto, Hidehiro Kato and Shoichi Tanaka. Tokyo: Koseisha Kouseikaku, 1991.

Otsuka, Kenji. "*Chyukokku toshi no jumin ishiki nmeru `kankyo mondai*'" (Awareness of `environmental problems' among China's urban populations). *World Trend* 13 (June 1996): 14-17.

Sakuramoto, Nagomi *et al*, eds. *Keirui Shigen no Kenkyu to Kanri* (The study and management of whale resources), Tokyo: Koseisha, 1991.

"*Sanseiu o kangaeru*" (Thinking about Acid Rain). Tokyo: Nihon Kankyo Kyokai, October 1991.

Saotome, Mitsuhiro. *Za, Borantea — NGO no Shakaigaku* (Volunteers! The Sociology of NGO). *International Development Journal* (1995).

"*Sekai no Shinrin Hozen o Kangaeru*" (Protecting the World's Forests). *Kankyo Series* 65. Tokyo: Nihon Kankyo Kyokai, December 1993.

Seki, Soichiro. "*Kaihatsutojokoku no Kankyo Osen*" (Environmental Pollution in Developing Countries). *Kankyo Kenkyu* 76 (1989): 72-76.

Shiba, Tatsuhiko. *Kujira to Nihonjin* (Whales and the Japanese), new ed. Tokyo: Yousensha, 1988.

———. *Sumi Mamoru—Houte Bunsho, Kujira Ichidai* (Sumi Mamoru—A First Generation Whaling Harpooner). Tokyo: Seiei Shaban, 1986.

Shimin Kyanping Tsushin 16. April 1994.

Shinrin Foramu Jikkou Iinkai, ed., *Nettai Rin soshite Nihon* (Tropical Forest and Japan). Tokyo: Nihon Keizai Hyoronsha, 1990.

Bibliography

Shogyo hogei zaikai hantai panfureto hatsuko iinkai, ed. "Another Voice," Vol.1 & 2. Tokyo: Shogyo hogei zaikai hantai panfureto hatsuko iinkai 1993.

Sumi, Kazuo. *Genjo no Genjitsu* (The Reality of Assistance). Tokyo: Iwanami Shoten, 1989.

Takagami, Shinobu and Osamu Kishimoto. *Nettai Nougyo 21 Seiki e no Tenbou* (Prospects of Tropical Agriculture in the 21st Century), Tokyo: Kokin Shoin, 1987.

Takahashi, Junichi. *Kujira no Nihon Bunkashi—Hogei Bunka no Kouseki o Todoru* (Whales in Japanese Cultural History—Tracing the Death of a Whaling Culture). Tokyo: Tankosha, 1992.

Takahashi, Toshio. "*Nihon no Hogei*" (Japanese Whaling). Tokyo: Greenpeace (Japan), 31 March 1994.

Takasu, Hisashi. "*Gokai ni Umoreta Nettai Rin Mondai: Chikyu Kankyo Hozen no Genten o Saguru*" (Burying Misunderstandings of the Tropical Forest Problem: Searching for the Origin of Global Environmental Protection). 1990.

Takeuchi, Naoto, ed. *Nettai Urin to Sarawaku Senju Minzoku: Jinken to Ekoroji o Mamorutatakai* (Tropical Rainforests and Indigenous Peoples in Sarawak: Human Rights and Ecology), Tokyo: Akashi Shoten, 1993.

Takeuchi, Tadashi. "*Kankyocho ni yoru Sanseiu Mondai e no tori gumi*" (The Environment Agency's Initiative for the Acid Rain Problem). *Kankyo Kenkyu* 99 (September 1995): 143-146.

"*Tokushyu 1 — Kei to Kujira*" (Special Issue 1: Whales and Whales), *Oikos Magazine* 2 (October 1987): 2-23.

Tsujinaka, Yutaka. *Rieki Shudan* (Profit Organizations). Tokyo: University Press, 1988.

Ui, Jun. "*Ajia to Nihon ni Kanrensuru Kankyomondai*" (Tying Asia and Japan with Environmental Problems). *Kankyo to Kogai,* 24:2 (October 1994): 8-13.

———. "*Kigyou to kogai taisaku*" (Policies toward Industry and Pollution). Tokyo: Iwanami, n.d.

———. "*Nihon no kogai to jumin undo*" (Pollution in Japan and Citizen Movements). *Shakai Undo*, n.d.

Umezaki, Yoshito. *Kujira to Inbo: Shoku Bunka Senso no Shirarezaru Uchi* (Whales and Conspiracy: The Unknown Inside Story of the War of Food Cultures). Tokyo: ABC Shupan, 1986.

Utsuki, Mieru. "*Nettai Rin no Hozen*" (Tropical Forest Protection), *Kankyo Kenkyu* 76 (1989): 66-71.

WWF (Japan), WWF Monthly Magazine, Special Issue: *Kujira Niku o kangaeru* (Thinking about whale meat) 24: 206 (April 1994).

318 *Bibliography*

Yamamoto, Shohei. *Chikyu Kankyo Mondai to wa Nanka* (What are Global Environmental Problems?). Tokyo: Iwanami Shinsho, 1994.

Yawata, Kazuo. *"Saraba Tsusansho"* (Farewell to MITI). *Bungei Shunju* (December 1997): 146-156.

World Wide Web

ourworld.compuserve.com/homepages/iwcoffice/press98.htm (1998 Annual Meeting, Muscat, Oman: Final Press Release) Viewed on 2 June 1998.

www.eic.or.jp/eanet/e/blaw/leaflet2.htm (Environmental Protection Policy in Japan: The Basic Environment Law) Viewed on 9 May 1998.

www.eic.or.jp/eanet/e/emad/design04.html (Design of the Acid Deposition Monitoring Network in East Asia.) Viewed on 9 May 1998.

www.eic.or.jp/eanet/e/emad/summ04.html (Chairman's Summary of the Fourth Expert Meeting on Acid Deposition Monitoring Network in East Asia") Viewed on 9 May 1998.

www.eic.or.jp/eanet/e/jeq/v001-01.html#4 (The ECO ASIA Long Term Perspective Project Workshop) Viewed on 9 May 1998.

www.eic.or.jp/eanet/e/jeq/v002-03.html (Statement by Prime Minister Ryutaro Hashimoto at UNGASS) Viewed on 9 May 1998.

www.eic.or.jp/eanet/e/jeq/v002-04.html#4 (ECO ASIA '97 Focuses on COP3) Viewed on 9 May 1998.

www.eic.or.jp/eanet/e/jeq/v003-01.html#7 (Acid Deposition Monitoring Network in East Asia) Viewed on 9 May 1998.

www.eic.or.jp/eanet/e/jeq/v003-01.html#7 (ECO ASIA Long-Term Project) Viewed on 9 May 1998.

www.eic.or.jp/eanet/e/jeq/v003-01.html#7 (ECO ASIA NET Workshop) Viewed on 9 May 1998.

www.eic.or.jp/eanet/en/org/fa/ged.html (Global Environment Department) Viewed on 10 March 2000.

www.eic.or.jp/eanet/en/org/jeq/v004-04.html (Japan Environment Quarterly) Viewed on 10 March 2000.

www.eic.or/jp/eanet/en/topic/eanet/attach.html (Components of Acid Deposition Monitoring During the Preparatory Phase) Viewed on 10 March 2000.

www.eic.or.jp/jec/eg/html.eng5.htm (Global Environmental Program) Viewed on 10 March 2000.

www.epa.gov/acidrain/overview.html (Acid Rain Program) Viewed on 12 May 1998.

www.geic.or.jp/geic-act.html (Activities of GEIC) Viewed on 10 March 2000.

Bibliography

www.iiasa.ac.at/`heyes/docs/rains.asia.html (RAINS-ASIA) Viewed on 11 May 1998.

www.iisd.ca/linkages/forestry/forest.html (Global Forest Policy) Viewed on 2 May 1998.

www.japantimes.co.jp/100/100-56.html (Japan adapting to global role) Viewed on 10 March 2000.

www.jca.ax.apc.org/janic.data.html (NGO-Data) Viewed on 10 March 2000.

www.keidanren.or.jp (Keidanren) Viewed on 10 May 1998.

www.maff.go.jp/mud.349.html (MAFF Update) Viewed on 10 March 2000.

www.maff.go.jp/soshiki/aguidetomaff/eguide/efishery5.html (Fishery) Viewed on 10 March 2000.

www.maff.go.jp/soshiki/aguidetomaff/eguide/eforest4.html (Forestry) Viewed on 10 March 2000.

www.maff.go.jp/soshiki/koukai/sekkei/isahaya-e.html (Message from the Japanese Ministry of Agriculture, Forestry and Fisheries on the Isahaya-Bay Sea Reclamation Project) Viewed on 9 May 1998.

www.mofa.go.jp/policy/199706/evn_sect.html (Japanese Economic Cooperation in the Environmental Sector) Viewed on 9 May 1998.

www.mofa.go/jp/policy/economy/fishery/whales/index.html (Japan and the Management of Whales) Viewed on 10 March 2000.

www.mofa.go.jp/policy/global/environment/pamph/1992/3.html (Environmental Protection: The Japanese Experience) Viewed on 9 May 1998.

www.mofa.go.jp/policy/global/environment/pamph/1994/coop.html (Japan's Environmental Cooperation) Viewed on 9 May 1998.

www.mofa.go.jp/policy/global/environment/pamph/199706/develop.html ("Energy Technology Development) Viewed on 9 May 1998.

www.mofa.go.jp/policy/global/environment/pamph/199706/enegy.html (Japan's Energy Conservation) Viewed on 11 May 1998.

www.mofa.go.jp/policy/oda/category/ngo/aid.html (NGO Support Schemes in Japan) Viewed on 9 May 1998.

www.mofa.go.jp/policy/oda/summary/1997/chart2.html (Initiatives for Sustainable Development (ISD) toward the 21st Century—Summary) Viewed on 11 May 1998.

www.mofa.go.jp/policy/oda/summary/1997.07.html (Special Interest Rates on ODA Loans for Environmental Projects and Japan-China Environmental Cooperation toward the 21st Century) Viewed on 11 May 1998.

www.mofa.go.jp/policy/oda/summary/1998/8.html (Efforts in Environmental Conservation) Viewed on 10 March 2000.

320   *Bibliography*

www.mofa.go.jp/policy/oda/summary/1998/12.html (The ODA Charter) Viewed on 10 March 2000.

www.nautilus.org/esena/choice.html (Dilemmas of Energy Choice in Northeast Asia) Viewed on 12 May 1998.

www.nautilus.org/esena/papers/carmichael.html (Gregory R. Carmichael and Richard Arndt, "Baseline Assessment of Acid Deposition in Northeast Asia) Viewed on 12 May 1998.

www.nautilus.org/esena/papers/streets.html (David G. Streets, Energy and Acid Rain Projections for Northeast Asia) Viewed on 12 May 1998.

ww.soc.titech.ac.jp/ngo/jp-ngoactivities.html (Japan's NGO Activities and the Public Support System) Viewed on 10 March 2000.

www.soc.titech.ac.jp/ngo/jpngo-face.html (The Changing Face of NGOs in Japan) Viewed on 10 March 2000.

www.soton.ac.uk/~engenvir/environment/air/acid.laws.html (Legislation) Viewed on 12 May 1998.

Index

Aboriginal subsistence whaling (see International Whaling Commission and Whaling)

Academia and policymaking in Japan, 74-75

Acid Deposition Monitoring Network (see Environment Agency of Japan)

Acid pollution
causes of, 16, 202, 204
effects of, 202-203, 209, 221-222
in Asia, 16-18, 203, 204, 206
in China, xxvi, 17, 204, 217, 222, 235-236
in Japan, 47, 204-205, 222-223, 228
in Europe, 203, 208-215, 229
in North America, 37, 203, 209, 214, 215-217
responses to, 9, 18, 204, 206, 207-208, 208-215, 215-217, 223

Agenda 21 Plan of Japan, 2, 49, 69

Amakudari, 67-68, 76

Asian financial crisis, xx, xxiv, 235

Asia Pacific Economic Cooperation, 204

Association of Southeast Asian Nations, 241

Bargaining in decision making, 3, 26, 28, 30, 31, 32, 34, 61-62 (see also Reverberations, Side payments, Transnational coalitions, Linkages, Issues)

Basic Environment Law 1967 (see Environment legislation in Japan)

Basic Environment Law 1993 (see Environment legislation in Japan)

Big business in Japan
activities to support global environmental protection, 65, 66
interest in international envi-

ronmental issues, 65, 68
relations with government bureaucracy, 67-68
relations with non-governmental organizations, 67, 70, 73
research think tanks and, 75-76

Biodiversity protection in Japanese policies, xix, 60

Brown issues, xix, 115

Brundtland Commission Report of 1987, 48

Bureaucratic leadership, 53, 60, 115, 261

Bureaucratic politics model
definition of, 33-34

Clean coal technologies, xix, 205, 206, 218, 234-235

Commission on Sustainable Development (see United Nations Commission on Sustainable Development)

Common property resources, 14, 94, 152

Complex interdependence, 27-28, 129, 130, 244, 265

Comprehensive National Security Strategy (see also Japanese perception of national security), 6-7

Consensus decision making in Japan, 61-62, 263, 263-264 (see also Government bureaucracy in Japan)

Consumptive use of natural resources, 13, 151-152, 189

Convention for the Regulation of Whaling, 92

Convention on International Trade in Endangered Species of Wild Fauna and Flora, xxiv, 59, 60, 95, 107, 108

Convention on Long-range Transboundary Air Pollution, 211, 212, 213

Creative conservatism, 50

Deforestation in the tropics
European countries and, 156
causes of, xxiv
environmental impacts of, 146
rate of, 145, 150, 162

Double-edged diplomacy (see Two-level games theory)

Earth Summit (*see* Rio Earth Summit)

Environment Agency of Japan
Acid Deposition Monitoring Network, xxvi, 240-242, 244
acid rain and, 56, 207, 231, 231-232, 233, 234, 244
acid rain pollution surveys, 226-227, 234
deforestation in the tropics and, 177, 188

Environment Congress for Asia and the Pacific (ECO ASIA), 234
Global Environment Department, 56
Global Environment Information Center, xxii, 57
Influence and powers, 54-55
Institute for Global Environmental Strategies, 56
Japan Fund for the Global Environment, 57, 63, 70

Index

mandate of, 52, 54-54
Ministry of Environment, xxiii
National Institute for Environment Studies, 56
origin of, 47, 52, 54
relations with non-governmental organizations, 56, 56-57, 69-70
structure and size, xxiii, 54
top concerns, 54, 56, 65
whaling and, 114-115, 128

Environment goods and services
sale/transfer of, 8-10, 230, 235-236

Environment legislation in Japan
Basic Environment Law, 1967, 46
Basic Environment Law 1993, 49-50, 57, 128
Basic Environment Plan, 50
Carbon tax proposal, 58
Environment impact assessment
Harmonization principle, 46
Nature Conservation Law 1972, 47
Pollution Prevention Act 1969, 47

Epistemic community, 37

Exclusive economic zone (see United Nations Convention on Law of the Sea)

External pressure and Japanese policies, 14, 114, 126-127, 128, 264

Federation of Economic Organizations (see Keidanren)

Forest Principles, 157-158

Forestry Agency of Japan (see Ministry of Agriculture, Forestry and Fisheries)

Friends of the Earth
International, 27, 183-184
Japan, 121, 123, 124

Global forest convention, xxiv, 156-158, 161

Global Legislators Organization for a Better Environment (GLOBE), 62

Global climate change, 47, 50, 56, 66

Government bureaucracy in Japan
administrative guidance, 79-80
consensus building and, 61-62, 79, 116, 119
dominance in policymaking, 2, 11, 51, 79, 114, 128
interest in international environmental affairs, 11, 231-232
intra-governmental rivalries, xx, 12, 50-51, 52, 58, 65, 76, 119
jurisdiction and leadership, 52, 61, 258-259
powers and resources, xx, 12, 52,
quasi-governmental think tanks and, 76-77
relations with big business, 67-68
relations with non-governmental organizations, xxi

Great Hanshin earthquake, 69

Green Aid Plan (see Ministry of International Trade and Industry)

Green consumption in Japan, 68

Green issues, xix

324   *Index*

Greenpeace
    International, 27, 95, 186
    Japan, 69

Hashimoto, Ryutaro (see Prime ministers of Japan)

Hironaka, Wakako (see also Politicians in Japan), 62

Illegal whaling (*see* Whaling)

Indonesia log export ban, 167-168

Information asymmetries, 33

Interdependence, 26, 28, 29-30 (see also Complex interdependence)

Intergovernmental Forum on Forests, 160
Intergovernmental Panel on Forests, 160

International Convention for the Regulation of Whaling, 92, 100, 127

International Fund for Animal Welfare, 121-122, 124

International Timber Organization, 161

International trade of tropical timber
    certification and labeling schemes, 152, 158-159
    competition from softwood timber, 151, 153
    China and, xxv
    European Union and, 155-156, 159, 165-166
    General Agreement on Trade and Tariff and, 159
    General trading companies and, 172, 181, 182-183
    Japan and, xxv, 147, 148, 149,

162-165, 169-170
    United States and, 165
    liberalization of, xxv
    size of, 147

International Tropical Timber Agreement 1983, 152

International Tropical Timber Agreement 1994, 153, 176

International Tropical Timber Organization, 152-154, 156, 158,174, 177, 178-179

International Union for the Conservation of Nature and Natural Resources (IUCN), 183

International Whaling Commission
    aboriginal subsistence whaling, 97, 107
    International Observer Program, 95
    management schemes, 90, 94, 95, 98, 99, 103
    mandate, 92, 100, 127
    membership, 93, 96, 97
    moratorium on commercial whaling, 14, 63, 90, 96, 97, 106, 107, 145
    opposition to moratorium, 97, 98
    Scientific Committee, 94, 94-95, 97, 98, 99
    Southern Ocean Sanctuary, 99
    structure, 93-94

Internet and citizen movement in Japan (see Non-governmental organizations in Japan)

Issue areas, 29
    hierarchy, 27, 30
    linkages, 29, 32, 188-189
    redefinition, 26, 32, 189

Index

Japan Agricultural Standard (JAS), 180

Japan-China relations, 63, 207, 208, 223, 225, 226, 229, 236, 237

Japan-U.S. relations, 63, 64, 117, 118-121, 130, 178-179

Japan fisheries industry, 110, 112, 116-117, 117-118, 121, 125-126, 129

Japan Tropical Forest Action Network (see also Non-governmental organizations in Japan), 183-184, 186

Japanese media, 12-13, 45, 47, 123, 185

Japanese perceptions of energy and resource security, 37, 47, 60
leadership in international affairs, 12, 48
national security, 6-7
nature, 37, 184
United Nations, 176
whales (see Whales)

Japanese whaling
growth and decline of whaling companies, 100-105
early history of, 100-101
economic importance of, 13, 102, 103, 107, 110, 111-112
end of, 104, 106, 111
government regulation of, 101-106
international criticisms of, 91, 92, 110111, 113
large-type commercial whaling, 101, 102, 103, 11
modern history of, 101-106
objection to international moratorium, 13, 91, 97, 112,

114, 115, 116, 119
pelagic whaling, 101, 111
perception of cultural imperialism and, 113, 122-123, 127
relief quota request, 99, 106
research whaling, xxiv, 13, 64, 91 97, 106, 113, 117, 118, 121, 126
Russo-Japanese War and, 101
small-type coastal whaling, 102, 106, 107, 111
traditional whaling communities, 90-91, 100-101, 103

Kaifu, Toshiki (see Prime ministers of Japan)

Keidanren, 15, 65-66, 66-67

Kosugi, Takagi, 62 (see also Global Legislator for a Better Environment)

Kyoto Protocol, xix, xxv

Level of analysis, 25-27, 31

Liberal Democratic Party, xxiii, 51, 62, 63, 120

Linkages, 29-32

Ministry of Agriculture, Forestry and Fisheries
acid rain and, 232
deforestation in the tropics and, 60, 177, 179, 191
fisheries and, 53, 115
fisheries industry and, 116, 118, 119
international environmental policy and, 60, 180-181
non-governmental organizations and, 60, 70, 181
whaling and, 13, 114, 115-118, 126, 128, 129, 130

Index

Ministry of Construction, 52, 53, 168, 177, 181

Ministry of Environment (see Environment Agency of Japan)

Ministry of Finance
international environmental policy and, 57, 58

Ministry of Foreign Affairs
acid rain and, 233, 234, 236-237
deforestation in the tropics and, 177-179, 187-188
international environmental policy and, 60-62
Japan International Cooperation Agency, 163, 225, 236
non-governmental organizations and, 61, 179, 263
whaling and, 114, 116, 118-120, 128-129, 259-260, 260, 261

Ministry of International Trade and Industry
acid rain and, 233, 234, 244
deforestation in the tropics and, 177, 181, 188
global warming and, 52, 54, 55, 58-59, 59, 65, 68, 225, 234
international environmental policy and, 58-59 , 115
relations with industry, 68
whaling and, 115, 126

Ministry of Health and Welfare, xxiii, 52

Ministry of Posts and Telecommunications, 70

Murazumi-Baldrige Agreement, 111, 119, 122, 126, 130

Naksone, Yasuhiro (see Prime ministers of Japan)

Newspapers in Japan, 123

Non-governmental organizations in Japan
acid deposition and, 237-238, 238-239
deforestation in the tropics and, 123, 181, 183-187
government funds for, 49, 70, 72, 187
image in Japanese society, xxi, 16, 69, 72, 73, 185-186
internet and, xxii, xxiii
laws governing, xxi, xxii, 70-72, 73
leadership and staff in, xxii, 71, 123, 187
origin of, 2, 46
relations with government bureaucracy, xxi, 2, 15-16, 49, 57, 69, 69-70, 70-72, 79-80, 113-114, 187
relations with non-Japanese non-governmental organizations and groups outside of Japan, 69-70, 73-74, 121, 122, 123-124, 183, 184, 186
size and strength, 69, 70-72, 114
whaling and, 121-125, 125

Non-profit organizations law, xxi, xxiii, 71

Non-state actors in international affairs, 27, 30, 36

North Atlantic Marine Mammal Commission, 98

Official Development Assistance of Japan
aid to China, 63, 68, 223-225,

Index

236-237
budget, xx, 11, 50, 231-232
criticisms of, 10, 172-173
environment aid, 1, 3, 6, 10, 48, 52, 168, 174, 223
Official Development Assistance Charter, 49
policy making, xxii, 57-58, 61
purposes of, xx, 3, 4, 48-49, 59
technology transfer, xix, 10, 59, 68, 223, 250

Oil Crises, 47, 215

Organization for Economic Cooperation and Development
review of Japan's environmental policy, 47, 56, 264

Participation expansion 31-32

Packwood-Magnuson Amendment, 109-110, 111, 116, 125, 128

Pelly Amendment to the Fisherman's Protection Act, 108-109, 128

Plaza Accord 1985, 47 (see also Yen appreciation)

Policymaking in Japan
bureaucratic leadership and, 115
bureaucratic model and, 34-36
gaiatsu, 36, 45-46, 61
patterned pluralism and, 34
transparency in, 50
role of bureaucracy (see Government bureaucracy in Japan)

Post-war housing boom in Japan, 162-163

Politicians in Japan, xxiii, 14, 45, 51-

62, 63, 64, 120, 257

Prime ministers in Japan
Hashimoto, Ryutaro, 50, 64
Kaifu, Toshiki, 63
Morihiro Hosokawa, 225
Noboru Takeshita, 48, 63, 64-65
role in policy making, 14
Yasuhiro Nakasone, 14, 63, 64, 114, 117, 118, 120-121, 128, 129

Reactive state, 35

Regimes, 28-30

Reverberations, 32, 264

Rio Earth Summit, 6, 49, 131, 151, 157-158, 160, 186, 227

Sarawak Campaign Committee, 184, 186

Science and scientists in policy making, 26, 98, 112-113, 238-239

Side-payments, 32

Sogo sosha (*see* Big business in Japan)

Stockholm Conference, 5, 47, 49, 54, 95, 209

Sustainable development, 7, 47

Takeshita, Noboru (see Prime Ministers in Japan)

Think tanks in Japan, 75-77

Transnational coalitions, 28, 32, 33, 36

Tropical Forest Action Plan, 155

Two-level games theory, 30-33

328 *Index*

United Nations Commission on Sustainable Development, 160

United Nations Conference on the Environment and Development (see Rio Earth Summit)

United Nations Conference on the Human Environment (see Stockholm Conference)

United Nations Convention on Law of the Sea, xx, 97, 119

United Nations Economic Commission for Europe, 209, 210, 211

United Nations Environment Program, 150, 227

United Nations Food and Agriculture Organization, 45, 150, 153

United Nations Forum on Forests, xxiv

United Nations Framework Convention on Climate Change

United Nations General Assembly Special Session on the Environment and Sustainable Development, 50, 160-161, 174

U.S. General International Fisheries Agreement, 110

Whale meat consumption and Japan, 89, 103, 113 (see also Whales)

Whale oil and spermaceti, 92, 103

Whales as commons, 93, 94
as symbols for environmental protection, 89, 90
commercial value of, 89, 92, 95, 99, 103, 107

consumptive versus non-consumptive use, 89, 90, 99, 113
decline in stocks and species (see also Whaling and International Whaling Commission), 90, 95, 103
international trade of, 95, 107, 109 (see also CITES)
Japanese perceptions of, 91, 113

Whale watching, 99, 100, 124

Whaling
aboriginal/subsistence, 90, 97, 99
American, 89
as fisheries, 93
Basque, 89
British, 89, 90
Canadian, 98, 99, 109
community-based, 90
Dutch, 89
Greenland, 90, 98
Icelandic, 90, 98, 119
illegal, 90, 94, 95
in Antarctic southern oceans, 89-90, 94
Inuit,
Norwegian, 89, 90, 97-98, 99, 109
Olympic, 94
opposition to, 94-100, 107
pelagic, 89
Soviet/Russian, 94, 98
traditional whaling, 91
U.S. legislation against, 108-110, 111, 116, 125, 128

Win-sets, 31

World Meteorological Organization (WMO), 211, 232

World Trade Organization (WTO), 237

World Wide Fund for Nature (WWF),

Index

121, 123, 183

Yen appreciation, 47 (see also Plaza Accord 1985)

Zero-sum game, 27-28